NOLO Products & Services

⇨ Books & Software

Get in-depth information. Nolo publishes hundreds of great books and software programs for consumers and business owners. Order a copy—or download an ebook version instantly—at Nolo.com.

⇨ Legal Encyclopedia

Free at Nolo.com. Here are more than 1,400 free articles and answers to common questions about everyday legal issues including wills, bankruptcy, small business formation, divorce, patents, employment and much more.

⇨ Plain-English Legal Dictionary

Free at Nolo.com. Stumped by jargon? Look it up in America's most up-to-date source for definitions of legal terms.

⇨ Online Legal Documents

Create documents at your computer. Go to Nolo.com to make a will or living trust, form an LLC or corporation or obtain a trademark or provisional patent. For simpler matters, download one of our hundreds of high-quality legal forms, including bills of sale, promissory notes, nondisclosure agreements and many more.

⇨ Lawyer Directory

Find an attorney at Nolo.com. Nolo's consumer-friendly lawyer directory provides in-depth profiles of lawyers all over America. From fees and experience to legal philosophy, education and special expertise, you'll find all the information you need to pick the right lawyer. Every lawyer listed has pledged to work diligently and respectfully with clients.

⇨ Free Legal Updates

Keep up to date. Check for free updates at Nolo.com. Under "Products," find this book and click "Legal Updates." You can also sign up for our free e-newsletters at Nolo.com/newsletters.

10th edition

How to Form a
Nonprofit
Corporation

Attorney Anthony Mancuso

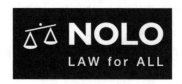

TENTH EDITION	MAY 2011
Editor	JINAH LEE
Cover Design	SUSAN PUTNEY
Production	MARGARET LIVINGSTON
CD-ROM Preparation	ELLEN BITTER
Proofreading	NICOLE THOMAS
Index	SONGBIRD INDEXING
Printing	DELTA PRINTING SOLUTIONS, INC.

Mancuso, Anthony.
  How to form a nonprofit corporation / By Anthony Mancuso.—10th ed.
      p. cm.
  Includes index.
  Summary: "Provides background information and step-by-step instructions that nonprofits need to apply for federal 501(c)(3) tax-exempt status and qualify as a public charity with the IRS. The 10th edition covers recent changes in the law"—Provided by publisher.
  ISBN-13: 978-1-4133-1386-4 (pbk.)
  ISBN-10: 1-4133-1386-8 (pbk.)
  ISBN-13: 978-1-4133-1476-2 (epub e-book)
  1. Nonprofit organizations—Law and legislation—United States—Popular works. 2. Incorporation—United States—Popular works. I. Title.
  KF1388.M36 2011
  346.73'064—dc22

                              2010052791

Please note

We believe accurate, plain-English legal information should help you solve many of your own legal problems. But this text is not a substitute for personalized advice from a knowledgeable lawyer. If you want the help of a trained professional—and we'll always point out situations in which we think that's a good idea—consult an attorney licensed to practice in your state.

Acknowledgments

The author extends a special thanks to my editor, Diana Fitzpatrick, and Stan Jacobsen for invaluable and thorough research assistance, and to all the hardworking people at Nolo.

About the Author

Anthony Mancuso is a corporations and limited liability company expert. Tony graduated from Hastings College of the Law in San Francisco, is an active member of the California State Bar, writes books and software in the fields of corporate and LLC law, and has studied advanced business taxation at Golden Gate University in San Francisco. He also has been a consultant for Silicon Valley EDA (Electronic Design Automation) and other technology companies, and currently works at Google in Mountain View, California.

He is the author of many Nolo books on forming and operating corporations (profit and nonprofit) and limited liability companies. Among his current books are *Incorporate Your Business; The Corporate Records Handbook; How to Form a Nonprofit Corporation in California; Nonprofit Meetings, Minutes & Records; Form Your Own Limited Liability Company; LLC or Corporation?*; and *Your Limited Liability Company: An Operating Manual*. His books have shown over a quarter of a million businesses and organizations how to form and operate a corporation or LLC.

He has lectured at Boalt School of Law on the University of California Berkeley campus ("Using the Law in Non-Traditional Settings") and at Stanford Law School ("How to Form a Nonprofit Corporation"). He taught Saturday Morning Law School business formation and operation courses for several years at Nolo's offices in Berkeley. He has also scripted and narrated several audio tapes and podcasts covering LLCs and corporate formations and other legal areas for Nolo as well as The Company Corporation. He has given many recorded and live radio and TV presentations and interviews over the years covering business, securities, and tax law issues. His law and tax articles and interviews have appeared in *The Wall Street Journal* and *TheStreet.com*.

Tony is a licensed helicopter pilot and has performed for years as a guitarist in various musical idioms.

Table of Contents

Part Two: Incorporating Your Nonprofit

9 Final Steps in Organizing Your Nonprofit Corporation

10 After Your Corporation Is Organized

11 Lawyers and Accountants

A Appendix A: How to Use the CD-ROM

Corporate Forms

Incorporation Checklist

Application for Reservation of Corporate Name

Articles of Incorporation

Articles Filing Letter

Bylaws

Waiver of Notice and Consent to Holding of First Meeting of Board of Directors

Minutes of First Meeting of Board of Directors

IRS Forms and Publications and Tax Articles

Form 1023: *Application for Recognition of Exemption (with Notice 1382)*

Instructions for Form 1023

Form SS-4: *Application for Employer Identification Number*

Instructions for Form SS-4

Form 5768: *Election/Revocation of Election By an Eligible Section* 501(c)(3) *Organization To Make Expenditures To Influence Legislation*

Publication 557: *Tax-Exempt Status for Your Organization*

Publication 4220: *Applying for 501(c)(3) Tax-Exempt Status*

Publication 4221-PC: *Compliance Guide for 501(c)(3) Public Charities*

Publication 4221-PF: *Compliance Guide for 501(c)(3) Private Foundations*

Publication 1828: *Tax Guide for Churches and Religious Organizations*

IRS Revenue Procedure 75-50

IRC Section 4958, Taxes on Excess Benefit Transactions

IRS Regulations Section 53.4958-0, Table of Contents

Public Charity or Private Foundation Status Issues Under IRC §§ 509(a)(1)–(4), 4942(j)(3), and 507

Disclosure, FOIA and the Privacy Act

Update: The Final Regulations on the Disclosure Requirements for Annual Information Returns and Applications for Exemption

Education, Propaganda, and the Methodology Test

Election Year Issues

Lobbying Issues

Private School Update

UBIT: Current Developments

Intermediate Sanctions (IRC Section 4958) Update

IRS Revenue Ruling 2007-41 *Political Campaign Prohibition Guidance*

Internal Revenue Bulletin (IRB 2008-18) with T.D. 9390 Final Regulation changes to Section 4958 regulations

Your Legal Companion for Forming a Nonprofit Corporation

Forming a nonprofit corporation may sound like a daunting task that you should hand over to a lawyer as quickly as you can—after all, aren't there a lot of paperwork and filings, and complicated IRS nonprofit tax laws to learn? There is paperwork, and you will need to deal with the IRS, but the truth is, you can do it yourself. Forming a nonprofit corporation in any state is actually a fairly straightforward process. And, with the help of our line-by-line instructions, you can also obtain tax-exempt status from the IRS for your newly-formed nonprofit corporation. Thousands of people have gone through the entire process of incorporating a nonprofit and obtaining 501(c)(3) tax-exempt status with this book to guide them.

Along the way, there may be decisions you need to make where you should seek professional advice. We'll let you know when you need outside help. And even if you do decide to hire a lawyer to handle some of the work for you, the information in this book will help you be an informed client—and get the most for your money.

This book explains, in plain English, how to incorporate your nonprofit in any state and obtain 501(c)(3) tax-exempt status from the IRS. We show you how to:

- prepare and file nonprofit corporation articles and bylaws in any of the 50 states

- apply for and obtain 501(c)(3) tax-exempt status from the IRS
- qualify as a 501(c)(3) public charity
- satisfy IRS conflict-of-interest and excess-benefit guidelines
- prepare minutes for your first board meeting, and
- take care of postincorporation filings and tasks.

In Appendix B we explain how you can locate each state's secretary of state's office and state tax agency online to find state forms and additional information.

There are legal and tax technicalities that nonprofits must deal with in exchange for the substantial benefits they receive as nonprofits. We give you the information and tools you need both to form your tax-exempt nonprofit and understand the practical and ongoing issues related to running a nonprofit.

We know that any legal process can be challenging. We hope this book, with its step-by-step approach to incorporation and obtaining tax-exempt status from the IRS, will help you through the legal hoops and over the hurdles of incorporating your nonprofit in any state and obtaining tax-exempt status from the IRS. Congratulations on taking your first steps toward success in your new nonprofit endeavor!

PART

1

How Nonprofit Corporations Work

Is Nonprofit Incorporation Right for You?

eciding to form a nonprofit corporation will be a big step for you and the members of your group. It will involve more paperwork and government forms, on both the state and federal level, than anyone will like; and you'll have to conduct your business within the legal framework of various state and federal laws. Fortunately, there are big payoffs to all this work and attention, including the ability to attract donors and grant funds, obtain real and personal property tax exemptions and special nonprofit mailing rates, avoid corporate income taxes, and shield officers and directors from legal liability. Before starting down the path of nonprofit incorporation, however, you'll want to learn a little more about who can form a nonprofit and the consequences of doing so. In this chapter, we'll explain:

- the kinds of groups that can—and can't—form a nonprofit using this book

- the benefits you'll enjoy as a nonprofit—and some of the disadvantages to choosing this route

- how nonprofits can raise start-up funds and earn money, should they wish to do so

- the process you'll go through (following the instructions in this book) to incorporate and obtain your tax-exempt status, and

- for those considering incorporating in another state, considerations to bear in mind before doing so.

References to IRS Articles and Materials

There are references in the book to IRS articles and materials included on the CD-ROM. Some of this material includes articles and information made available by the IRS on its website as part of its Exempt Organizations Continuing Professional Education Technical Instruction Program, which regularly publishes articles for tax-exempt organizations. The IRS has the following statement on its website regarding this material: "These materials were designed specifically for training purposes only. Under no circumstances should the contents of these articles be used or cited as authority for setting or sustaining a technical position."

In other words, use this material to learn about IRS tax issues, but don't expect to be able to rely on it if you end up in a dispute with the IRS. Nolo includes this material on the CD-ROM as a convenience to the reader and as an alternative to directing you to an IRS website link to this material. This material is taken from the exempt organization tax law training articles available from the IRS website at www.irs.gov (select "Charities & Non-Profits," "More Topics," then "EO Tax Law Training Articles"). If you are interested in one of the issues, you should check the IRS website for any updated articles or information on your topic.

Is Your Group a Nonprofit That Can Use This Book?

For-profit corporations can usually be formed for "any lawful purpose" under state statutes. Nonprofit corporations, on the other hand, generally must be established to accomplish one or more specific purposes that benefit either the public at large, a segment of the community, or a particular membership. While it may be easy for your group to incorporate as a nonprofit in your state, this is only the first hurdle. The next important step is to obtain tax-exempt status under state and federal tax statutes. To do this, your group must meet specific-purpose requirements contained in state and federal tax statutes.

This book has been written specifically for nonprofits that want to qualify for federal income tax exemption under Section 501(c)(3) of the Internal Revenue Code. This means that your nonprofit corporation must be formed for religious, charitable, scientific, literary, and/or educational purposes. There are other types of groups—labor unions, chambers of commerce, social and recreational clubs, fraternal societies, credit unions, farmers' co-ops, and legal service organizations, to name a few—that may be eligible for tax-exempt status under other sections of the Internal Revenue Code. (See "Special Nonprofit Tax-Exempt Organizations," in Appendix C, for a list of organizations that can qualify for tax-exempt status under a subsection of 501(c) other than Subsection 3).

These groups often have more leeway to provide direct financial benefits to their members, but they don't receive the same tax benefits as a 501(c)(3) group. If you are planning on forming one of these non-501(c)(3) nonprofits, this book can help acquaint you with the process of forming a nonprofit. It will not, however, guide you step-by-step through the process of preparing articles of incorporation and bylaws for your group or the tax exemption applications you will need for your nonprofit.

If your group falls within one of the 501(c)(3) purposes, however, you can rest assured that this book will help you step-by-step through the process of incorporating and obtaining tax-exempt status. First, we'll help you create your corporate entity by showing you how to prepare and file articles of incorporation that meet your state's corporate law requirements. Then we'll show you how to obtain your state and federal nonprofit income tax exemptions for Section 501(c)(3) tax-exempt status.

TIP

If you are forming a nonprofit in California. If you plan to incorporate your nonprofit in California and want additional information about incorporating there, see *How to Form a Nonprofit Corporation in California*, by Anthony Mancuso (Nolo).

Corporation Basics

You don't have to understand all there is to know about corporations in order to follow this book or form your nonprofit. But there are a few basic concepts you'll want to have under your belt as we go through the process. Here they are, with special emphasis on any differences between for-profit corporations and nonprofits.

- **A corporation is a separate legal entity.** A corporation is a legal entity that allows a group of people to pool energy, time, and money for profit or nonprofit activities. It acquires legal existence after its founders comply with their state's incorporation procedures and formalities. The law treats a corporation as a separate person, distinct from the people who own, manage, or operate it. The corporation can enter into contracts, incur debts, and pay taxes. Corporations are either for-profit (business corporations) or nonprofits.

- **For-profit, or business, corporations versus nonprofits.** Business corporations can be formed for any legal purpose. They can issue shares of stock to investors in return for money or property, or services performed for the corporation. Shareholders receive a return on their investment if dividends are paid or if, upon dissolution of the corporation, any

corporate assets remain to be divided among the shareholders after payment of all creditors. Nonprofits, on the other hand, generally cannot issue shares of stock or pay dividends under state law (unless they are some type of hybrid such as consumer or producer co-ops). The federal tax code also prohibits 501(c)(3) tax-exempt nonprofit corporations from paying dividends or profits to their members or other individuals. When a 501(c)(3) tax-exempt nonprofit corporation dissolves, it must distribute its remaining assets to another tax-exempt nonprofit group.

- **In-state and out-of-state corporations.** Corporations formed in a particular state are known as domestic corporations in their state. Corporations formed in other states, even if physically present and engaging in activities in a state, are called foreign corporations in that state. For example, a corporation formed in California is a domestic corporation as far as California is concerned, but a foreign corporation when considered by other states. We give more information on deciding whether to incorporate in a particular state below, in "Where Should You Incorporate?"

Benefits of the Nonprofit Corporation

Now that you understand that this book is intended for nonprofit corporations organized for religious, charitable, scientific, literary, and/or educational purposes that want to qualify for a tax exemption under Section 501(c)(3) of the Internal Revenue Code (and hopefully your nonprofit is among them), let's look at the benefits you'll enjoy as a 501(c)(3) tax-exempt nonprofit corporation. The relative importance of each of the following benefits will vary from group to group, but at least one of them should be very significant for your organization.

If you finish this section and conclude that nothing here is very important for your group, you'll want to consider whether it makes sense to incorporate at all. Many groups accomplish their nonprofit purposes just fine as unincorporated nonprofit associations, without formal organizational paperwork or written operational rules. If you can continue to accomplish your nonprofit purposes and goals informally, you may be happier staying small.

Tax Exemptions

Nonprofit corporations are eligible for state and federal exemptions from payment of corporate income taxes, as well as other tax exemptions and benefits. At federal corporate tax rates of 15% on the first $50,000 of taxable income, 25% on the next $25,000, and 34% and higher on income over $75,000, it goes without saying—at least if you expect to earn a substantial amount of money (from services, exhibits, or performances, for example)—that you'll want to apply for an exemption. In states with a corporate income tax, a state income tax exemption is equally attractive, as are local county, real, and personal property tax exemptions. Chapters 3, 4, and 5 cover tax exemptions in detail.

SEE AN EXPERT

Get the help of a competent tax adviser as soon as you decide to incorporate. Make sure you choose someone experienced in the special field of nonprofit bookkeeping and reporting. Ask the advisor to help you (especially your treasurer) set up a good record-keeping system, which you can use to prepare your annual federal and state nonprofit tax forms and reports. Have the tax helper periodically review the system to be sure that you are maintaining your financial records properly and have filed your tax forms on time.

Receiving Public and Private Donations

One of the primary reasons for becoming a 501(c)(3) nonprofit corporation is that it increases your ability to attract and receive public and private grant funds and donations.

- **Public sources.** Tax-exempt government foundations (like the National Endowment for the Arts, the National Endowment for the Humanities, or the Corporation for Public Broadcasting), as well as private foundations and charities (such as the Ford Foundation, the United Way, or the American Cancer Society), are usually required by their own operating rules and federal tax regulations to donate their funds to only 501(c)(3) tax-exempt organizations.

- **Individual private donors** can claim personal federal income tax deductions for contributions made to 501(c)(3) tax-exempt groups. At a donor's death, a complete federal estate tax exemption is available for bequests made to 501(c)(3) groups.

In short, if you plan to ask people to give you significant amounts of money in furtherance of your nonprofit purpose, you need to demonstrate to your donors that you have 501(c)(3) tax-exempt status.

Protection From Personal Liability

Protecting the members of your group from personal liability is one of the main reasons for forming a corporation (either profit or nonprofit). Once you're incorporated, directors or trustees, officers, employees, and members of a corporation usually won't be personally liable for corporate debts or liabilities, including unpaid organizational debts and unsatisfied lawsuit judgments against the organization, as they normally would be if they conducted their affairs without incorporating. Creditors can go after only corporate assets to satisfy liabilities incurred by the corporation—not the personal assets (cars, homes, or bank accounts) of the people who manage, work for, or volunteer to help the nonprofit corporation.

EXAMPLE:

A member of the audience sued a nonprofit symphony orchestra when the patron fell during a concert, claiming that the symphony (which also owned the concert hall) provided an unsafe ramp. The patron won a judgment that exceeded the orchestra's insurance policy limits. The amount of the judgment in excess of insurance is a debt of the corporation, but not of its individual directors, members, managers, or officers. By contrast, had the orchestra been an unincorporated association of musicians, the principals of the unincorporated group could be held personally liable for the excess judgment amount.

In a few situations, however, people involved with a nonprofit corporation may be personally liable for the corporation's liabilities. Here are some major areas of potential personal liability:

- **Taxes.** State and federal governments can hold the corporate employee who is responsible for reporting and paying corporate taxes personally liable for any unpaid taxes, penalties, and interest due for failure to pay taxes or file necessary returns (for example, the treasurer if the nonprofit board has given this officer full authority to pay all taxes as they become due). With proper planning, your nonprofit corporation should be tax exempt, but you still have to file federal and state informational returns and annual reports to the secretary of state and state attorney general, as well as pay employee withholding and other payroll taxes and taxes on income unrelated to your nonprofit purposes. IRS penalties for delinquent tax payments and returns are substantial, so keep this exception to limited liability in mind—particularly if you will be the treasurer or a board member who specifically approves the payment of taxes on behalf of your corporation.

- **Dues.** Members of a nonprofit corporation are personally liable for any membership fees and dues they owe the corporation. In most cases, this is a minor obligation because dues are normally set at modest amounts.

- **Violations of statutory duties.** Corporate directors are legally required to act responsibly (not recklessly) when managing the corporation. They may be held personally financially liable if they fail to act responsibly. Personal liability of this sort is the exception, not the rule. Generally, as long as directors attend meetings and carry out corporate responsibilities conscientiously, they should have little to worry about—the corporate limited liability shield insulates directors from all but the most reckless and irresponsible decisions.

- **Intermingling funds or other business dealings.** A nonprofit corporation must act so that its separate existence is clear and respected. If it mixes up corporate funds with the personal funds of those in charge, fails to follow legal formalities (such as failing to operate according to bylaws, hold director meetings, or keep minutes of meetings), or risks financial liability without sufficient backup in cash or other assets, a court may disregard the corporate entity and hold the principals responsible for debts and other liabilities of the corporation. In legalese, this is known as piercing the corporate veil. Piercing the veil is the exception, not the rule, and only happens when a court decides that it is necessary to prevent a gross injustice or fraud perpetrated by the founders or principals of a corporation.

- **Private foundation managers.** If the nonprofit corporation is classified as a private foundation, foundation managers can be held personally liable for federal excise taxes associated with certain prohibited transactions. They may also be held personally liable for penalties and interest charged for failing to file certain tax returns or pay required excise taxes. (As explained in Chapter 4, a private foundation is a 501(c)(3) corporation that does not qualify as a public charity—you'll see that most 501(c)(3) nonprofits qualify as public charities and are not subject to the private foundation requirements.)

- **Loans.** When a nonprofit corporation takes a loan to cover its operating costs or buys property subject to a mortgage, banks and commercial lending institutions sometimes insist on the personal guarantee of its directors or officers. If the directors or officers agree to personally guarantee the loan or mortgage, the protection that they would normally enjoy as a result of their organization's corporate status goes away. It is somewhat unusual for nonprofit directors or officers to sign a personal guarantee. Obviously, if they do, they will be liable to repay the loan if the corporation cannot do so.

Separate and Perpetual Legal Existence

A corporation is a legal entity that is separate from the people who work for it. Again, one benefit of this separate existence is that corporate liabilities are not the liabilities of the managers, officers, or members of the corporation (known as the corporate characteristic of limited liability). Another benefit is that this corporate legal person is, in a sense, immortal; the nonprofit corporation continues to exist as a legal entity despite changes in management or other corporate personnel caused by the resignation, removal, or death of the people associated with it. It may, of course, be dissolved or drastically affected by the loss of key people, but its inherent perpetual existence makes it more likely that the group's activities will continue, an attractive feature to the private or public donor who prefers funding activities that are organized to operate over the long term.

Employee Benefits

Another benefit of the nonprofit corporation is that its principals can also be employees and, therefore, eligible for employee fringe benefits not generally available to the workers in unincorporated organizations. These benefits include group term life insurance, reimbursement of medical expenses, and coverage by a qualified corporate employee pension or retirement income plan.

Formality and Structure

The formal corporate documents—the articles, bylaws, minutes of meetings, and board resolutions—that you'll prepare as a nonprofit will actually be quite useful to your organization. They'll outline the group's purposes, embody its operating rules, and provide structure and procedures for decision making and dispute resolution. This is important for any collective activity, but for nonprofit groups it is vital, especially if the board includes members of the community with diverse interests and viewpoints. Without the clear-cut delegation of authority and specific operating rules in the articles and bylaws, running the organization might be a divisive, if not futile, affair.

Miscellaneous Benefits

Additional advantages are available to nonprofits that engage in particular types of activities or operations. These benefits can be helpful, and in some cases are critical, to the success of a nonprofit organization. Here are examples of some of the benefits available to certain types of tax-exempt nonprofits.

- Your nonprofit may qualify for exemptions from county real and personal property taxes.

- 501(c)(3) organizations receive lower postal rates on third-class bulk mailings.

- Many publications offer cheaper classified advertising rates to nonprofit organizations.

- Nonprofits are the exclusive beneficiaries of free radio and television public service announcements (PSAs) provided by local media outlets.

- Many stores offer lower membership rates to nonprofit employees.

- Nonprofit employees are often eligible to participate in job training, student intern, work-study, and other federal, state, and local employment incentive programs (where salaries are paid substantially out of federal and state funds).

- 501(c)(3) performing arts groups are qualified to participate in the performance programs sponsored by federally supported colleges and universities.

- Certain 501(c)(3) educational organizations are eligible for a tax refund for gasoline expenses (for example, in running school buses).

Does Incorporation Make Sense for Your Group?

A senior citizens botany club began as an informal organization. Initially, six members took a monthly nature walk to study and photograph regional flora. Everyone chipped in to buy gas for whoever drove to the hike's starting point. Recently, however, membership increased to 15 and the group decided to collect dues from members to pay the increased expenses—gas money, guidebooks, maps, and club T-shirts—associated with more frequent field trips. To avoid mixing club monies with personal funds, a treasurer was designated to open a bank account on behalf of the organization. Several people suggest that it is time to incorporate the club.

Does incorporation make sense at this time? Probably not. There is no new pressing need to adopt the corporate form or to obtain formal recognition as a tax-exempt nonprofit. Most banks will allow an unincorporated group without a federal Employer Identification Number or IRS tax exemption to open up a non-interest-bearing account. However, should the club decide to seek funding and contributions to spearhead a drive to save open space in the community, it might be a good idea to incorporate.

The Disadvantages of Going Nonprofit

If your group has come together for 501(c)(3) tax-exempt purposes, and if reading about the benefits of becoming a nonprofit above prompted a "Wow! We would really like to be able to do *that!*" then chances are you've decided to tackle the rules and forms necessary to establish your status as a legal nonprofit. Before jumping in, however, take a minute to read the following descriptions of some of the hurdles and work you'll encounter along the way, especially if you have been operating informally (and successfully) without financial or employee record keeping or controls. If any of the following appear insurmountable to you, think again about incorporating.

Official Paperwork

One disadvantage in forming any corporation is the red tape and paperwork. You'll begin by preparing initial incorporation documents (articles of incorporation, bylaws, and minutes of first meeting of the board of directors). Although this book will show you how to prepare your own incorporation forms and bylaws with a minimum of time and trouble, the process will still take you a few hours. You and your compatriots must be prepared for some old-fashioned hard work.

After you've set up your corporation, you'll need to file annual tax and reporting returns with the state (the state tax or revenue office and the attorney general) as well as the Internal Revenue Service. Also, you will need to regularly prepare minutes of ongoing corporate meetings, and, occasionally, forms for amending articles and bylaws. The annual tax reporting forms will require the implementation of an organized bookkeeping system plus the help of an experienced nonprofit tax advisor as explained below. Fortunately, keeping minutes of these meetings is not all that difficult to do once someone volunteers for the task (typically the person you appoint as corporate secretary). Sample forms for amending nonprofit articles are usually available from the state corporate filing office online (see Appendix B to locate the website address of your state's corporate filing office).

Annual nonprofit tax and information returns do present a challenge to a new group unfamiliar with state tax reporting forms and requirements. Other record-keeping and reporting chores, such as double-entry accounting procedures and payroll tax withholding and reporting, can be equally daunting. At least at the start, most nonprofits rely on the experience of a tax advisor, bookkeeper, or other legal or tax specialist on the board or in the community to help them set up their books and establish a system for preparing tax forms on time. See Chapter 11 for recommendations on finding legal and tax professionals for your nonprofit.

Incorporation Costs and Fees

For nonprofit incorporators unwilling to do the job themselves, a main disadvantage of incorporating a nonprofit organization is the cost of paying an attorney to prepare the incorporation forms and tax exemption applications. Putting some time and effort into understanding the material in this book can help you eliminate this disadvantage, leaving you with only the actual cost of incorporation. Including the typical $400 federal tax exemption application fee, total fees to incorporate are approximately $450–$600. (Costs are $450 higher for nonprofits that anticipate gross receipts of more than $10,000. These groups pay an $850, rather than a $400, federal tax exemption application fee.) The IRS may allow you to use an online "Cyber Assistant" application for a lower $200 application fee. Go to www.irs.gov and search for "user fee information" to get the latest fee information.

Time and Energy Needed to Run the Nonprofit

When a group decides to incorporate, the legal decision is often part of a broader decision to increase not just the structure, but the overall scope, scale, and visibility of the nonprofit. With a larger, more accountable organization comes a number of new tasks: setting up and balancing books and bank accounts, depositing and reporting payroll taxes, and meeting with an accountant to extract and report year-end figures for annual informational returns. Although these financial, payroll, and tax concerns are not exclusively corporate chores, you'll find that most unincorporated nonprofits keep a low employment, tax, and financial profile and get by with minimum attention to legal and tax formalities.

EXAMPLE:

A women's health collective operates as an unincorporated nonprofit organization. It keeps an office open a few days a week where people stop by to read and exchange information on community and women's health issues. The two founders donate their time and the office space and pay operating costs (such as phone, utilities, and photocopying) that aren't covered by contributions from visitors. The organization has never made a profit, there is no payroll, and tax returns have never been filed. There is a minimum of paperwork and record keeping.

The founders could decide to continue this way indefinitely. However, the founders want to expand the activities and revenues of the collective. They decide to form a 501(c)(3) nonprofit corporation in order to be eligible for tax-deductible contributions and grant funds from the city, and to qualify the group to employ student interns and work-study students. This will require them to prepare and file articles of incorporation and a federal corporate income tax exemption application. They must select an initial board of directors and prepare organizational bylaws and formal written minutes of the first board of directors' meeting.

After incorporation, the group holds regular board meetings documented with written minutes, sets up and uses a double-entry bookkeeping system, implements regular federal and state payroll and tax procedures and controls, files exempt organization tax returns each year, and expands its operations. A full-time staff person is assigned to handle the increased paperwork and bookkeeping chores brought about by the change in structure and increased operations of the organization.

This example highlights what should be one of the first things you consider before you decide to incorporate: Make sure that you and your coworkers can put in the extra time and effort that an incorporated nonprofit organization will require. If the extra work would overwhelm or overtax your current resources, we suggest you hold off on your incorporation until you get the extra help you need to accomplish this task smoothly (or at least more easily).

Restrictions on Paying Directors and Officers

As a matter of state corporation law and the tax exemption requirements, nonprofits are restricted in how they deal with their directors, officers, and members. None of the gains, profits, or dividends of the corporation can go to individuals associated with the corporation, including directors, officers, and those defined as members in the corporation's articles or bylaws. State self-dealing rules apply as well, regulating action by the board of directors if a director has a financial interest in a transaction.

Officers and staff can be paid a reasonable salary for work they do for the corporation. State laws often provide for this type of compensation, and even if nothing is specified, it is permissible. Directors can also be paid for their expenses and time for attending director meetings. In all cases, however, these payments should be reasonable. Lavish payments or undeserved payouts characterized as "salaries" or "compensation" can be challenged by the IRS and can lead to penalties and even a loss of tax exemption (see "Other Requirements for 501(c)(3) Groups" in Chapter 3).

Restrictions Upon Dissolution

One of the requirements for the 501(c)(3) tax exemption is that upon dissolution of the corporation, any assets remaining after the corporation's debts and liabilities are paid must go to another tax-exempt nonprofit, not to members of the former corporation.

Restrictions on Your Political Activities

Section 501(c)(3) of the Internal Revenue Code establishes a number of restrictions and limitations that apply to nonprofits. Here, we discuss a limitation that may be very significant to some groups—the limitation on your political activities. Specifically, your organization may not participate in political campaigns for or against candidates for public office, and cannot substantially engage in legislative or grassroots political activities except as permitted under federal tax regulations (for more on this, see "Other Requirements for 501(c)(3) Groups" in Chapter 3).

EXAMPLE:

Society for a Saner World, Inc., has as one of its primary objectives lobbying hard to pass federal and local legislation that seeks to lessen societal dependency on fossil fuels. Since a substantial portion of the group's efforts will consist of legislative lobbying, the group's 501(c)(3) tax exemption probably will be denied by the IRS. Instead, the group should seek a tax-exemption under IRC § 501(c)(4) as a social welfare group, which is not limited in the amount of lobbying the group can undertake. Of course, the benefits of 501(c)(4) tax exemption are fewer too—contributions to the group are not tax deductible, and grant funds will be more difficult to obtain (see "Special Nonprofit Tax-Exempt Organizations," in Appendix C).

Oversight by the Attorney General

Each state's attorney general has broad power to oversee the operations of 501(c)(3) nonprofits. The attorney general can take the corporation to court to make sure it complies with the state corporation law. This usually doesn't happen, however, unless an organization commits a serious offense (such as the founders' diverting contributions for their personal use) and the organization is on the state attorney general's enforcement division radar (through a complaint filed by a disgruntled group or a member of the public who feels aggrieved by the nonprofit's actions or policies).

Religious 501(c)(3) nonprofit corporations have wider flexibility in managing their internal affairs. A state attorney general is less likely to step in and sue a religious nonprofit to enforce compliance with state corporate laws, except in the most extreme and unusual cases of fraud or misappropriation by the principals of a religious-purpose nonprofit.

How Nonprofits Raise, Spend, and Make Money

Most nonprofits need to deal with money—indeed, being able to attract donations is a prime reason for choosing nonprofit status. Nonprofits can also make money. Nonprofit does not literally mean that a nonprofit corporation cannot make a profit. Under federal tax law and state law, as long as your nonprofit is organized and operating for a recognized nonprofit purpose, it can take in more money than it spends in conducting its activities. A nonprofit may use its tax-free profits for its operating expenses (including salaries for officers, directors, and employees) or for the benefit of its organization. What it cannot do under IRC § 501(c)(3) is distribute any of the profits for the benefit of its officers, directors, or employees (as dividends, for example).

This section explains how nonprofits raise initial funds and how they make money on an ongoing basis.

Initial Fundraising

Under state corporate statutes, a nonprofit corporation is not legally required to have a specified amount of money in the corporate bank account before commencing operations. This is fortunate, of course, because many beginning nonprofits start out on a shoestring of meager public and private support.

So, where will your seed money come from? As you know, nonprofit corporations cannot issue shares, nor can they provide investment incentives, such as a return on capital through the payment of dividends to investors, benefactors, or participants in the corporation (see "Corporation Basics," at the beginning of this chapter). Nonprofits have their own means and methods of obtaining start-up funds. Obviously, the most common method is to obtain revenue in the form of contributions, grants, and dues from the people, organizations, and governmental agencies that support the nonprofit's purpose and goals. Also, if you are incorporating an existing organization, the organization's assets are usually transferred to the new corporation—these assets may include the cash reserves of an unincorporated group, which can help your corporation begin operations. You can also borrow start-up funds from a bank, although for newly formed corporations a bank will usually require that incorporators secure the loan with their personal assets—a pledge most nonprofit directors are understandably reluctant to make.

Often, of course, nonprofits receive initial and ongoing revenues from services or activities provided in the pursuit of their exempt purposes (ticket sales, payments for art lessons or dance courses, school tuition, or clinic charges). Section 501(c)(3) nonprofits are allowed to earn this type of revenue under federal and state tax laws and still maintain their tax-exempt status.

Making Money From Related Activities

Many nonprofits make money while they further the goals of the organization. The nonprofit can use this tax-exempt revenue to pay for operating expenses (including reasonable salaries) and to further its nonprofit purposes. For example, an organization dedicated to the identification and preservation of shorebirds might advertise a bird-watching and counting hike for which they charge a fee; the group could then use the proceeds to fund their bird rescue operations. What it cannot do with the money, however, is distribute it for the benefit of officers, directors, or employees of the corporation (as the payment of a patronage dividend, for example).

EXAMPLE:

Friends of the Library, Inc., is a 501(c)(3) nonprofit organized to encourage literary appreciation in the community and to raise money for the support and improvement of the public library. It makes a profit from its sold-out lecture series featuring famous authors and from its annual sale of donated books. Friends can use this tax-exempt profit for its own operating expenses, including salaries for officers and employees, or to benefit the library.

Making Money From Unrelated Activities (Unrelated Income)

Nonprofits can also make money in ways unrelated to their nonprofit purpose. Often this income is essential to the survival of the nonprofit group. This unrelated income, however, is usually taxed as unrelated business income under state and federal corporate income tax rules. While earning money this way is permissible, it's best not to let unrelated business activities reach the point where you start to look more like a for-profit business than a nonprofit one. This can happen if the unrelated income-generating activities are absorbing a substantial amount of staff time, requiring additional paid staff or volunteers, or producing more income than your exempt-purpose activities. If the unrelated revenue or activities of your tax-exempt nonprofit reach a substantial level, the IRS can decide to revoke

the group's 501(c)(3) tax exemption—a result your nonprofit will no doubt wish to avoid. (For more information, see "Other Requirements for 501(c)(3) Groups" in Chapter 3.)

EXAMPLE:

Many thousands of books are donated to Friends of the Library for its annual book sale, one of its major fundraising events. Although the sale is always highly successful, thousands of books are left over. Friends decides to sell the more valuable books by advertising in the rare and out-of-print books classified sections in various magazines. The response is overwhelming; soon, there are six employees cataloguing books. In addition, Friends begins a business purchasing books from other dealers and reselling them to the public. Such a situation could attract attention from the IRS and prompt it to reconsider Friends' 501(c)(3) tax-exempt status.

Making Money from Passive Sources

Although it's not typical for the average nonprofit, a nonprofit corporation can make money from passive sources such as rents, royalties, interest, and investments. This income is nontaxable in some cases.

Your Path to Nonprofit Status

Nonprofit organizations first obtain nonprofit corporate status with the state corporate filing office—usually the corporations division of the secretary of state's office. This is a simple formality accomplished by filing articles of incorporation. Then they go on to obtain a corporate income tax exemption with the Internal Revenue Service. Once the IRS exemption is obtained, a copy of the federal tax exemption determination letter is filed with the state tax or revenue office. This automatically qualifies the nonprofit for a state corporate income tax exemption (assuming the state imposes a corporate tax). In a few states, you must apply for a separate state nonprofit corporate income tax exemption.

In sum, your path to nonprofit status is a usually a two-step process—first you incorporate with the state, then you apply for tax-exempt recognition from the IRS. When you're done with this book, you'll have completed each of these steps, plus additional follow-up steps to make sure your corporation is off to a good legal and tax start.

Where Should You Incorporate?

Corporations formed in a particular state are known in that state as domestic corporations. When viewed from outside that state, these corporations are considered foreign. A foreign corporation that plans to engage in a regular or repeated pattern of activity in another state must qualify to do business there by obtaining a certificate of authority from the secretary of state. For example, a corporation formed in Nevada that intends to do regular business in California is a foreign corporation in California, and must qualify with the California Secretary of State.

Incorporators who plan to operate in another state besides their home state might wonder whether it makes sense to incorporate in that other state. Maybe the incorporation fees or corporate taxes are lower than those in the home state or the nonprofit statutes are more flexible. Then, the reasoning goes, one could qualify the corporation in the home state as a

foreign corporation. As tempting as this end run may appear, it's usually not worth it. This section explains why, and also advises you of out-of-state activities that you can engage in without worrying about qualifying in another state.

Qualifying as a Foreign Corporation in Your Home State Will Cost You More

The process of qualifying a foreign corporation to operate in your home state takes about as much time and expense as incorporating a domestic corporation in your home state. This means that you will pay more to incorporate out-of-state since you must pay the regular home state qualification fees plus out-of-state incorporation fees.

Two Sets of Tax Exemptions

Your corporation will still be subject to taxation in each state in which it earns or derives income or funds. If the state of incorporation, which we here assume is a "foreign" state, imposes a corporate income tax, then the nonprofit corporation will need to file for and obtain two state corporate tax exemptions—one for its home state (the state where the corporation will be active and qualify to do business) and one for the foreign state of incorporation. Similarly, double sales, property, and other state tax exemptions may often be necessary or appropriate.

Two Sets of State Laws

Your out-of-state corporation will still be subject to many of the laws that affect corporations in your home state. Many state corporate statutes that apply to domestic corporations also apply to foreign corporations.

Out-of-State Activities Below the Radar

For the above reasons, most readers who flirt with the idea of incorporating in a state other than their home state would be well advised to skip it. This doesn't mean, however, that you'll have to trim all of your activities to stay within your home state. Fortunately, there are many things nonprofits can do as a foreign corporation in another state without obtaining a certificate of authority from the secretary of that state. Here are some activities that can be done in most states without qualifying to do business there:

- maintaining, defending, or settling any legal action or administrative proceeding, including securing or collecting debts and enforcing property rights

- holding meetings of corporate directors or of the membership and distributing information to members

- maintaining bank accounts and making grants of funds

- making sales through independent contractors and engaging in interstate or foreign commerce

- conducting a so-called isolated transaction that is completed within 30 days and is not one of a series of similar transactions, and

- exercising powers as an executor, administrator, or trustee, as long as none of the activities required of the position amount to transacting business.

When Out-of-State Incorporation Makes Sense

There may be a few of you for whom incorporation in another state makes sense. If you plan to set up a multistate nonprofit with corporate offices and activities in more than one state (a tristate environmental fund for example), you may want to consider incorporating in the state that offers the greatest legal, tax, and practical advantages. To help you decide where to incorporate, go online to each state's corporate filing office website (see Appendix B). Another approach is to check a nonprofit resource center library. For nonprofit library resources online, type "nonprofit resource libraries" into your browser—you'll find a host of online libraries at your disposal. An experienced nonprofit lawyer or consultant can also help you determine which state is the most convenient and least costly to use as the legal home for your new nonprofit corporation. ●

Legal Rights and Duties of Incorporators, Directors, Officers, Employees, and Members

Even though a corporation is a legal person capable of making contracts, incurring liabilities, and engaging in other activities, it still needs real people to act on its behalf to carry out its activities. These people decide to incorporate, select those who will be responsible for running the organization, and actually manage and carry out the nonprofit's goals and activities.

This chapter explains the rights and responsibilities of those in your group who will organize and operate your nonprofit corporation. These incorporators, directors, officers, members, and employees have separate legal rights and responsibilities. Later, after your nonprofit is up and running, you may want to refer back to this chapter if you have questions regarding the powers and duties of these important people.

How Many People Are Needed to Form a Nonprofit Corporation?

Roughly half of the states take the modern permissive approach and allow only one person to form a nonprofit corporation. In these states, one person can be the corporation's sole director, president, secretary, and treasurer. Of course in the nonprofit context, it is rare to form a one-person corporation, because a nonprofit usually must rely on the talent and energy of at least several people to make a go of it. And just as important, the IRS will look askance at a one-person corporation, because it expects multiple people to pitch in to advance the public purposes of a 501(c)(3) organization. If only one person (or even just two or three)

organize and operate the nonprofit, the IRS is going to need to be convinced that the nonprofit is not being organized and operated simply to advance the self-interested agenda of such a small group of individuals. (See Chapters 3 and 4 for more on IRS requirements.)

In many states, more than one person is needed to organize and operate the corporation. We list these states, below. If you want to be sure these are the latest minimum-number-of-people rules, check your state's nonprofit corporation law (see Appendix B). Another easy way to check the latest rules is to go to your state's filing office website and read the instructions for your state's nonprofit articles form—typically, these instructions contain the latest state law requirements for the number of incorporators, directors, and officers. If they don't, look elsewhere on the website—many states maintain lists of basic organizational rules directly on their websites.

Incorporator

Most states allow a nonprofit corporation to have one incorporator (only one person is needed to sign the articles of incorporation). But in Alaska, the District of Columbia, Oklahoma, and South Dakota, local law requires at least three incorporators; New Hampshire requires at least five.

Directors

Many states allow the corporation to have just one director. However, several states require the corporation to have more than one director and/or have other special director-selection rules, as noted below.

States That Require More Than One Director	
Alabama, Alaska, Arkansas, Connecticut, District of Columbia, Florida, Hawaii, Illinois, Indiana, Kentucky, Michigan, Minnesota, Missouri, Montana, Nebraska, New Jersey, New Mexico, New York, Rhode Island, South Carolina, South Dakota, Tennessee, Texas, Utah, Vermont, West Virginia, Wisconsin, Wyoming	A minimum of three directors is required.
California	A majority of the directors of a public benefit corporation—generally, this includes non-religious 501(c)(3) nonprofits—must be financially disinterested (must not receive payment from the corporation during the preceding 12 months nor be related to such a paid person). See the state filing office website for more information.
Idaho	A minimum of three directors is required. If the nonprofit is a religious corporation, one director is allowed.
Louisiana	A minimum of three directors is required in a membership corporation. If there are less than three members, then the number of directors can equal the number of directors.
Maine	A minimum of three directors is required. A majority of the directors of a public benefit corporation must be financially disinterested (must not receive payment from the corporation during the preceding 12 months nor be related to such a paid person). See the state filing office website for more information.
New Hampshire	A minimum of five directors is required; for non-religious charitable nonprofits, these five directors cannot be related unless the corporation receives a waiver from this requirement. See the state filing office website for more information.
North Dakota	A minimum of three directors is required (or at least the number of voting members if there are fewer than three voting members). A majority of the board must be unpaid (in a capacity other than director) and unrelated to paid directors. See the state filing office website for more information.
Ohio	A minimum of three directors is required. If there are fewer than three members, the number of directors must be at least equal to the number of members.
Oregon	A minimum of three directors is required for public benefit corporation; religious or mutual benefit corporations may have only one director.

Officers

Most states require the corporation to have a president, secretary, and treasurer, but allow one person to fill two or more of these officer positions. However, the states listed in the chart below specify that one person cannot be both the president and the secretary of the nonprofit corporation (some states have a different or an additional rule, which we note in the chart).

Incorporators and Their Role as Promoters

An incorporator is the person (or persons) who signs and delivers the articles of incorporation to the secretary of state for filing. In practice, the incorporator is often selected from among the people who serve as the initial directors of the corporation. Once the corporation is formed, the incorporator's legal role is finished. Attorneys often serve as the incorporator for a corporation. Because you are doing the paperwork yourself with the help of this book,

you won't need to pay a lawyer to act as your incorporator—one or more of your founders can act as the incorporator(s) of your nonprofit.

During the organizational phase, it's not unusual for an incorporator to become a "promoter" of the corporation. An incorporator's promotional activities can quickly go beyond enthusiastic talk about the organization. Promotional activities may involve obtaining money, property, personnel, and whatever else it takes to get the nonprofit corporation started. Arranging for a loan or renting office space will require signatures and promises—to repay the loan and pay the rent. But will the newly formed corporation automatically become responsible? Future directors may hesitate to join a new organization that is saddled already by contracts negotiated by an eager (but perhaps naive) promoter. The promoters themselves will naturally be nervous that they'll be personally responsible if the incorporation plans go awry. And what about the third parties? They may not be inclined to do business with promoters unless they are

States That Prohibit One Person From Being Both President and Secretary	
District of Columbia, New York, Rhode Island, Tennessee, Texas, Vermont	One person cannot be both the president and the secretary.
Alabama, Alaska, South Dakota, Washington	One person cannot be both the president and the secretary. At least one vice president is also required.
California	Neither secretary nor treasurer can also be president or chairperson of the board.
Idaho	One person cannot be both the president and the secretary, but religious corporations are not required to have any officers.
Massachusetts	The clerk (a secretary-like officer role) must be a Massachusetts resident unless the corporation designates a registered agent (as most do).
New Hampshire	No employee of a non-religious charitable nonprofit corporation shall hold the position of chairperson or presiding officer of the board (this requirement is waivable by the approval of the director of charitable trusts; see the state filing office website for more information).

Ways to Reassure Potential Officers and Directors

Before you start looking for people to help run your nonprofit, take a moment for a reality check: Many potential helpers will hesitate to become involved because they've read in the press about a few notorious, high-visibility lawsuits where nonprofit directors have been held personally liable for misconduct by executives of the nonprofit (for example, the executive of a large, public membership nonprofit misappropriates program funds to buy a yacht or high-priced apartment for personal use). On a more down-to-earth level, a potential treasurer for your nonprofit may hesitate to serve if that person thinks he or she will be personally responsible for the organization's tax reporting penalties, or a potential director may be worried about being personally sued by a fired employee of the nonprofit. Fortunately, these types of personal liability are extremely rare. Most nonprofits should be able to assure potential director and officer candidates that the nonprofit will be run accountably and sensibly without undue risk of tax or legal liability for the directors.

One obvious way to reassure candidates is to purchase directors' and officers' liability insurance from an insurance broker who handles nonprofit corporate insurance (called "D&O errors and omissions insurance"). This type of insurance, however, is expensive and usually beyond the reach of newly formed small nonprofits. Also, D&O coverage often excludes the sorts of potential liabilities that your directors and officers may be worried about (personal injury and other types of legal tort actions, claims of illegality, or intentional misconduct and the like). If you decide to investigate the cost of D&O insurance, you will want to make sure to go over the areas of coverage and exclusion in the policy very carefully before you buy in.

State legislators recognize that nonprofits often can't afford D&O liability insurance with adequate claim coverage, and many states have enacted nonprofit law provisions that help limit *volunteer* directors' and officers' exposure to liability. State laws also often require corporations to indemnify (advance or pay back) a director for legal expenses incurred in a lawsuit under certain conditions. These laws can provide added comfort to people considering serving as a nonprofit corporation director or officer. If you want more information about the laws in your state, browse your state's nonprofit laws online (see Appendix B for information on how to locate your state's nonprofit law online) or consult with a nonprofit lawyer in your state. Again, we believe the best and most practical way to reassure directors and officers to hitch their wagon to your nonprofit organization's star is to be able to show them that you will operate your nonprofit fairly, responsibly, and safely without undue risk of lawsuits by employees or complaints by the public.

assured that there will be a responsible party at the other end. After explaining how a promoter must approach every transaction—with the corporation's best interests in mind—we'll show you how to address the concerns of the eventual directors, the promoters themselves, and the third parties with whom they do business.

A Promoter Must Act With the Corporation's Best Interests in Mind

When an incorporator acts as a promoter, he or she is considered by law to be its fiduciary. This legal jargon simply means the incorporator has a duty to act in the best interests of the corporation, and must make full disclosure of any personal interest and potential benefits he or she may derive from business transacted for the nonprofit.

EXAMPLE:

When the incorporator/promoter arranges to sell property to the nonprofit corporation, the promoter must disclose to the nonprofit's board of directors any personal ownership interest in the property and also any gain he or she stands to make on the sale.

Directors Must Ratify a Promoter's Actions

Most of the time, a nonprofit corporation will not be bound by an incorporator's preincorporation contract with a third party unless the board of directors ratifies the contract or the corporation accepts the benefits of the contract. For example, if a nonprofit board votes to ratify the lease signed by an incorporator before the date of incorporation, the corporation will be bound to honor the lease. Similarly, if the nonprofit staff moves into its new offices and

conducts business there, their actions will constitute a ratification and the nonprofit will be bound.

Promoters Can Avoid Personal Liability

Fortunately, if promoters carefully draft documents—such as any loan papers and leases—they can avoid the risk of personal liability in the event that the corporation doesn't ratify the deal (or if the corporation never comes into being). Incorporators will not be personally liable for these contracts if they sign in the name of a proposed corporation, not in their individual name, clearly inform the third party that the corporation does not yet exist and may never come into existence, and tell the third party that even if it does come into existence, it may not ratify the contract.

Convincing Third Parties to Do Business With a Promoter

As you might imagine, a cautious third party may balk at doing business with an individual whose yet-to-be-formed nonprofit may repudiate the deal. One way to provide some assurance to a third party is for an incorporator to bind himself personally to the contract—in essence, become a guarantor for the loan, lease, or other contract. Understandably, few incorporators will be able or willing to put their personal finances on the line, unless they are absolutely sure that the corporation will in fact be formed and will ratify the deal. The other solution is to incorporate quickly—which you can do with the help of this book!

EXAMPLE:

An incorporator/promoter enters into an agreement to lease office space for its organization. Six months later, the organization obtains nonprofit corporate status. The newly formed nonprofit is not bound by the lease agreement unless its board of directors ratifies the agreement or the organization used the office space during the preincorporation period.

Directors

Directors meet collectively as the board of directors, and are responsible—legally, financially, and morally—for the management and operation of your nonprofit corporation.

Before we discuss legalities and state law requirements, let's look at an overriding practical concern: how to select the best directors for your organization.

Selecting Directors

Choosing directors is one of the most important decisions you will make when organizing your nonprofit. Here are some important things to consider that will help you make the best possible choice for your organization.

Commitment to Your Nonprofit's Purpose

Your directors are a crucial link between your organization and its supporters and benefactors. Make sure that the members of the community that you plan to serve will see your directors as credible and competent representatives of your group and its nonprofit goals. Their status and integrity will be crucial to encouraging and protecting public trust in your organization, and their connections will be vital to attracting recognition, clients, donations, and other support.

- Consider members of the communities you will serve who have a proven commitment to the goals of your organization. There may be more than one community that

you'll want to consider. For example, your draw may be local (city, county, or state), regional, or national. If you are an environmental group concerned with issues in the southern part of the state, you have both a geographic community (people in the area) and a community of interest (environmentalists generally). Your board should reflect a cross section of interested and competent people from both of these communities.

- Look for people with contacts and real-world knowledge and experience in the specific area of your nonprofit's interest. If you are starting a new private school or health clinic, someone familiar with your state's educational or public health bureaucracy would be a big help.

- If your organization is set up to do good works that will benefit a particular group, don't overlook the value of including a member of that recipient group. You may learn important things about your mission and get valuable buy-in from the beneficiaries of your hard work.

Business Knowledge and Expertise

Directors' responsibilities include developing and overseeing organizational policies and goals, budgeting, fundraising, and disbursing a group's funds. The board of directors may hire an administrator or executive director to supervise staff and daily operations, or it may supervise them directly. Either way, your board of directors should be a practical-minded group with strong managerial, technical, and financial skills. In making your selection, try to find people with the following skills and experience:

- **Fundraising experience.** While many large nonprofits have a staff fundraiser, smaller groups often can benefit from the advice of an experienced board member.

- **Experience managing money.** A professional accountant or someone with expertise in record keeping and budgeting can be a godsend. Many nonprofits get into difficulty because their record keeping and reporting techniques aren't adequate to produce the information required by the federal and state governments. Many are simply inattentive to financial responsibilities, such as paying withholding taxes or accounting properly for public or private grant monies.

- **Useful practical skills.** Do you need the professional expertise of a doctor, lawyer, or architect; or operational assistance in areas such as public relations, marketing, or publishing? If so, make finding one of these professionals a high priority during your board search.

Public Officials Are a Good Choice

The IRS likes to see that you have a representative (and financially disinterested) governing body that reflects a range of public interests, not simply the personal interests of a small number of donors. While it's by no means required, the presence of a sympathetic public official on your board can enhance its credibility with both the IRS and the community.

Avoid Conflicts of Interest

When selecting board members, you may need to inquire about, or at least consider, a prospective member's agenda or motives for joining the board. Obviously, people who want to join for personal benefit rather than for the benefit of the organization or the public should not be asked to serve. This doesn't mean that everyone with a remote or potential conflict of interest should be automatically disqualified. It does mean that any slight or possible conflict of interest should be fully recognized and discussed. If the conflict is limited, the director may be able to serve constructively if he or she refrains from voting on certain issues. The bylaws included in this book have conflict of interest provisions that contain rules and procedures for avoiding or approving transactions, including compensation arrangements, that benefit the nonprofit's directors, officers, employees, or contractors. See Article 9 of the bylaws and "Limitation on Profits and Benefits," in Chapter 3, for more information on this topic.

Develop a Realistic Job Description

Your board of directors should be prepared to put time and energy into the organization. Make sure every prospective director has a realistic and clear understanding of what the job entails. Before you contact prospective candidates, we suggest that you prepare a job description that specifies at least the following:

- the scope of the nonprofit's proposed activities and programs

- board member responsibilities and time commitments (expected frequency and length of board meetings, extra duties that may be assigned to directors), and

- the rewards of serving on your board (such as the satisfaction of working on behalf of a cause you care about or the experience of community service).

A clear and comprehensive job description will help with decision making and will also help avoid future misunderstandings with board members over what is expected of them.

Train Your New Directors

The organizers of a nonprofit corporation often need to give initial directors orientation and training about the nonprofit's operations and activities. This training should continue so that board members can handle ongoing operational issues as well. For example, if your nonprofit corporation is organized to provide health care services, board members may need to learn city, state, and federal program requirements that impact your operations, and should get regular updates on changes made to these rules and regulations.

 TIP

Choose the right number of directors. You'll want enough to ensure a wide basis of support (particularly with respect to fundraising), but not so many as to impede efficiency in the board's operation. Boards with between nine and 15 directors often work well.

Paying Your Directors

Nonprofit directors usually serve without compensation. We believe this is generally wise. Having nonprofit directors serve without pay reinforces one of the important legal and ethical distinctions of the nonprofit corporation: Unlike its for-profit counterpart, its assets are used to promote its goals, not for the private enrichment of its incorporators, directors, agents, members, or employees.

If you compensate directors, do so at a reasonable rate, related to the actual performance of services and established in advance by a board resolution. (See Article 9 of the bylaws included in this book for specific procedures to follow when approving compensation arrangements.) Most nonprofits reimburse directors only for necessary expenses incurred in performing director duties, such as travel expenses—typically a gas or mileage allowance—to attend board meetings. Sometimes directors are paid a set fee for attending meetings. In most cases,

however, director compensation is minimal or nominal, if it is paid at all.

Term of Office

The term of office for directors is usually specified in the corporation's bylaws. Some states set a maximum term for directors (typically one year) only if the term is not specified in the articles or bylaws; other states specify a maximum term in all cases. Most states let you specify any term for directors in your bylaws.

Staggered Elections for Board Members

In the interest of continuity, staggered elections of board members may be a good idea. For example, rather than replacing the entire board at each annual election, you may wish to reelect one-third of the board members each year to serve a three-year term. To start this staggered system out with a 15-member board, five of the initial directors would serve for one year, five for two years, and the remaining five for the full three-year term. At each annual reelection, one-third of the board would be elected to serve three-year terms.

Quorum Rules

For the board of directors to take action at a meeting, a specified number of directors of the corporation—called a quorum—must be present. Generally, state nonprofit statutes require a majority quorum. This means that a majority of the full board must be present to hold a meeting.

Director Action by Written Consent or Conference Call

Your board of directors doesn't necessarily have to meet in person to take action affecting the corporation. Many states authorize directors to take action by written consent or by a conference telephone call. In some states, the directors must consent unanimously, in writing, to this procedure; in others, only the number of directors needed to pass the resolution (normally a majority of a quorum) must consent. If you're interested in having your board take action without a meeting, check your state's nonprofit corporation law. Look for a section titled "Action by Written Consent" in the part dealing with "Directors."

Voting Rules

Once a quorum is present at a meeting, a specified number of votes is needed to pass a board resolution. Unless otherwise stated in the articles or bylaws, a resolution normally must be passed by a majority vote of the directors present at a meeting where there is a quorum. In some cases, the votes of interested directors cannot be counted. This is discussed more in "How to Avoid Self-Dealing," below.

EXAMPLE:

The bylaws of a corporation with ten board members specify that a quorum consists of a majority of the board and that action by the board can be taken by a majority of the directors present. This means that a quorum of at least six people (a majority of the ten-person board) must be present to hold a board meeting and, at the very least, four votes (a majority of the six members present at a meeting) are required to pass a resolution. If eight of the ten directors attend the meeting, action must be approved by at least five votes—a majority of those present at the meeting.

If a quorum is present initially at a meeting and one or more board members leave, action can often still be taken even if you lose your quorum. As long you can still obtain the number of votes that represents a majority of the required quorum stated in the bylaws, the board normally can take action even though a quorum is no longer present at the meeting (this is known as the initial quorum rule). Going back to the example above, in a ten-director board, the required quorum for board action is six directors (a majority of the ten) and at least four votes (a majority of those present) are needed to take board action. Under the initial-quorum rule, two directors can leave the meeting and the four remaining votes will still be sufficient to pass a resolution. Why? Because a quorum was initially present and four board members, representing a majority of the required quorum of six, can vote to pass a resolution.

Executive Committees

The board of directors can delegate some or even a significant part of the board's duties to an executive committee, usually consisting of two or more directors. This arrangement is often used when some directors are more involved in running and managing the nonprofit's affairs and business than others.

Even the passive directors, however, should still keep an eye on what their more active colleagues are up to and actively participate in regular meetings of the full board. To encourage passive directors to stay involved, courts have held the full board responsible for the actions of the executive committee.

Fortunately, keeping the full board abreast of executive committee actions isn't very difficult. The full board should receive regular, timely minutes of executive committee meetings and should review and, if necessary, reconsider important executive committee decisions at each regularly scheduled meeting of the full board. The full board should retain the power to override decisions of the executive committee.

Under state law, there are certain actions that can't be delegated to an executive committee. Typically, an executive committee cannot be given authority to do one or more of the following:

- approve action that requires approval by the membership
- fill vacancies on the board or other committees
- fix directors' compensation
- alter bylaws, or
- use corporate funds to support a nominee to the board after more people have been nominated than can be elected.

Don't confuse this special executive committee of directors with other corporate committees. The board typically appoints several specialized committees to keep track of and report on corporate operations and programs. These committees act as working groups that are more manageable in size and help make better use of the board's time and its members' talents. They may include finance, personnel, buildings and grounds, new projects, fundraising, or other committees. These committees, often consisting of a mix of directors, officers, and paid staff, do not normally have the power to take legal action on behalf of the corporation; their purpose is to report and make recommendations to the full board or the executive committee.

EXAMPLE:

The board of directors appoints a finance committee charged with overseeing the organization's fundraising, budgeting, expenditures, and bookkeeping. The corporation's treasurer chairs the committee. Periodically, this committee makes financial recommendations to the full board. The board could also appoint a personnel committee to establish hiring and employment policies and to interview candidates for important positions. A plans and programs committee might be selected to put together the overall action plan for accomplishing the goals of the organization. Any action taken based on a committee's report or recommendation would be subject to approval by the board.

Directors' Duty of Care

Corporate directors and officers have a legal duty to act responsibly and in the best interests of the corporation—this is called their statutory "duty of care." The statutes defining this phrase use general, imprecise legal terms that are not very helpful in understanding what exactly it means. As a result, the meaning of the term has developed over time as judges and juries, faced with lawsuits, decide whether a director's acts did (or did not) live up to the duty of care. Fortunately, most of it boils down to common sense, as the following discussions show.

Personal Liability for Directors' Acts

In general, you shouldn't be overly concerned about the prospect of personal liability for your directors. Broadly speaking, courts are reluctant to hold nonprofit directors personally liable, except in the clearest cases of dereliction of duty or misuse of corporate funds or property. In the rare cases when liability is found, the penalties are usually not onerous or punitive—typically, the court orders directors to repay the losses their actions caused.

Ordinary negligence or poor judgment is usually not enough to show a director breached the duty of care. Instead, there generally must be some type of fraudulent or grossly negligent behavior. *Volunteer* directors and executive officers of nonprofits enjoy extra protection from personal liability. These personal immunity laws are discussed in detail in "Director Indemnification and Insurance," below.

EXAMPLE:

A committee of the nonprofit advises the board of an unsafe condition on the corporation's property. The committee recommends certain remedial actions to get rid of the problem. If the board fails to implement any remedial measures or otherwise take steps to deal with the problem, a court could hold the directors personally liable for any ensuing damage or injuries.

Although the risk of being held personally liable is small, there are some things a director can and should do to minimize the risk of personal liability. Most importantly, all directors, whether active participants or casual community observers, should attend board meetings and stay informed of, and participate in, all major board decisions. If the board makes a woefully wrongheaded or ill-advised decision that leads to monetary damages, the best defense for any board member is a "No" vote recorded in the corporate minutes.

Also, all boards should try to get an experienced financial manager on their board or use the services of a prudent accountant who demands regular audited financial statements of the group's books. Legalities aside, what is

most likely to put nonprofit directors at risk of personal liability is bad financial management, such as failing to pay taxes, not keeping proper records of how much money is collected and how it is disbursed, and commingling funds, either mixing directors' personal funds with corporate funds or restricted with nonrestricted funds.

Reliance on Regular Business Reports: A Safe Haven

To help directors accomplish their managerial duties, state law as well as IRS regulations and procedures often allow directors to rely on information from reliable, competent sources within the corporation (officers, committees, and supervisory staff), or on outside professional sources (lawyers, accountants, and investment advisors). If this information later turns out to be faulty or incorrect, the directors will not be held personally liable for any decision made in reliance on the information, unless the directors had good reason to question and look beyond the information presented to the board and failed to do so.

For example, if a nonprofit's treasurer tells the board that the organization has sufficient cash to meet ongoing payroll tax requirements, and the report seems reasonable (perhaps because the nonprofit has a budget surplus), the IRS will probably find that the individual board members were entitled to rely on the treasurer's report, even if there is not enough money to pay the taxes. However, if the board knows or should have known that the nonprofit is having a difficult time paying its bills despite reports to the contrary by the treasurer, and the board does not direct the treasurer to make sure to set money aside to pay payroll taxes, the IRS may try to hold board members personally liable for unpaid taxes.

Investment Decisions Involving Corporate Assets

Directors of 501(c)(3) nonprofit corporations must use more caution when making investment decisions than when they decide routine business matters. That's because when they make investment decisions involving corporate funds, directors usually have an added duty of care under state nonprofit law to avoid speculation and protect those funds—a stricter standard of care than the normal standard discussed above. A typical phrasing of this stricter standard of care, known as the directors' fiduciary duty to the corporation, is that the directors must "avoid speculation, looking instead to the permanent disposition of the funds, considering the probable income, as well as the probable safety of the corporation's capital."

EXAMPLE:

The treasurer of a performing arts group tells the group's directors that the group has a hefty surplus of funds because of its recent road tour. The board decides to invest this money in a stable asset mutual fund rather than one of several high-risk equity funds that reported double-digit declines in the last several quarters. If challenged by the state attorney general or a complaining member, the directors should be able to show that they've met their fiduciary duty to the corporation—they have attempted to preserve the capital of the corporation by investing in a stable fund with a predictable positive return track record rather than a riskier fund that was more likely to lose money.

Directors Must Be Loyal

A director has a duty of loyalty to the corporation. In most states, this is commonly understood to mean that the director must give the corporation a right of first refusal on business opportunities that the director becomes aware of in his or her capacity as director. If the corporation fails to take advantage of the opportunity after full disclosure, or if the corporation clearly would not be interested in the opportunity, the director can take advantage of the opportunity as an individual.

EXAMPLE:

Bob is a volunteer director on the board of Help Hospices, a nonprofit hospice and shelter organization. He agrees to shop around for a low-rent location in a reasonably safe neighborhood for the next nonprofit hospice site. He learns of three low-rent locations, one of which would also be ideal as a low-cost rental studio for his son who wants to move out of his parents' house as soon as possible. Bob reports all three locations to the board, and tells them that he plans to apply for a lease in his son's name on one of the rental units only if the board decides that it is not interested in leasing the space for nonprofit purposes. This type of specific disclosure is exactly what is required for Bob to meet his duty of loyalty to the nonprofit. Bob can apply for the lease for his son if the board gives him the go-ahead after deciding the nonprofit is not interested in leasing the space for itself.

How to Avoid Self-Dealing

Directors must guard against unauthorized self-dealing—that is, involving the corporation in any transaction in which the director has a material, or significant, financial interest— without proper approval. The self-dealing rules and proper approval requirements can arise in many different types of transactions, including the purchase or sale of corporate property, the investment of corporate funds, or the payment of corporate fees or compensation.

The nonprofit corporation laws of most states include special rules for validating self-interested director decisions of this sort. In most cases, the interest of the director must be disclosed prior to voting, and only disinterested members of the board may vote on the proposal.

EXAMPLE:

A board votes to authorize the corporation to lease or buy property owned by a director, or to purchase services or goods from another corporation in which a director owns a substantial amount of stock. Either of these could be considered a prohibited self-dealing transaction if not properly disclosed and approved, because a director has a material financial interest in each transaction and neither falls within one of the specific statutory exceptions.

See Article 9 of the bylaws included in this book for specific procedures to follow when approving transactions that benefit directors, officers, employees, or contractors associated with the nonprofit.

Loans and Guarantees

Most states expressly prohibit nonprofits from making or guaranteeing a loan to a director, or require approval by special disclosure or voting rules. Because of the strict rules prohibiting individuals involved with a nonprofit's operations from personally benefiting from the nonprofit, it's easy to see why a loan to a director from tax-exempt funds over which he or she exercises control might appear questionable. We suggest that you carefully review your state's nonprofit statutes before considering approval of loans or guarantees

to directors—and, as always, ask a nonprofit lawyer for advice if you have questions.

Director Indemnification and Insurance

In addition to director and officer immunity statutes, most states have director indemnification laws. These laws typically require a corporation to indemnify (reimburse) a director for legal expenses incurred as a result of acts done on behalf of the corporation, if the director is successful in the legal proceeding.

Directors' (and officers') liability coverage (also called errors and omissions coverage) is, of course, one way to insulate directors from possible personal liability for their actions on behalf of the corporation. This type of insurance, however, is normally priced far beyond the reach of the average small nonprofit organization. Rather than worrying about trying to obtain this kind of coverage, it often makes more sense to do everything possible to minimize potential risks that might arise in the pursuit of your nonprofit purposes.

For example, try to make sure that employees perform their work in a safe manner and that anyone required to perform skilled tasks is properly trained and licensed. In addition, the corporation should obtain specific coverage for any likely risks: motor vehicle insurance to cover drivers of corporate vehicles, general commercial liability insurance to cover the group's premises, and so on.

Officers

Most states require a nonprofit corporation to have a president, a secretary, and a treasurer. A vice president usually is optional under state statutes. In most states, one person can hold two or more offices. However, some states prohibit one person from serving simultaneously as both the president and secretary of the corporation. See "How Many People Are Needed to Form a Nonprofit Corporation?" at the beginning of this chapter.

Duties and Responsibilities

The powers, duties, and responsibilities of officers are specified in the corporation's articles or bylaws, or by resolution of the board of directors. Generally, officers are in charge of supervising and implementing the day-to-day business of the corporation. This authority does not usually include the authority to enter into major business transactions, such as the mortgage or sale of corporate property. These kinds of major transactions are left to the board of directors. If the board wants the officers to have the power to make one or more major business decisions, special authority should be delegated by board resolution.

Officers have a duty to act honestly and in the best interests of the corporation. Officers are considered agents of the corporation and can subject the corporation to liability for their negligent or intentional acts if their acts cause damage and are performed in the scope of their employment.

Officers May Bind the Corporation

Generally, the actions and transactions of an officer are legally binding on the corporation. A third party is entitled to rely on the apparent authority of an officer and can require the corporation to honor a deal, regardless of whether the officer was actually empowered by the board to enter into the transaction. To avoid confusion, if you delegate a special task to an officer outside the realm of the officer's normal duties, it's best to have your board pass a resolution granting the officer special authority

to enter into the transaction on behalf of the corporation.

And, of course, any action taken by an officer on behalf of a corporation will be binding if the corporation accepts the benefits of the transaction or if the board ratifies the action, regardless of whether or not the officer had the legal authority to act on the corporation's behalf.

Compensation of Officers

Officers can receive reasonable compensation for services they perform for a nonprofit corporation. It is appropriate to pay officers who have day-to-day operational authority, and not to pay the officers who limit themselves to presiding over the board of directors or making overall nonprofit policy decisions. In smaller nonprofits, it is more common for officers and directors to also assume staff positions and be paid for performing these operational tasks.

EXAMPLE:

In a larger nonprofit organization, a paid executive director or medical director (these are staff positions, not board of director posts) might oversee routine operations of a medical clinic, and the paid principal or administrator (also staff positions) will do the same for a private school. However, in a smaller nonprofit, the corporate president or other officer may assume these salaried tasks.

See Article 9 of the bylaws included in this book for specific procedures to follow when approving transactions that benefit directors, officers, employees, or contractors associated with the nonprofit.

Loans, Guarantees, and Immunity Laws

Loans and guarantees to nonprofit officers are either prohibited or very strictly regulated, as they are with directors (see "Loans and Guarantees," above). Officers have a duty to act honestly and in the best interests of the corporation. Officers can be insured or indemnified against personal liabilities, and they can benefit from the same immunity statutes that relieve volunteer, and in some states paid, directors from personal liability for monetary damages. See your state nonprofit statutes before approving loans or guarantees to officers.

Employees

Employees of nonprofit corporations work for and under the supervision of the corporation and are paid a salary in return for their services. Paid directors and officers are considered employees for purposes of individual income tax withholding, Social Security, state unemployment, and other payroll taxes the employer must pay. Employees have the usual duties to report and pay their taxes, and the usual personal liability for failing to do so.

Employee Immunity

Employees are generally not personally liable for any financial loss their acts or omissions may cause to the corporation or to outsiders, as long as they are acting within the course and scope of their employment. If the harm is done to outsiders, it is the corporation, not the employees, which must assume the burden of paying for the loss.

CAUTION

Employees may be personally liable for taxes. An important exception to the rule of employee nonliability concerns the employee whose duty it is to report or pay federal or state corporate or employment taxes. The responsible employee (or officer or director) can be held personally liable for failure to report or pay such taxes. The IRS may take a broad view as to who is responsible for such duties—see "Federal Corporate Tax Returns" in Chapter 10.

Employee Compensation

Salaries paid to officers or regular employees should be reasonable and given in return for services actually performed. A reasonable salary is one roughly equal to that received by employees rendering similar services elsewhere. If salaries are unreasonably high, they are apt to be treated as a simple distribution of net corporate earnings and could jeopardize the nonprofit's tax-exempt status. Nonprofits should avoid paying discretionary bonuses at the end of a good year—this may look like a payment from the earnings and profits of the corporation, a no-no for nonprofits. In reality, since the pay scale for nonprofit personnel is usually lower than that of their for-profit counterparts, most of this cautionary advice shouldn't be needed for smaller nonprofits.

Employee Benefits

Among the major advantages associated with being an employee of a corporation are the employment benefits it can provide, such as corporate pension plans, corporate medical expense reimbursement plans, and term life insurance. Generally, amounts the corporation pays to provide these benefits are not included in the employee's individual gross income and therefore are not taxed to the employee. Also, the benefits themselves are often not taxed when the employee receives them.

The nonprofit itself enjoys a tax break when offering benefits in certain situations. Benefits are deductible by a nonprofit corporation if taxes are owed by the corporation in connection with an activity that uses the services of these employees. For example, if a nonprofit generates $20,000 in gross revenue unrelated to its exempt purposes, but pays wages of $10,000 plus benefits of $5,000 to generate this income, its net unrelated business income is reduced to $5,000.

Nonprofits may establish some of the employee benefit plans available to employees of business corporations. The rules are complicated, however. For information on setting up qualified employee plans and other benefits, consult your tax advisor or a benefit plan specialist.

Membership Nonprofits

If a nonprofit corporation establishes a formal membership structure in its articles of incorporation or bylaws, then members of the corporation will be granted basic rights to participate in the affairs and future of the nonprofit corporation. We refer to members who are given these special legal rights as formal members.

It is optional for a nonprofit corporation to have formal members with legal voting rights. To avoid the problems (including the paperwork and expense) of having to put elections of directors and other major corporate decisions to a vote of the members, most smaller nonprofits choose not to have formal membership structures.

Not having formal members is organizationally simpler than adopting a formal membership structure because only the directors

are legally entitled to participate in the operation of the corporation. People interested in a nonmembership nonprofit, although they may play fundamental advisory roles, need not be notified nor allowed to vote for directors or approve changes to the corporation's articles or bylaws. Normally this works well—because most people become involved in nonprofit organizations out of interest in the group's activities and purposes, or in some cases because they receive attendance privileges or discounts to nonprofit events or programs, not because they wish to participate in the legal affairs of the corporation.

Interested people who work with a nonprofit corporation to help it achieve its goals (and who may pay annual dues or fees) but are not formal members are often called supporters, patrons, contributors, or advisors. For example, a patron may be issued an informal museum membership that entitles the person to free admissions, participation in educational programs and events, use of a special facility, or attendance at exhibition previews, but does not give the person any say as a formal (legal) member in the museum's operation and management. We discuss the decision to set up (or do without) a formal membership structure and show you how to adopt membership or nonmembership bylaws in Chapter 7.

Classes of Membership

If you decide to set up a formal membership structure, you may establish different classes of membership, such as voting and nonvoting membership classes. If so, the rights, privileges, restrictions, and obligations associated with each class of membership must normally be stated in the articles of incorporation. (Again, most smaller corporations are better off without a formal membership structure and won't choose this option.)

Membership Quorum and Voting Rules

Most states allow nonprofits to set their own quorum requirement in the articles or bylaws for members' meetings. If the corporation does not adopt a membership quorum provision, some state statutes set a quorum for members' meetings at a low percentage of the full membership. Other states specify a limit (such as one-third of the membership) below which the quorum cannot be set in any case. Some states simply say that a quorum is the actual number of voting members that attend the meeting (under this circularly phrased rule, a meeting of members can always be held if one or more members show up for the meeting).

Despite this flexibility under state statutes, many membership nonprofits will wish to set the members' quorum requirement at a majority (or some higher percentage) of the voting membership to ensure that representational meetings are attended by a sufficient cross section of the voting membership.

TIP

Use proxy voting with large membership groups. Larger membership nonprofits rarely call and hold meetings of the membership with the expectation that members will attend and vote at the meeting in person. Instead, membership proxies (written votes) are usually solicited by mail well in advance of the meeting. The corporate secretary tallies and reports these votes at the membership meeting. The main business of the membership—the reelection of the board—is usually accomplished through this proxy-by-mail or email procedure (or by relying on a specific nomination and balloting by mail procedure authorized by the state's nonprofit corporation statutes).

The membership provisions in the bylaws included in this book provide a simple membership balloting procedure that allows members to elect directors and transact other business by mail without a meeting.

Unless the articles or bylaws state otherwise, each member is entitled to cast one vote on any matter submitted for approval to the members. Again, it's possible to have several classes of membership with different voting rights attached to each membership.

Formal Membership Rights in a Nonprofit Corporation

A formal (legally recognized) member of a nonprofit corporation is usually entitled, under the state's nonprofit corporation law, to vote on the following matters:

- election and removal of directors
- amendment of articles and bylaws
- approval of merger or consolidation with another corporation
- election to wind up or dissolve the corporation
- sale of corporate assets, and
- approval of a transaction involving an interested director or officer.

Requirements for Section 501(c)(3) Tax Exemption

Corporations, like individuals, are normally subject to federal and state income taxation. One reason to establish a nonprofit corporation is to obtain an exemption from corporate income taxes. Exemption is not automatic—a corporation must apply and show that it is in compliance with nonprofit exemption requirements to receive it. This chapter focuses on the basic federal tax exemption available to nonprofits under Section 501(c)(3) of the Internal Revenue Code and what is required to obtain tax-exempt status under this provision. In later chapters, we discuss the state exemption (which is very similar to the federal exemption) and also take you line by line through the federal tax exemption application.

You'll notice in going through the material in this chapter that many IRS tax exemption requirements are broad and seemingly applicable to a wide range of activities, both commercial and noncommercial. In fact, many commercial organizations are engaged in activities that could qualify for 501(c)(3) tax-exempt status. For example, there are for-profit scientific organizations that perform research that could qualify as 501(c)(3) scientific research. Similarly, many commercial publishing houses publish educational materials that could qualify the organization for 501(c)(3) status.

So why do only certain organizations obtain tax-exempt status? Because a corporation must choose to apply for tax-exempt status from the IRS. Many organizations that might be eligible for 501(c)(3) status prefer to operate as commercial enterprises because they do not want to be subject to the moneymaking, profit distribution, and other restrictions applicable to nonprofits. (See Chapter 1 for a discussion of these restrictions). By defining and organizing your activities as eligible for 501(c)(3) status and then seeking tax-exempt status from the IRS, you distinguish your organization from similar commercial endeavors.

Section 501(c)(3) Organizational Test

Under Section 501(c)(3) of the Internal Revenue Code, groups organized and operated exclusively for charitable, religious, scientific, literary, and educational purposes can obtain an exemption from the payment of federal income taxes. The articles of incorporation of a 501(c)(3) corporation must limit the group's corporate purposes to one or more of the allowable 501(c)(3) purposes and must not empower it to engage (other than as an insubstantial part of its activities) in activities that don't further one or more of these tax-exempt purposes. This formal requirement is known as the 501(c)(3) organizational test.

A group can engage in more than one 501(c)(3) tax-exempt activity. For example, a group's activities can be characterized as charitable and educational, such as a school for blind or physically handicapped children.

A nonprofit cannot, however, engage simultaneously in a 501(c)(3) exempt purpose activity and an activity that is exempt under a different subsection of Section 501(c). Thus, a group cannot be formed for educational *and* social or recreational purposes because social and recreational groups are exempt under Section 501(c)(7) of the Internal Revenue Code (see "Is Your Group a Nonprofit That Can Use This Book?" in Chapter 1, for a discussion of non-501(c)(3) tax-exempt groups). As a practical matter, this problem rarely occurs because the non-501(c)(3) subsections are custom-tailored to specific types of organizations, such as war veterans' organizations and cemetery companies.

Valid Purposes Under Section 501(c)(3)

Now let's take a closer look at the most common 501(c)(3) purposes—charitable, religious, scientific, literary, and educational—and the requirements for each of these purposes. In addition to the valid purpose requirements discussed in this section, there are other general requirements that all 501(c)(3) groups must comply with to obtain 501(c)(3) status. These other requirements are discussed below in "Other Requirements for 501(c)(3) Groups."

Humane Societies and Sports Organizations

There are other, less commonly used exemptions available under Section 501(c)(3), which we do not cover in this book. For example, groups organized to prevent cruelty to children or animals, or to foster national or international amateur sports competitions, can claim a tax exemption under Section 501(c)(3). However, these groups must meet narrowly defined 501(c)(3) requirements, and, for humane societies, special state requirements. See IRS Publication 557 for specifics on each of these special 501(c)(3) groups and contact your state attorney general's office for special incorporation requirements for humane societies.

Charitable Purposes

The charitable purpose exemption is the broadest, most all-encompassing exemption under Section 501(c)(3). Not surprisingly, it is also the most commonly used exemption.

Benefit to the Public

The word charitable as used in Section 501(c)(3) is broadly defined to mean "providing services beneficial to the public interest." In fact, other 501(c)(3) purpose groups—educational, religious, and scientific groups—are often also considered charitable in nature because their activities usually benefit the public. Even groups not directly engaged in a religious, educational, or scientific activity but whose activities indirectly benefit or promote a 501(c)(3) purpose can qualify as a 501(c)(3) charitable-purpose group.

Groups that seek to promote the welfare of specific groups of people in the community (handicapped or elderly persons or members of a particular ethnic group) or groups that seek to advance other exempt activities (environmental or educational) will generally be considered organized for charitable purposes because these activities benefit the public at large and are charitable in nature.

Groups that advance religion, even if they do not have a strictly religious purpose or function, are often considered charitable purpose organizations under Section 501(c)(3). The IRS reasons that the advancement of religion is itself a charitable purpose. Examples of some of these charitable purpose groups include:

- **Monthly Newspaper.** A group that published and distributed a monthly newspaper with church news of interdenominational interest was held to accomplish a charitable purpose because it contributed to the advancement of religion.

- **Coffeehouse.** A nonprofit organization formed by local churches to operate a supervised facility known as a coffeehouse was found to have a valid 501(c)(3) charitable purpose because it advanced religion and education by bringing together college-age people with church leaders, educators, and leaders from the business community for discussions and counseling on religion, current events, social, and vocational problems.

- **Genealogical Research.** An organization formed to compile genealogical research data on its family members in order to perform religious observances in accordance with the precepts of their faith was held to advance religion and be a charitable organization under 501(c)(3).

- **Missionary Assistance.** A missionary group established to provide temporary low-cost housing and related services for missionary families on furlough in the United States from their assignments abroad was held to be a charitable purpose organization under Section 501(c)(3).

Other examples of activities and purposes that have met the IRS organizational test for charitable purpose (and possibly another 501(c)(3) purpose as well) include:

- relieving the poor, distressed, or under-privileged
- advancing education or science
- erecting or maintaining public buildings, monuments, or works
- lessening the burdens of government
- lessening neighborhood tensions
- eliminating prejudice and discrimination
- promoting and developing the arts
- defending human and civil rights secured by law
- providing facilities and services to senior citizens
- maintaining a charitable hospital
- providing a community fund to support family relief and service agencies in the community

- providing loans for charitable or educational purposes, and
- maintaining a public-interest law firm.

Class or Group of Beneficiaries

A charitable organization must be set up to benefit an indefinite class of people, not particular persons. The number of beneficiaries can be relatively small as long as the benefited class is open and the beneficiaries of the group are not specifically identified.

EXAMPLE 1:

A charitable nonprofit corporation cannot be established under Section 501(c)(3) to benefit Jeffrey Smith, an impoverished individual. But Jeffrey Smith can be selected as a beneficiary of a 501(c)(3) charitable group whose purpose is to benefit needy individuals in a particular community (as long as he is a member of that community).

EXAMPLE 2:

A foundation that awards scholarships solely to undergraduate members of a designated fraternity was found to be a valid charitable organization under 501(c)(3), even though the number of members in the benefited group is small.

The following groups, all charitable in nature and benefiting a defined but indefinite group of people, were found to be valid charitable purpose organizations under Section 501(c)(3):

- an organization formed to build new housing and renovate existing housing for sale to low-income families on long-term, low-payment plans
- a day care center for children of needy, working parents

- a group created to market the cooking and needlework of needy women
- a self-help housing program for low-income families
- homes for the aged where the organization satisfies the special needs of an aged person for housing, health care, and financial security. (The requirements for housing and health care will be satisfied if the organization is committed to housing residents who become unable to pay and if services are provided at the lowest possible cost.)
- an organization that takes care of patients' nonmedical needs (reading, writing letters, and so on) in a privately owned hospital
- an organization that provides emergency and rescue services for stranded, injured, or lost persons
- a drug crisis center and a telephone hotline for persons with drug problems, and
- a legal aid society offering free legal services to indigent persons.

Health care nonprofits, whether hospitals or less formal, noninstitutional health care facilities or programs, can qualify as charitable 501(c)(3) organizations. However, the IRS is particularly concerned about conflicts of interest and business dealings between doctors who do work for the nonprofit and also rent space or have other commercial dealings with the nonprofit. The IRS recommends that the health care nonprofit form a community board and have conflict of interest provisions in its bylaws.

Services Need Not Be Free

Section 501(c)(3) charitable organizations are not required to offer services or products free or at cost. Nevertheless, doing so, or at least providing services at a substantial discount

from the going commercial rate, can help convince the IRS of your group's bona fide charitable intentions. Charging full retail prices for services or products does not usually demonstrate a benefit to the public. Other restrictions applicable to a nonprofit's ability to make money are discussed below in "Other Requirements for 501(c)(3) Groups."

Religious Purposes

For Section 501(c)(3) purposes, religious purpose groups can be either a loosely defined religious organization that practices or promotes religious beliefs in some way or a formal institutional church. Groups formed to advance religion often qualify as charitable purpose organizations under Section 501(c)(3).

Qualifying as a Religious Organization

Traditionally, the IRS and the courts have been reluctant to question the validity or sincerity of religious beliefs or practices held by a group trying to establish itself as a religious purpose organization. As long as the organization's beliefs appear to be "truly and sincerely held" and their related practices and rituals are not illegal or against public policy, the IRS generally does not challenge the validity of the religious tenets or practices. However, the IRS will question the nature and extent of religious activities (as opposed to religious beliefs) if they do not appear to foster religious worship or advance a religious purpose, or if they appear commercial in nature.

EXAMPLE:

A group that holds weekly meetings and publishes material celebrating the divine presence in all natural phenomena should qualify as a religious purpose group. However, an organization that sells a large volume of literature to the general public, some of which has little or no connection to the religious beliefs held by the organization, could be regarded by the IRS as a regular trade or business, not as a tax-exempt religious organization.

A religious group need not profess belief in a supreme being to qualify as a religious organization under Section 501(c)(3).

Religious corporations also have the widest flexibility in managing their internal affairs.

Qualifying as a Church

You can also qualify under the 501(c)(3) religious purpose category as a church, but doing so is more difficult than simply qualifying as a 501(c)(3) religious organization. One of the advantages of qualifying as a church is that a church automatically qualifies for 501(c)(3) *public charity status*—a status that all 501(c)(3) groups want to obtain, as we explain later, in Chapter 4.

CD-ROM

The IRS has a guide to assist churches and clergy in complying with the religious purpose requirement of the Internal Revenue Code. The publication is intended to be a user-friendly compilation, set forth in question-and-answer format. A copy of this guide, IRS Publication 1828, *Tax Guide for Churches and Religious Organizations*, is included on the CD-ROM. Most church and religious-purpose groups will find the information in this publication extremely helpful when preparing their federal exemption application (see Chapter 8).

Under IRS rulings, a religious organization should have the following characteristics to qualify as a church (not all are necessary but the more the better):

- a recognized creed or form of worship
- a definite and distinct ecclesiastical government
- a formal code of doctrine and discipline
- a distinct religious history
- a membership not associated with any other church or denomination
- a complete organization of ordained ministers
- a literature of its own
- established places of worship
- regular congregations, and
- regular religious services.

Courts have used similar criteria to determine whether or not a religious organization qualifies as a church. In one case, the court looked for the presence of the following "church" factors:

- services held on a regular basis
- ordained ministers or other representatives
- a record of the performance of marriage, other ceremonies, and sacraments
- a place of worship
- some support required from members
- formal operations, and
- satisfaction of all other requirements of federal tax law for religious organizations.

All religious purpose groups that claim church status must complete a special IRS schedule with specific questions on some of the church characteristics listed above. We discuss this tax application and the special IRS schedule for churches in Chapter 8.

Traditional churches, synagogues, associations, or conventions of churches (and religious orders or organizations that are an integral part of a church and engaged in carrying out its functions) can qualify as 501(c)(3) churches without difficulty. Less traditional and less formal religious organizations may have a harder time. These groups often have to answer additional questions to convince the IRS that they qualify as tax-exempt churches.

Some churches stand a greater chance of being audited by the IRS than others. Not surprisingly, the IRS is more likely to examine and question groups that promise members substantial tax benefits for organizing their households as tax-deductible church organizations.

Scientific Purposes

Groups that engage in scientific research carried on in the public interest are also eligible for tax-exempt status under 501(c)(3). Under IRS regulations, research incidental to commercial or industrial operations (such as the normal inspection or testing of materials or products, or the design or construction of equipment and buildings) does not qualify as a scientific purpose under Section 501(c)(3). In an IRS case involving a pharmaceutical company, the company's clinical testing of drugs was held not to be "scientific" under Section 501(c)(3) because the clinical testing in question was incidental to the pharmaceutical company's commercial operations.

Generally, research is considered in the public interest if the results (including any patents, copyrights, processes, or formulas) are made available to the public; that is, the scientific research must be published for others to study and use. Research is also considered in the public interest if it is performed for the United States or a state, county, or city government, or if it is conducted to accomplish one of the following purposes:

- to aid in the scientific education of college or university students

- to discover a cure for a disease, or

- to aid a community or region by attracting new industry, or by encouraging the development or retention of an existing industry.

EXAMPLE:

An organization was formed by a group of physicians specializing in heart defects to research the causes and treatment of cardiac and cardiovascular conditions and diseases. The physicians practiced medicine in a private practice facility that was separate and apart from the organization's research facility and that was used exclusively for the research program. Although some patients from the physicians' private practice were accepted for the research program, they were selected on the same criteria as other patients. The IRS found that the physician's research group met the scientific purpose organizational test for Section 501(c)(3) purposes.

If you are applying for a scientific exemption under Section 501(c)(3), your federal exemption application (covered in Chapter 8) should show that your organization is conducting public interest research, and you should provide the following information:

- an explanation of the nature of the research

- a description of past and present research projects

- how and by whom research projects are determined and selected, and

- who will retain ownership or control of any patents, copyrights, processes, or formulas resulting from the research.

RESOURCE

For a list of the specific information the IRS requires from scientific groups, see the "Scientific Organizations" section in IRS Publication 557.

Literary Purposes

This is a seldom-used Section 501(c)(3) category because most literary purpose nonprofits are classified as educational by the IRS. Nevertheless, valid 501(c)(3) literary purposes include traditional literary efforts, such as publishing, distribution, and book sales. These activities must be directed toward promoting the public interest as opposed to engaging in a commercial literary enterprise or serving the interests of particular individuals (such as the proprietors of a publishing house). Generally, this means that literary material must be available to the general public and must pertain to the betterment of the community.

A combination of factors helps distinguish public interest publishing from private publishing. If you publish materials that are clearly educational and make them available to the public at cost, or at least below standard commercial rates, then you might qualify as a 501(c)(3) literary purpose organization. However, if your material seems aimed primarily at a commercial market and is sold at standard rates through regular commercial channels, chances are that your literary organization will be viewed by the IRS as a regular business enterprise, ineligible for a 501(c)(3) tax exemption. For example, publishing textbooks at standard rates will probably not qualify as a tax-exempt literary purpose under Section 501(c)(3) because the activity is more private than public in nature. On the other hand, publishing material to promote highway safety or the education of handicapped children is likely to qualify as a bona fide 501(c)(3) literary purpose.

EXAMPLE:

A publishing house that only published books related to esoteric Eastern philosophical thought applied for 501(c)(3) literary exemption. Their books were sold commercially but at modest prices. The IRS granted the tax exemption after requesting and reviewing the manuscript for the nonprofit's first publication. The IRS found that the material was sufficiently specialized to render it noncommercial in nature.

Educational Purposes

The type of educational activities that qualify as educational purpose under 501(c)(3) are broad, encompassing instruction both for self-development and for the benefit of the community. The IRS allows advocacy of a particular intellectual position or viewpoint if there is a "sufficiently full and fair exposition of pertinent facts to permit an individual or the public to form an independent opinion or conclusion. However, mere presentation of unsupported opinion is not (considered) educational."

If a group takes political positions, it may not qualify for an exemption (see discussion on political activities in "Other Requirements for 501(c)(3) Groups," below). An educational group that publishes a newsletter with a balanced analysis of issues, or at least with some room devoted to debate or presentation of opposing opinions, should qualify as a 501(c)(3) educational purpose group. If its newsletter is simply devoted to espousing one side of an issue, platform, or agenda, the educational purpose tax exemption may not be granted.

Examples of activities that qualify as educational purpose include:

- publishing public interest educational materials
- conducting public discussion groups, forums, panels, lectures, and workshops

- offering a correspondence course or a course that uses other media, such as television or radio

- operating a museum, zoo, planetarium, symphony, orchestra, or performance group

- serving an educational institution, such as a college bookstore, alumni association, or athletic organization, or

- publishing educational newsletters, pamphlets, books, or other material.

CD-ROM

See the CD-ROM file Education, Propaganda, and the Methodology Test for guidelines used by the IRS and courts to determine if a nonprofit qualifies as an educational purpose organization under Section 501(c)(3).

Formal School Not Necessary

To qualify as a 501(c)(3) educational organization, a group does not need to provide instruction in traditional school subjects or organize as a formal school facility with a regular faculty, established curriculum, and a regularly enrolled student body.

CAUTION

You may need formal school attributes for other reasons. People setting up nontraditional schools should remember that although they do not need a regular faculty, full-time students, or even a fixed curriculum to qualify for a 501(c)(3) educational purpose tax exemption, as a practical matter, they may need some or all of these things to qualify for state or federal support, participate in federal student loan programs, and obtain accreditation.

Child Care Centers

Providing child care outside the home qualifies as a 501(c)(3) educational purpose under special provisions contained in Internal Revenue Code Section 501(k) if:

- the care enables parent(s) to be employed, and

- the child care services are available to the general public.

A child care facility that gives enrollment preference to children of employees of a specific employer, however, will not be considered a 501(c)(3) educational purpose organization.

Private School Nondiscrimination Requirements

If you set up a 501(c)(3) private school, you must include a nondiscrimination statement in your bylaws and publicize this statement to the community served by the school. This statement must make it clear that the school does not discriminate against students or applicants on the basis of race, color, or national or ethnic origin.

Here is a sample statement taken from *IRS Revenue Procedure 75-50*:

Notice of Nondiscriminatory Policy as to Students

The [name of school] admits students of any race, color, national and ethnic origin to all the rights, privileges, programs, and activities generally accorded or made available to students at the school. It does not discriminate on the basis of race, color, national and ethnic origin in administration of its educational policies, admissions policies, scholarship, and loan programs, and athletic and other school-administered programs.

RESOURCE

Additional information on the history and status of 501(c)(3) private school nondiscrimination requirements is on the IRS website (www.irs.gov), in a tax topic update titled "Private School Update." For further information on IRS private school antidiscrimination rules and procedures, see *IRS Revenue Procedure 75-50* and "Private Schools," in IRS Publication 557.

CD-ROM

The CD-ROM at the back of this book contains the following related IRS material:

- Publication 557, *Tax-Exempt Status for Your Organization*
- Private School Update, and
- *IRS Revenue Procedure 75-50.*

Other Requirements for 501(c)(3) Groups

In addition to being organized primarily for one or more allowable tax-exempt purposes, a nonprofit must not engage in other activities that conflict or substantially interfere with its valid 501(c)(3) purposes. This section discusses some of the requirements that keep a 501(c)(3) from straying too far from its exempt-purpose activities.

Unrelated Business Activities

To obtain 501(c)(3) status, a corporation cannot substantially engage in activities unrelated to the group's tax-exempt purposes. Or, put differently, your nonprofit corporation can conduct activities not directly related to its exempt purpose as long as these activities don't represent a substantial portion of your total activities. Some unrelated activity is allowed because as a practical matter, most nonprofits need to do some unrelated business to survive. For example, a nonprofit dance group might rent unused portions of its studio space to an outside group for storage. Another nonprofit might invest surplus funds to augment its income.

Most groups need not be overly concerned with this limitation unless activities unrelated to exempt purposes start to involve a significant amount of the group's energy or time, or if these activities produce "substantial" income. If the activities are themselves nonprofit, they should be included in the organization's exempt purposes and classified as related activities. The IRS keeps an eye out for tax-exempt groups that regularly engage in profit-making businesses with little or no connection to their exempt purposes (a church running a trucking company). Business activities necessary to further the group's exempt purposes, such as hiring and paying employees and paying rent for space used for the group's exempt purpose, are considered related activities.

Most new nonprofits work full time simply tending to their exempt purposes and do not explore unrelated moneymaking activities until later, if at all. However, if you plan to engage in unrelated business from the start, be careful. It's hard to pin down exactly when these activities become substantial enough to jeopardize the corporation's tax-exempt status. Also, income derived from unrelated business activities is subject to federal and state corporate income tax, even if it is not substantial enough to affect the group's 501(c)(3) tax-exempt status.

CD-ROM

For more information on the federal unrelated business income tax that applies to nonprofit 501(c)(3) groups, see the CD-ROM file UBIT: Current Developments.

Limitation on Profits and Benefits

A 501(c)(3) nonprofit corporation cannot be organized or operated to benefit individuals associated with the corporation (directors, officers, or members) or other persons or entities related to, or controlled by, these individuals (such as another corporation controlled by a director). In tax language, this limitation is known as the prohibition on private inurement, and means that 501(c)(3) groups can't pay profits to, or otherwise benefit, private interests.

Two specific 501(c)(3) requirements implement this prohibition on self-inurement:

- no part of the net earnings of the corporation can be distributed to individuals associated with the corporation, and

- upon dissolution, the assets of a 501(c)(3) group must be irrevocably dedicated to another tax-exempt group (another 501(c)(3) or a federal, state, or local government for a public purpose).

These federal tax exemption requirements often are mirrored in the state's nonprofit corporation law. Note that the IRS and state law allow a nonprofit to pay reasonable salaries to directors, officers, employees, or agents for services rendered in furtherance of the corporation's tax-exempt purposes.

Excess Benefit Rules

The IRS has adopted strict rules and regulations regarding the payment of money, benefits, or property to nonprofit directors, officers, sponsors, donors, and others associated with the nonprofit. The main purpose for these rules, called the excess benefit rules, is to make sure nonprofit organizations do not pay out lavish benefits or skim off program funds to line the pockets or serve the private interests of individuals associated with the nonprofit.

The excess benefit rules are also called the IRS intermediate sanctions, a euphemism that is meant to have an appropriately harsh ring. These rules are contained in Section 4958 of the Internal Revenue Code and Section 53.4958 of the IRS Regulations.

The excess benefit rules apply to individuals associated with 501(c)(3) nonprofit public charities. (As explained more fully in Chapter 4, in all likelihood you will be forming a public charity nonprofit.) The individuals subject to the rules include nonprofit directors, officers, and trustees, as well as major sponsors, donors, or anyone else in a position to exercise substantial influence over the affairs of the nonprofit. The rules also apply to family members and entities owned by any of the individuals subject to the rules.

Under the rules, an excessive benefit transaction is any transaction where the nonprofit gives cash, property, or anything of value to a recipient that exceeds the value of the services performed by the recipient (or the value of any other cash, property, or thing of value given to the nonprofit by the recipient). If a nonprofit pays $100 to an officer who has contributed $75 worth of services, the excess benefit is $25. Of course, the IRS is looking for much bigger numbers, sometimes in the realm of thousands, or hundreds of thousands of dollars worth of extra benefits paid by the nonprofit to directors, officers, consultants, sponsors, and donors.

The sanctions include a tax that must be paid by both the recipient of the excess benefit as well as the nonprofit managers (the directors and executive officers) who approved the excess benefit transaction. The recipient of the excess benefit can be assessed a 25% tax on the excess benefit, and the manager or managers who approved it can be assessed a 10% tax, with a limit on a manager's liability capped at $20,000 per transaction. A director must object to the transaction to be excluded from those considered to have approved it—silence or abstention at a board meeting that results in the excess benefit payment is not a defense. The recipient must repay or return the excess benefit to the nonprofit or the recipient will be charged an additional 200% tax. The message is clear— if you receive an undeserved benefit from your nonprofit, you and others in your nonprofit may have to pay large penalties.

The IRS regulations add detail about the scope and operation of the excess benefit rules. For example, disqualified persons are broadly defined to include all sorts of people paid by or associated with the nonprofit organization. Excess salaries, contract payments, benefits, privileges, goods, services, or anything else of value paid or provided to almost anyone associated with your nonprofit can potentially trigger the excess benefit tax rules.

The regulations also contain a safe harbor provision for deals or decisions that provide an economic benefit to a director, officer, contractor, or other key nonprofit person. To qualify for the protection of the safe harbor rule, a number of conditions must be met, including:

- disinterested members of the board or committee must approve the transaction in advance
- the decision must be based on "comparability" data reviewed and relied on by the board that shows the property is transferred at fair market value or compensation is paid at a rate similar to that paid by other organizations for comparable services, and
- the decision must be documented in the corporate records at the time the transaction is approved.

Falling within the safe harbor provision creates a presumption that your deal or decision

was fair. The IRS can rebut this presumption if it obtains evidence to the contrary.

If you are interested in reading more information about these rules, you can use the CD-ROM files listed below.

CD-ROM

The CD-ROM at the back of this book contains the following files with information on the excess benefit rules and regulations.

- IRC Section 4958, Taxes on Excess Benefit Transactions
- IRS Regulations Section 53.4958-0, Table of Contents. This file contains the IRS regulations promulgated under Section 4958.
- Final 4958 regulation changes. See Internal Revenue Bulletin No. 2008-18, T.D. 9390.
- Intermediate Sanctions (IRC Section 4958) Update

Conflict of Interest Provisions

Article 9 of the bylaws included in this book contains rules and procedures for approving or avoiding conflict of interest transactions, including compensation arrangements. This bylaw provision contains the conflict of interest language recommended by the IRS (included in the sample conflict of interest policy in the instructions to IRS Form 1023 in Appendix A). It also has language for the approval of compensation arrangements that attempts to comply with the safe harbor provisions of the excess benefit rules (See Article 9, Section 5). You will need to become familiar with Article 9 of your bylaws and refer to those provisions whenever your board, or a committee of your board, decides to set or increase salaries, enter into contracts, or approve deals with individuals or other organizations.

If you have any question about whether a transaction, contract, compensation decision, or other economic decision is reasonable or whether it may be outside the safe harbor provisions of the excess benefit rules, ask a nonprofit lawyer for help. The last thing you want to have happen is to subject board members, officers, contractors, sponsors, donors, and others who deal with your nonprofit to the prospect of having to pay back money or the value of benefits previously paid out or provided by your nonprofit plus very hefty taxes, interest, and penalties.

Limitation on Political Activities

A 501(c)(3) corporation is prohibited from participating in any political campaigns for or against any candidate for public office. Participation in or contributions to political campaigns can result in the revocation of 501(c)(3) tax-exempt status and the assessment of special excise taxes against the organization and its managers. (See Internal Revenue Code §§ 4955, 6852, and 7409.)

Voter Education Activities

Section 501(c)(3) groups can conduct certain voter education activities if they are done in a nonpartisan manner (see IRS Revenue Ruling 78-248). If you want to engage in this type of political activity, we recommend you consult an attorney. Your organization can request an IRS letter ruling on its voter education activities by writing to the address listed in IRS Publication 557, Chapter 3, "Political Activity."

CD-ROM

For information on restrictions on political candidate campaign activity by 501(c)(3) organizations, see Election Year Issues, in the CD-ROM. It also contains information about other laws and restrictions applicable to political campaign nonprofits—non-501(c)(3) groups organized

primarily to support or oppose political candidates, under Internal Revenue Code § 527.

Influencing Legislation

Section 501(c)(3) organizations are prohibited from acting to influence legislation, "except to an insubstantial degree." In the past, courts have found that spending more than 5% of an organization's budget, time, or effort on political activity was substantial. More recently, courts have tended to look at the individual facts of each case. Generally, if a nonprofit corporation contacts, or urges the public to contact, members of a legislative body, or if it advocates the adoption or rejection of legislation, the IRS considers it to be acting to influence legislation.

Lobbying to influence legislation also includes:

- any attempt to affect the opinions of the general public or a segment of the public, and

- communication with any member or employee of a legislative body, or with any government official or employee who might participate in the formulation of legislation.

However, lobbying to influence legislation does not include:

- making available the results of nonpartisan analysis, study, or research

- providing technical advice or assistance to a government body, or to its committee or other subdivision, in response to a written request from it, where such advice would otherwise constitute the influencing of legislation

- appearing before, or communicating with, any legislative body with respect to a possible decision that might affect the organization's existence, powers, tax-exempt status, or the deductibility of contributions to it, or

- communicating with a government official or employee, other than for the purpose of influencing legislation.

Also excluded from the definition of lobbying efforts are communications between an organization and its members about legislation (or proposed legislation) of direct interest to the organization and the members, unless these communications directly encourage members to influence legislation.

EXAMPLE:

A housing information exchange keeps its members informed of proposed legislation affecting low-income renters. This should not be considered legislative lobbying activity unless members are urged to contact their political representatives in support of, or in opposition to, the proposed legislation.

In determining whether a group's legislative activities are substantial in scope, the IRS looks at the amount of time, money, or effort the group spends on legislative lobbying. If they are substantial in relation to other activities, 501(c)(3) tax status might be revoked and, again, special excise taxes can be levied against the organization and its managers. See IRC § 4912.

Political Expenditures Test

Under the political expenditures test in IRC § 501(h), limitations are imposed on two types of political activities: lobbying expenditures and grassroots expenditures. Lobbying expenditures are those made for the purpose of influencing legislation, while grassroots expenditures are those made to influence public opinion.

For examples of these two types of activities, see IRS Publication 557, the "Lobbying Expenditures" section. The monetary limits are different for each of the categories, and the formulas for computing them are somewhat complicated.

If your 501(c)(3) nonprofit elects the political expenditures test, you must file IRS Form 5768, *Election-Revocation of Election by an Eligible Section 501(c)(3) Organization To Make Expenditures To Influence Legislation*, within the tax year in which you wish the election to be effective. This election is also available under similar rules at the state level. A copy of this form is included on the CD-ROM provided with this book.

The Alternative Political Expenditures Test

Since it is impossible to know ahead of time how the IRS will assess the substantiality of a group's legislative activity, the IRC allows 501(c)(3) public charities (most 501(c)(3) groups will qualify as public charities—see Chapter 4) to elect an alternative expenditures test to measure permissible legislative activity. Under this test, a group may spend up to 20% of the first $500,000 of its annual expenditures on lobbying, 15% of the next $500,000, 10% of the next $500,000, and 5% of its expenditures beyond that, up to a total limit of $1 million each year.

> **CAUTION**
>
> **Some groups can't use the political expenditures test.** This expenditures test and its provisions for lobbying and grassroots expenditures are not available to churches, an integrated auxiliary of a church, a member of an affiliated group of organizations that includes a church, or to private foundations.

If your nonprofit corporation plans to do considerable lobbying activity, mostly by unpaid volunteers, then electing the expenditures test might be a good idea. Why? Because the minimal outlay of money to engage in these activities will probably keep you under the applicable expenditure limits. If you didn't make this election, your 501(c)(3) tax exemption might be placed in jeopardy if the IRS considers your political activities to be a substantial part of your overall purposes and program.

If you plan to engage in more than a minimum amount of political lobbying or legislative efforts, you need to decide whether it is to your advantage to elect the expenditures test based on the facts of your situation. If you find that these alternative political expenditures rules are still too restrictive, you might consider forming a social welfare organization or civic league under Section 501(c)(4) of the Internal Revenue Code—this exemption requires a different federal exemption application, IRS Form 1024, and does not carry with it all the attractive benefits of 501(c)(3) status (access to grant funds, tax deductible contributions, etc.). See "Is Your Group a Nonprofit That Can Use This Book?" in Chapter 1 and IRS Publication 557 for further information on 501(c)(4) organizations.

> **CAUTION**
>
> **Additional limitations for certain groups.** Federally funded groups may be subject to even more stringent political expenditure tests than those discussed here (for example, political activity and expenditure restrictions imposed by the federal Office of Management and Budget).

> **CD-ROM**
>
> **For a thorough discussion of the rules that apply to lobbying activities by 501(c)(3) organizations** and detailed information on the Section 501(h) political expenditures test election, see Lobbying Issues, in the CD-ROM.

Political Action Organizations

The IRS can also challenge a 501(c)(3) group's political activities by finding that it is an action organization: one so involved in political activities that it is not organized exclusively for a 501(c)(3) tax-exempt purpose. Under these circumstances the IRS can revoke the organization's tax-exempt status. Intervention in political campaigns or substantial attempts to influence legislation, as discussed above, are grounds for applying this sanction. In addition, if a group has the following two characteristics, it will be classified as an action organization and lose its 501(c)(3) status:

- Its main or primary objective or objectives —not incidental or secondary objectives— may be attained only by legislation or defeat of proposed legislation.

- It advocates or campaigns for the attainment of such objectives rather than engaging in nonpartisan analysis, study, or research and making the results available to the public.

In determining whether a group has these characteristics, the IRS looks at the surrounding facts and circumstances, including the group's articles and activities, and its organizational and operational structure.

The point here is to be careful not to state your exempt purposes in such a way that they seem attainable only by political action. Even if you indicate that your activities will not be substantially involved with legislative or lobbying efforts, the IRS may decide otherwise and invoke this special classification to deny or rescind 501(c)(3) status.

If the IRS classifies a group as an action organization, the group can still qualify as a social welfare group under 501(c)(4).

EXAMPLE:

A group that has a primary purpose of "reforming the judicial system in the United States" will likely sound like a political action organization to the IRS, because this sounds like a political goal that must be accomplished mostly by political means. However, if the group rephrases its primary purpose as "educating the public on the efficacy of mediation, arbitration, and other alternative nonjudicial dispute resolution mechanisms," it stands a better chance of having the IRS approve its application, even if it lists some political activity as incidental to its primary educational purpose.

CAUTION

Check the Federal Election Commission (FEC) website. Politically active groups should go to the FEC website at www.fec.gov to read about the ever-changing federal election laws and how they may impact their nonprofit's activities.

RESOURCE

IRS provides illustrations for clarification on what constitutes political campaign activities. IRS Revenue Ruling 2007-41 (included on the CD-ROM) has 21 fact situations that help explain when the IRS will and will not consider a group to be conducting unpermitted political campaign activities.

Information for Specific Questions About Your Group's Activities

Even after reading through this chapter, you might still have some questions about whether your specific nonprofit activities meet the IRS definition of educational, charitable, or religious purposes under Section 501(c)(3) of the Internal Revenue Code. Or, after you take a closer look at Chapter 4, you might wonder whether your nonprofit can qualify for special public charity treatment as a school or church.

Answers to these types of questions used to be left to the expertise of highly paid lawyers and tax professionals—this is no longer true. It is remarkably easy to find out more about how the IRS might look at your nonprofit organization when it reviews your tax exemption application. The IRS website disseminates most of the material necessary to answer many technical questions as long as you are persistent enough to search the site thoroughly and uncover the material. Specifically, IRS publications and regulations, as well as the technical manuals the IRS examiners use when reviewing tax exemption applications, are available online.

This chapter refers to special IRS training materials from the IRS website and includes this material on the CD-ROM that accompanies this book. We describe how each of these articles helps explain and illustrate a specific issue related to obtaining and maintaining a 501(c)(3) tax exemption. There is a lot more helpful material on the IRS website, and we encourage you to browse it to learn as much as you'd like about nonprofit organization tax issues.

Here is one way to search the IRS site for nonprofit tax exemption answers:

Go to the main page of the IRS website at www.irs.gov and click the Charities & Non-Profits tab. This page contains special nonprofit tax topics, resources, and links to additional information. If you don't find what you're looking for, in the search box type in a word or phrase which succinctly describes your question.

You can also try to find your topic by clicking on the Site Map link that appears at the top of most of the site's Web pages. You should see a list of links for Charities & Non-Profits, which you can use to navigate through the site to find the material you're looking for.

Another, more advanced approach is to click the Site Map link at the top of the Web page, then click the Internal Revenue Manual, listed under the Tax Professionals heading. This link takes you to a table that lists different sections of the internal IRS procedures manual used by IRS examiners and field agents. It contains a wealth of technical material about IRS procedures, rulings, and policies. Part 7 is the main area of interest for nonprofit groups applying for their 501(c)(3) tax exemption. Select this link, then scroll down the heading list until you see the heading, "7.25 Exempt Organizations Determinations Manual." Click on the link under this heading to "7.25.3, Religious, Charitable, Educational, Etc.,

Organizations." This chapter contains examples of groups that have and have not qualified under each of the 501(c)(3) tax-exempt purposes.

If you want to learn even more, you can examine any of the IRS rulings and cases that you uncover in your website search. Rulings are compiled in IRS *Cumulative Bulletins,* the most recent of which are available for browsing on the IRS website. Click the Site Map link at the top of any IRS site Web page, then under the Tax Professionals heading, select Resources for Tax Professionals and scroll down and select the Internal Revenue Bulletins link. Then select the volume for the year when the ruling was issued and scroll through the beginning table of contents to find the page where the ruling begins (the first two numbers of a ruling indicate its year—for example, Ruling 2004-51 was issued in 2004, so you would look at the *Bulletin* for 2004 to find the text of the ruling). Most years have more than one *Bulletin* volume, and some rulings are placed in the next year's volume. It takes persistence to track down rulings, but they can be enormously helpful in understanding why the IRS accepted or rejected a nonprofit organization's application for a 501(c)(3) tax exemption. For more information on doing your own research, see Chapter 11.

RESOURCE

For an in-depth discussion and analysis of the requirements that apply to each type of 501(c)(3) nonprofit, supplemented annually with the latest IRS and court rulings in each area, see *The Law of Tax-Exempt Organizations*, by Bruce R. Hopkins, (John Wiley & Sons, Inc., Hoboken, NJ).

Public Charities and Private Foundations

In this chapter, we explain why it is not enough to simply obtain your 501(c)(3) tax-exempt status—you also need to be recognized as a 501(c)(3) public charity. Getting this extra recognition is essential to make your life as a nonprofit easier to manage. Even though the last thing you may be interested in at this point is delving into more tax technicalities, it will help you enormously to have a general understanding of the distinction between public charity and private foundation tax status before you do your federal tax exemption application. You will understand the importance of some of the most technical questions on the application and you'll know how to answer questions to show you qualify for public charity tax status.

We help you get through this information by explaining the different public charity classifications and requirements in plain English. You don't need to master this material. In fact, many nonprofits let the IRS decide which public charity category works for them. For now, simply read through the information to get a general understanding of the concepts. You can come back to this chapter when you do your federal tax exemption application and reread the sections that apply to you.

Throughout this chapter, we refer to the Internal Revenue Code sections that apply to the different public charity classifications. You don't need to pay attention to these section references. They will be useful later as references when you prepare your federal tax exemption application.

The Importance of Public Charity Status

The IRS classifies all 501(c)(3) tax-exempt nonprofit corporations as either private foundations or public charities. Initially, most 501(c)(3) corporations are presumed to be private foundations. It's extremely important to understand that your group, too, will initially be viewed as a private foundation. The problem with this classification is that private foundations are subject to strict operating rules and regulations that don't apply to groups classified as public charities. You'll want to get yourself out from under this presumption because, like most 501(c)(3) groups, you would probably find it impossible to operate under the rules and restrictions imposed on private foundations. To overcome this presumption, you must show on your federal 501(c)(3) tax exemption application that you qualify as a public charity.

A few special groups are not presumed to be private foundations and do not have to apply for public charity status—the same groups that are not required to file a 501(c)(3) tax exemption application. We think it's foolhardy in most cases not to apply for, and obtain, official notification from the IRS that you are a public charity. (For a discussion of this issue, see "Do You Need to File Form 1023?" in Chapter 8.)

How to Start Out as a Public Charity

Under the latest IRS regulations, a new 501(c)(3) group can qualify as a public charity for the first five years if the group can demonstrate in its Form 1023 application that it reasonably expects to receive qualifying public support. Under the old rules, a new organization had to seek an advance ruling that it would be publicly supported when it applied for its tax exemption and then had to file a special tax form at the end of five years that showed it met the required public support test.

The current IRS Form 1023 tax exemption application, dated June 2006, does not reflect the new rules. It contains instructions and questions on electing an advance ruling of public charity status (which no longer applies). Before filling in your Form 1023 application, go to the IRS website at www.irs.gov to see if a newer Form 1023 is available. If not, fill out the Form 1023 (June 2006 version) according to the instructions in the book, which we have updated to reflect the new rules. You'll see that the 2009 notice that is included at the beginning of the 2006 1023 form contains a brief description of the new rules. Again, we have used these new rules in the instructions in this book.

For more information on the latest public charity qualification rules, including transition rules that apply to organizations that have already received their advance ruling, search for "Elimination of the Advance Ruling Process" on the IRS website at www.irs.gov.

How to Qualify for Public Charity Status

As explained above, almost all 501(c)(3) nonprofits want to overcome the private foundation presumption and establish themselves as a public charity. There are three basic ways to do this:

- **Form one of the types of nonprofits that automatically qualify.** Particular types of nonprofit organizations, such as churches, schools, or hospitals, automatically qualify for public charity status because of the nature of their activities.

EXAMPLE:

A church that maintains a facility for religious worship would most easily obtain automatic public charity status. A church qualifies for recognition as a public charity because of the nature of its activities rather than its sources of support.

- **Derive most of your support from the public.** If your group receives support primarily from individual contributions, government, or other public sources, you can qualify for public charity status as a publicly supported organization.

EXAMPLE:

An organization formed to operate a center for rehabilitation, counseling, or similar services that plans to carry on a broad-based solicitation program and depend primarily on government grants, corporate contributions, and individual donations would most likely seek public charity status as a publicly supported organization.

- **Receive most of your revenue from activities related to your tax-exempt purposes.** If your group receives most of its revenue from activities related to its tax-exempt purposes, you can qualify under a special public charity support test (the exempt activities support test) that applies to many smaller nonprofits.

EXAMPLE:

An arts group deriving most of its income from exempt-purpose activities (lessons, performances, and renting studio facilities to other arts groups) would probably choose the support test. This public charity test, unlike those that apply to publicly supported organizations, allows groups to count income derived from the performance of their exempt purposes as qualified support.

CD-ROM

For additional information on the rules that apply to each of the three public charity tests, see the file, Public Charity or Private Foundation Status Issues under IRC §§ 509(a)(1)–(4), 4942(j)(3), and 507, on the CD-ROM included at the back of this book. For information on the public charity requirements associated with each type of automatically recognized public charity (churches, schools, hospitals, and others), see the section titled, "Type A. Organizations That Engage in Inherently Public Activity (IRC § 509(a)(1) and IRC §§ 170(b)(1) (A)(i)–(v))." For information on the public charity test we call the public support test, see the section titled, "Publicly Supported Organizations Described in IRC §§ 509(a)(1) and 170(b)(1)(A)(vi)." For information on the public charity test we call the exempt-activities support test, see the section titled, "Publicly Supported Organizations Described in IRC § 509(a)(2)."

> ### You Can Let the IRS Decide Your Public Charity Classification
>
> It's sometimes hard to figure out whether your organization will meet the public support test or the exempt activities test discussed below. To make this decision, an organization must second-guess future sources of support and tackle quite a few tax technicalities. Fortunately, if you have doubts, the IRS will help. Simply check a box on the federal tax exemption application and the IRS will decide this question for you based upon the financial and program information you submit with your application.
>
> For the specifics on making this election, see the Chapter 8 instructions to Part X, Line 5(i), of the federal tax exemption application.

Automatic Public Charity Status

The IRS automatically recognizes certain 501(c)(3) groups as public charities because they perform particular services or engage in certain charitable activities. The following groups automatically qualify:

Churches

Religious purpose groups that qualify as churches for 501(c)(3) tax exemption purposes also automatically qualify as a public charity. (IRC §§ 509(a)(1) and 170(b)(1)(A)(i).) Qualifying as a church under Section 501(c)(3) is more difficult than qualifying as a 501(c)(3) religious-purpose organization. To qualify as a church, the organization must have the institutional and formal characteristics of a church. (See "Religious Purposes" in Chapter 3.) If your religious-purpose 501(c)(3) group does not qualify as a church, it can still qualify for public charity status under one of the other public charity tests described below.

Schools

Certain educational institutions that have the institutional attributes of a school automatically qualify as public charities. (IRC §§ 509(a)(1) and 170(b)(1)(A)(ii).) Generally, these are educational organizations whose primary function is to present formal instruction. These schools usually have a regular faculty and curriculum, a regularly enrolled body of students, and a place where their educational activities are carried on.

This school category for automatic public charity recognition is geared toward primary or secondary preparatory or high schools, and colleges and universities with regularly enrolled student bodies. The farther an educational group strays from the institutional criteria mentioned above, the harder it will be to qualify as a public charity. This doesn't mean that less structured educational institutions can't automatically qualify for public charity status as schools, it just may be more difficult. Nontraditional groups have a better chance of obtaining automatic public charity status if they have some conventional institutional attributes, such as regional accreditation and a state-approved curriculum. If your educational-purpose 501(c)(3) group does not fall within this school category for automatic recognition, it can still qualify for public charity status under the public support test or exempt activities support test, described below.

Hospitals and Medical Research Organizations

Nonprofit health care groups that operate charitable hospitals or facilities and whose main function is to provide hospital or medical care, medical education, or medical research automatically qualify as public charities. (IRC §§ 509(a)(1) and 170(b)(1)(A)(iii).) These charitable hospitals generally have the following characteristics:

- doctors selected from the community at large, who are part of the courtesy staff
- a community-oriented board of directors
- emergency room facilities available on a community-access basis
- admission of at least some patients without charge (on a charitable basis)
- nondiscrimination with respect to all admissions (particularly Medicare or Medicaid patients), and
- a medical training and research program that benefits the community.

Other 501(c)(3) health care organizations, such as rehabilitation groups, outpatient clinics, community mental health programs, or drug treatment centers, can qualify as hospitals if their principal purpose is to provide hospital or medical care. A health organization that uses consultation services of certified medical personnel such as doctors and nurses will have an easier time meeting the hospital criteria. The IRS does not, however, recognize convalescent homes, homes for children or the aged, or institutions that provide vocational training for the handicapped as fitting within this public charity category.

Medical education and research organizations do not qualify under these IRC sections unless they actively provide on-site medical or hospital care to patients as an integral part of their functions. Medical research groups must also be directly and continuously active in medical research with a hospital, and this research must be the organization's principal purpose.

TIP

Hospitals and other tax-exempt health care organizations may want to adopt a community board and a conflict of interest policy in their bylaws. We explain how hospitals and medical care groups can modify the conflict of interest provisions in the bylaws included in this book to add provisions recommended by the IRS in Chapter 8, Part VIII, Line 20.

Public Safety Organizations

Groups organized and operated exclusively for public safety testing automatically qualify for public charity status. Generally, these organizations test consumer products to determine their fitness for use by the general public. (IRC § 509(a)(4).)

Government Organizations

Certain government organizations operated for the benefit of a college or university automatically qualify as public charities. (IRC §§ 509(a)(1) and 170(b)(1)(A)(iv).) You won't be forming a government corporation, but we mention it because this type of organization is included in the list of public charities on the federal tax exemption application form.

Supporting Organizations

Organizations operated solely for the benefit of, or in connection with, one or more of the above organizations, or publicly supported groups or groups that meet the exempt activities support test (described below in "Public Support Test" and "Exempt Activities Support Test"), are also automatically classified as public charities (except those that benefit a public safety organization). (IRC § 509(a)(3).)

RESOURCE

For further information on organizations listed above, see IRS Publication 557, *Tax Exempt Status for Your Organization*, "Section 509(a)(1) Organizations." For supporting organizations, see Publication 557, "Section 509(a)(3) Organizations." Also note that as part of the Pension Protection Act of 2006 federal rules have been enacted that impose additional requirements on supporting organizations

and private foundations that fund them. Ask your tax adviser for more information.

Public Support Test

To be classified as a publicly supported public charity, a group must regularly solicit funds from the general community. It must normally receive money from government agencies and/or from a number of different private contributors or agencies. (IRC §§ 509(a)(1) and 170(b)(1)(A)(vi).) The term "normally" has a special meaning in this context, which is explained below. We call this public charity test the public support test because the main requirement is that the organization must receive a substantial portion of its funds from broad-based public support sources.

In general, museums, libraries, and community centers that promote the arts should qualify under this public charity test if they rely on broad-based support from individual members of the community or from various public and private sources. Organizations that expect to rely primarily on a few private sources or occasional large grants to fund their operations will probably not meet the requirements of this section. This support test is difficult for small, grassroots groups to meet because income from the performance of tax-exempt purposes does not count as qualifying public support income—a source of support commonly relied upon by these groups.

To determine whether your group qualifies as a publicly supported public charity, you will need to do some basic math and understand some technical rules. Try not to get overwhelmed or discouraged by this technical material. For now, you can simply read through the information to get a sense of the basic criteria for this test and whether or not you might qualify. You can revisit anything that might seem applicable to you later when you fill in your federal tax exemption application.

More importantly, you may decide to let the IRS figure out which public support test works for you. In most cases, unless you know your nonprofit easily fits within the automatic public charity classification discussed above, the best and easiest approach is to let the IRS decide whether the public support test (covered in this section) or the exempt activities support test (discussed below) works for your nonprofit. After all, the technical experts on the IRS Exempt Organizations Determinations staff know this material inside out. Why not use their expertise and let them apply the public charity support tests to your group's past and projected sources of public support, which you will disclose in your federal tax exemption application?

RESOURCE

For more detailed information on qualifying as a public charity using the public support test, see IRS Publication 557 (included on the CD-ROM, which is at the back of the book), *Tax Exempt Status for Your Organization*, "Publicly Supported Organizations." Also check the IRS website at www.irs.gov under the "Public Charities & Non-Profits" section.

How Much Public Support Do You Need?

The IRS will usually consider an organization qualified under the public support test if it meets one of the following tests:

- The group normally receives at least one-third of its total support from governmental units, from contributions made directly or indirectly by the general public, or from a combination of the two (including contributions from other publicly supported organizations), or

- The organization receives at least one-tenth of its support from these sources *and* meets an additional "attraction of public support"

requirement (we discuss the attraction of public support test, below).

We call this one-third or one-tenth figure public support. To keep your percentage high enough, you'll want the IRS to classify as much of your income as possible as public support (the numerator amount), and keep your total support figure (the denominator amount) as low as possible. This will make your final percentage of public support as high as possible. Of course, the IRS has many rules, and exceptions to the rules, to define public support and total support. We provide a guide to the basic technical terms used, below.

Some basic math must be used to estimate your organization's percentage of support. As we explain later, only certain types of support can be included in the numerator of the fraction— the support funds classified as qualified public support. The denominator of the fraction includes the organization's total support, which includes most sources of support received by the nonprofit. You will want as much support as possible to show up in the numerator as qualified public support. If some support received by the nonprofit does not qualify as public support, then it is better to have the support also excluded from the total support. This will keep the excluded support from reducing your public support percentage, since both the numerator and denominator will be left intact.

What Is Public Support?

Qualified public support (support included in the numerator of the fraction) includes funds from private and public agencies as well as contributions from corporate and individual donors. However, the IRS limits how much qualified support your group can receive from one individual or corporation. Also, some membership fees can be included as qualified support. We discuss these special rules in more detail, below.

What Does "Normally" Mean?

An organization must "normally" receive either one-third or one-tenth of its total support from public support sources. This means that one tax year won't make or break your chances of meeting the test—the IRS bases its decision on five years' cumulative receipts. Your organization will meet either the one-third or one-tenth support test for the current tax year if, during the current tax year and the four prior tax years (five years total), its cumulative public support equals one-third or one-tenth of its cumulative total support.

If your nonprofit meets the support test in the current year (based on support received over the five-year testing period, which includes the current tax year and the previous four tax years), it will be classified as a public charity for the current and the next tax year.

EXAMPLE:

Open Range, Inc. is a nonprofit organization conducting medical research on the healthful effects of organic cattle ranching. ORI's cumulative total support was $60,000 for 2007 through 2011, and its cumulative public support was $25,000. The organization will, therefore, be considered a publicly supported public charity for 2011 and the following tax year, 2012. This remains true even if, for one or more of the previous four years or the current tax year (which we're asssuming is 2011), public support did not equal one-third of the total support—it's the cumulative total that counts.

EXAMPLE:

If World Relief, a 501(c)(3) nonprofit, meets the public support test for the year 2012 because of grants and contributions received from the public from the start of 2008 through the end of 2012 (the five-year testing period that includes the current year), the nonprofit will be classified as a public charity for both 2012 and 2013. Let's assume that in 2013 World Relief fails the support test (using the new five-year testing period of 2009 through and including 2013). It retains its public charity status for 2013 because it met the support test in the prior year. But if World Relief also fails the support test in 2014 (using a new five-year testing period of 2010 to and through 2014), it will lose its public charity status as of the start of its 2014 tax year. In other words, it will be classified as a private foundation as of the beginning of its 2014 tax year.

What Is a "Government Unit"?

Money received from a government unit is considered public support. Government units include federal or state governmental agencies, county and city agencies, and so on. The most common example of governmental support is a federal or state grant.

The 2% Limit Rule

Direct or indirect contributions from the general public are considered public support. Indirect contributions include grants from private trusts or agencies also funded by contributions from the general public, such as grants from Community Chest or the United Fund.

However, there is a major restriction applicable to these contributions. The total contributions from one individual, trust, or corporation made during the current year and preceding four tax years can be counted only to the extent that they do not exceed 2% of the corporation's total support for those five years. Contributions from government units, publicly supported organizations, and unusual grants are not subject to this 2% limit. These exceptions are discussed below.

EXAMPLE:

If your total support over the current year and previous four-year period was $60,000, then only $1,200 (2% of $60,000) contributed by any one person, private agency, or other source can count as public support.

Note that the total amount of any one contribution, even if it exceeds this 2%, five-year limitation, is included in the corporation's total support. Paradoxically, therefore, large contributions from an individual or private agency can have a disastrous effect on your status as a publicly supported charity. You get to include such contributions as public support only to the extent of 2% of the current year and previous four years' total income, but the total income figure is increased by the full amount of the contribution. This makes it more difficult for you to meet the one-third or one-tenth public support requirement.

EXAMPLE:

On Your Toes, a ballet troupe, received the following contributions from 2007 through 2011:

2007	$10,000	from individual X
2008	20,000	from individual Y
2009	50,000	from Z Community Chest
2010	10,000	as an additional contribution from individual X
2011	10,000	additional contribution from Z Community Chest
	$100,000	Total Support

All support for the five-year period is from contributions, direct or indirect, from the general public. However, in view of the 2% limit, On Your Toes will have trouble maintaining its publicly supported public charity status. While all contributions count toward total support, only $2,000 (2% x $100,000) from any one contributor counts as public support.

Therefore, the troupe's public support for this period is only $6,000 ($2,000 from each contributor, X, Y, and Z), which falls $4,000 short of the minimum one-tenth public support requirement.

Now, suppose On Your Toes received $2,000 each from 50 contributors over the five-year period. It still has $100,000 total support, but because no one contributor gave more than 2% of the five years' total support, it can count the entire $100,000 as public support.

TIP

Increase your chances of qualifying as a publicly supported public charity. One way to do this is to solicit smaller contributions through a broad-based fundraising program and don't rely constantly on the same major sources. This way, you'll beat the 2% limit and have a better chance of qualifying contributions as public support.

Exceptions to the 2% Limit Rule

There are two major exceptions to the 2% limit, as described below.

Money From Government Units or Publicly Supported Organizations

Contributions received from a government unit or other publicly supported organization are not subject to the 2% limit, except those specifically earmarked for your organization by the original donor.

EXAMPLE:

Ebeneezer Sax gives $1 million to National Public Music, a national government foundation that promotes musical arts. NPM then gives your organization the million dollars as a grant. If Sax made the contribution to NPM on the condition that the foundation give it to your organization, it is considered earmarked for you and the 2% limit applies. If not, the limit doesn't apply—and you can count the whole donation as public support.

Except for earmarked contributions or grants, you can rely on large contributions or grants from specific government agencies or other publicly supported organizations every year, since all such contributions will be counted as public support.

Money From Unusual Grants

Another major exception to the 2% limit is for unusual grants from the private or public sector. A grant is unusual if it:

- is attracted by the publicly supported nature of your organization
- is unusual—this means you don't regularly rely on the particular grant and it is an unexpectedly large amount, and
- would, because of its large size, adversely affect the publicly supported status of your organization (as we've seen, because of the 2% limit, large grants can cause trouble).

If a grant qualifies as an unusual grant, you can exclude the grant funds from both your public support and total support figures for the year in which it is given.

EXAMPLE:

The National Museum of Computer Memorabilia, Inc. is a nonprofit corporation that operates a museum of computers and artificial intelligence memorabilia. The years 2008 through 2011 are difficult ones, and the museum raises very little money. But in 2012 the organization receives an unexpected windfall grant. A look at the receipts for 2008 to 2011 helps illustrate the importance of the unusual grant exception. All amounts are individual contributions from the general public unless indicated otherwise:

2008	$1,000	from A
2009	1,000	from B
2010	1,000	from C
2011	1,000	from D
	1,000	from E
2012	100,000	from Z, a private grant agency
	$105,000	Total Receipts

Assume that the 2012 grant qualifies as an unusual grant. The total support computation for the five-year period would be:

2008	$1,000	from A
2009	1,000	from B
2010	1,000	from C
2011	1,000	from D
	1,000	from E
2012	0	the $100,000 grant drops out from total support
	$5,000	Total Support

Because the total support is $5,000, the museum can only count a maximum of 2% times $5,000, or $100, received from any one individual during this period as public support. Therefore, the public support computation for this period looks like this:

2008	$100	from A
2009	100	from B
2010	100	from C
2011	100	from D
	100	from E
2012	0	the $100,000 contribution also drops out from the public support computation
	$500	Total Public Support

The museum meets the 10% support test because total public support of $500 equals 10% of the total support of $5,000 received over the five-year period. If the organization also meets the attraction of public support requirement (which must be met by groups whose public support is less than one-third of total support), it will qualify as a publicly supported public charity for 2012 and 2013. (If you meet the five-year support test, you qualify as a public charity for the current and next tax years).

If the $100,000 contribution did not qualify as an unusual grant, the nonprofit would not meet the 10% public support test. Total support would equal total receipts of $105,000; a maximum of 2% times $105,000, or $2,100, from each individual and the grant agency would be classified as public support. Public support received over the five-year period would consist of $1,000 from individuals A, B, C, D, and E and the maximum allowable sum of $2,100 from the grant agency, for a total public support figure of $7,100. The percentage of public support for the five-year period would equal $7,100 divided by $105,000, or less than 7%, and the group would not meet the support test in 2012. Again, you can see how a large grant can hurt you if it does not qualify as an unusual grant.

Membership Fees as Public Support

Membership fees are considered public support as long as the member does not receive something valuable in return, such as admissions, merchandise, or the use of facilities or services. If a member does receive direct benefits in exchange for fees, the fees are not considered public support. These fees are, however, always included in the total support computation.

What's Not Public Support?

We've already mentioned some sources of support that are excluded because of special circumstances (they exceed the 2% limit or are paid by members in return for something of value). There are additional types of support that are never included as public support. The following types of income are not considered public support and, in some cases, are also not included in the total support figure (in which case they would drop entirely from the percentage of one-third or one-tenth support calculation).

Unrelated Activities and Investment

Net income from activities unrelated to exempt purposes as well as gross investment income, which includes rents, dividends, royalties, and returns on investments, are not considered public support. Both these types of income are added to the total support figure (they stay in the denominator of your one-third or one-tenth support calculation).

Sales of Assets or Performing Tax-Exempt Activity

The following types of income are not considered as public support or part of total support (as with unusual grants, they drop out of both computations):

- **Gains from selling a capital asset.** Generally, capital assets are property owned by the corporation for use in its activities. Note that capital assets do not include any business inventory or resale merchandise, business accounts or notes receivable, or real property used in a trade or business. Gains from selling these noncapital asset items are characterized as gross investment income and are not considered public support, but are added to the total support figure.

- **Receipts from performing tax-exempt purposes.** Examples include money received from admissions to performances of a tax-exempt symphony, fees for classes given by a dance studio, and tuition, or other charges paid for attending seminars, lectures, or classes given by an exempt educational organization.

Since we're dealing with tax laws, you'd probably expect at least one complicating exception. Here it is. If your organization relies primarily on gross receipts from activities related to its exempt purposes (such as an educational nonprofit that receives most of its support from class tuition), this exempt-purpose income will not be considered public support. Instead it will be computed in total support (so it will decrease your percentage of support calculation by making the fraction smaller). If your group falls in this category, it will probably not be able to qualify as a publicly supported public charity and should attempt to qualify under the public charity exempt activities support test, discussed below.

Attraction of Public Support Test

Groups that can't meet the one-third public support requirements can qualify for public charity status if they receive at least one-tenth of their total support from qualified public income sources and meet the additional attraction of public support requirement. Only groups trying to qualify for public charity status using the one-tenth (as opposed to one-third) public support requirements must satisfy this attraction of public support test. The IRS considers a number of factors in determining whether a group meets the test. Only Factor 1, below, must be met; none of the other factors are required.

The IRS looks favorably on organizations that meet one or more of the attraction of public support factors listed below. Meeting as many of these factors as possible will not only help you obtain public charity status, it also shows that you satisfy the basic 501(c)(3) tax-exempt status requirements—namely, that your nonprofit is organized and operated in the public interest and has broad-based community support and participation.

Factor 1. Continuous Solicitation of Funds Program

Your group must continually attract new public or governmental support. You will meet this requirement if you maintain a continuous program for soliciting money from the general public, community, or membership—or if you solicit support from governmental agencies, churches, schools, or hospitals that also qualify as public charities (see "Automatic Public Charity Status," above). Although this factor concerns broad-based support, the IRS allows new groups to limit initial campaigns to seeking seed money from a select number of the most promising agencies or people.

Factor 2. Percentage of Financial Support

At least 10% of your group's total support must come from the public. However, the greater the percentage of public support, the better.

Remember that if your public support amounts to one-third or more, you do not have to meet the attraction of public support factors listed in this section.

Factor 3. Support From a Representative Number of People

If your group gets most of its money from government agencies or from a broad cross section of people as opposed to one particular individual or a group with a special interest in your activities, it will more likely meet the attraction of public support requirement.

Factor 4. Representative Governing Body

A nonprofit corporation whose governing body represents broad public interests, rather than the personal interest of a limited number of donors, is considered favorably by the IRS. The IRS is more likely to treat an organization's governing body as representative if it includes:

- public officials
- people selected by public officials
- people recognized as experts in the organization's area of operations
- community leaders or others representing a cross section of community views and interests (such as members of the clergy, teachers, and civic leaders), or
- for membership organizations, people elected under the corporate articles or bylaws by a broad-based membership.

Factor 5. Availability of Public Facilities or Services

If an organization continuously provides facilities or services to the general public, the IRS will consider this favorably. These facilities and services might include a museum open to the public, an orchestra that gives public performances, a group that distributes educational literature to the public, or a senior citizens' home that provides nursing or other services to low-income members of the community.

Factor 6. Additional Factors

Corporations are also more likely to meet the attraction of public support requirement if:

- members of the public with special knowledge or expertise (such as public officials, or civic or community leaders) participate in or sponsor programs
- the organization maintains a program to do charitable work in the community (such as job development or low-income housing rehabilitation), or
- the organization gets a significant portion of its funds from another public charity or a governmental agency to which it is, in some way, held accountable as a condition of the grant, contract, or contribution.

Factor 7. Additional Factors for Membership Groups Only

A membership organization is more likely to meet the attraction of public support requirement if:

- the solicitation for dues-paying members attempts to enroll a substantial number of people in the community or area, or in a particular profession or field of special interest
- membership dues are affordable to a broad cross section of the interested public, or
- the organization's activities are likely to appeal to people with some broad common interest or purpose—such as musical activities in the case of an orchestra or different forms of dance in the case of a dance studio.

Exempt Activities Support Test

Don't worry if your Section 501(c)(3) group does not qualify as a public charity either automatically or through the one-third or one-tenth public support test described above. There is another way to qualify as a public charity. The exempt activities support test is likely to meet your needs if your 501(c)(3) group intends to derive income from performing exempt-purpose activities and services (IRC § 509(a)(2)).

Although IRS publications sometimes include groups that meet the support test described in this section as publicly-supported organizations, we do not in this chapter. For purposes of this chapter, publicly-supported organizations are those that qualify under the public support test described above. We use the term "exempt activities support test" in this chapter to describe this test.

For more detailed information on this public charity category, see IRS Publication 557, *Tax Exempt Status for Your Organization,* "509(a)(2) Organizations."

TIP

Let the IRS do the work for you. You can let the IRS do the hard part of deciding how each of the special rules described below applies to your group's anticipated sources of financial support. We show you how to check a box on the federal exemption application to do this. For now, just read through this material and you can come back to a particular section if you need to later when you fill in your IRS tax exemption application.

What Type of Support Qualifies and How Much Do You Need?

To qualify under the exempt activities public charity support test, a 501(c)(3) nonprofit organization must meet two requirements:

1. The organization must normally receive more than one-third of its total support in each tax year as qualified public support. Qualified public support is support from any of the following sources:

   • gifts, grants, contributions, or membership fees, and

   • gross receipts from admissions, selling merchandise, performing services, or providing facilities in an activity related to the exempt purposes of the nonprofit organization.

2. The organization also must normally not receive more than one-third of its annual support from unrelated trades or businesses or gross investment income. Gross investment income includes rent from unrelated sources, interest, dividends, and royalties—sources of support far removed from the activities of most small nonprofit organizations. However, it does not include any taxes you pay on income from unrelated businesses or activities—these amounts are deducted before the one-third figure is calculated.

Again, the most important aspect of this test, and the one that makes it appropriate for many 501(c)(3) groups, is that it allows the one-third qualified public support amount to include the group's receipts from performing its exempt purposes. Hence, this public charity classification is appropriate for many self-sustaining nonprofits that raise income from their tax-exempt activities, such as performing arts groups, schools, and other educational-purpose organizations, and nonprofit service organizations. School tuition, admissions to concerts or plays, or payments for classes at a pottery studio count as qualified public support under this public charity test.

Support Must Be From Permitted Sources

Qualified public support under this test must come from permitted sources including:

- individuals
- government agencies, and
- other 501(c)(3) public charities—generally, those that qualify as public charities under one of the tests described in "Automatic Public Charity Status" or "Public Support Test," above.

Permitted sources do not include disqualified persons (defined under IRC Section 4946)—people who would be considered disqualified if the organization were classified as a private foundation. These include substantial contributors, the organization's founders, and certain related persons.

Membership Fees and Dues Get Special Treatment

Dues paid to provide support for or to participate in the nonprofit organization, or in return for services or facilities provided only to members, are considered valid membership dues and can be counted in full as qualified public support. On the other hand, fees or dues paid in return for a discount on products or services provided to the public, or in return for some other monetary benefit, are not valid membership fees. However, these payments can still be counted as qualified public support if the fee entitles the member to special rates for exempt-purpose activities—in which case the payments would qualify as receipts related to the group's exempt purposes, but the payments may be subject to the 1% or $5,000 limitation, discussed below.

EXAMPLE:

People pay $50 to become members of All Thumbs, a nonprofit group dedicated to rebuilding interest in the unitar, a near-extinct one-stringed guitar-like musical instrument. All Thumbs' members are allowed $50 worth of reduced rate passes to all unitar concerts nationwide. Although these fees can't be counted as valid membership fees because they are paid in return for an equivalent monetary benefit (a $50 discount at unitar concerts), they still count as receipts related to the performance of the group's exempt purposes (putting on these concerts is an exempt purpose and activity of the group). Therefore, the fees can be counted by the organization as qualified public support (we assume the fees paid by each individual do not exceed the 1% or $5,000 limitation that applies to exempt-purpose receipts, as discussed in the next section, below).

Are You Selling Services or Information That the Federal Government Offers for Free?

If your nonprofit plans to sell services or information, check to see if the same service or information is readily available free (or for a nominal fee) from the federal government. If so, you may need to tell potential clients and customers of this alternate source. This rule applies to all tax-exempt nonprofits (including any 501(c)(3) organization, whether classified as a public charity or private foundation). (IRC § 6711.) Failure to comply with this disclosure requirement can result in a substantial fine. For further information on these disclosure requirements, see IRS Publication 557.

The 1% or $5,000 Limit for Exempt-Purpose Income

There is one major limitation on the amount of income from exempt-purpose activities that can be included in the one-third qualified public support figure. In any tax year, receipts from individuals or government units from the performance of exempt-purpose services that exceed $5,000 or 1% of the organization's total support for the year, whichever is greater, must be excluded from the organization's qualified public support figure. This limitation applies only to exempt-purpose receipts and not to gifts, grants, contributions, or membership fees received by the organization.

EXAMPLE:

Van-Go is a visual arts group that makes art available to people around the nation by toting it around in specially marked vans. In 2012, Van-Go derives $30,000 total support from the sale of paintings. The funds are receipts related to the performance of the group's exempt purposes. Any amount over $5,000 paid by any one individual cannot be included in computing Van-Go's qualified public support for the year, although the full amount is included in total support. Of course, if Van-Go's total support for any year is more than $500,000, then the limitation on individual contributions will be 1% of the year's total support, since this figure exceeds $5,000.

Some Gifts Are Gross Receipts

When someone gives money or property without getting anything of value in return, we think of it as a gift or contribution. But when people give a nonprofit money or property in return for admissions, merchandise, services performed, or facilities furnished to the contributor, these aren't gifts. They are considered gross receipts from exempt-purpose activities and are subject to the $5,000 or 1% limitation.

EXAMPLE:

At its annual fundraising drive, the National Cormorant Preservation League rewards $100 contributors with a book containing color prints of cormorants. The book normally retails for $25. Only $75 of each contribution is considered a gift; the remaining $25 payments are classified as gross receipts from the performance of the group's exempt purposes and are subject to the $5,000 or 1% limitation.

Some Grants Are Gross Receipts

It is sometimes hard to distinguish money received as a grant from exempt-purpose gross receipts. The IRS rule is that when the granting agency gets some economic or physical benefit in return for its grant, such as a service, facility, or product, the grant is classified as gross receipts related to the exempt activities of the nonprofit organization. This means that the funds will be subject to the 1% or $5,000 limitation that applies to exempt-purpose receipts. Money contributed to benefit the public will be treated as bona fide grants by the IRS, not as exempt-purpose receipts. This type of bona fide grant is not subject to the 1% or $5,000 limitation.

EXAMPLE 1:

A pharmaceutical company, Amalgamated Mortar & Pestle, provides a research grant to a nonprofit scientific and medical research organization, Safer Sciences, Inc. The company specifies that the nonprofit must use the grant to develop a more reliable childproof cap for prescription drug containers (the results of the nonprofit

CHAPTER 4 | PUBLIC CHARITIES AND PRIVATE FOUNDATIONS | 75

research will be shared with the commercial company). The money is treated as receipts received by Safer Sciences in carrying out its exempt purposes and is subject to the $5,000 or 1% limitation.

EXAMPLE 2:

Safer Sciences gets a grant from the federal Centers for Disease Control and Prevention to build a better petri dish for epidemiological research. Since the money is used to benefit the public, the full amount will be included in the nonprofit organization's qualified public support figure.

Unusual Grants Drop Out of the Support Computation

To be included as qualified support (in the numerator of the support fraction), the support must be from permitted sources. Disqualified persons include founders, directors, or executive officers of the nonprofit. A large grant from one of these sources could undermine the ability of the nonprofit to qualify under this public charity test.

To avoid this result for nonprofits that would otherwise qualify under the exempt activities support test, unusual grants are ignored—that is, they drop out of both the numerator and denominator of the support calculation. (There is a similar exclusion for unusual grants under the public support test, discussed above.) A grant will be classified as unusual if the source of the grant is not regularly relied on or actively sought out by the nonprofit as part of its support outreach program and if certain other conditions are met. If you want to learn more about these unusual grant requirements for groups that qualify as a public charity under the exempt-activities support test, see IRS Publication 557 (included on the CD-ROM).

Rents Related to Exempt Purposes Are Not Gross Investment Income

Rents received from people or groups whose activities in the rented premises are related to the group's exempt purpose are generally not considered gross investment income. This is a good thing. Why? Remember: Under this public charity test, the organization must normally not receive more than one-third of its total support from unrelated trades or businesses or from gross investment income.

EXAMPLE:

Good Crafts, Inc., a studio that provides facilities for public education in historic crafts, rents a portion of its premises to an instructor who teaches stained glass classes. This rent would probably not fall into the gross investment income category. However, if the tenant's activities in the leased premises were not related to the nonprofit's purposes, then the rent would be included as gross investment income and, if all the unrelated and investment income of the nonprofit exceeded one-third of its total support, the nonprofit could lose its public charity status under the exempt activities support test.

Keep this exception in mind if your group owns or rents premises with extra space. It may be important to rent (or sublease, if you are renting, too) to another person or group whose activities are directly related to your exempt purposes. (If you're renting, be sure the terms of your lease allow you to sublease; most of the time, you'll need your landlord's permission.)

SEE AN EXPERT

When to consult a tax expert. If you plan to supplement your support with income from activities unrelated to your exempt purposes (as more and more nonprofits must), check with your tax adviser. You'll want to make sure this additional income will not exceed one-third of your total support and jeopardize your ability to qualify under this public charity category.

There's That Word "Normally" Again

To qualify as a public charity under the support test, groups must "normally" meet the one-third qualified support requirements set forth in "Public Support Test," above. As with publicly supported organizations, this means that the IRS looks at the total amount of support over the current tax year and previous four years to decide if the organization meets the support text for the current tax year. (See "What Does 'Normally' Mean?" above.)

Private Foundations

Initially, the IRS will classify your 501(c)(3) corporation as a private foundation. As we mentioned at the beginning of this chapter, almost all nonprofits will want to overcome this presumption and establish themselves as a public charity instead. Because you are probably interested in public charity status, you can skip this section or read through it quickly if you want learn about private foundations and the operating limitations and restrictions applicable to them. If you want to form a private foundation, you can use this book as an introduction to the subject, but you will probably also need the help of a nonprofit lawyer or tax specialist with experience setting up private foundations. The rules that apply to private foundations are very complicated and the penalties for not obeying the rules are stiff.

RESOURCE

Need more information on private foundations? See IRS Publication 4221-PF, *Compliance Guide for 501(c)(3) Private Foundations*, available at the IRS website at www.irs.gov.

Background

Broadly speaking, the reason that private foundations are subject to strict operating limitations and special taxes, while public charities are not, is to counter tax abuse schemes by wealthy individuals and families. Before the existence of private foundation restrictions, a person with a lot of money could set up his own 501(c)(3) tax-exempt organization (such as The Jonathan Smith Foundation) with a high-sounding purpose (to wipe out the potato bug in Northern Louisiana). The potato bugs, though, were never in any danger, because the real purpose of the foundation was to hire all of Jonathan Smith's relatives and friends down to the third generation. Instead of leaving the money in a will and paying heavy estate taxes, Jonathan Smith neatly transferred money to the next generation tax free by use of a tax-exempt foundation that just happened to hire all of his relatives.

To prevent schemes such as this, Congress enacted the private foundation operating restrictions, special excise taxes, and other private foundation disincentives discussed in the next section.

Operating Restrictions

Private foundations must comply with operating restrictions and detailed rules, including:

- restrictions on self-dealing between private foundations and their substantial contributors and other disqualified persons
- requirements that the foundation annually distribute its net income for charitable purposes
- limitations on holdings in private businesses
- provisions that investments must not jeopardize the carrying out of the group's 501(c)(3) tax-exempt purposes, and
- provisions to assure that expenditures further the group's exempt purposes.

Violations of these provisions result in substantial excise taxes and penalties against the private foundation and, in some cases, against its managers, major contributors, and certain related persons. Keeping track of and meeting these restrictions is unworkable for the average 501(c)(3) group, which is the main reason why you'll want to avoid being classified by the IRS as a private foundation.

Limitation on Deductibility of Contributions

Generally, a donor can take personal income tax deductions for individual contributions to private foundations of up to only 30% of the donor's adjusted gross income. Donations to public charities, on the other hand, are generally deductible up to 50% of the donor's adjusted gross income.

Of course, the overwhelming number of individual contributors do not contribute an amount even close to the 30% limit, so this limitation is not very important. The real question of importance to contributors is whether you are a qualified 501(c)(3) organization so that charitable contributions to your group are tax deductible.

 **RESOURCE**

For more on IRS rules about deduction limitations. IRS Publication 526, *Charitable Contributions*, discusses the rules limiting deductions to private foundations (called 30% limit organizations) and public charities (50% limit organizations), including special rules that apply to donations of real estate, securities, and certain types of tangible personal property. Qualifying 501(c)(3) organizations (both public charities and private foundations) and other qualified groups eligible to receive tax-deductible charitable contributions are listed in IRS Publication 78, *Cumulative List of Organizations*. You can search this list online at the IRS website (www.irs.gov). Enter "Publication 78" in the search box, then select the link to "Publication 78, Search for Exempt Organizations."

Special Types of Private Foundations

The IRS recognizes two special types of private foundations that have some of the advantages of public charities: private operating and private nonoperating foundations. We mention them briefly below because they are included in IRS nonprofit tax publications and forms. Few readers will be interested in forming either of these special organizations.

Private Operating Foundations

To qualify as a private operating foundation, the organization generally must distribute most of its income to tax-exempt activities and must meet one of three special tests (an assets, support, or endowment test). This special type of 501(c)(3) private foundation enjoys a few benefits not granted to regular private foundations, including the following:

- **More generous deductions for donors.** As with public charities, individual donors can deduct up to 50% of adjusted gross income for contributions to the organization.

- **Extended time to distribute funds.** The organization can receive grants from a private foundation without having to distribute the funds received within one year (and these funds can be treated as qualifying distributions by the donating private foundation).

- **No excise tax.** The private foundation excise tax on net investment income does not apply.

All other private foundation restrictions and excise taxes apply to private operating foundations.

CD-ROM

For additional information on the rules that apply to private operating foundations, see the file, Public Charity or Private Foundation Status Issues under IRC §§ 509(a)(1)–(4), 4942(j)(3), and 507, on the CD-ROM included at the back of this book. See the section titled, "IRC 4942(j)(3)—Private Operating Foundations."

Private Nonoperating Foundations

This special type of private foundation is one that either:

- distributes all the contributions it receives to public charities and private operating foundations (discussed just above) each year, or

- pools its contributions into a common trust fund and distributes the income and funds to public charities.

Individual contributors to private non-operating foundations can deduct 50% of their donations. However, these organizations are subject to all excise taxes and operating restrictions applicable to regular private foundations. ●

Other Tax Benefits and Reporting Requirements

In this chapter we discuss additional federal tax issues that affect nonprofits, such as the deductibility of contributions made to 501(c)(3) nonprofits and what happens if a 501(c)(3) makes money from activities not related to its tax-exempt purposes. We also cover nonprofit tax benefits and tax and nontax requirements that apply to 501(c)(3) nonprofits under state law.

Federal and State Tax Deductions for Contributions

A donor (corporate or individual) can claim a personal federal income tax deduction for contributions made to a 501(c)(3) tax-exempt organization. These contributions are called charitable contributions. Generally, states follow the federal tax deductibility rules for charitable contributions made to nonprofit corporations.

Corporations can make deductible charitable contributions of up to 10% of their annual taxable income. Individuals can deduct up to 50% of their adjusted gross income in any year for contributions made to 501(c)(3) public charities and to some types of 501(c)(3) private foundations, as explained in Chapter 4. Donations to most types of private foundations are limited to 30% of an individual's adjusted gross income in each year.

What Can Be Deducted

A donor can deduct the following types of contributions:

- **Cash.**
- **Property.** Generally, donors can deduct the fair market (resale) value of donated property. Technical rules apply to gifts of appreciated property (property that has increased in value) that may require donors to decrease the deduction they take for donat-

ing appreciated property—see IRS Publication 526, *Charitable Contributions*, "Giving Property That Has Increased In Value."

- **Unreimbursed car expenses.** These include the cost of gas and oil incurred by the donor while performing services for the nonprofit organization.
- **Unreimbursed travel expenses.** These include expenses incurred by the donor while away from home and performing services for the nonprofit organization, such as the cost of transportation, meals, and lodging.

What Cannot Be Deducted

Certain types of gifts cannot be deducted as charitable contributions. Nondeductible gifts include:

- **The value of volunteer services.** For example, if you normally are paid $40 per hour for bookkeeping work, and you volunteer ten hours of your time to a nonprofit to help them prepare their annual financial statements, you cannot claim a charitable deduction for the value of your time donated to the nonprofit (you can't claim a charitable deduction of $400).
- **The right to use property.** If you rent out office space for $1,000 per month and allow a nonprofit to use one-tenth of the total space for a small office, you cannot claim a charitable deduction of $100 per month for letting the nonprofit use the space for free.
- **Contributions to political parties.** These contributions, however, can be taken as a tax credit, subject to dollar and percentage limitations.
- **Direct contributions to needy individuals.**
- **Tuition.** Even amounts designated as donations, which must be paid in addition to tuition as a condition of enrollment, are not deductible.

- **Dues paid to labor unions.**
- **The cost of raffle, bingo, or lottery tickets, or other games of chance.**
- **Child care costs paid while performing services for a nonprofit organization.**

Donations That Can Be Partially Deducted

Contributions that a nonprofit receives in return for a service, product, or other benefit (such as membership fees paid in return for special membership incentives or promotional products, or donations charged for attending a performance) are only partially deductible. Donors may deduct for these only to the extent that the value of the contribution exceeds the fair market value of the service, product, or benefit received by the donor.

EXAMPLE:

If a member of a 501(c)(3) organization pays a $30 membership fee and receives a record album that sells for $30, nothing is deductible. But if a $20 product is given in return for the $30 payment, $10 of the fee paid is a bona fide donation and may be deducted by the member as a charitable contribution.

501(c)(3) nonprofit groups should always clearly state the dollar amount that is deductible when receiving contributions, donations, or membership fees in return for providing a service, product, discount, or other benefit to the donor.

Reporting Requirements

Individuals can claim deductions for charitable contributions by itemizing the gifts on IRS Schedule A and filing this form with their annual 1040 income tax return. IRS rules require donors to obtain receipts for all charitable contributions claimed on their tax returns. Receipts must describe the contribution and show the value of any goods or services received from the nonprofit by the donor as part of the transaction. See IRS publications mentioned below for more information on how to prepare donor receipts for your organization.

RESOURCE

The IRS requirements for deducting and reporting charitable contributions change from year to year. For current information, see IRS Publication 526, *Charitable Contributions*. For information on valuing gifts, see IRS Publication 561, *Determining the Value of Donated Property*.

Federal Estate and Gift Tax Exemptions

Gifts made as part of an individual's estate plan (through a will or trust document) can be an important source of contributions for 501(c)(3) nonprofits. When the individual dies, the 501(c)(3) organization receives the money and the money is excluded from the taxable estate of the individual.

In the past, this provided significant tax savings for donors. However, the estate tax has been in a state of flux in recent years. There was no estate tax in effect for 2010, and for tax years 2011 and 2012, only estates worth more than $5 million must pay a tax. (The $5 million exemption amount could change.) Nevertheless, many people are motivated to engage in estate planning, including making charitable gifts to nonprofit organizations.

Traditionally, colleges and universities and larger environmental and health organizations have actively solicited estate charitable giving by providing information to members and donors about estate planning and the benefits of charitable bequests. Increasingly, smaller nonprofits are starting to understand the game and are pursuing similar strategies in their fundraising efforts. If you understand how charitable giving affects the donor's taxes, you'll be better able to persuade potential donors to give to your cause.

An individual does not pay taxes on gifts made during his lifetime. However, gifts to an individual (who isn't the giver's spouse) or to a nonqualified organization will reduce the donor's unified estate and gift tax credit to the extent the gifts exceed $13,000 in one calendar year. For example, a $14,000 gift to a struggling writer, who will use the money to support himself while he writes the great American novel, will not be taxed to you. But the excess of $1,000 will be counted as part of your estate tax credit. On the other hand, gifts made to a 501(c)(3) nonprofit (even if they exceed $13,000) do not reduce this federal and estate gift tax credit. Tax-wise, you might be better off giving the money to a literary nonprofit that, in turn, gives grants to promising writers (unfortunately, you could not earmark the money for a particular writer, as explained in "Charitable Purposes," in Chapter 3).

RESOURCE

For further information on federal and state estate and gift taxes and individual estate planning techniques, see *Plan Your Estate*, by Denis Clifford (Nolo).

Federal Unrelated Business Income Tax

All tax-exempt nonprofit corporations, whether private foundations or public charities, may have to pay tax on income derived from activities unrelated to their exempt purposes.

The first $1,000 of unrelated business income is not taxed. After that, the normal federal corporate tax rate applies: 15% on the first $50,000 of taxable corporate income; 25% on the next $25,000; and 34% on taxable income over $75,000 (with a 5% surtax on taxable income between $100,000 and $335,000). Higher corporate tax rates (35% and an interim 38% surtax) apply to corporate taxable incomes over ten million dollars.

CAUTION

Be careful with unrelated income. As explained in "Unrelated Business Activities," in Chapter 3, if unrelated income is substantial, it may jeopardize the organization's 501(c)(3) tax exemption.

CD-ROM

For past history and current developments in the federal treatment of an exempt organization's unrelated business income tax, see UBIT: Current Developments, contained on the CD-ROM included at the back of this book.

Activities That Are Taxed

Unrelated business income comes from activities that are not directly related to a group's exempt purposes. An unrelated trade or business is one that is regularly carried on and not substantially related to a nonprofit group's exempt purposes. It is irrelevant that the organization uses the profits to conduct its exempt-purpose activities.

EXAMPLE 1:

Enviro-Home Institute is a 501(c)(3) nonprofit organized to educate the public about environmentally sound home design and home construction techniques. Enviro-Home develops a model home kit that applies its ideas of appropriate environmental construction and is very successful in selling the kit. The IRS considers this unrelated business income because it is not directly related to the educational purposes of the organization.

EXAMPLE 2:

A halfway house that offers room, board, therapy, and counseling to recently released prison inmates also operates a furniture shop to provide full-time employment for its residents. This is not an unrelated trade or business because the shop directly benefits the residents (even though it also produces income).

Activities That Are Not Taxed

A number of activities are specifically excluded from the definition of unrelated trades or businesses. These include activities in which nearly all work is done by volunteers, and those that:

- are carried on by 501(c)(3) tax-exempt organizations primarily for the benefit of members, students, patients, officers, or employees (such as a hospital gift shop for patients or employees)

- involve the sale of mostly donated merchandise, such as thrift shops

- consist of the exchange or rental of lists of donors or members

- involve the distribution of low-cost items, such as stamps or mailing labels worth less than $5, in the course of soliciting funds, and

- involve sponsoring trade shows by 501(c)(3) groups—this exclusion extends to the exempt organization's suppliers, who may educate trade show attendees on new developments or products related to the organization's exempt activities.

Some of these exceptions have been hotly contested by commercial business interests at congressional hearings. The primary objection is that nonprofits receive an unfair advantage by being allowed to engage, tax free, in activities that compete with their for-profit counterparts. Expect more hearings and future developments in this volatile area of nonprofit tax law.

Also excluded from this tax is income not derived from services (termed gross investment income in the Internal Revenue Code). Remember, this tax applies to unrelated activities, not necessarily to unrelated income. Examples of nontaxable income include:

- dividends, interest, and royalties

- rent from land, buildings, furniture, and equipment (some forms of rent are taxed if the rental property was purchased or improved subject to a mortgage, or if the rental income is based on the profits earned by the tenant), and

- gains or losses from the sale or exchange of property.

See Section 512(b) of the Internal Revenue Code for the complete list of these untaxed sources of income and the exceptions that exist for certain items.

SEE AN EXPERT

It is often difficult to predict whether the IRS will tax an activity or income as unrelated business. Furthermore, IRS regulations and rulings and U.S. Tax Court decisions contain a number of rules classifying specific activities as unrelated businesses that are subject to tax. In short, you should do more research or consult a tax specialist if you plan to engage in activities or derive income from sources not directly related to your exempt purposes. Please note, this isn't the same thing as saying you shouldn't engage in an unrelated activity—many nonprofits must engage in commercial businesses unrelated to their exempt purposes to survive. But to avoid jeopardizing your 501(c)(3) tax-exempt status and to understand the tax effects of engaging in unrelated business, you simply need good tax advice.

State Corporate Income Tax Exemptions

Most states have a corporate income tax, but nonprofit groups are eligible to apply for an exemption in all cases. Fortunately, in the overwhelming majority of states, there is little or nothing to do, as state authorities will rely on your federal 501(c)(3) exemption determination as proof that you are also entitled to a state corporate income tax exemption.

In many states, a nonprofit corporation that has received its federal exemption is automatically exempt from state corporate income taxes. A few states exempt nonprofits if they file nonprofit articles with the secretary of state (obtaining a federal tax exemption is not necessary to obtain the state tax exemption).

Some states require you to notify the department of revenue or complete a separate exemption application, but their decision is based on the federal determination. Finally, only a handful of states make an independent evaluation of nonprofit purposes, activities, and financial statements to determine whether to grant an exemption.

Generally, a corporation that has filed for its federal tax exemption need not pay state corporate income taxes prior to receiving a federal determination, which can take a few months or more in special cases. If the federal application is denied—and the state exemption determination is based upon obtaining the federal exemption—the corporation may have to pay the state income taxes it would have paid as a for-profit corporation while the application was pending. Check with a tax adviser for the rules in your state.

Even if your organization receives a state tax exemption, it may still be required to file an informational tax return yearly. For forms and information about your state's exemption requirements, contact your state tax agency online (see Appendix B for contact information).

Also keep in mind that just as at the federal level, there are state taxes on unrelated business income generated by a regular activity that has nothing to do with your exempt purposes. If you will have unrelated business income, you might wish to see a tax accountant in your state to be certain about your state corporate tax liabilities and necessary state filings.

> **TIP**
> **Don't forget about state unrelated business income taxes.** Like the IRS, each state with a corporate income tax scheme normally will assess regular state corporate income tax on income earned by a nonprofit within the state from activities that are unrelated to the nonprofit's tax-exempt purposes. Your state tax office can provide the specific details of your state's unrelated business income tax—again, see Appendix B for contact information.

Other State Taxes

Each state imposes additional taxes that may apply to your nonprofit activities and operations. In many cases, your tax-exempt 501(c)(3) can apply for an exemption from one or more of these additional taxes.

Most states have enacted a sales tax. Some states exempt nonprofits from payment when purchasing goods. Only a few exempt nonprofits from collecting sales tax when selling goods, and then only under restricted circumstances, such as fundraising events—bake sales, crafts fairs, benefit dinners, or performances, for example—that take place occasionally during the year.

In addition, a nonprofit corporation may be eligible to apply for exemption from state and local use, excise, and property taxes, hotel and meal taxes, and business license fees.

Contact your state's tax agency online (see Appendix B) to learn more about your tax responsibilities—and exemption possibilities.

Some States Require an Advance Tax Payment

In a small number of states, incorporators must make a franchise tax, trust fund, or other advance payment when filing nonprofit articles of incorporation with the secretary of state. Check with your state tax agency by going to its online website. (See Appendix B.)

State Solicitation Regulations

Fundraising is a way of life for most nonprofit organizations, which must depend either on public or private grants, or on contributions solicited from the general public, for all operating funds. This activity—solicitation of contributions from the general public by a 501(c)(3) public charity—is regulated by most states.

Generally, state regulation of charitable solicitations is meant to serve two purposes:

- to curb fundraising abuses by monitoring the people involved and their activities, and
- to give the public access to information on how much an organization spends to raise whatever ultimately goes into funding its charitable, educational, religious, or other nonprofit purposes.

A majority of states require groups that solicit within the state to register, usually with the attorney general. Most of these states also require the registration of paid fundraisers and solicitors, both the people who administer the programs and those who go door-to-door or use the telephone or other media to solicit money. A registration fee, a bond, or both, may also be required for solicitors, ranging from as little as $15 to $800 or more.

The U.S. Supreme Court has decided several cases affecting how much information solicitors must disclose about their methods of solicitation and what happens to the money they collect. At present, states may require professional solicitors to tell prospective donors where to check for financial information on their campaigns, including what percentage of the money collected actually goes to charity, but fundraisers needn't submit scripts of their pitches to the state for review.

In addition to solicitor regulation, many states have detailed contribution reporting requirements, and demand information on the amount spent (on paid solicitors, advertising and promotion, mailings, and so on) to raise the total amount solicited. The organization may have to supply this information either annually or for each individual fundraising campaign.

While large-scale fundraising operations—those that use telemarketing and massive direct mail solicitation—are the targets of these regulations, all organizations must comply with these rules. Find out what your obligations are by checking with your city government. At the state level, the attorney general's office is usually in charge of solicitation registration; if not, find out from your secretary of state what registration and reporting requirements, if any, you must meet.

Regulation of charitable solicitation is currently an active area of both legislation and litigation. At the federal level, Congress has proposed putting multistate nonprofit fundraising activities under Federal Trade Commission (FTC) regulation, and thereby under federal court jurisdiction; single-state efforts would remain under state and local jurisdiction. Many state legislatures have also enacted laws or tightened existing ones regulating charitable solicitation.

RESOURCE

For more information on fundraising registration requirements, see *Nonprofit Fundraising Registration: The 50-State Guide,* by Stephen Fishman (Nolo).

Exceptions to State Solicitation Regulations

Typically, grants, unrestricted gifts, bona fide membership fees, and payments for goods and services not received in connection with a solicitation are exempted from state solicitation rules and regulations.

State Nonprofit Corporate Report Requirements

Nonprofit corporations in most states must periodically file reports with the secretary of state, in effect reregistering their existence. Generally this is an annual report, but in a few states a report is required less frequently.

The contents of the state corporate report—generally submitted on a form supplied by the secretary of state—vary. Most states want only a simple recital of minimal information to confirm that a corporation is still operating, under the same name, at the same address, and for the purposes stated in its articles of incorporation. Sometimes the names and addresses of directors and/or officers must be included, and the report must be signed by one of these people. Many states also collect a filing fee with the annual report.

A few states, however, require more detailed financial and other information, such as:

- a disclosure of salaries, loans, guarantees, and other payments or benefits made to or conferred on directors and officers

- the amount of money invested in real or personal property in the state, or

- a complete financial statement listing all assets and liabilities, revenues and receipts, and expenses and disbursements (except for the smallest nonprofits; your accountant or treasurer should prepare a balance sheet and income statement at least annually).

Each state has its own filing date or period; you can get this information from your secretary of state. (Go to your state's corporate filing office website—Appendix B.) Although completing the corporate report is a mere formality in most states, requiring the submission of very little information, compliance is important. Failing to file may, in some cases, result in the imposition of a fine and the suspension of corporate powers by the secretary of state. ●

PART

2

Incorporating Your Nonprofit

Choose a Name and File Your Articles of Incorporation

This chapter shows you how to form your nonprofit corporation in a sequence of small, manageable steps. Fortunately, most incorporation steps are relatively easy and straightforward. For the most part, you will fill in blanks on standard incorporation forms based on information you already have at your fingertips. Take your time and relax—you'll be surprised at how easy it all is when you follow our instructions one step at a time.

TIP

Forming your corporation will be the first step you take to obtain nonprofit status. Your corporation must be in existence when you apply for your federal tax exemption. We recommend, however, that before you file your articles, you read through and prepare some of the other documents required later in the process, such as your bylaws and tax exemption application. That way you'll know what is required to complete the process before you form your corporation. (See discussion in "Check Your State Filing Office Website," below).

Because the content and format of certain corporate documents differ from state to state, it's essential that you contact your secretary of state or other corporate official to obtain official incorporation forms and information. We show you how to do this. We provide sample clauses, forms, and information designed to show you how to use this state-specific information to prepare your nonprofit incorporation forms.

As you begin the process of forming your corporation, we suggest that you use the tear-out Incorporation Checklist, in Appendix C (or, access the checklist file on the CD-ROM), to chart your way through the incorporation steps in chapters 6 through 10. This will help you keep track of where you are and can greatly simplify the incorporation process for you.

Nonprofit Nomenclature

Different states use different words in their nonprofit statutes, regulations, and bureaucracies. We have tried to use the most common terms to describe nonprofit forms, procedures, and officials. For example, we refer to the charter document used to form the nonprofit corporation as the articles of incorporation. In some states, this document is given another name such as the certificate of incorporation. Similarly, we refer to the office that handles corporate filings as the secretary of state's office—this is the official designation used in most states for this function. Just keep in mind that your state may occasionally use different corporate terminology than we use in the text.

CAUTION

We strongly recommend you go to the IRS website, at www.irs.gov, and browse IRS Form 1023 (the 501(c)(3) exemption application) and IRS Form 990 (the annual exempt organization information return) and the instructions to both forms. Looking over the forms will give you a sense of the amount of organizational and financial work that looms ahead after you form a tax-exempt nonprofit. We help you get through the exemption application in Chapter 8, but you will need all the additional help and expertise you can get to be able to gather and report the detailed program, fundraising, and financial data required on the annual 990 return and its associated schedules. We are not trying to scare you off—we just want to make a realistic assessment of your ability to handle the required level of record keeping and reporting before you form your nonprofit.

Setting up procedures to assemble and report the required information on your annual federal 990 return is one of the prices you pay for tax exemption (unless you are exempt from filing a 990 return). Your workload will be lessened if you qualify to file Form 990-EZ.

View Materials From Your Secretary of State

To get started, you will need to view nonprofit incorporation information and forms provided by your secretary of state's office. You can go online to your state's filing office (see Appendix B) to see your state's nonprofit forms, instructions, and other information.

Most states' corporate filing office websites provide a nonprofit articles of incorporation form with instructions for filling it in, and a link to the nonprofit corporation statutes that contain the technical requirements for organizing and operating a nonprofit corporation in your state. In most states, the non-profit laws are contained in a separate nonprofit statute or act. In a few states, the nonprofit laws are mixed in with, and can be obtained as part of, the state's regular business corporation act or law. In Appendix B we explain how you can locate your state's statute online. This is the fastest and most efficient way to access your state's nonprofit law. You may need to refer to these statutes when completing your articles of incorporation and corporate bylaws.

Most secretary of state's websites also provide:

- a fee schedule showing current charges for filing, copying, and certifying various corporate forms
- forms and instructions to check corporate name availability and reserve a corporate name, and
- forms and instructions for postincorporation procedures. These may include materials to amend articles, change the corporation's registered office or registered agent, or register an assumed corporate name (one that is different from the corporate name shown in the incorporation papers).

Many states also allow you to check name availability, reserve a corporate name, and prepare and file your articles online. If your state's website provides these services, we recommend you use them as an efficient alternative to using the mail.

To Obtain Your Nonprofit Material

Check your state's website (see Appendix B). The site probably has everything you need online.

You can call your secretary of state for special questions. The phone number of the corporations division or similar office in your state is listed on the state corporate filing office website.

Choose a Corporate Name

Your first step in forming your corporation is to choose a name that you like and one that also meets the requirements of state law. The state corporate filing office (typically the secretary of state) will approve your corporate name when you file your articles of incorporation. As explained more below, you can check name availability and reserve a corporate name before you file your articles.

The Importance of Your Corporate Name

As a practical matter, your corporate name is one of your most important assets. It represents the goodwill of your organization. We don't use the term goodwill here in any legal, accounting, or tax sense; rather, your name is significant because people in the community, grant agencies, other nonprofits, and those with whom you do business will identify your nonprofit primarily by its name. For this

---

Keeping or Changing Your Name

If you are incorporating an existing organization, you may want to use your current name as your corporate name, particularly if it has become associated with your group, its activities, fundraising efforts, products, or services. Many new corporations do this by simply adding "Inc." to their old name (for example, The World Betterment Fund decides to incorporate as The World Betterment Fund, Inc.). Using your old name is not required, however. If you have been thinking about a new name for your organization, this is your chance to change it.

---

reason, as well as to avoid having to print new stationery, change promotional literature, or create new logos, you should pick a name you'll be happy with for a long time.

Corporate Name Legal Requirements

Let's look at the basic legal name requirements applicable in most states for nonprofit corporations.

Your Name Must Be Unique

Your proposed corporate name (the name stated in your articles of incorporation) must not be the same as, or confusingly similar to, a name already on file with the secretary of state.

The list of names maintained by the secretaries of state includes:

- existing corporations formed in your state
- out-of-state corporations qualified to do business in your state
- names reserved for use by individuals planning to incorporate in your state (name

reservation periods vary from 30 to 120 days and often can be renewed at least once)

- names registered in your state by out-of-state corporations, and
- in some states, names registered as trademarks or service marks and those registered as assumed corporate names (we discuss these special types of business names below).

In deciding whether a corporate name is too similar to one already on file, the secretary's office will usually look only at similarities between the names themselves, not at similarities in the types and locations of the businesses using the names. If you attempt to form a corporation with a name that is similar in sound or wording to the name of another corporation on the corporate name list, the secretary's office may reject your name and return your articles of incorporation to you.

EXAMPLE:

Your proposed corporate name is Open Spaces Society, Inc. If another corporation has filed the name Open Spaces International, Inc., with the secretary of state, your name will probably be rejected as too similar.

Corporate Designator Requirements

In many states, your corporate name must include a corporate designator, such as Incorporated, Corporation, Company, Limited, or one of their abbreviations.

Although corporate designators are typically included at the end of a corporate name (The Foundation for Health, Incorporated), the designator may generally be placed anywhere in your corporate name (The Incorporated Healthcare Foundation).

RESOURCE

Corporate name requirements. See the instructions to your state's articles form (you can find them online—see Appendix B) to determine the nonprofit corporate name requirements in your state.

Prohibited Names

The statutes of various states forbid the use of specific words in the name of a nonprofit corporation. Mostly, prohibited names are those associated with specialized business, nonprofit, professional or governmental entities, or corporations. Try to avoid names from each of these categories—here are several examples of specialized corporate names whose use is limited by state laws:

Accounting	Insurance
Attorney	Physician
Banking	Reserve
Cooperative	Trust
Engineering	United States
Federal	

Of course, if you are forming a specialized nonprofit corporation, such as a consumers' or producers' cooperative or a nonprofit organization named "Solar Engineering Data Sciences" that collects research on solar engineering, you may be entitled to use one of these special words in your corporate name.

Using Two Names and Changing Your Name

If you want to adopt a formal corporate name in your articles that's different than the one you have used (or plan to use) to identify your nonprofit organization, you can do so. You'll need to file a fictitious business name statement (also known as an assumed business name statement or a dba statement in some states) with the local county clerk.

You can also change your corporate name after you've filed your articles. After making sure that the new name is available for use (as explained further, below), you can amend your articles and file the amendment with the secretary of state.

CAUTION

Having your name approved by the corporate filing office when you file your articles of incorporation does not guarantee that you will have the absolute legal right to use that name. As explained in more detail below, another organization or business may already be using the name as its business name or may be using it as a trademark or service mark. If someone else is using the name, they may be able to prevent you from using it, depending on their location, type of business, and other circumstances. We show you how to do some checking on your own to be relatively sure that no one else has a prior claim to your proposed corporate name based on trademark or service mark.

Practical Suggestions When Selecting a Name

Now that we've looked at the basic legal requirements related to your choice of a corporate name, here are some practical suggestions to help you do it.

Use Common Nonprofit Terms in Your Name

There are a number of words that broadly suggest 501(c)(3) nonprofit purposes or activities. Choosing one of these names can simplify the task of finding the right name for your organization and will alert others to the nonprofit nature of your corporate activities. Here are just a few:

Aid
American
Appreciation
Assistance
Association
Benefit
Betterment
Care
Center
Charitable
Coalition
Community
Congress
Conservation
Consortium
Council
Cultural
Education
Educational
Environmental
Exchange
Fellowship
Foundation
Friends
Fund
Health
Help
Heritage
Home
Hope
Hospice
Hospital

Human
Humane
Institute
International
Learning
Literary
Mission
Music
Orchestra
Organization
Philanthropic
Philharmonic
Program
Project
Protection
Public
Refuge
Relief
Religious
Research
Resource
Scholarship
Scientific
Service
Shelter
Social
Society
Study
Troupe
Voluntary
Welfare

Names to Avoid

When selecting a corporate name, we suggest you avoid, or use with caution, the types of words described and listed below. Of course, there are exceptions. If one of these words relates to your particular nonprofit purposes or activities, it may make sense to use the word in your name.

Avoid words that, taken together, signify a profit-making business or venture, such as Booksellers Corporation, Jeff Baxter & Company, Commercial Products Inc., or Entrepreneurial Services Corp.

Avoid words that describe or are related to special types of nonprofit organizations (those that are tax exempt under provisions of the IRC other than Section 501(c)(3)), such as Business League, Chamber of Commerce, Civic League, Hobby, Recreational or Social Club, Labor, Agricultural or Horticultural Organization, Political Action Organization, Real Estate Board, or Trade Group.

RELATED TOPIC

For a listing of these special tax-exempt nonprofit groups and a brief description of each group, see "Special Nonprofit Tax-Exempt Organizations," in Appendix C.

EXAMPLE:

The name Westbrook Social Club, Inc., would clearly identify a social club, tax exempt under IRC § 501(c)(7). For this reason, you shouldn't use this type of name for your 501(c)(3) nonprofit. However, The Social Consciousness Society might be an appropriate name for a 501(c)(3) educational-purpose organization. Also, although The Trade Betterment League of Pottersville would identify a 501(c)(6) business league, and The Millbrae Civic

Betterment League a 501(c)(4) civic league, The Philanthropic League of Castlemont might be a suitable name for a 501(c)(3) charitable giving group.

Avoid words or abbreviations associated with nationally known nonprofit causes, organizations, programs, or trademarks. You can bet that the well-known group has taken steps to protect its name as a trademark or service mark. Steer clear of the names in "These Names Are Already Taken," below.

These Names Are Already Taken

Here is a small sampling of some well-known —and off-limits—nonprofit names and abbreviations:

AAA

American Red Cross

American Ballet Theatre or ABT

American Conservatory Theatre or ACT

Audubon

Blue Cross

Blue Shield

Environmental Defense Fund

National Geographic

National Public Radio or NPR

Sierra Club

Public Broadcasting System or PBS

Avoid words with special symbols or punctuation that might confuse the secretary of state's computer name-search software, such as: @ # $ % ^ & * () + ? > or <.

Pick a Descriptive Name

It's often a good idea to pick a name that clearly reflects your purposes or activities (for example, Downtown Ballet Theater, Inc.; Good Health Society, Ltd.; or Endangered Fish Protection League, Inc.). Doing this allows potential members, donors, beneficiaries, and others to easily locate and identify you. More fanciful names (The Wave Project, Inc. or Serendipity Unlimited Inc.) are usually less advisable because it might take a while for people to figure out what they stand for, although occasionally their uniqueness can provide better identification over the long term.

EXAMPLE:

> Although the name Northern Counties Feline Shelter, Inc., will alert people at the start to the charitable purposes of the nonprofit group, Cats' Cradle, Inc., may stay with people longer once they are familiar with the activities of the organization.

Limit Your Name Geographically or Regionally

If you use general or descriptive terms in your name, you may need to further qualify it by geographic or regional descriptions to avoid conflicts or public confusion.

EXAMPLE 1:

> Your proposed name is The Philharmonic Society, Inc. Your secretary of state rejects this name as too close to a number of philharmonic orchestras on file. You refile using the proposed name, The Philharmonic Society of East Creek, and your name is accepted.

EXAMPLE 2:

> Suppose you are incorporating the AIDS Support Group, Inc. Even if this name does not conflict with the name of another corporation on file in your state, it is still a good idea to limit or qualify the name to avoid confusion by the public with other

groups in other parts of the country that share the same purposes or goals. You could do this by changing the name to the AIDS Support Group of Middleville.

Choose a New Name Instead of Trying to Distinguish Yourself

Instead of trying to distinguish your proposed name from another established group by using a regional or other identifier, it's usually better to choose a new and different name if the public is still likely to confuse your group with the other group.

EXAMPLE:

Your proposed nonprofit name is The Park School, Inc. If another corporation (specializing in a nationwide network of apprentice training colleges) is already listed with the name Park Training Schools, your secretary of state may reject your name as too similar.

You may be able to limit your name and make it acceptable (The Park Street School of Westmont, Inc.) but this may not be a good idea for two reasons: First, members of the public who have heard of the Park Training Schools might think that your school is simply a Westmont affiliate of the national training program. Second, you might still be infringing the trademark rights of the national group (they may have registered their name as a state or federal trademark).

Check Name Availability

The secretary of state will reject your articles of incorporation if the name you've chosen for your corporation is not available. Any name already being used by another corporation on file with the secretary of state's office is considered unavailable. To avoid having your articles rejected, it's often wise to check if the name you want is available before you try to file your articles.

Check Online or by Phone

In many states, you can check corporate name availability online by going to the state filing office website listed (see Appendix B), or you can call the main number of the corporate filings office listed on the state website and ask to speak to someone in the corporate name availability section.

If your proposed corporate name is not the same as or similar to an existing name listed online, you may decide it's safe to go ahead and file your articles without formally checking name availability or reserving your name with the secretary of state. If you discover a match to your proposed name, and the corporation is still active (the name search tells you whether the corporation is active or not), you need to look for another name. If you discover a similar corporate name, the secretary of state may find that it is too similar to your proposed name to let you use it. The only way to tell whether the secretary of state will allow you to use a name that is similar to an existing corporate name is to do a formal name availability check or try to reserve the name. If the secretary of state reports that the name is not available or won't reserve it for your use, you know the name was too similar to the existing corporation's name.

TIP

Don't use an LLC name for your corporation. Even though the corporate filing office may let you use a corporate name that conflicts with an LLC name, we advise against doing this. To avoid legal disputes, it's best to stay clear of any business name (whether a corporate, LLC, or unincorporated business name) that is the same as or similar to your proposed corporate name. The fact that an LLC name has a different ending than your corporate name (for example, "Racafrax, LLC" and you want to use "Racafrax" as your corporate name) does not mean you will be allowed to use your proposed name. If the names are substantially similar, a court may stop you from using your proposed name, even if you use it for a corporation and the competing business name is used by an LLC.

Do You Want to Bypass Name Checking Procedures?

Even if your proposed corporate name is available when you check with the secretary of state, this does not guarantee that your name will be available when you later file your articles of incorporation. For this reason, you may wish to dispense with a written name availability check and attempt to reserve your corporate name, as explained below, or file your articles and hope that your name is available for use.

Filing your articles without preliminary name checking or reservation makes sense if your state allows you to form your corporation online—if your proposed name is unavailable, the website will tell you. Also, if your state offers an expedited (24-hour) filing procedure for a small additional fee, you'll know in a day or two if your proposed name is available and if your articles were filed. Of course, if your state allows you to check a proposed corporate name online or over the phone, we suggest you take the time to do this in all cases.

What to Do When There's a Name Conflict

If using your proposed name is crucial to you and the secretary of state's office tells you that it is too similar to an existing corporate name already on file, there are a few things you can do, as explained below.

Appeal the Decision

You can ask the corporate filing office's legal counsel to review the staff's determination regarding your name's acceptability. This will involve filing a written request, and you may decide to seek the help of a lawyer. Here's why: The legal question of whether or not a name is so close to another name so as to cause confusion to the public is a difficult one, and involves looking at a number of criteria contained in court decisions. Factors such as the nature of each trade name user's business (the term trade name simply means a name used in conjunction with the operation of a trade or business), the geographical proximity of the two businesses, and other factors work together in ways that are difficult to predict. We cover trade name issues in more detail below but, for now, we simply note that if you do get into this sort of debate, you will probably want to see a lawyer who is versed in the complexities of trade name or trademark law or do some additional reading on your own.

Get Permission

An obvious resolution would be to obtain the written consent of the other corporation. Sometimes, profit corporations that have registered a name similar to the proposed name of a nonprofit corporation will be willing to allow the nonprofit corporation to use the similar name. We think this is too much trouble. Besides, most businesses jealously guard their name, and it is unlikely any business or organization will let you ride on the coattails of their existing name. If you are told your proposed corporate name is too similar to another name, we recommend you move on and choose another name that is available for your use.

Pick Another Name

You may decide that it's simpler (and less trouble all the way around) to pick another name for your nonprofit corporation. We usually recommend this approach.

> **CAUTION**
>
> **A name check is just a preliminary indication of the availability of your proposed corporate name.** Don't order your stationery, cards, or office signs until the secretary of state has formally accepted your name by approving a reservation of corporate name or filing your articles of incorporation.

Reserve Your Corporate Name

Most states allow you to reserve an available corporate name with the secretary of state. During the reservation period, only you may file articles with this name or a similar name. The reservation period and the fees vary. In many states, you can renew your reservation if you don't get around to filing your articles during the first reservation period.

Once you have decided on a corporate name and established its availability, it makes sense to reserve it if you will not be filing your articles immediately because:

- available corporate names are becoming hard to find, particularly in states with a lot of corporate filing activity, and
- reserving a name allows you to hold on to it while you complete your initial paperwork.

To reserve a corporate name, follow the instructions on your secretary of state website —most states provide an online reservation of name form, which you can download. Some even let you reserve your name online and pay for the reservation by credit card. If you have no information, call the corporations filings office of your secretary of state and ask for instructions. If the secretary does not provide a form, you can use the reservation of corporate name letter, shown below.

> **CD-ROM**
>
> The CD-ROM includes a copy of the Application for Reservation of Corporate Name form, and Appendix C includes a blank, tear-out copy.

> **CAUTION**
>
> **The person who signs the letter must also sign the articles.** Make sure that the person signing this reservation letter will be available to sign articles of incorporation on behalf of your organization—the corporate name is reserved for this person's use only.

> **CAUTION**
>
> **Reservation fees are subject to change.** To be sure the fee amounts are correct, call your secretary of state's office or check current fee information at your state's website.

Perform a Name Search

Approval by the secretary of state's office doesn't necessarily mean that you have the legal right to use a name; it simply means that your name does not conflict with that of another corporation already on file with the secretary of state and that you are presumed to have the legal right to use it within your state. Another organization (corporate or noncorporate, profit or nonprofit) may, in fact, already have the legal right to use this same name as a federal

Application for Reservation of Corporate Name

Date: _____

[Name and address of secretary of state office—see Appendix B]

_____

_____

Re: Corporate Name Reservation

Please reserve the following corporate name for my use for the allowable period specified under the state's corporation statutes.

[your proposed corporate name] _____

I enclose the required payment of $ _____[fee]_____. My name, address, and phone number are included below if you wish to contact me regarding this request.

Name: _____

Address: _____

Phone: _____

Thank you for your assistance.

[your signature] _____

---

or state trademark or service mark used to identify their goods or services. Most secretaries of state do not check state trademark/service mark registration lists to see if your proposed corporate name is available; none check the federal trademark register. Also, another organization may already be presumed to have the legal right to the name in a particular county if they are using it as a tradename (as the name of their business or organization) and have filed an assumed (or fictitious) business name statement with their county clerk. The secretaries of state of many states do not register or check assumed names, even assumed corporate names—this is most often done at the county level.

Who Needs to Do a Name Search

In many circumstances, you will know that your name is unique and unlikely to infringe on another organization's name. This would probably be the case, for example, if you called your group the Sumner County Crisis Hotline, or the Southern Wisconsin Medieval Music Society. By qualifying your name this way, you know that you are the only nonprofit in your area using the name. However, in some circumstances you may be less sure of your right to use a name. For example, the names Legal Rights for All or The Society to Cure Lyme Disease may be in use by a group in any part of the country.

Who Gets to Use a Name

The basic rule is that the ultimate right to use a particular name will usually be decided based on who was first in time to actually use the name in connection with a particular trade, business, activity, service, or product. In deciding who has the right to a name, the similarity of the types of businesses or organizations and their geographical proximity are usually taken into account.

Do Your Own Search

Below we list self-help name checking procedures you may want to use to be more certain that your proposed corporate name is unique. Do these name search procedures before you file your articles. Obviously, you can't be 100% certain—you can't possibly check all names in use by all other groups. However, you can check obvious sources likely to expose names similar to the one you wish to use. Here are some places to start.

- **State and county assumed business name files.** Your secretary of state website should indicate whether assumed (or fictitious) corporate names (different from the name a corporation uses in its articles) are registered with your secretary of state's office, at the county level, or both. If they are registered at the state level, call the assumed name section at the secretary of state's office and ask whether your proposed corporate name is the same as or similar to a registered assumed (or fictitious) corporate name. Also, call your local county clerk's office to ask how you

can check assumed business name filings—in most states, noncorporate assumed or fictitious business name statements, or "doing business as" (dba) statements, are filed with the county clerk's office. In most cases, you will have to go in and check the assumed business name files in person—it takes just a few minutes to do this.

- **State trademarks and service marks.** Call the trademark section of your secretary of state's office and ask if your proposed corporate name is the same as or similar to trademarks and service marks registered with the state (some offices may ask for a written request and a small fee before performing this search).

- **Directories.** Check major metropolitan phone book listings, nonprofit directories, business and trade directories, and other directories to see if another company or group is using a name similar to your proposed corporate name. Large public libraries keep phone directories for many major cities throughout the country, as well as trade and nonprofit directories. A local nonprofit resource center or business branch of a public library may have a special collection of nonprofit research materials—check these first for listings of local and national nonprofits. One commonly consulted national directory of nonprofit names is the *Encyclopedia of Associations* published by Gale Research Company (www.gale.cengage.com).

- **The *Federal Trademark Register.*** If your name is the type that might be used to market a service or product or to identify a business activity of your nonprofit corporation, you should check federal trademarks and service marks. You can check the *Federal Trademark Register* for free at www.uspto.gov. You can also go to a large public library or special business and government library in your area that carries the *Federal Trademark Register*, which lists trademark and service mark names broken into categories of goods and services.

- **Internet databases.** Most of the business name listings mentioned above, including Yellow Page listings, business directory databases, and the federal and state trademark registers, are available as part of several commercial computer databases. For example, the federal and state registers can be accessed through the TrademarkScan databases using SAEGIS, Dialog, or Westlaw online services. (Use your browser's search engine to find links to these services.) Subscription databases charge fees for your research time (unlike the www.uspto.gov site, which is free).

Outside Help

Of course, if you wish to go farther in your name search, you can pay a private record search company to check various databases and name listings. Alternatively, or in conjunction with your own efforts or search procedures, you can pay a trademark lawyer to oversee or undertake these searches for you (or to render a legal opinion if your search turns up a similar name). Most organizers of smaller nonprofits, particularly those who believe that a specialized or locally based name is not likely to conflict with anyone else's name, will not feel the need to do this and will be content to undertake the more modest self-help search procedures mentioned above.

The Consequences of Using Another's Name

To avoid problems, we suggest using the name selection techniques and performing the kind of commonsense checking described earlier. Disputes involving trade names, trademarks, and service marks tend to arise in the private, commercial sector. It is unlikely that your nonprofit will wish to market products and services as aggressively as a regular commercial concern and thereby run afoul of another business's trademark or service mark (you'd also be jeopardizing your tax-exempt status by engaging in a substantial amount of commercial activity). Nonetheless, as a matter of common sense, and to avoid legal disputes later on, you should do your best to avoid names already in use by other profit and nonprofit organizations, or in use as trademarks or service marks.

Legal remedies for violation of trade name or trademark rights vary under federal and state laws and court decisions. Most of the time, the business with the prior claim to the name can sue to enjoin (stop) you from using your name or can force you to change it. The court may also award the prior owner money damages for loss of sales or goodwill caused by your use of the name. If you violate a trademark or service mark registered with the U.S. Patent and Trademark Office, the court may award treble damages (three times the actual money damages suffered as a result of the infringement), any profits you make from using the name, and court costs; and may order that the goods with the offending labels or marks be confiscated and destroyed.

EXAMPLE:

A company called Foul Weather Gearheads has been in business for ten years selling foul weather gear such as rain slicks and hip boots via catalogues and the Internet. For the first seven to eight years, Foul Weather averaged gross annual sales of approximately $2 million. Another company, calling itself Rainy Day Gearheads, starts selling competing products, and Foul Weather's gross revenues slip by about 25% over the next two years. If Foul Weather can prove that the Rainy Day Gearheads trademark likely caused customer confusion that resulted in Foul Weather's decrease in sales, Foul Weather can recover its lost profits. Or if, prior to the infringement, Foul Weather had registered its name on the Principal Trademark Register maintained by the U.S. Patent and Trademark Office, it could choose to go after Rainy Day's profits (instead of recovering its own losses), attorneys' fees, and treble damages.

RELATED TOPIC

For further information, see *Patent, Copyright & Trademark: An Intellectual Property Desk Reference*, by Richard Stim (Nolo).

Protect Your Name

Once you have filed your articles of incorporation, you may want to take some additional steps to protect your name against later users. For example, if your name is also used to identify your products or services, you may wish to register it with your state of incorporation and the United States Patent and Trademark Office as a trademark or service mark. You may also want to register in other states if you plan to conduct operations there.

You can register your name with the U.S. Patent and Trademark Office if:

- you have actually used the name in interstate commerce (that is, in two or more states) in connection with the marketing of goods or services, or

- you intend to use the name in interstate commerce in connection with the marketing of goods or services.

If you specify the second ground in your trademark application, you must file an affidavit (sworn statement) within six months stating that the name has been placed in actual use—and pay an additional fee. This six-month period may be extended for additional six-month periods (at an additional fee for each extension), up to a total extension of two and one-half years. To obtain these extensions, you have to convince the Patent and Trademark Office that you have good cause for delaying your use of the name. Because trademark application procedures are relatively simple and inexpensive, you may wish to tackle this task yourself—your local county law library should have practice guides available to help you handle state and federal trademark and service mark filing formalities.

Applying for a Federal Trademark

To apply for a federal trademark, go to the website of the Patent and Trademark Office (PTO) at www.uspto.gov and download a trademark application. Fill out the form following the instructions. A month or so after mailing the form, you should hear from the PTO. If there are any problems, you will receive a written list of questions together with the telephone number of a trademark examiner. The examiner should be able to address any questions and issues you can't handle yourself and should help you finalize your application without undue difficulty or delay.

Prepare Your Articles of Incorporation

The next step in organizing your nonprofit corporation is to prepare articles of incorporation. This is your primary incorporation document—your corporation comes into existence on the date you file your articles with your secretary of state. You must complete this step before you send in your federal tax exemption application because the IRS requires a filed copy of your articles with your tax exemption application.

Check Your State Filing Office Website

Most secretaries of state provide sample or ready-to-use forms for articles of incorporation that meet the statutory requirements. You can download these forms from their websites (see Appendix B). Before you do anything else, check your state's corporate filing office website. Here's what you can expect to find:

- **Sample forms and instructions.** Many secretaries of state provide a sample articles form with instructions. You will need to retype your final form using the format and content of the sample form.

- **Ready-to-use articles.** Some states provide a form that you can print, fill in, and file with the secretary of state. Instructions for filling in the blanks are often provided on the printed form.

- **Online filing.** Some states let you prepare and file articles online. If this option is available, we suggest you use it—it's fast and efficient.

- **Links to nonprofit statutes.** Most state websites provide a link to the state's nonprofit corporation laws.

- **Filing checklist.** Some websites include a checklist showing both the filing requirements and some common reasons for rejection of articles. This information can help you comply with some of the less obvious substantive and formal requirements of the secretary of state's office (such as whether you can show a P.O. box as an address, how to properly sign and acknowledge the form, how much space to leave at the top of the first page for the secretary's file stamp, and so on).

Some States Require Special Nonprofit Articles Forms

Some states classify nonprofit corporations as public benefit, religious, or mutual benefit corporations and provide a separate articles form for each type of nonprofit; others provide one form and ask you to specify the type of nonprofit you are organizing. (See your state's filing office website for instructions on completing any special articles form.) In these states, most 501(c)(3) tax-exempt nonprofit corporations organized for charitable, educational, literary, or scientific purposes are classified as public benefit corporations. Religious-purpose 501(c)(3) nonprofits are, naturally, classified as religious corporations. The states that classify nonprofits as public benefit, religious, or mutual benefit corporations, or a variation on this scheme, are listed in the chart below.

States That Classify Nonprofits as Public Benefit, Religious, or Mutual Benefit Corporations	
Arkansas, California, Indiana, Missouri, Montana, Nebraska, South Carolina, Wyoming	Articles must specify whether the nonprofit corporation being formed is a public benefit, religious, or mutual benefit corporation.
Maine	Articles must specify whether the nonprofit corporation being formed is a public benefit or mutual corporation; there is no separate religious corporation category. All 501(c)(3) tax-exempt nonprofit corporations are considered public benefit corporations.
Nevada	All 501(c)(3) tax-exempt nonprofit corporations are classified as public benefit corporations that are subject to regulation and enforcement proceedings by the state attorney general's office.
Oregon	Articles must specify whether the nonprofit corporation being formed is a public benefit, religious, or mutual benefit corporation. Most 501(c)(3)s are formed as either public benefit or religious corporations. Religious corporations can be formed with one person as a founder under special rules as a "corporation sole"—see the state filing office website.
Tennessee	A corporation must identify itself in its charter as a public benefit or mutual benefit corporation; 501(c)(3) tax-exempt nonprofit corporations are classified as public benefit corporations. If the corporation is a religious corporation, this fact also must be stated in the charter; a 501(c)(3) religious nonprofit is classified as a public benefit corporation *and* as a religious corporation.
Vermont	The articles must specify whether the corporation being formed is a public benefit or mutual benefit corporation. All 501(c)(3)s, including 501(c)(3) religious nonprofits, are classified as public benefit corporations.

Typical Secretary of State Guidelines for Retyping Articles

- Write all text in English (no foreign language characters, punctuation, or diacritical marks).

- Type your responses to blank items (or retype your form) using a black ink ribbon. Some secretaries may allow hand-printed responses—check your secretary of state's instructions.

- Use letter-sized (8½" × 11") paper.

- Fasten pages with staples, not rivet-type fasteners.

- Make sure all typing and signatures (and any hand-printed responses) are of sufficient contrast to be legibly photocopied by the secretary's office; black ink is usually specified.

Preparing Articles of Incorporation in Iowa and Nebraska

Only Iowa and Nebraska do not provide a complete or sample articles form for you to follow or use. If you are forming a nonprofit in either state, first go online to the state's filing office website (see Appendix B) to see if they now provide a form. If not, follow our instructions below to prepare an articles form from scratch.

Iowa

The state filing office website has a link in the Nonprofit Forms section to Section 504.202 of the Iowa Nonprofit Corporation Act. This section specifies the mandatory and optional contents of nonprofit articles of incorporation (the link provided sends you to the law retrieval page—insert "504.202" in the search box to view the articles statute). The articles statute says that the articles must contain the name of the corporation, the address of the corporation's registered agent and the name of the registered agent at this office, the name and address of each incorporator (only one is needed), whether the corporation will have members, and provisions regarding the distribution of assets of the corporation upon its dissolution.

Additional optional provisions also are listed in the statue. To draft these, use our sample clauses in this chapter for each of these provisions: Article 1. Name of Corporation, Article 2. Registered Agent and Office, Article 5. Name and Addresses of Incorporators, Article 7. Membership Provisions, and the dedication of assets clause shown in the "Additional Federal Tax Exemption Language" section in this chapter. Also include any other provisions you wish or that we recommend to obtain your federal tax exemption. The Iowa nonprofit corporation name requirements are contained in Section 504.401 of the Iowa statutes—just insert this section in the law retrieval search box to see the requirements (a corporate designator is not required).

Nebraska

The Nebraska nonprofit corporation articles statute is contained in Section 21-1921 of the Revised Nebraska Statutes (available at the website of the Nebraska Legislature at www.nebraskalegislature.gov; enter "12-1921" in the Search Laws, Keywords box and click Go). Articles must state the name of the corporation; whether the corporation is a public benefit, religious, or mutual benefit corporation; the street address of the registered office and the name of the registered agent at that office; the name and street address of each incorporator; whether the corporation will have members; and an asset dedication clause.

To complete your own Nebraska articles, see the following sample articles in this chapter: Article 1. Name of Corporation, Article 2.

Registered Agent and Office, Article 5. Name and Addresses of Incorporators, Article 7. Membership Provisions, and the dedication of assets clause shown in the "Additional Federal Tax Exemption Language" section in this chapter. Also include any other provisions you wish or that we recommend to obtain your federal tax exemption. The Nebraska nonprofit corporation name requirements are contained in Section 21-1931 of the Nebraska statutes (go to http://nebraskalegislature.gov; enter "21-1931" in the Search Laws, Keywords box; and click Go)—a corporate designator is not required. You will need to add your own article to state if you are forming a Nebraska public benefit, mutual benefit, or religious corporation. Generally, most 501(c)(3) nonprofits are formed for either religious purposes (as a religious corporation), or as a public benefit corporation (formed for charitable, educational, or other public-benefit 501(c)(3) purposes).

Complete Your Articles

The basic clauses various states require in articles of incorporation are similar. By following the material below and referring to the specific instructions for preparing articles provided by your secretary of state, you should be able to prepare your form without undue difficulty. Here are some hints to make this job easier:

- Scan this information to get a general idea of the various types of clauses and provisions traditionally included in standard articles of incorporation. This information will help you understand the specific form and instructions provided by your secretary of state.
- If your secretary provides a sample form that must be retyped, type or write out a draft copy first.

- Complete as much of the form as you can, following your secretary of state's form and specific instructions. If you get stuck with a particular article or provision, refer to our instructions below.
- To locate a particular incorporation requirement in your state (for example, the number of directors to be named in your articles) see the instructions to the state's form. If you want more information, browse your state's nonprofit corporation statute. (See Appendix B for instructions on locating your state's nonprofit law online.)

Sample Article Provisions

Below we provide sample language and explanations of the provisions you are likely to find in the articles of incorporation provided by your secretary of state. An article number and heading identifies the subject matter of the provision or clause and explanatory text follows each sample article. Blanks indicate information that needs to be inserted in the text of the provision or clause.

Heading and Format of Articles

Articles of Incorporation

of

_____

a Nonprofit Corporation

Article 1.	....
Article 2.	....
Article 3.	....

State law does not normally specify any format for the heading or body of the articles. Typically, the name of the corporation is shown in the heading of the articles and each provision is numbered sequentially. Your secretary of state's office may provide guidelines for retyping articles.

Statement of Statutory Authority

The undersigned incorporator(s), in order to form a corporation under the _[name of state's nonprofit corporation law]_ , adopt the following Articles of Incorporation:

Although not required in many states, a statement of statutory authority often is included at the beginning of the articles stating the name or section numbers of the state's nonprofit corporation act under which the corporation is being formed.

In some states, it is customary to recite that the incorporators or the corporation meet specific statutory requirements (for example, that the incorporators are of legal age or that the corporation is not formed for pecuniary profit).

Here is an example of a statutory authority clause taken from an official state form:

> The undersigned natural person(s) of the age of eighteen years or more for the purpose of forming a corporation under the _____ Nonprofit Corporation Act adopt(s) the following Articles of Incorporation.

RESOURCE

Specific forms and instructions for forming a California nonprofit are contained in _How to Form a Nonprofit Corporation in California_, by Anthony Mancuso (Nolo). Use this more specialized book if you are incorporating in California.

Article 1. Name of Corporation

The name of this CORPORATION is _____

_____.

The heading to the articles and the first article of incorporation normally specify the name of the corporation. See "Choose a Corporate Name," above, to select a name for your corporation. If you have reserved a corporate name, make sure to use the exact spelling of the reserved name in your articles.

Article 2. Registered Agent and Office

The name and address of the registered agent of this corporation are: _____

_____.

Most states require that articles include the name and address of the corporation's initial registered agent (or agent for service of process). The agent is the person authorized to receive legal papers on behalf of the corporation; the agent's office is also known as the registered office of the corporation. Generally, the agent must be a resident of the state and at least 18 years of age. Although the registered office may be different from the principal office of the corporation in many states, most nonprofits keep things simple and appoint one of the directors as the initial agent, showing the principal address of the corporation as the registered office of the corporation.

TIP

You must usually use a street address, not a post office box, as your agent's address. Also, some states require the filing of a separate designation of registered agent form with the articles. See your state's instructions to the official article's form.

Article 3. Statement of Purpose

The purposes for which this corporation is organized are: _____

_____.

A statement of purpose clause is a standard feature in nonprofit articles of incorporation. Your statement of purpose should be used to satisfy state corporate law and federal 501(c)(3) tax exemption requirements. Let's look at the federal requirements first.

Federal 501(c)(3) Tax-Exempt Purpose Clause

In the purpose clause in your articles of incorporation, you must include language stating that your corporation is organized for 501(c)(3) tax-exempt purposes. We refer to this language in later discussions as your *statement of tax-exempt purposes*.

Here is the standard IRS-approved language (see IRS Publication 557) for this statement of tax-exempt purposes:

> Article 3. The purposes for which this corporation is organized are:
>
> This corporation is organized exclusively for charitable, religious, educational, and scientific purposes, including, for such purposes, the making of distributions to organizations that qualify as exempt organizations under Section 501(c)(3) of the Internal Revenue Code, or the corresponding section of any future federal tax code.

This general statement authorizes the corporation to engage in one or more 501(c)(3) tax-exempt purposes, including making distributions to other 501(c)(3) organizations.

While this general statement will satisfy IRS requirements, we think it makes more sense (and also meets IRS requirements) to specify the real 501(c)(3) purpose or purposes of your nonprofit in a brief tax-exempt purpose statement. Here is an example of a specific tax-exempt purpose statement that we prefer instead of a general statement:

> Article 3. The purposes for which this corporation is organized are:
>
> This corporation is organized and operated exclusively for [*state one or more of your actual tax-exempt purposes, such as "charitable,"*

"religious," "educational," "literary," and/or "scientific"] purposes within the meaning of 501(c)(3) of the Internal Revenue Code.

This specific tax-exempt purpose statement eliminates the purpose related to distributing funds to other 501(c)(3)s. The additional purpose is usually only relevant to feeder organizations set up to support other nonprofits. This specific purpose statement also makes it clear that the nonprofit is organized and operated for 501(c)(3) purposes—the IRS likes to see this additional "operational" language.

The official form of articles promulgated by your secretary of state may already contain a boilerplate or fill-in statement of tax-exempt purposes (or a slight variation on one of the clauses shown above). Some official forms include this clause in a statement of purposes

---

If You Get Stuck on Your Statement of Nonprofit Purposes

We provide instructions for dealing with the types of purpose clauses required in the majority of states. However, if you encounter special language or special format requirements not covered in our discussion, here are two suggestions:

- Rely primarily on the instructions to the sample and printed forms on your secretary of state's website—these will usually show you how to cope with any special state statutory requirements.

- For further assistance, check your state's articles statute (see Appendix B to locate your state's law online) for the special statutory language you must include or special requirements you must follow to complete your purpose clause.

article; others include it under a space set aside on the form for "additional provisions." In all cases, if this (or similar) tax-exempt purpose language does not appear in your articles, make sure to include it somewhere on the form. You'll need it to get your federal income tax exemption.

RELATED TOPIC

Your secretary of state form may include other tax exemption provisions. See Article 8, below, for a discussion of additional federal tax exemption language that is required, or may be included, in your articles.

Additional Statements of Purpose Required Under State Law

In many states, a statement of 501(c)(3) tax-exempt purposes will be all you need to satisfy the requirements for completing the purpose clause in your articles. Some states, however, have their own unique requirements for purpose clause wording in the articles. Below we look at the most common types of statements required under state statutes.

TIP

These special statements of purpose satisfy state law requirements. To satisfy the federal 501(c)(3) tax requirements, make sure to also include a statement of your federal tax-exempt purposes somewhere in your articles (see above).

Statement of Lawful Purpose

Some states require that the articles contain specific statutory wording indicating that the corporation is formed for a lawful purpose under the laws of the state (we call this a *statement of lawful purposes*).

A typical statement of lawful purposes reads as follows:

> The purpose of the corporation is to engage in any lawful act or activity for which corporations may be organized under the Nonprofit Corporation Law of _____.

If your articles include this lawful purpose statement (in addition, of course, to a tax-exempt purpose statement, as explained above), we recommend that you add language to limit it to make it clear that your nonprofit will only pursue lawful activities that satisfy the IRC 501(c)(3) requirements. Here's one way to do this (see the language in italics added to the end of the standard lawful purpose statement below):

> The purpose of the corporation is to engage in any lawful act or activity for which corporations may be organized under the Nonprofit Corporation Law of _____, *provided, however, that the corporation shall only engage in acts or activities that are consistent with and in furtherance of its 501(c)(3) tax-exempt purposes, which are described in other provisions of these articles.*

Statement of Specific Purposes

Some states also require a brief, one- or two-sentence description of the purposes and activities of your corporation in the purpose clause of the articles (we call this a *statement of specific purposes*). If you can't determine whether your state requires a statement of specific purpose by reading your state's instructions, we suggest you include one just to be safe.

Tips on Preparing a Statement of Specific Purposes

Make sure to keep your specific purpose statement brief—one or two short sentences is best (for example, to set up a child care center, home for the aged, AIDS hotline, or dance or musical troupe; to provide scholarships to needy students or establish a book fair; and so on). The secretary of state usually doesn't want much detail or narrative here. You will provide a fuller description of your nonprofit purposes and activities in your bylaws and on your federal tax exemption application.

If possible, describe the kinds of activities you pursue in language that will clearly identify them as ones that the IRS considers to be tax-exempt.

For example, if your specific purpose is to set up a hospital, indicate that you are forming a *charitable hospital*; if establishing a child care center, state that *it is open to the general public and will allow parents to be gainfully employed*; if setting up a scientific organization, that *scientific research will be carried on in the public interest.*

Avoid using keywords, terms, or phrases associated with organizations exempt from taxation under other (non-501(c)(3)) sections of the Internal Revenue Code, such as *social, fraternal, recreational, political*, and so on.

Environmental Education. Here is a sample statement of specific purposes for an environmental group:

> Article 3. The specific purposes for which this corporation is organized are:
> to publish a newsletter providing information to the public on preserving tropical rain forests.

Publishing and Lectures. Here is a sample specific purpose clause for a group that wishes to publish books and give public lectures:

> Article 3. The specific purposes for which this corporation is organized are:
> to develop an institution to teach and disseminate educational material to the public, including, but not limited to, material relating to   *[the areas of instruction are mentioned here]*   , through publications, lectures, or otherwise.

Dance Group. The following sample specific purpose clause is for a group that wishes to set up studios where it can teach dance and hold performances. The educational purposes of the group are clearly identified in the specific purpose clause and the general public is identified as the recipient of these services. For future flexibility, the group leaves itself the option of teaching and promoting other art forms.

> Article 3. The specific purposes for which this corporation is organized are:
> to educate the general public in dance and other art forms. The means of providing such education includes, but is not limited to, maintaining facilities for instruction and public performances of dance and other art forms.

Housing Improvement. Here is a sample clause for a group planning to get grants and tax exemptions to improve housing conditions for low- and moderate-income people by organizing a housing information and research exchange. Note that the following example simply and succinctly states the group's specific purposes, characterizing them as charitable and educational purposes in the interests of the general public—no further embellishment or narrative in the specific purpose clause is needed here.

Article 3. The specific purposes for which this corporation is organized are:

to provide education and charitable assistance to the general public by organizing a housing information and research exchange.

Medical Clinic. This sample specific purpose clause is for a community health care clinic for low-income individuals.

Article 3. The specific purposes for which this corporation is organized are:

to establish and maintain a comprehensive system of family-oriented health care aimed primarily at the medically underserved areas of ___[city and county]___ .

Religious Teachings and Publishing. Here is a specific purpose statement that is appropriate for a religious group devoted to the teachings and works of a particular religious leader or religious order:

Article 3. The specific purposes for which this corporation is organized are:

to establish a religious organization to promote the teachings of, and publish materials of and concerning, _[name of spiritual leader or religious order]_ .

Scientific Research. Sometimes, a reference to the tax-exempt purposes of the group will suffice as a specific purpose statement, as follows:

Article 3. The purposes for which this corporation is organized are:

to engage in scientific research in the public interest.

Article 4. Number, Names, and Addresses of Initial Directors

The number of initial directors of this corporations is

_____.

Their names and addresses are as follows: _____

_____.

Many states require you to include the number of persons who will serve on the first board of directors, followed by their names and addresses. In some states, this information is not (or is only optionally) included in the articles provided by the secretary of state.

RELATED TOPIC

Directors. The instructions to your state's articles should indicate the minimum number of directors required in your state. Also see "How Many People are Needed to Form a Nonprofit Corporation" in Chapter 2.

To fill in this article, type the number of directors of your corporation, then list the names and addresses (street, not P.O. box) of the persons appointed to your initial board. Initial board members serve until the first meeting held to reelect directors—the date of this meeting will be specified in your bylaws.

Article 5. Names and Addresses of Incorporators

The names and addresses of the incorporators of this corporation are: _____

_____.

The incorporator is the person or persons who form the corporation by signing and filing articles of incorporation. Although more than one incorporator may be used, most nonprofits, if allowed, designate one person to assume this responsibility. Most articles of incorporation require the name and address of the incorporator (or incorporators) of the corporation either in the body of the articles or at the end of the document after the signature line.

Although the incorporator is usually one of the initial directors of the corporation, usually any person may be designated the incorporator and prepare, sign, and file articles on behalf of your corporation.

RELATED TOPIC

Incorporators. Your state's articles instructions should indicate any special incorporator requirements in your state (for example, if you must have more than one incorporator). Also see "How Many People are Needed to Form a Nonprofit Corporation" in Chapter 2.

Article 6. Duration of Corporation

The period of duration of this corporation is: _____
_____.

In some states, the articles include a provision specifying the duration of the corporation. Almost all nonprofit corporations wish to continue into the indefinite future and will insert the word "perpetual" in this provision. In the extremely rare circumstance that you wish to limit the duration of your corporation's existence, insert a specific period or date in this clause.

Article 7. Membership Provisions

The classes, rights, privileges, qualifications, and obligations of members of this corporation are as follows: _____
_____.

In some states, the articles of incorporation include a membership clause similar to the sample shown above.

As explained in Chapter 2, most smaller nonprofit corporations will not wish to set up a formal membership structure and will indicate

"No Members" if this clause appears in their articles. If you do decide to adopt a formal membership structure, it's usually best to indicate here that "The membership provisions of this corporation shall be stated in the bylaws of this corporation." This approach gives you the most flexibility—bylaw provisions may be repealed, changed, and added with relative ease, while amendments to articles must be filed with the secretary of state.

Finally, if you wish to adopt membership provisions and your state requires you to summarize these provisions in your articles, here is some standard language you may wish to use that provides for one class of dues-paying membership in the corporation:

> This corporation shall have one class of membership. Any person shall be qualified to become a member upon payment of the initial dues and shall continue as a member upon paying the annual dues. The amount, method, and time of payment of dues shall be determined, and may be changed, from time to time, by the board of directors. Additional provisions specifying the rights and obligations of members shall be contained in the bylaws of this corporation pursuant to, and in accordance with, the laws of this state.

RELATED TOPIC

For further information and suggested language to set up a formal membership structure in your bylaws, see Chapter 7.

Article 8. Additional Provisions

Insert additional provisions for operating the corporation in the space provided below:

[Insert required and optional 501(c)(3) tax exemption provisions, special language from state statutes for the operation of the corporation, and so on].

In many states, a blank article for additional provisions is included in the standard articles form. In some states, this blank article begins with wording similar to the language shown above (with suggestions for the types of optional clauses that may be inserted given in parentheses).

Below, we discuss some required and optional federal and state language you should include in this portion of your articles if it is not already included on your state's form.

Additional Federal Tax Exemption Language

To be eligible for your 501(c)(3) tax exemption, your articles must dedicate the assets of the corporation to exempt purposes. Technically, this dedication clause is not required in a few states (including Arkansas, California, Louisiana, Massachusetts, Minnesota, Missouri, Ohio, and Oklahoma—see Part III of the instructions to Form 1023: *Application for Recognition of Exemption,* on the CD-ROM). Nonetheless, we recommend all incorporators make sure a dedication of assets clause appears in their articles. This will help you to minimize delay in the processing of your federal tax exemption and avoid problems if your state laws change in the future. Here is a general dedication of assets clause you can include in the Additional Provisions article (adapted from example language in the IRS Instructions to Form 1023):

> Article 8. Additional Provisions
>
> Upon the dissolution of this corporation, its assets remaining after payment, or provision for payment, of all debts and liabilities of this corporation shall be distributed for one or more exempt purposes within the meaning of Section 501(c)(3) of the Internal Revenue Code or shall be distributed to the federal government, or to a state or local government, for a public purpose.

CAUTION

Always include a dedication statement. Make sure to include this dedication of assets statement in your articles if one does not already appear on your form.

Alternative Wording for Specific Dedication Clause: The sample dedication language above dedicates the assets of the nonprofit corporation to one or more allowable 501(c)(3) tax-exempt purposes. Most nonprofits, however, prefer using a specific dedication clause that dedicates its assets to one or more of its specific 501(c)(3) purposes. Here is an example of a specific dedication clause of this type:

> The property of this corporation is irrevocably dedicated to ____ [*state one or more of your actual tax-exempt purposes, such as "charitable," "religious," "educational," "literary," and/or "scientific"*] ____ purposes. Upon the dissolution or winding up of the corporation, its assets remaining after payment, or provision for payment, of all debts and liabilities of this corporation shall be distributed to a nonprofit fund, foundation, or corporation which is organized and operated exclusively for ____ [*repeat the same purpose or purposes stated in the first blank*] ____ purposes and which has established its tax-exempt status under Section 501(c)(3) of the Internal Revenue Code.

There is one other type of dedication of assets clause you can use in your articles—one which dedicates your assets to a specific nonprofit organization. Of course, the organization should be a qualified 501(c)(3) and you should provide that the assets will be distributed to another 501(c)(3) in case the named organization is not in existence or tax-exempt when your nonprofit dissolves. If you want to specify a named organization to which you will dedicate your assets, see the instructions to Form 1023 and IRS Publication 557.

Optional 501(c)(3) Tax Exemption Language

Now let's look at optional federal tax exemption language which is commonly included in nonprofit articles. We recommend that all nonprofits include the first three optional paragraphs shown below (if these federal tax exemption provisions are not already included on your secretary's sample or printed form). Many states allow you to expand the portion of the articles set aside for additional provisions by attaching a typewritten page to your form.

Limitation on Political Activities. The following clause shows that your nonprofit group will comply with the 501(c)(3) limitation on political activities as discussed in "Limitation on Political Activities," in Chapter 3:

> No substantial part of the activities of this corporation shall consist of carrying on propaganda, or otherwise attempting to influence legislation (except as otherwise provided by Section 501(h) of the Internal Revenue Code), and this corporation shall not participate in, or intervene in (including the publishing or distribution of statements), any political campaign on behalf of, or in opposition to, any candidate for public office.

Limitation on Private Inurement (Private Benefits). Below is standard IRS-approved language prohibiting private inurement— private or personal benefit to individuals associated with the nonprofit corporation, such as directors, officers, employees, and so on, as discussed in Chapter 3. The last portion of this clause indicates that reasonable compensation for services rendered is allowed under federal tax law.

> No part of the net earnings of this corporation shall inure to the benefit of, or be distributable to, its members, directors, officers, or other private persons, except that this corporation shall be authorized and empowered to pay reasonable compensation for services rendered and to make payments and distributions in furtherance of the purposes set forth in these articles.

General Limitation on Nonprofit Activities. The statement below limits the activities of the corporation to those permitted to 501(c)(3) organizations and those allowed to corporations to which contributions are deductible under Section 170(c)(2) of the Internal Revenue Code:

> Notwithstanding any other provision of these articles, this corporation shall not carry on any other activities not permitted to be carried on (1) by a corporation exempt from federal income tax under Section 501(c)(3) of the Internal Revenue Code or (2) by a corporation contributions to which are deductible under Section 170(c)(2) of the Internal Revenue Code.

RELATED TOPIC

For a discussion of the deductibility of charitable contributions made to 501(c)(3) organizations, see Chapter 4.

Private Foundation Restrictions. The following language relates to technical aspects of the 501(c)(3) tax exemption and states that the corporation will comply with all the operating restrictions that apply to private foundations if the corporation is classified as a private foundation by the IRS. Because you will want your nonprofit to be classified as a 501(c)(3) public charity rather than a private foundation, you do not need to include this language in your articles. We mention it only because it may appear in the official form promulgated by your secretary of state (it is required only for private foundations formed in Arizona and New Mexico).

> In any taxable year in which this corporation is a private foundation as described in Section 509(a) of the Internal Revenue Code, the corporation

(1) shall distribute its income for said period at such time and manner as not to subject it to tax under Section 4942 of the Internal Revenue Code; (2) shall not engage in any act of self-dealing as defined in Section 4941(d) of the Internal Revenue Code; (3) shall not retain any excess business holdings as defined in Section 4943(c) of the Internal Revenue Code; (4) shall not make any investments in such manner as to subject the corporation to tax under Section 4944 of the Internal Revenue Code; and (5) shall not make any taxable expenditures as defined in Section 4945(d) of the Internal Revenue Code.

RELATED TOPIC

For a discussion of private foundation and public charity tax status, see Chapter 4.

Sample Completed Articles

We've covered a lot of ground in the individual sample articles of incorporation and explanations above. To help you tie all this information together, we include a sample completed articles below together with our comments (which appear in italicized type).

CD-ROM

Articles of incorporation. The CD-ROM includes a copy of a blank articles of incorporation form. A copy has also been included in Appendix C.

Customizing Your Articles

Although the standard articles discussed in this chapter and included in your secretary of state form will be sufficient for most incorporators, some may wish to adopt special operating rules or provisions. Although it is preferable to include these special rules in the bylaws (which can be adopted and changed with relative ease), some special provisions must, under state law, be included in the articles to be effective. For example, the following types of provisions, if adopted by the corporation, must often be included in the articles:

- establishing different classes of membership (such as voting and nonvoting members)
- allowing specific members of the board to be designated by individuals rather than elected by the board or voting membership
- requiring a supermajority vote (such as two-thirds or three-fourths) of directors or members for the approval of certain matters, and
- providing for special indemnification or immunity for directors and officers.

Your state website instructions may list the special provisions you have to include in your articles.

Articles of Incorporation

of

The Bluegrass Music Society of the Appalachians, Inc.

A Nonprofit Corporation

Pursuant to the provision of the Nonprofit Corporation Act of this state, the undersigned incorporators hereby adopt the following Articles of Incorporation:

Article 1

The name of this corporation is: The Bluegrass Music Society of the Appalachians, Inc.

Article 2

The name and address of the registered agent and registered office of this corporation is:
 [*Name of one of the initial directors, address of corporation.*]

Article 3

The specific purposes for which this corporation is organized are: To establish a musical society open to the general public to foster an appreciation of American bluegrass music, through lectures, seminars, study groups, public and classroom performances, exhibits, and any and all other appropriate means. [*This is a statement of specific purposes requested by the secretary of state.*]

   This corporation is organized and operated exclusively for educational purposes within the meaning of 501(c)(3) of the Internal Revenue Code. [*This is a statement of tax-exempt purposes required under IRC Section 501(c)(3).*]

Article 4

The number of initial directors of this corporation shall be   three   and the names and addresses of the initial directors are as follows:
 [*Names and addresses of three initial directors*]

Article 5

The name and address of the incorporators of this corporation are:

 [*Name and address of one of the initial directors listed above*]

Article 6

The period of the duration of this corporation is: perpetual.

Article 7

The classes, rights, privileges, qualifications, and obligations of members of this corporation are as follows:

    As stated in the bylaws of this corporation.

Article 8

Additional provisions (attach separate page if necessary):

    The property of this corporation is irrevocably dedicated to educational purposes. Upon the dissolution or winding up of the corporation, its assets remaining after payment, or provision for payment, of all debts and liabilities of this corporation shall be distributed to a nonprofit fund, foundation, or corporation which is organized and operated exclusively for educational purposes and which has established its tax-exempt status under Section 501(c)(3) of the Internal Revenue Code. [*This is the dedication of assets statement required under IRC Section 501(c)(3).*]

    No substantial part of the activities of this corporation shall consist of carrying on propaganda, or otherwise attempting to influence legislation (except as otherwise provided by Section 501(h) of the Internal Revenue Code), and this corporation shall not participate in, or intervene in (including the publishing or distribution of statements), any political campaign on behalf of, or in opposition to, any candidate for public office. [*This is the optional limitation on political activities statement under IRC Section 501(c)(3).*]

    No part of the net earnings of this corporation shall inure to the benefit of, or be distributable to, its members, directors, officers, or other private persons, except that this corporation shall be authorized and empowered to pay reasonable compensation for services rendered and to make payments and distributions in furtherance of the purposes set forth in these articles. [*This is the optional limitation on private inurement statement under IRC Section 501(c)(3).*]

    Notwithstanding any other provision of these articles, this corporation shall not carry on any other activities not permitted to be carried on (1) by a corporation exempt from federal income tax under Section 501(c)(3) of the Internal Revenue Code or (2) by a corporation contributions to which are deductible under Section 170(c)(2) of the Internal Revenue Code. [*This is the optional general limitation on activities statement under IRC Section 501(c)(3).*]

The undersigned incorporators hereby declare under penalty of perjury that the statements made in the foregoing Articles of Incorporation are true.

Dated: _____

 [*signature of incorporator*] _____

Name and Address of Incorporator: _____

_____

_____

[*Normally, the incorporator(s) must sign the articles. Some states require initial directors, if named in articles, to sign instead. If notarization is required, the signature(s) must be given in the presence of a notary.*]

File Your Articles of Incorporation

File your articles with your secretary of state following the instructions on your secretary of state's website. Most corporations file by mail, although many offices will accept articles in person. Some states allow you to fill in and file your articles online (see your state filing office website for any online filing information). Some states provide their own articles filing letter. If your state does and you file by mail, use it instead of ours, below.

CD-ROM

The CD-ROM disk includes a copy of the Articles Filing Letter, and there is a blank tearout copy in Appendix C. You may wish to use (or modify) it to submit your articles of incorporation by mail to the secretary of state. Complete it as indicated on the following sample and special instructions, below.

Special Instructions for the Articles Filing Letter

❶ A person who signs your articles should prepare and sign this cover letter.

Note: If you have reserved a corporate name, the person who reserved the corporate name should prepare and sign this letter—the corporate name will be reserved for this person's use only.

❷ In some states, you need only submit an original of the articles—the secretary will file the original and send you a certificate of incorporation as proof of filing. In other states, you need to submit the original and one or more copies. The secretary will file the original and file-stamp and return one or more copies to you. In some states, an additional fee is

charged for submitting more than one copy of your articles for file-stamping. One copy should be sufficient—you can make copies of this file-stamped copy to send to financial institutions, grant agencies, and others when necessary as proof of your incorporation.

❸ Include a check for the total fees, made payable to the "Secretary of State" or other official title of the office that files articles in your state. Check your secretary of state instructions carefully to make sure your total fee payment is correct—otherwise, your articles may be returned to you unfiled.

❹ If you have reserved your corporate name, fill in the blanks here to show the certificate number and/or date your reservation was issued. In some states, the secretary simply sends you a file-stamped copy of your reservation letter—if so, just show the file-stamped date on the letter in the second blank.

Your next step is to wait. The secretary of state will make sure your corporate name is available for use and that your articles conform to law. If there are no problems, the secretary of state will mail you a certificate of incorporation (or file-stamped copy of your articles). If there are any problems with your articles, the secretary of state will usually return your articles, indicating the items that need correction. Often the problem is technical, not substantive, and easy to fix. If the problem is more complicated (such as an improper or insufficient corporate purpose clause), you may be able to solve the problem by rereading our examples and suggestions for completing the articles. If you get stuck, you will need to do a little research or obtain further help from a nonprofit lawyer with experience in drafting and filing nonprofit articles (see Chapter 11).

Articles Filing Letter

[Name and address of Incorporator] ❶ _____

_____

_____

_____

Date: _____

[Name and address of secretary of state office—see Appendix B]

_____

_____

Re: Articles of Incorporation Filing

I enclose an original and _[number]_ ❷ _____ copies of the proposed Articles of Incorporation of

[name of corporation] _____ .

Please file the Articles of Incorporation and return a Certificate of Incorporation (or file-stamped copy of the original Articles) to me at the above address.

A check/money order in the amount of $_____ ❸ _____, made payable to your office, for total filing and processing fees is enclosed.

The above corporate name was reserved for my use pursuant to reservation # _____ ❹ _____ issued on

_____ .

Sincerely,

[signature of incorporator] ❶ _____

_____ , Incorporator

[typed name]

Sign Documents on Behalf of the Corporation

Congratulations! Once your articles are filed, your organization is a legally recognized nonprofit corporation. But before you rush out to pursue your nonprofit objectives, remember that your corporation is the one who is now doing business, not you as an individual. This means that signatures on any document, such as an agreement with a vendor, application for a grant, lease, or other financial or legal form must clearly show that you're acting on behalf of the corporation (and not for yourself). Your signature should be a block of information (plus a signature), which looks like this:

Parents for a Better Society, Inc.

By: _____[*your signature*]_____
   [*your corporate title, such as
   director, president, or secretary*]

If you fail to sign documents on behalf of the corporation and in your capacity as a corporate director, officer, or employee, you are leaving yourself open to possible personal liability for corporate obligations. From now on, it is extremely important for you to maintain the distinction between the corporation that you've organized and yourself. As we've said, the corporation is a separate legal "person" and you want to make sure that other organizations, businesses, the IRS, and the courts respect this distinction.

It's also very important to realize that until you obtain your federal and state tax exemptions, your corporation is liable for the payment of state and federal income taxes. Furthermore, until you apply for and obtain your federal 501(c)(3) tax exemption and public charity status, your corporation will be unable to receive most public and private grant funds, and will be unable to assure donors that contributions made to the corporation are tax deductible. Therefore, make sure to follow through with the procedures contained in the succeeding chapters—doing so is vital to the success of your new corporation. ●

C H A P T E R

Prepare Your Bylaws

Choose a Membership or Nonmembership Structure 124

Purpose and Scope of Our Bylaws..125

Prepare Your Bylaws 127

Prepare Membership Provisions..138

Your next step is to prepare your bylaws. This document is, for all practical purposes, your corporation's internal affairs manual. It sets forth the rules and procedures for holding meetings, electing directors and officers, and taking care of other essential corporate formalities. Specifically, the bylaws:

- Contain information central to the organization and operation of your particular corporation (for example, dates of meetings, quorum requirements).

- Restate the most significant legal and tax provisions applicable to tax-exempt nonprofit corporations. This is useful for your own reference and necessary to assure the IRS and the state that you are eligible for these tax exemptions.

- Provide a practical, yet formal, set of rules for the orderly operation of your corporation: to resolve disputes, provide certainty regarding procedures, and manage corporate operations.

Preparing bylaws for a nonprofit corporation is not difficult. It simply involves filling in blanks. Before you begin work on your bylaws, you'll need to decide whether your nonprofit will have members.

CAUTION

Don't think of your bylaws as meaningless fine print. On the contrary, bylaws are crucial to the functioning of your organization. Be sure to read through them carefully, making sure you understand the purpose and effect of the different provisions included.

Choose a Membership or Nonmembership Structure

Your first step in preparing bylaws is to decide whether you want your nonprofit corporation to be a membership or nonmembership corporation. There are significant differences between the two structures and significant legal consequences that will result from your decision.

RELATED TOPIC

See "Membership Nonprofits," in Chapter 2, for a discussion of the two different types of structures and the legal consequences of setting up a membership versus a nonmembership structure.

Most smaller groups will probably want to form a nonmembership corporation. Why? Because a nonmembership corporation is simpler to establish and operate. Nonmembership corporations are run by a board of directors, as opposed to membership corporations, where members have the right to vote on major corporate decisions. And you don't lose any significant advantages by not having members—most people who want to support your group aren't interested in having the technical legal rights given to members.

Some groups, however, will decide that the nature of their activities requires a membership structure. This is a reasonable decision in circumstances where membership participation in the affairs of the nonprofit corporation is essential or desirable (for example, to increase member involvement in the nonprofit's mission and program). Members of a nonprofit corporation are given specific legal rights under state law to participate in corporate affairs. Such membership rights typically include the right to:

- vote for the election of the board of directors

- approve changes to the articles or bylaws of the corporation

- vote for a dissolution of the corporation, and

- approve a sale of substantially all of the corporation's assets.

Some nonprofits may even decide to combine a legal, voting membership structure with a larger group of dues-paying supporters.

EXAMPLE:

A large botanical society may have one class of formal members who elect the board of directors and an informal group of dues-paying supporters who receive the society's magazine and attend special events sponsored by the society.

If you do decide to adopt a formal membership structure for your nonprofit corporation, we show you below how to add basic membership provisions to your bylaws.

Purpose and Scope of Our Bylaws

Appendix C contains a tear-out bylaws form that is suitable for all types of 501(c)(3) nonprofits—nonmembership and membership groups alike. This form is also included on the CD-ROM. The provisions contained in this document were drafted to serve the following purposes:

- they contain information central to the organization and operation of your corporation (time, place, date, call, notice, and quorum requirements for meetings)

- they restate the most significant provisions applicable to tax-exempt nonprofit

corporations, useful for your own reference and necessary to assure the IRS that your corporation is eligible for its tax exemptions

- they provide a practical, yet formal, set of rules for the orderly operation of your corporation—to resolve disputes, to provide certainty regarding legal procedures, and to ensure at least minimum control over corporate operations, and

---

Why Not Having Members Makes Sense

Here are some reasons why most nonprofit incorporators prefer not to have members:

- Setting up a formal membership with voting rights dilutes directorship control over corporate operations.

- It isn't always easy to expel a member. State law may require that members only be expelled for good cause following a formal hearing.

- Nonmembership groups can still receive support from subscribers, sponsors, patrons, friends, benefactors, and so on. You can offer discounts or other benefits to outsiders who participate in the activities and programs of the corporation without giving them a legal right to participate in the management and other affairs of the corporation.

In some states, you may even call these outside supporters "members" of the corporation without running the risk of entitling these persons to voting and other legal membership rights in the corporation. Nonetheless, to be safe and to avoid confusion and controversy later on, we suggest you use another term for persons who will not be legal members of your corporation but who will otherwise contribute to, or participate in, corporate affairs and activities.

- they contain provisions intended to help you get and keep your 501(c)(3) tax exemption. For example, we include conflict of interest and compensation approval provisions that the IRS recommends, as one way to comply with the IRS regulations. You'll see that the IRS asks you if you have these provisions in place when you complete your federal income tax exemption application and your annual federal 990 returns. Although these are optional provisions, including these and other IRS-recommended provisions in your bylaws can go a long way toward making your dealings with the IRS a lot easier, both now and in future years.

RESOURCE

For an excellent guide to the type of governance policies the IRS likes to see in an organization's bylaws, see the Panel on the Nonprofit Sector's *The Principles Noticebook: Steering Your Board Toward Good Governance and Ethical Practice*, available at www.nonprofitpanel.org.

Form 990—See What the IRS Looks for in Bylaws

The IRS 990 annual nonprofit return and instructions reveal a lot about what the IRS likes to see in bylaws. By going through the form, you'll see what the IRS asks about (and likes to see) in bylaws. Namely, you'll see that the IRS is interested in:

- the avoidance of excess benefit and conflict of interest transactions
- the contemporaneous recording of nonprofit minutes of meetings and written consents
- independent (noncompensated) board members
- the ability of nonprofit insiders to report wrongdoing (documented by a written whistleblowing policy)
- document retention and destruction (evidenced by a written document retention and destruction policy), and
- public disclosure of the organization's exemption application and annual tax returns on its website and/or on request by the pubic (through a written public disclosure policy)

Our bylaws help you meet the first two recommendations. We suggest you give thought to adding provisions to your bylaws that address one or more of the additional policies listed above. This will help you meet the other good governance policies and practices the IRS asks about.

What the IRS doesn't like to see authorized or allowed in bylaws is:

- a small board of directors comprised of related people. (Even for a smaller nonprofit, four or five board members looks better than just two or three.)
- board members who are paid or related to paid people. If all or most of the board is paid or related to paid people in your nonprofit, expect questions from the IRS (which will be trying to determine whether your nonprofit is set up to benefit the paid directors instead of the public).

As you know, nonprofit corporation laws vary slightly from state to state. The provisions contained in our general-purpose bylaws will conform to the statutory requirements of most states. In areas where state legal rules do diverge somewhat, our bylaw provisions simply refer to the laws of your state. For example, the indemnification provisions in the bylaws state that your directors and officers are entitled to indemnification *to the fullest extent permissible under the law of this state.*

If a specific area of nonprofit law or procedure is particularly important to you or your legal advisor, you can easily replace the general-purpose provisions in the bylaws with the exact provisions contained in your state's nonprofit corporation code. See Appendix B to locate your state's nonprofit law online. For a discussion about looking up the law yourself, see Chapter 11.

RESOURCE

Should you consult a nonprofit professional? The primary practical reason to adopt the rules contained in the bylaws is to allow the incorporators to arrive at a good, workable consensus regarding the ground rules of the corporation. However, these may not meet all your needs or you may have questions about one or more of them. If so, check the provisions in our form against your state's nonprofit statutes or have them reviewed and customized by a lawyer with nonprofit experience.

Prepare Your Bylaws

Tear-out bylaws are contained in Appendix C; the CD-ROM also contains a bylaws form. Make a photocopy of this form and fill in the blanks on the form as you follow the instructions below. Or fill in the blanks on the CD-ROM version of the form. Instructions are provided for bylaws containing blanks or for special bylaw provisions that warrant a further explanation.

Making Modifications to the Bylaws

In the text, we discussed various reasons why some groups may wish to insert specific statutory rules from their state's nonprofit corporation law in the tear-out bylaws. There are many good reasons why groups may wish to customize their bylaws to add special language or provisions.

For example, if your nonprofit corporation plans to receive federal or other public grants or monies, some funding agencies may require that you include special provisions in your bylaws that state that no member of the board, officer, or other person exercising supervisory power in the corporation, or any of their close relatives can individually benefit from the receipt of grant funds. Generally, provisions of this sort are meant to prohibit board members, officers (president, vice president, secretary, and treasurer), and their families from being paid from, or directly benefited by, grant monies given to the organization.

Don't Worry About References to Members in the Bylaws

There are certain provisions in the bylaws that refer to "the members, if any," of the corporation or use other language making certain provisions applicable to the corporation only if the corporation has members. These provisions have no effect for nonmembership corporations using these bylaws—they simply allow membership corporations to add membership provisions to the bylaws, as explained in "Prepare Membership Provisions," below.

Below we go over the sample bylaw provisions. An article number and heading identifies the subject matter of each provision, and explanatory text with examples or blanks, if applicable, follows.

Heading

Type the name of your corporation.

Article I, Section 1.
Principal Office

Type the name of the county and state where the corporation's principal office is located— this is the corporate office where you will keep a copy of your bylaws, records of meetings, and other formal corporate records mentioned in various bylaw provisions. Customarily, the principal office designated here will be the same as the legal office of the corporation (the address specified in the articles as the registered office of the corporation where legal papers must be served on the corporation).

! **CAUTION**

Don't fill in the blanks for change of address at the end of Section 2. Use these blanks later, if necessary, to change the principal office of the corporation to another location within the same county, by showing the new address and date of the address change.

Article 2, Section 1.
IRC Section 501(c)(3) Purposes

This section contains a standard statement of 501(c)(3) tax-exempt purposes (similar to the tax-exempt purpose clause discussed earlier for the articles of incorporation). We include this statement in the bylaws to remind the IRS that your corporation is organized exclusively for a bona fide 501(c)(3) purpose.

Article 2, Section 2.
Specific Objectives and Purposes

Use the space provided here to state the specific tax-exempt objectives and purposes of your nonprofit corporation. If you included a statement of specific purposes in your articles of incorporation, it should have been brief. Here you can go into as much detail as you want in describing the specific purposes and activities of your corporation. We suggest you list your major purposes and activities, showing your nonprofit goals and the means by which you plan to achieve them. This will be useful not only as an exercise to help define and clarify your nonprofit objectives, but also as a way to give the IRS additional information regarding the tax-exempt purposes and activities of your corporation.

Dance Group. Here's an example of an expanded list of objectives and purposes that might be used by an educational-purpose, nonprofit dance group. It is illustrative of the large number of 501(c)(3) nonprofit corporations that will derive tax-exempt revenue primarily from the performance of services related to their exempt purposes, rather than from grants and contributions:

Section 2. Specific Objectives and Purposes
The specific objectives and purposes of this corporation shall be:

(a) to provide instruction in dance forms such as jazz, ballet, tap, and modern dance;

(b) to provide instruction in body movement and relaxation art forms such as tumbling, tai-chi, and yoga;

(c) to give public performances in dance forms and creative dramatics;

(d) to sponsor special events involving the public performance of any or all of the above art forms as well as other performing arts by the corporation's performing troupe as well as by other community performing arts groups; and

(e) to directly engage in and to provide facilities for others to engage in the promotion of the arts, generally.

Nonprofit Book Festival. Here's a completed statement of specific objectives and purposes for a nonprofit educational-purpose group that sponsors a book fair and promotes book reading and publishing in the local community:

Section 2. Specific Objectives and Purposes
The specific objectives and purposes of this corporation shall be:

(a) to sponsor an annual book fair with an emphasis on exhibiting books created and published in our community;

(b) to sponsor other informational events open to the public which focus on books;

(c) to educate the public concerning our community's contributions to book creation, publication, and distribution;

(d) generally, through educative and other efforts, to help make books and reading as inviting and accessible to as broad an audience as possible; and

(e) to engage in other activities related to educating the public about book writing, publishing, and distribution in our community.

Women's Health Information Resource Center. Here's a completed statement for a women's health group:

Section 2. Specific Objectives and Purposes
The specific objectives and purposes of this corporation shall be:

(a) to maintain a women's health library open to the public containing books, articles, and other material related to women's health issues;

(b) to maintain a physicians referral listing containing patient evaluations of physicians practicing in the community;

(c) to sponsor seminars and workshops open to the general public where ideas, opinions, and writings relating to women's health issues and health concerns may be expressed and shared with others;

(d) to publish a monthly newsletter containing articles informative of women's health issues; and

(e) to engage in other activities related to educating the public concerning women's health issues and health concerns.

Environmental Conservation and Protection Organization. Here's a sample for an environmental group:

Section 2. Specific Objectives and Purposes
The specific objectives and purposes of this corporation shall be:

(a) to educate the public concerning the necessity of preserving the nation's wetlands;

(b) to publish a newsletter that focuses on information related to wetlands preservation efforts and developments;

(c) to sponsor seminars and other educational events where community and environmental leaders, governmental and organizational representatives, and other concerned members of the public and government may meet to exchange ideas, suggest solutions, and implement strategies to protect the nation's wetlands;

(d) to meet with governmental representatives; to report to governmental committees, agencies, and boards; and generally to attempt to help local, state, and federal lawmakers establish enforceable legislation to help protect wetland areas; and

(e) to expand and redefine our educational and environmental program from time to time as necessary to meet the continuing challenge of protecting the nation's wetland resources.

Private College. Here's a completed statement for a private school:

Section 2. Specific Objectives and Purposes
The specific objectives and purposes of this corporation shall be:

(a) to establish a private university, licensed by the state and accredited by a recognized regional accreditation organization;

(b) to maintain a regularly enrolled student body, an established curriculum, and a full-time faculty;

(c) to participate in federal and state student loan and other student educational and financial incentive programs; and

(d) to have the normal functions, operations, programs, and pursuits incidental to a fully recognized and operational nonprofit center of learning and higher education.

 TIP

Be sure to authorize related activities. The last item in each of the above examples contains a clause that authorizes the corporation to engage in activities necessary or incidental to its main purposes and pursuits. We suggest you use similar language to allow your corporation to engage in activities related to its specific objectives and purposes.

Article 3, Section 1.
Number of Directors

Insert the total number of directors who will serve on your board. Make sure the number of directors you specify here is equal to or greater than the minimum number required in your state (see the instructions to your state's articles form; also see "How Many People Are Needed to Form a Nonprofit Corporation" in Chaper 2). Also, consider how many directors you will need to efficiently run your nonprofit corporation. We discuss this point further in Chapter 2.

Often, the number shown here will be the same as the number of initial directors specified in your articles (if initial directors are listed in the articles). However, you may state a greater number at this time if you wish to allow additional directors to be elected to your board.

Article 3, Section 2.
Qualifications for Directors

Our bylaws provide that directors must be of the age of majority in your state. Although not a legal requirement in every state, we think this is a sensible provision to avoid legal problems that can occur if minors conduct or manage business.

We suggest that you not add additional qualifications to limit the makeup of your board to a particular group of individuals (for example, to educators or enrolled students of a school or to parents of children who attend a nonprofit day care center). The IRS likes to see various segments of the community represented on the board of a 501(c)(3) tax-exempt group, not just a select group with a singular nonprofit perspective or interest.

Instead of imposing a blanket qualification requirement on all board positions, it often makes sense to allocate a certain number of director positions to specific groups of individuals. This type of "selective diversity" is, in fact, encouraged by the IRS.

EXAMPLE:

A nonprofit hospital wishes to set aside three board positions for physicians, three for health care administrators, and three for community representatives. This section of the bylaws is completed as follows:

Section 2. Qualifications

Directors shall be of the age of majority in this state. Other qualifications for directors of this corporation shall be as follows:

Three board positions shall be filled by licensed physicians in private practice in Jefferson County; three board positions shall be filled by health care administrators of nonprofit hospitals in Jefferson County; and three board positions shall be filled by representatives of the Jefferson County community who are not health care professionals.

Article 3, Section 5.
Term of Office of Directors

Indicate the length of the term of office for directors in this blank.

Most states specify an annual (one year) term for directors. Many states allow you to provide for a longer term (subject to a maximum, typically of three to six years). We recommend you state a one-year term. This way you will meet your state's requirements, and you can re-elect your directors to successive one-year terms each year if they are performing satisfactorily. If you want to specify a term of more than one year, check your state's nonprofit law to make sure you can do so.

Here is a sample bylaw for appointing directors for one year:

Each director shall hold office for a period of one year and until his or her successor is elected and qualifies.

Customizing Director Provisions. Some nonprofits with larger boards or other special requirements may wish to draft their own term of office or board election provisions. For example, some may wish to provide for a staggered board, in which only a portion of the full board is elected each term to guarantee that there will always be a majority of experienced members. Or some may want to allow certain members of the board to be appointed by specified individuals or organizations (such as a city council, board of directors of a hospital, or committee of an environmental organization). There are other possibilities as well. For example, you may wish to provide that a director can only serve two or three consecutive terms so as to bring in new directors periodically.

 CAUTION

Check before you use alternative bylaw provisions. In all cases, we suggest that you check your nonprofit corporation law to determine whether the alternate provisions are permitted by your state's statutes. See Appendix B for instructions on how to locate your state's nonprofit law online.

Staggered Board Provision. Here's an example of a substitute bylaw that provides for the election of a staggered board. A corporation with a 12-person board, for instance, could use this provision to elect four directors each year:

Each year, one-third [*or some other percentage or number*] of the authorized number of directors shall be elected to serve on the board of directors. Each director shall hold office until his or her successor is elected and qualifies.

The above provision can be used to elect a portion of the board each term. Of course, more complicated schemes are possible with different classes of directors serving for different lengths of time.

Are Staggered Boards Allowed in Your State?

The nonprofit laws of some states specifically allow staggered boards. Staggered boards are also allowed in a number of states whose nonprofit statutes are silent on this issue (for example, in states whose statutes only specify particular terms of office for directors). However, if your state law doesn't address this issue but requires that all directors must be elected at an annual (or other periodic) meeting for the election of directors, staggered boards may not be valid—the statutes can be read to require that all board members be elected at one time. Check with a nonprofit lawyer if you wish to authorize a staggered board and have a question regarding your state's statute on directors' terms of office.

By the way, how do you tell which members of the initial board should first be selected to serve staggered terms? Here's one idea (simply a fancy way of saying that the corporate secretary can draw straws to make this selection):

> If, at a meeting for the election of directors, more than one group of initial board members is elected to serve for a first staggered term of office, then the secretary of the corporation shall assign each director to a numbered group and shall make a chance selection between or among the numbered groups (by selecting among numbered lots or by some other chance selection procedure). The group corresponding to the number so chosen shall be subject to election to a staggered term at the meeting.

Article 3, Section 6. Director Compensation

As we've said, nonprofit directors customarily serve without compensation because the IRS will probably view substantial payments to directors for performing director duties as instances of prohibited private inurement. This is the wise approach. This bylaw section, however, does allow the corporation to pay directors a reasonable fee for attending meetings as well as reasonable advancement or reimbursement for expenses incurred in performing director duties. In practice, many nonprofits do not pay directors even these lesser amounts except to reimburse directors who must travel a long distance to attend board meetings. However, some nonprofits may authorize minimal payments as incentives to individuals for serving on the board.

Article 3, Section 8. Regular Board Meetings

In the blanks in the first paragraph, specify the date(s) and time(s) when regular meetings of the board will be held. Many nonprofits with active agendas hold regular board meetings on a monthly or more frequent basis. Smaller or less active organizations may schedule a regular board meeting less frequently (quarterly, semiannually, or even annually) and call special meetings during the year to take care of specific items of business.

We recommend that you use this bylaw provision to schedule regular board meetings on at least a monthly basis. The majority of nonprofit corporations, whether large, mid-sized, or small, should keep their boards busy managing corporate projects and programs; setting up, supervising, and hearing back from a number of corporate committees; and just generally taking care of business on an ongoing basis. And remember, to help avoid personal liability for management decisions, each board member should be able to show that he or she is as fully informed of, and actively involved in, corporate business as possible. Corporate records showing director attendance at, and participation in, regular meetings of the board are an excellent way to show that your directors meet this standard of corporate conduct. Here is a sample bylaw calling for regular board meetings:

> Regular meetings of Directors shall be held on the second Tuesday of each month at 7:30 p.m.

In the second paragraph of this section, nonmembership nonprofits should fill in the blank to indicate which one of the regular board meetings will be specified for election (or reelection) of corporate directors.

Membership Note: The provisions in the second paragraph of this section take effect only for nonmembership corporations—membership corporations can leave this item blank because they will add provisions to their bylaws that specify that the members, not the directors, elect directors of the corporation.

In a nonmembership corporation, the directors vote for their own reelection or replacement. The frequency of this regular meeting to elect directors depends upon their term of office. If the term is one year, then one regular meeting per year will be designated for election of the board. Likewise, if you have specified a three-year term for directors, then one regular meeting every third year will be designated as the meeting to elect directors. Under the terms of this bylaw, each director casts one vote for each candidate (up to the number of candidates to be elected), and the candidates receiving the highest number of votes are elected.

Directors Elected Annually. Here's an example of a bylaw for a nonmember corporation where the directors are to be elected annually:

> If this corporation makes no provision for members, then, at the regular meeting of directors held on January 1 of each year, directors shall be elected by the board of directors. Voting for the election of directors shall be by written ballot. Each director shall cast one vote per candidate, and may vote for as many candidates as the number of candidates to be elected to the board. The candidates receiving the highest number of votes up to the number of directors to be elected shall be elected to serve on the board.

EXAMPLE:

Your nonprofit board consists of 15 members. The names of 20 candidates to the board are placed in nomination at the beginning of the regular meeting for election of the board. Pursuant to this bylaw provision, each director casts one vote for 15 (of the 20) candidates. The 15 candidates receiving the highest number of votes are elected to the board. Smaller nonmembership nonprofits commonly hold uncontested elections in which each director simply places him- or herself in nomination and the board votes itself in for another annual term.

 RESOURCE

If you wish to add special nomination, balloting, or other director election procedures to your bylaws in place of this standard provision, check your state's nonprofit statutes before doing so (look for a section heading entitled "Election of Directors").

Article 3, Section 10. Notice of Board Meetings

Section (a) of this bylaw dispenses with notice of all regular meetings of directors (this includes the regular meeting for the election of directors). This is a standard provision codified in the nonprofit statutes of most states. It is assumed that directors will keep track of, and attend, regular meetings, once they have been given the schedule. As a practical matter, you may wish to call and remind less active directors of all upcoming meetings of the board.

Section (b) requires that the date, time, place, and purpose of special director meetings be communicated to each director at least one week in advance. Our bylaw specifies that notice may be given in person, or by mail, telephone, or fax machine. Since fax messages may go unnoticed or unread (or occasionally be eaten by the machine), they must be acknowledged by a return fax or telephone call within 24 hours.

Section (c) allows the corporation to obtain a written consent from a director prior to or after a meeting. Written consents and waivers of this sort are specifically authorized under the nonprofit statutes of many states and are a good way to ensure that a director is informed of the meeting. Also, this avoids having to worry about complying with any special statutory rules that may exist for calling, noticing, or holding the meeting. If a director consents in writing to the meeting, he or she cannot protest later that the corporation failed to comply with a formality contained in your nonprofit corporation code.

TIP

You may want to customize your notice provisions. We think these are reasonable notification provisions, which keep all directors informed of special business while eliminating premeeting preliminaries and delays for all regular meetings. You may wish to adopt provisions that match exactly any special requirements in your state or you may wish to customize these provisions to suit your own needs or circumstances. For example, you may wish to mail written notice and agendas of all regular and special board meetings to each director one week prior to the meeting date. Or, if allowed in your state, you may wish to allow email notice and acknowledgement of notice procedures.

Article 3, Section 11.
Quorum for Board Meetings

Indicate the percentage of the full board (or the number of directors) who must be present at a directors' meeting to constitute a quorum so that business can be conducted. We recommend a majority quorum as a sensible rule that will satisfy the director quorum requirements in most states. Some states let you lower the requirement to less than a majority, but check your state's nonprofit law if you want to do this.

Quorum Specified as Percentage of Full Board. Here is a sample bylaw, which defines a quorum as a percentage of the board:

> A quorum shall consist of <u>a majority</u> of the members of the board of directors.

Quorum Specified as Number of Directors. Here is a sample bylaw that qualifies a quorum as a specific number of members of the board:

> A quorum shall consist of three of the members of the board of directors.

Most corporations specify a majority of the board as the director quorum requirement, even if state law allows a smaller percentage or number of directors to be specified. Of course, you can set a larger quorum requirement if you wish. Whatever you decide, you should realize that this section of the bylaws concerns a quorum, not a vote requirement. Under the provisions of the next section in the bylaws, normal board action can be taken by a majority of directors at a meeting at which a quorum is present.

EXAMPLE:

If a six-director corporation requires a majority quorum and a meeting is held at which a minimum quorum (four) is present, action can be taken by the vote of three directors, a majority of those present at the meeting.

Article 3, Section 13.
Conduct of Board Meetings

Use this blank to specify the rules of order which will be used at directors' meetings. Some larger nonprofits use *Robert's Rules of Order* (major editions change every ten years or so), but you may indicate any set of procedures for proposing, approving, and tabling motions that you wish. You may also want to look at *Robert's Rules of Order*, a procedural guide for holding nonprofit meetings (see www.robertsrules.com). If you will have a small informal board, you may wish to leave this line blank if you see no need to specify formal procedures for introducing and discussing items of business at board meetings, or you may wish to specify "such procedures as may be approved from time to time by the board of directors" to allow your board to develop its own set of procedures for conducting meetings.

Article 4, Section 1.
Designation of Officers

This section provides for the four standard officer positions of president, vice president, secretary, and treasurer and allows the board to designate and fill other corporate officer positions as needed. In most nonprofits, directors are appointed to serve as the unpaid officers of the corporation. The officers, in turn, oversee the salaried staff. For a list of the formal duties and responsibilities associated with each officer position, see sections 6 through 9 of this article in the form.

TIP

In some states, one or more corporate officer positions cannot be filled by the same person. For example, the same person cannot serve as both the corporate president and corporate secretary. See your state's nonprofit law if you want to see any special rules that apply in your state

(also see "How Many People Are Needed to Form a Nonprofit Corporation?" in Chapter 2).

Even if you set up a small nonprofit run by just a few individuals, it is customary to fill these four primary officer slots with different people. You will elect officers when you hold your first meeting of directors. Under this bylaw provision, your board may designate and fill other officer titles and positions whenever it wishes to do so.

Article 5, Section 1.
Executive Committee of the Board

This section allows the board to appoint an executive committee of directors to make management decisions for the corporation. If you wish to use this provision, insert the number of directors who will serve on this committee. Note that this provision requires that the designation of an executive committee be approved by a majority of directors.

Typically, under state law, a committee of the board can't approve major decisions, such as amendments to articles or bylaws or major structural changes. See your state's nonprofit law for more information.

While we do not necessarily recommend that board authority be delegated, establishing an executive committee of directors may be advisable in certain nonprofits where action must routinely be taken in between formal board meetings or where distance, time, or other constraints sometimes make it difficult to achieve a quorum for board meetings. In all cases, the executive committee should keep minutes of its meetings and document all formal action. Regular and timely reports of executive committee actions should be presented to the full board.

CAUTION

Directors can be personally liable for board action. Under state law and court decisions, less active board members (those who sit on the full board and approve actions taken by the more active executive committee members) can be held personally accountable (and, in extreme cases, personally liable) for executive committee decisions. Mostly, such personal liability occurs if members of the full board are willfully or grossly negligent in carrying out their duties, which include reasonably monitoring executive committee action.

Article 7, Sections 3 and 4. Director and Member Inspection Rights

These provisions give directors and members broad rights to inspect the corporation's properties and financial and corporate records. State law may impose additional inspection rights and obligations (or may allow you to restrict these rights). For the details of any additional inspection provisions that may apply in your state, see your nonprofit corporation law.

Article 7, Section 6. Periodic Report Requirements

In most states, nonprofit corporations must file an annual or other periodic report form with the secretary of state, the attorney general's office, or some other state office or agency showing the names and addresses of the corporation's directors and officers and other information. Standard corporate financial statements and reports of charitable solicitation programs and finances may also be required.

TIP

Go online for your state's form. Your state's corporate filing office website should provide —or show you how to order—a copy of your state's corporate annual report form.

Special Membership Reports

Your state's nonprofit corporation act may also require you to furnish annual corporate financial statements to members. In addition, it may require you to make an annual written report to members detailing specific transactions, such as the making of loans or guarantees to directors or officers. Your state nonprofit law will contain any special membership reporting requirements that apply in your state.

Article 8. 501(c)(3) Tax Provisions

The various sections in this article contain language that will help show the IRS and, if applicable, your state revenue or tax department, that you qualify for tax-exempt status:

- Section 1 contains specific and general limitations on your nonprofit activities. The first paragraph indicates that you will comply with the specific 501(c)(3) prohibitions against substantial lobbying activities and involvement with political campaigns for public candidates (the reference to IRC Section 501(h) is a reminder that you may elect to fall under the alternative political expenditures test available to 501(c)(3) public charities—see "Limitation on Political Activities" in Chapter 3). The second paragraph limits the activities of the corporation, generally, to those permitted to 501(c)(3) organizations and to organizations that qualify for tax deductible charitable contributions (under IRC § 170(c)(2)).

- Section 2 restates the 501(c)(3) prohibition against private inurement (benefiting individuals associated with the nonprofit organization). Payments made to individuals as reasonable compensation for services rendered and to further the tax-exempt purposes of the group are specifically authorized.

- Section 3 irrevocably dedicates the assets of the organization to another 501(c)(3) group or to a governmental office or agency for a public purpose. The last sentence is a reminder that such assets must be distributed in accordance with state law.

- Section 4 contains technical language restating the requirements applicable to 501(c)(3) organizations classified as private foundations. These provisions state that for any year the corporation is classified as a 501(c)(3) private foundation, it will operate in such a way as to avoid all private foundation excise taxes imposed under various sections of the Internal Revenue Code. As you will not want to be classified as a private foundation (but, rather, as a public charity), why include these provisions in the bylaws? Simply to show the IRS that you mean business (in a nonprofit sense of course) and will comply with any and all 501(c)(3) restrictions— whether your organization is classified as a public charity or as a private foundation.

Article 9. Conflict of Interest and Compensation Approval Policies

Article 9 of the bylaws included in this book contains rules and procedures for approving or avoiding conflict of interest transactions, including compensation arrangements, between your nonprofit and its directors, officers, employees, contractors, and others. This bylaw provision contains the conflict of interest language recommended by the IRS (included in the sample conflict of interest policy in Appendix A of the instructions to IRS Form 1023). It also contains language for the approval of compensation arrangements that attempts to

comply with the safe harbor provisions of the excess benefit rules (see "Limitation on Profits and Benefits" in Chapter 3). You will need to become familiar with this provision, and make sure you are comfortable with its procedures for the approval and review of financial transactions with, and salary and other compensation paid to, your directors, officers, and others who are in a position to influence your nonprofit. If you decide to make changes to this provision, do so only after reading "Prepare Your Tax Exemption Application," in Chapter 8, instructions to Part V, where we refer to this bylaw provision when providing sample responses to question on the application. If you make any changes, you will need to create your own responses to some of the questions on the 501(c)(3) application.

Adoption of Bylaws

Use the Adoption of Bylaws page as the last page of your completed bylaws. In the blank, specify the number of preceding pages in your bylaws. Fill in the date and have each of the persons named as an initial director in your articles sign on a blank line below the first paragraph. If directors were not named in your articles, have each of your incorporators (the person or persons who signed your articles) sign here.

After you adopt your bylaws, make sure to keep a copy with your corporate records (so the organization can refer to them as needed in the future). You will also need to make a copy of your bylaws to attach to your federal tax exemption application, as explained in the next chapter.

Prepare Membership Provisions

This section shows how to add membership provisions to the bylaws prepared in the preceding section.

SKIP AHEAD

If you have decided to form a nonmembership corporation (as most nonprofits will), this section does not apply to you and you should skip ahead to Chapter 8.

To add membership provisions to your bylaws, fill in the blanks in the tear-out membership provisions in Appendix C or in the bylaws form on the CD-ROM, following the instructions below.

Customizing Your Membership Provisions

There are significant state law differences with respect to membership rules and procedures. In drafting the membership provisions, we have specified general membership rules that avoid significant state differences and provide a skeletal membership structure for your corporation to help you complete your bylaws and continue with your incorporation process (apply for your tax exemptions, and so on).

You may need to customize your membership rules—for example, to provide for different classes of membership, proxy voting, special director nomination or selection procedures, additional grounds and procedures for terminating memberships, and so on. Drafting extra membership provisions that comply with your state's rules will require legal research or a consultation with a nonprofit lawyer.

Heading

Type the name of your corporation in this blank.

Article 12. Membership Provisions

The membership provisions start with Article 12. You will include these membership provision pages at the end of the basic bylaw pages, as explained below.

Article 12, Section 2. Qualifications of Members

Use this blank to indicate any special qualifications required of members in your corporation. We suggest you do not limit or qualify membership in your corporation unless the qualification is of obvious utility (members must be of the age of majority) or is clearly related to the tax-exempt purposes or activities of your organization.

EXAMPLE:

A nonprofit private college decides to limit membership to alumni because the founders wish to confer legal membership power only on those who have attended and completed the educational program. Because any person may enroll in the school, the IRS should have no objection.

EXAMPLE:

A specialized philanthropic and fundraising newsletter only admits as members persons who can show a few years' prior experience working with or for nonprofit organizations. This selection criterion is intended to generate a membership that is involved in the organization's areas of interest, and should be acceptable to the IRS.

No Specified Membership Qualification. If you do not wish to limit or qualify membership in your corporation, complete this blank as follows:

> The qualifications for membership in this corporation are as follows: Any person is qualified to become a member of this corporation.

CAUTION

Dues and fees go in Section 4, below. Do not use this blank to limit your membership to those who pay membership fees or dues—you will specify any initial and ongoing payments required of members in separate membership provisions, as explained below.

Article 12, Section 3.
Admission of Members

Most smaller nonprofit corporations do not require formal application for membership in the corporation. A few, however, may do this to determine if prospective members meet the qualification requirements set forth in Article 12, Section 2, as discussed above. Others will use this bylaw to indicate that members must pay an admission fee and/or annual dues prior to acceptance as a member in the corporation.

Specified Membership Qualification. Here is a sample bylaw which provides for membership qualification, an application fee, and annual dues:

> Applicants shall be admitted to membership on making application therefore in writing and upon approval of the application by the membership committee of this corporation [*and/or*] upon payment of the application fee and first annual dues, as specified in the following sections of this bylaw.

The actual amounts paid by members will be specified in the following sections of this bylaw.

Article 12, Section 4.
Membership Fees and Dues

Use these blanks to authorize or specify any application fee or annual dues charged to members:

> (a) The following fee shall be charged for making application for membership in the corporation: *[state specific admission fee, leave to discretion of board (for example, "in such amount as may be specified from time to time by resolution of the Board of Directors charged for, and payable with, the application for membership"), or, if no fee, type "None"]* .
>
> (b) The annual dues payable to the corporation by members shall be *[state amount of annual dues, leave to discretion of board (for example, "in such amount as may be determined from time to time by resolution of the Board of Directors"), or type "None"]*.

Article 12, Section 9.
Termination of Membership

The termination of membership provisions here are basic ones. Membership can be terminated voluntarily by a member or by the corporation if the member fails to pay dues. The corporation may also terminate a member for cause if the member is provided written notice and an opportunity to be heard.

RESOURCE

The statutes and court decisions of your state may contain specific substantive and procedural rules for terminating membership in a nonprofit corporation. If you do need to expel a member, we suggest you do so only after checking the latest annotated nonprofit statutes in your state (look under Membership Provisions in your state's nonprofit corporation act).

Article 13, Section 2.
Regular Meetings of Members

In the blanks in the first paragraph of this section, indicate the date and time of the regular meeting of members held to elect the board of directors. Typically membership nonprofits will specify an annual meeting to elect the board here. The frequency of this meeting will, of course, depend on the length of the term of office for your directors (see the instructions for Article 3, Section 5, above).

Directors Elected Annually. Here is a sample bylaw for electing directors annually:

> A regular meeting of members shall be held on January 2 of each year , at 1 p.m., for the purpose of electing directors and transacting other business as may come before the meeting.

In the second paragraph, type the date and time of any *additional* regular meetings of members you wish to schedule. Although we encourage frequent membership meetings, some smaller membership nonprofits may not wish to provide for regular meetings (other than the regular meeting to elect directors as specified in the preceding paragraph of the bylaws) and will leave these items blank. Others with a more active membership will use these blanks to specify frequent or occasional (for example, monthly or semiannual) regular meetings of members.

TIP

Remember special meetings. Your non-profit membership corporation can also call and hold special meetings of members during the year—see the discussion below.

Article 13, Section 3.
Special Meetings of Members

This provision allows the chairperson of the board or the president of the corporation to call special meetings of members—this represents standard practice (and the standard state rule) for most nonprofits. Your nonprofit corporation law may allow other special meetings to be called by a specified percentage of the membership of the corporation—see your nonprofit corporation law if you wish to allow members to call special meetings (look under "Special Meetings of Members").

Article 13, Section 4.
Notice of Members' Meetings

Our notice provisions for members' meetings are, for the most part, standard provisions found in state nonprofit statutes, requiring personal or mailed notice for regular and special membership meetings. If you wish to extend or shorten the notice period (ten to 50 days), dispense with notice for regular meetings, or make other changes, check that your language conforms to your state's nonprofit law before making your changes.

As with the director notice provisions, members can waive notice of a meeting in writing—this procedure can come in handy if you don't have time to give formal notice of a meeting to members.

TIP

You can use telephone and fax machine notice. Our bylaw permits personal notification by telephone or fax machine. Again, a fax notice must be personally acknowledged by a return fax message or telephone call within 24 hours. If you want to allow email notification and acknowledgement of notice, check your state nonprofit law to make sure doing so is allowed.

Article 13, Section 5.
Quorum for Members' Meetings

Most smaller nonprofits indicate a majority quorum rule here (a majority of the members must be present to hold a members' meeting). The nonprofit corporation laws of a number of states are flexible on this point and allow the corporation to set its own member meeting quorum requirement. If you wish to provide for less than a majority membership quorum, check your state nonprofit law first to see any limits that apply to setting a quorum at less than a majority.

Specifying a Quorum as a Majority of Voting Members.

A quorum shall consist of a majority of the voting members of the corporation.

TIP

For membership approval at a meeting, the vote of a majority of those present is required. (See Article 13, Section 6, of the membership provisions.) For example, in a corporation with 50 members and a majority-quorum rule for membership meetings, a quorum for meetings consists of 26 members. If 26 members attend a meeting, action can be approved at the meeting by 14 members, a majority of those present.

Article 13, Section 8.
Action by Written Ballot

To make membership provisions more applicable and realistic, we have included this written ballot procedure to allow members to elect directors and transact other membership business by mail. These are standard, workable provisions—but they may not cover all the technical requirements found in your state's nonprofit statutes. To be certain, check our provisions against the membership written consent or written ballot procedures in your nonprofit statute or check with a lawyer.

Many states authorize membership action by written consent but require follow-up notice of any action taken to any nonconsenting members. See your state's nonprofit law for specific information.

Article 13, Section 9.
Conduct of Members' Meetings

Indicate, if you wish, the set of rules that will govern the proposing and taking of action at your membership meetings. *Robert's Rules of Order* is the standard, of course, but you may specify another set of procedures if you wish or leave this item blank if you see no reason to adopt formal rules for conducting membership meetings.

Completion of Membership Bylaws

Assemble your membership bylaws by adding the completed membership provision pages to the end of your completed bylaw pages. Then use the Adoption of Bylaws page as the last page of your bylaws—this page is included as the last page of the tear-out bylaws in Appendix C and the bylaws form on the CD-ROM. Fill in this page according to the Adoption of Bylaws instructions, given earlier. ●

Apply for Your Federal 501(c)(3) Tax Exemption

Now that you've filed your articles and prepared your bylaws, it's time to prepare your federal exemption application (IRS Form 1023). Obtaining your federal exemption is a critical step in forming your nonprofit organization because most of the real benefits of being a nonprofit flow from 501(c)(3) tax-exempt status. Most groups complete and submit their federal tax exemption application before obtaining their state tax exemption because state exemptions often are contingent on a nonprofit obtaining its federal tax exemption first—see "Obtain State Corporate Income Tax Exemption" in Chapter 9. To make your tax exemption retroactive to the date of your incorporation, your 1023 application must be postmarked within 27 months from the end of the month in which you filed your articles of incorporation.

The IRS recently revised the 1023 tax exemption application to make it a gentler, friendlier form. However, it still remains a daunting task to understand and complete the application. The official instructions to Form 1023 say that it takes an average of approximately ten hours to complete the form (plus more time for each schedule), and almost another hour to assemble the material for mailing. Hopefully, by reading and following our line-by-line instructions, below, you will accomplish this task in substantially less time. We provide a lot of handholding and suggestions for responses to make the task easier and less time consuming. And keep the following suggestion in mind: If you get stuck on a difficult question or run low on energy (as many do), take a break and return to it when you feel better able to follow and absorb the material. You will be well rewarded in the end for the time and effort you devote to this task.

> **CAUTION**
>
> **Special purpose nonprofits use a different IRS form.** If yours is a special purpose nonprofit group (formed for other than religious, educational, charitable, scientific, or literary purposes), you're likely to be exempt under subsections of Section 501(c) other than Subsection (3). To apply for your federal tax exemption, you'll need IRS Form 1024 instead of IRS Form 1023. Certain cooperative hospital service organizations and cooperative educational service organizations can use Form 1023—see the General Instructions to Form 1023, "Other Organizations that may file Form 1023."

Getting Started

Before diving into the task at hand, take a moment to read this section, which sets out the various tax forms and other IRS publications you'll encounter. We'll also give you tips on how to fill out the forms and deal with the additional information you may need to supply. Think of this portion of the chapter as your orientation.

Forms and Publications

You'll encounter several IRS forms as you make your way toward federal exempt status. We've provided the following federal forms with this book, in tear-out form in Appendix C, on the CD-ROM included with this book, or both (as indicated below):

- IRS Form 1023. Package 1023: *Application for Recognition of Exemption* (June 2006) (CD-ROM and tear-out) (includes September 2009 notice of changes)

- Instructions for Form 1023 (June 2006) (CD-ROM only)

- Form SS-4. *Application for Employer Identification Number* (January 2010) (CD-ROM and tear-out)

- Instructions for Form SS-4 (January 2010) (CD-ROM only)

Check that your IRS 1023 form is current. If you are using the IRS 1023 form included with this book (whether in Appendix C or on the CD-ROM), check to see that the form is current. Go to the IRS website (www.irs.gov) and access the form online (see instructions below under "Ways to Complete the Exemption Application"). The heading on the form will tell you the revision date for the most current 1023 form. If the date of the online form is more recent than the version included with this book (June 2006), use the newer online version. You also can obtain the latest IRS forms by calling 800-TAX-FORM.

The form that is currently available (June 2006) is likely to be updated soon. The IRS adopted regulations in 2008 that eliminated the advance ruling process for 501(c)(3) organizations. The 1023 tax exemption application dated June 2006 (the most current available at the time this book was published) has not been updated to reflect these changes. The IRS includes a notice of changes at the beginning of the 2006 form that explains how to use the 2006 form.

We have included the latest IRS instructions in our instructions, below (and added some additional information). If a new Form 1023 is available, you should still be able to use the instructions in this chapter, as well as the official instructions to the new form, to help you fill in the updated form. If a newer form contains questions not covered in this chapter, call the IRS Exempt Organizations Customer Account Services (877-829-5500) and ask a tax-exempt organization specialist for help with the new material. Or check Nolo's website for instructions for the new form (look for updates to this book).

We have also included some federal tax publications on the CD-ROM. These publications are surprisingly readable and give a lot of practical information. You can get copies or updated versions by going online to www.irs.gov or by calling the IRS forms and publications request number, 800-TAX-FORM.

- Publication 557, *Tax-Exempt Status for Your Organization* (October 2010)
- Publication 4220, *Applying for 501(c)(3) Tax-Exempt Status* (August 2009)
- Publication 4221-PC, *Compliance Guide for 501(c)(3) Public Charities* (July 2009)
- Publication 4221-PF, *Compliance Guide for 501(c)(3) Private Foundations* (June 2007)
- Publication 1828, *Tax Guide for Churches and Religious Organizations* (November 2009)

TIP

You can find additional helpful information, including articles on special exempt organization issues, on the IRS website at www.irs.gov. Check the "Charities & Non-Profits" page. Also see the *Stay Exempt-Tax Basics for Exempt Organizations*, at www.stayexempt.org.

Ways to Complete the Exemption Application

There are several ways to complete the federal tax exemption application. You can:

- use the tear-out form in the back of the book and fill it in by hand (print with a black ink pen) or typewriter (using a black ribbon)
- use the IRS Form 1023 included on the CD-ROM file at the back of this book, or
- go to the IRS website and obtain the form online.

Also, be on the lookout for the launch of the IRS "Cyber Assistant" at the IRS *Charities & Non-Profits* page (www.irs.gov/charities/index .html). This online program, expected some time after 2010, will allow you to prepare your 1023 exemption application online following IRS instructions (and for a lower filing fee). Of course, the instructions in this chapter should make your job even easier. Check to see if this online service is available before you begin working on your 1023 application.

If you use the tear-out form from this book or the form on the CD-ROM, check the IRS website to make sure the date on the form you are using is the same as the date on the form available on the IRS website. To access the IRS form, go to the IRS website at www.irs.gov. In the search box, type "1023." You should see links to both Form 1023 and to the separate instructions for the form at the top of the list.

The 1023 form on the IRS website is provided in PDF format. Save and work with a backup copy of the form—you will fill in and save your responses on your working copy. You will need the latest version of Adobe's *Reader* program (available free from Adobe.com) to fill in and save your responses. For more information on installing and using PDF files, see Appendix A.

Preliminary Reading

Before starting your federal tax exemption application, read the Instructions for Form 1023 (available on the CD-ROM or from the IRS website). Also skim through Chapters 1, 2, and 3 of IRS Publication 557 and Publications 4220 and 4221-PC—the information there covers the basic requirements for obtaining a 501(c)(3) tax exemption.

Also, be sure to read the IRS Form 990 Annual Return and Instructions. This form, called *Return of Organization Exempt From Income Tax*, must be filed each year with the IRS by 501(c)(3) organizations whose annual receipts are more than $25,000 a year (if your nonprofit has receipts of $25,000 or less,

it must file Form 990-N (e-Postcard)). It is an information return that the IRS uses to monitor the structure, activities, and finances of 501(c)(3) nonprofits. The annual disclosure requirements of the Form 990 are substantial, so look at the form and its schedules before you leap into applying for your tax exemption. You'll see that you will need to monitor and account for many of your nonprofit's financial and operational details throughout its life. Smaller nonprofits can file a simplified 990-EZ form instead of the 990 form (see the instructions to the 990-EZ form at the IRS website, at www.irs.gov, for the latest information).

If you find this reading a bit technical, don't let it bog you down. The information in this book, together with our line-by-line instructions for the forms, should be enough to get you through the process. If necessary, you can always refer back to the IRS publications and instructions when answering questions or filling out schedules.

Form 1023 Schedules, Attachments, and Exhibits

Form 1023 contains several schedules that only certain nonprofits (such as schools, churches, and hospitals) need to complete. Don't worry about these schedules—we will tell you if your group needs to complete a schedule as you go through the line-by-line instructions for Form 1023. We provide instructions for filling out the schedules.

You may need to answer or continue your response to some questions on the form on an attachment page or pages. Use letter-sized paper (8½" × 11") and include the following information:

- the name and EIN (Employer Identification Number) of your corporation, at the top of each attachment page

- for each response, state the part and line number to which the response relates. Also provide a description, if appropriate (see the sample attachment page, below).
- the page number in the header or footer of each page if you include more than one attachment page to your application. (Many groups will have multiple attachment pages.)

You do not need to have a separate attachment page for each response—just list your responses one after the other on your attachment pages (as shown on the sample below). The federal form has space under each question for your response, but often this space is insufficient. You can use attachment pages to continue any responses you start on the form.

You also can use attachments to indicate you are including additional information as exhibits. For example, you will need to attach documents, such as articles and bylaws, and other materials, such as copies of solicitations for financial support, to your application. Mark each document as an exhibit and label them in alphabetical order. You can write the exhibit letter at the top of the document, or you can staple a page or note to the first page of the document and write the exhibit reference (for example, "Exhibit A") on the cover page or note. We recommend that you use a separate cover page or note for your certified copy of your articles of incorporation because the articles you include as an exhibit should exactly match the articles you filed with the secretary of state. Make sure each document has a heading that identifies its content and the name and EIN of your nonprofit. The copies of your legal documents should have headings printed on the first page already, such as "Articles of [name of your corporation]" or "Bylaws of [name of your corporation]." Put similar identifying headings on all financial statements and other exhibits you prepare yourself and number each page if the document has multiple pages.

Attachment Page

Attachment to Form 1023, Page 1

GoodWorks, Inc.

EIN # XXXXXXXX

Part IV, Narrative Description of Activities: The nonprofit organization also will engage in the following activities: ...

Part V, Line 1a, Names, titles, mailing addresses, and compensation of officers, directors, and trustees (continuation):

Name	Title	Mailing Address	Compensation (actual or proposed)

Public Inspection Rights

As you begin entering information on the federal form, keep in mind that your readership may at some point be members of the public, not just some unknown bureaucrat at the IRS. Your federal 1023 tax exemption application, any papers submitted with the application, and your tax exemption determination letter from the IRS must be made available by your organization for public inspection during regular business hours at your organization's principal office. However, any information that has been submitted to the IRS and approved by it as confidential is not required to be publicly disclosed (see "How to Keep Form 1023 Information Confidential," below), and you do not have to disclose the names and addresses of contributors if you qualify as a public charity—which we assume you will.

If your organization regularly maintains one or more regional or district offices having three or more employees (defined as offices that have a payroll consisting of at least 120 paid hours per week), you must make copies of the documents available for public inspection at each of these offices. Copies of your organization's three most recent annual information returns must also be available for public inspection at your principal office (and, if applicable, your regional or district office).

Members of the public can also make a written request for copies of your organization's tax exemption application and its tax returns for the last three years. You must comply within 30 days and are allowed to charge only reasonable copying and postage costs. The public also can request copies or public inspection of your organization's exemption application or its annual returns by calling IRS Exempt Organizations Customer Account Services at 877-829-5500. These public inspection requirements apply to 501(c)(3) public charities, not to 501(c)(3) private foundations—again, we expect most incorporators to qualify as public charities.

It's important to comply with inspection requests. If you don't permit public inspection, you could face a $20-per-day penalty. The IRS will impose an automatic $5,000 additional penalty if your failure to comply is willful. These penalties are not imposed on the organization—they are applied against "the person failing to meet (these) requirements." See IRS Publication 557 and IRC §§ 6104(e), 5562(c)(1)(C) and (D), and 6685 for further information on these rules.

CD-ROM

For additional information about IRS regulations on required disclosures by 501(c)(3) nonprofits, see the CD-ROM file: Update: The Final Regulations on the Disclosure Requirements for Annual Information Returns and Applications for Exemption.

How to Keep Form 1023 Information Confidential

Any information submitted with your 1023 is open to public inspection. However, if an attachment or response to your application contains information regarding trade secrets, patents, or other information that would adversely affect your organization if released to the public, you can clearly state "NOT SUBJECT TO PUBLIC INSPECTION" next to the material and include your reasons for requesting secrecy. If the IRS agrees, the information will not be open to public inspection.

IRS Regulation § 301.6104(a)-5 says that the IRS will agree if you convince them that "the disclosure of such information would adversely affect the organization."

CD-ROM

See the CD-ROM file, Disclosure, FOIA and the Privacy Act, for additional information on the restrictions applicable to the IRS and its employees regarding disclosures of information submitted to the IRS.

The Consequences of Filing Late

You should file your 1023 within 27 months after the end of the month in which you filed your articles of incorporation. In our experience, the most common problem faced by nonprofits is failing to file their Form 1023 on time. What happens if you file late?

First, if you file on time (within 27 months of incorporating) and the IRS grants your exemption, the exemption takes effect on the date on which you filed your articles. The same is true if you can show "reasonable cause" for your delay (this means you have convinced the IRS that your tardiness was understandable and excusable). If you file late and don't have reasonable cause (or the IRS doesn't buy your story), your tax-exempt status will begin as of the postmark date on your form. For more information, see "Prepare Your Tax Exemption Application," Part VII, below and the instructions to Schedule E in "Filling Out the Schedules," below.

If your nonprofit has been organized for several years and you're just now getting around to filing your Form 1023, don't despair—you've got plenty of good company. The important point here is to persevere, complete your application, and mail it to the IRS as soon as possible.

Do You Need to File Form 1023?

Almost all nonprofit groups that want 501(c)(3) tax-exempt status will file Form 1023. Form 1023 serves two important purposes:

- It is used by nonprofit organizations to apply for 501(c)(3) tax-exempt status.
- It serves as your notice to the IRS that your organization is a public charity, not a private foundation. Remember, as discussed earlier, the IRS will presume that 501(c)(3) nonprofit groups are private foundations unless you notify the IRS that you qualify for public charity status.

This said, there are a few groups that are not required to file a Form 1023. You aren't required to file if you are:

- a group that qualifies for public charity status and normally has gross receipts of not more than $5,000 in each tax year (the IRS uses a special formula to determine whether a group "normally" has annual gross receipts of not more than $5,000—for specifics, see IRS Publication 557, "Organizations Not Required to File Form 1023," "Gross Receipts Test")
- a church (a church includes synagogues, temples, and mosques), interchurch organization, local unit of a church, convention, or association of churches, or an integrated auxiliary of a church, or
- a subordinate organization covered by a group exemption letter (but only if the parent organization timely submits a notice to the IRS covering the subordinate organization—see the group exemption letter requirements in IRS Publication 557).

Even if one of the above exceptions applies to you, we recommend that you file a Form 1023 anyway. Why? First, it's risky to second-guess the IRS. If you're wrong and the IRS denies your claim to 501(c)(3) tax status several years from now, your organization may have to pay substantial back taxes and penalties. Second, the only way, on a practical and legal level, to assure others that you are a bona fide 501(c)(3) group is to apply for an exemption. If the IRS agrees and grants your tax exemption, then, and only then, can you assure contributors, grant agencies, and others that you are a qualified 501(c)(3) tax-exempt, tax-deductible organization listed with the IRS.

Prepare Your Tax Exemption Application

Now it's time to go through Form 1023 line by line and fill it in. The form is divided into numerous parts. As you go through the form, you will find out whether you need to complete any of the schedules included with the application. Instructions for the schedules are covered separately below.

Part I: Identification of Applicant

Line 1: Write the name of your corporation exactly as it appears in your articles of incorporation.

Line 2: If you have designated one person in your organization to receive return mail from the IRS regarding your 1023 application, such as one of the founders, list this person's name as the "c/o name." Otherwise, insert "not applicable."

Line 3: Provide the mailing address of the corporation. If you do not have a street address, provide a post office box address. The IRS wants you to include the full nine-digit zip code in your address. Include it if you know it. (Zip code information can be obtained online at the U.S. Postal Service zip code lookup page.)

Line 4: All nonprofit corporations (whether or not they have employees) must obtain a federal Employer Identification Number (EIN) prior to applying for 501(c)(3) tax exemption. You will insert this number here on your 1023 form and use this identification number on all your future nonprofit federal information, income, and employee tax returns. Even if your organization held an EIN prior to incorporation, you must obtain a new one for the nonprofit corporate entity. If your nonprofit corporation has not yet obtained an EIN, it should do so now.

The easiest and quickest way to get an EIN is to apply online from the IRS website. Go to www.irs.gov and type "EIN" in the upper search box. Then click "Go" to open a page that lists links to EIN-related Web pages. You should see a link to the online EIN application. The online form is an electronically fileable version of IRS Form SS-4, *Application for Employer Identification Number.* Fill in the online version of the SS-4 form and submit the application to receive your EIN immediately.

Follow the instructions, below, when completing the SS-4 form:

- **Name and SSN of officer.** You will need to specify the name and Social Security Number of one of your principal officers. Normally the chief financial officer or treasurer will provide a name and SSN here.

- **Type of entity.** Check "church or church-controlled organization" if you are forming one; if not, check "other nonprofit organization" and specify its 501(c)(3) purpose (educational, charitable, and so on).

- **GEN number.** Most groups will ignore this item—it applies only to a group exemption application request. Members of an affiliated group of nonprofits can specify a previously assigned Group Exemption Number.

- **Reason for applying.** Check "started new business," then specify "formed nonprofit corporation" in the blank. If you are converting an existing unincorporated association (that has previously filed any appropriate tax returns for its association tax years with the IRS) to a nonprofit corporation, you can check "changed type of organization" instead, then insert "incorporation" in the blank.

- **Date Business Started.** The date you started your business is the date your articles were filed with the state filing office. Use the file-stamped date on the copy of your articles returned by the state office.

- **Employees.** You can enter zeros in the next item that asks the number of employees you expect to have in the next 12 months.

Make sure to write down your EIN immediately before changing Web pages—you will not be able to back up and retrieve the EIN after you navigate away from the Web page. Print a copy of the online form (you can do this by clicking the "Print Form" button on the IRS Web page after receiving your EIN), write the assigned EIN in the upper-right space of the printed form, then date and sign it, and place the copy in your corporate records.

You also can apply for an EIN by phone. To do this, fill in the SS-4 form (included as a tear-out and on the CD-ROM, with separate instructions, or available on the IRS's website). Then call the IRS at 800-829-4933—be sure to complete the form before making the phone call. If you apply by phone, you will be assigned an EIN immediately. Write this number in the upper right-hand box of a printed SS-4 form, then date and sign it, and keep a copy for your records. The IRS telephone representative may ask you to mail or fax a copy of your signed SS-4 form to the IRS.

You also can apply for an EIN by fax and get your EIN faxed back to you within four business days. See the instructions to Form SS-4 for more information on using the IRS Fax-TIN program.

Finally, you can get an EIN the slow way by simply mailing your SS-4 form to the IRS. Have an officer—typically the CFO or treasurer—sign the form, stating his or her title. Expect to wait at least four weeks. Remember, you can't complete line 4 of your 1023 form until you have your EIN.

Line 5: Specify the month your accounting period will end. Use the month number for your response. For example, if your accounting period will end December 31, insert "12." The accounting period must be the same as your corporation's tax year. Most nonprofits use a calendar year as their accounting period and tax year. If you choose to do the same, specify "12" here.

If you anticipate special seasonal cycles for your activities or noncalendar year record keeping or grant accountability procedures, you may wish to select a noncalendar accounting period for your corporation. For example, a federally funded school may wish to specify June ("6") in this blank, which reflects an accounting period of July 1 to June 30.

If you have any questions regarding the best accounting period and tax year for your group, check with your (probable) funding sources and consult your accountant or bookkeeper for further guidance.

Line 6(a)–6(c): State the name of a director or officer the IRS can contact regarding your application, the phone number where this person can be contacted during business hours, and a fax number. The fax number is optional—if you don't want to provide one, insert "not applicable." We suggest you list the name and telephone number of the director or officer who is preparing and will sign your tax exemption application (see Part XI, below). Nevertheless, don't expect the IRS to call to ask questions. If the IRS has questions about your application, it will usually contact you by mail.

Line 7: We assume you are filling in your 1023 form yourself, and will mark "no" to this item. However, if you are being helped by a lawyer, accountant, or other professional representative, mark "yes" to allow the representative to talk on your behalf with the IRS about your 1023 application. If you mark "yes," you will need to complete and attach an IRS Form 2848, *Power of Attorney and Declaration of Representative* (available from the IRS website), to your 1023 application.

Line 8: We assume most readers will answer "no" here. However, if you have paid or plan to pay an outside lawyer, accountant, or other professional or consultant to help you set up your nonprofit or advise you about its tax status, and the person is not acting as your formal representative (named in Form 2848, as explained in line 7, above) and the person is not a director, officer, or employee of your nonprofit, answer "yes" and provide the requested information. Traditionally, many nonprofits get professional guidance from unpaid lawyers and accountants who serve as volunteers to their board. If this is your situation, you can answer "no," since this item is asking about paid advice from an outsider. There is nothing wrong in paying an outsider for help. The purpose of this question is to require full disclosure of any paid relationships between your nonprofit and its advisers, to make sure the compensation arrangement is fair to the nonprofit, and to see that there is no obvious conflict of interest between the person's role and his or her paid status. An overriding concern of the IRS is to make sure that one person is not personally directing the organization and operation of your nonprofit to further personal financial interests and agendas.

Many professionals are being more careful these days and will shy away from providing professional advice on nonprofit boards unless they are indemnified and covered by directors' liability insurance. Some paid advisers will automatically say "no" when asked to sit on a nonprofit board because they do not want to confuse their role as adviser to the nonprofit entity (their real client to whom they owe a professional duty) with the separate task of acting as an adviser to the board and its individual members.

Line 9(a) and 9(b): Insert the URL for your nonprofit's website, if you have one. Any website content should be consistent with your nonprofit purposes and program as described in your 1023 application. Also, provide an email address to receive educational information from the IRS in the future. The email address is optional. If you leave out either of these items, insert "not applicable" in the blank.

Line 10: Some nonprofits using this box will be eligible for an exemption from filing IRS Form 990, the annual information return for nonprofits, or the shorter 990-EZ form for smaller groups—see "Federal Corporate Tax Returns" in Chapter 10. If you are reasonably sure you will be exempt—for example, if you are forming a church or know that you will have gross receipts of less than $25,000 per year—mark "yes" and state the reason why you are exempt on an attachment page. All other nonprofits using this book should mark "no" here. Remember, even if your nonprofit has $25,000 or less in gross receipts, it must file Form 990-N (e-Postcard) each year.

We think it is wise to file 990 returns each year, even if you and the IRS initially agree that your group should be exempt from filing the returns. Why? Because you may fail to continue to meet the requirements for the exemption from filing, and may get hit with late-filing penalties if you have to go back and file your returns for prior years that you missed. By filing a return, even if not required, you normally start the running of the time frame during which the IRS can go back and audit your nonprofit tax returns. And your filed 990 can come in handy in many states for meeting your state income tax and any state attorney general filing requirements. Groups exempt from the 990 filing requirements may still have to file a Form 990-N postcard or make the 990-N filing online from the IRS website. See Chapter 10 for the federal tax filing requirements.

Line 11: Insert the date your articles were filed by the secretary of state in mm/dd/yyyy format, such as 01/05/2011.

Line 12: We assume you will mark "no." If you are seeking an IRS 501(c)(3) tax exemption for a corporation formed abroad, mark "yes," insert the name of the country, and seek additional help from an advisor who can assist you through your more complicated tax-exemption application process.

Part II: Organizational Structure

Line 1: Most tax-exempt nonprofits are formed as nonprofit corporate entities, and we expect you to follow the standard practice of forming a corporation too. Check "yes" to indicate that your group is a corporation and attach a copy of your articles to your application. The copy should be a certified copy you received from the state filing office. It should show a file-date stamp on the first page or include a certification statement or page that states it was filed with the state and is a correct copy of the original filed document.

Line 2: We assume you will check "no" to indicate that you are not seeking a tax exemption for an LLC. Very few nonprofits are formed as limited liability companies. If this is what you are attempting to do, you should consult with an experienced lawyer.

Line 3: We assume you will check "no" here because we expect readers to form a traditional nonprofit tax-exempt corporation, not an unincorporated association. An unincorporated association requires special paperwork (association charter or articles and association operating agreement), and it leaves the members potentially personally liable for the debts of and claims made against the association. If you are applying for a tax exemption for an unincorporated association, you should check with a lawyer before applying for your tax exemption.

Line 4(a) and 4(b): Check "no" to show that you are not applying for a tax exemption for a nonprofit trust. If you are interested in establishing a tax-exempt trust, see an expert.

Line 5: Check "yes" and attach a copy of the bylaws you have prepared as part of Chapter 7. Make sure you have filled in all the blanks in your printed bylaws and include a completed Adoption of Bylaws page at the end of your bylaws. The adoption page should show the date of adoption and include the signatures of your initial directors.

Part III: Required Provisions in Your Organizing Document

Line 1: Your articles must contain a 501(c)(3) tax-exempt purpose clause (see "Federal 501(c)(3) Tax-Exempt Purpose Clause" in "Complete Your Articles" in Chapter 6). Check the box, and on the line provided insert the page, article, and paragraph where the 501(c)(3) purpose clause appears. Make sure you reference the 501(c)(3) purpose clause, not any state-required lawful purpose or specific purpose clause also included in your articles. For example, the following articles contain both a 501(c)(3) tax-exempt purpose clause and a state-required specific purpose clause:

> Article 3. The purposes for which this corporation is organized are:
>
> This corporation is organized and operated exclusively for educational purposes within the meaning of 501(c)(3) of the Internal Revenue Code.
>
> The specific purposes for which this corporation is organized are to educate the general public in dance and other art forms. The means of providing such education includes, but is not limited to, maintaining facilities for instruction and public performances of dance and other art forms.

The group would check the box in line 1, and then, in the space provided at the end of the text in line 1, insert "page 1, Article 3, paragraph 1"—because the 501(c)(3) tax-exempt purpose clause appears in the first paragraph of Article 3 on page one of the articles.

This group specified only one 501(c)(3) purpose—educational—in its 501(c)(3) exempt-purpose clause. You can choose to use a more general statement that specifies one or more or all of the allowable 501(c)(3) exempt purposes (see "Sample Completed Articles" in Chapter 6).

Line 2: Check the 2(a) box to indicate that your articles contain a 501(c)(3) asset dedication clause (we assume your articles will contain a dedication clause as explained below), and fill in the blank in 2(b) to state the page, article, and paragraph where the dissolution clause appears in your articles. Leave the box in 2(c) unchecked—it applies to groups whose articles do not contain a dissolution clause and are instead relying on specific state law provision as explained below.

A requirement for 501(c)(3) tax-exempt status is that any assets of a nonprofit that

remain after the entity dissolves be distributed to another 501(c)(3) tax-exempt nonprofit—or to a federal, state, or local government for a public purpose (see "Limitation on Profits and Benefits" in Chapter 3, and "Additional Federal Tax Exemption Language" in "Complete Your Articles" in Chapter 6). You can meet this irrevocable dedication of assets requirement by including an explicit dedication clause in your articles of incorporation or by relying on state law, if you live in a state that has adopted a 501(c)(3) default dedication clause. Some states have laws requiring all 501(c)(3)s formed in the state to dedicate their remaining assets upon dissolution to another 501(c)(3). We believe that, even if you live in a state that has a default dedication provision, you should always include an explicit dedication clause in your articles. It's best to state any major restrictions on assets and operations explicitly in your articles as a cautionary reminder to your directors, officers, members, and others. And you won't have to research your state law to find out if you have an applicable default provision, or be at risk of your state law changing or the IRS deciding that your state's dissolution clause is not sufficient to meet the 501(c)(3) dedication of assets requirement.

For example, assume a nonprofit has the following asset dedication clause on page 3 of its articles:

> **Article 8. Additional Provisions**
>
> The property of this corporation is irrevocably dedicated to _[state one or more of your actual tax-exempt purposes , such as "charitable," "religious," "educational," "literary," and/or "scientific"]_ purposes and no part of the net income or assets of this corporation shall inure to the benefit of any director, officer, or member thereof or to the benefit of any private person. Upon the dissolution or winding up of the corporation, its assets remaining after payment, or

provision for payment, of all debts and liabilities of this corporation shall be distributed to a nonprofit fund, foundation, or corporation that is organized and operated exclusively for   *[repeat the same purpose or purposes stated in the first blank]*   purposes and that has established its tax-exempt status under Section 501(c)(3) of the Internal Revenue Code.

No substantial part of the activities of this corporation shall consist of carrying on propaganda, or otherwise attempting to influence legislation (except as otherwise provided by Section 501(h) of the Internal Revenue Code), and this corporation shall not participate in, or intervene in (including the publishing or distribution of statements), any political campaign on behalf of, or in opposition to, any candidate for public office.

No part of the net earnings of this corporation shall inure to the benefit of, or be distributable to, its members, directors, officers, or other private persons, except that this corporation shall be authorized and empowered to pay reasonable compensation for services rendered and to make payments and distributions in furtherance of the purposes set forth in these articles.

Notwithstanding any other provision of these articles, this corporation shall not carry on any other activities not permitted to be carried on (1) by a corporation exempt from federal income tax under Section 501(c)(3) of the Internal Revenue Code or (2) by a corporation contributions to which are deductible under Section 170(c)(2) of the Internal Revenue Code.

It would check the box in 2(a), and insert the following on the line in 2(b): "page 3, Article 8, first paragraph." This article provision (which is taken from "Complete Your Articles," in Chapter 6, Article 8 instructions) contains additional optional 501(c)(3) compliance language that we recommend all groups include in their articles (see "Optional 501(c)(3) Tax Exemption Language" under "Complete Your Articles" in Chapter 6).

Do not check the 2(c) box. To be thorough, you can insert "Not Applicable" on the line at the end of line 2(c).

The boxes that appear in line 2 will not apply to most incorporators and should be ignored by most groups.

Part IV: Narrative Description of Your Activities

You should be familiar with the material in Chapter 3 concerning the basic requirements for obtaining a 501(c)(3) tax exemption before providing the information requested in this part of the form. We will refer to earlier explanations as we go along, but you may want to look over Chapter 3 now before you proceed.

TIP

Tell it like it is. When you describe your proposed activities, don't limit your narrative to only those activities that fit neatly within the 501(c)(3) framework if you're simply "gilding the lily" to gain IRS approval. Sure, you'll probably get your tax exemption, but you may not keep it. The IRS can always decide later, after examining your actual sources of support, that your actual activities go beyond the scope of the activities disclosed in your application. In short, it's a lot more painful and expensive to shut down your nonprofit if it loses its tax exemption rather than deciding at the outset not to apply for 501(c)(3) status because your proposed mission does not qualify for tax-exempt status.

On an attachment page, provide a detailed description of all of your organization's activities—past, present, and future—in their order of importance (that is, in order of the amount of time and resources devoted to each activity). For each activity, explain in detail:

- the activity itself, how it furthers an exempt purpose(s) of your organization, and the percentage of time your group will devote to it

- when it was begun (or, if it hasn't yet begun, when it will begin)

- where and by whom it will be conducted, and

- how it will be funded (the financial information or projections you provide later in your application should be consistent with the funding methods or mechanisms you mention here). For example, if your application shows you will be obtaining the bulk of your tax-exempt revenue from providing program-related services, such as tuition or admission fees, and/or from grant funds, you will want to mention these sources of support here (see additional instructions on describing your financial support below).

Many new groups will be describing proposed activities that are not yet operational, but you must still provide very thorough information.

If you plan to conduct any unrelated business (business that doesn't directly further your nonprofit goals), describe it here. Most nonprofits will not have planned unrelated business activities at this point. If you have, you will not want to stress the importance or scope of these incidental unrelated activities (for an explanation of the tricky issues surrounding unrelated business activities, see Chapter 3).

Tempting though it might be, resist copying the language that already appears in the purpose clause in your articles—the IRS wants a narrative, not an abbreviated, legal description of your proposed activities. You may include a reference to, or repeat the language of, the longer statement of specific objectives and purposes included in Article 2, Section 2, of your bylaws. However, unless your bylaw

language includes a detailed narrative of both your activities and purposes, we suggest you use it only as a starting point for a fuller response here. Generally, we recommend starting over with a fresh, straightforward statement of your group's nonprofit activities.

EXAMPLE 1:

A response by an environmental organization might read in part as follows:

The organization's activities will consist primarily of educating the public on environmental issues with an emphasis on energy conservation. Since January 20___, the organization has published brochures promoting solar energy heating systems as an alternative to traditional energy sources. The price for the brochures is slightly above cost—see copies of educational material enclosed, Attachments A–D. The brochures are published in-house at [*address of principal office*] . Both paid and volunteer staff contribute to the research, writing, editing, and production process. This work constitutes approximately 80% of the group's activities. In addition to publishing, the organization's other activities include the following [*list in order of importance other current, past, or planned activities and percentage of time devoted to each, where performed, etc.*].

EXAMPLE 2:

A nonprofit organization plans to sponsor activities for the purpose of supporting other nonprofit charities. It should describe both the activities in which it will engage to obtain revenue at special events and the manner in which this money will be spent to support other groups. Percentages of time and resources devoted to each should be given.

If you are forming an organization that automatically qualifies for public charity status (a church, school, hospital, or medical research organization) or has special tax-exemption requirements, you will want to show that your organization meets the criteria that apply to your type of organization. See "Automatic Public Charity Status," in Chapter 4, for a discussion of each of these special types of nonprofits. In the 1023 form, you'll find schedules and instructions that apply to each type of special group (for example, Schedule A for churches, Schedule B for schools, and Schedule C for hospitals—see the table below). If you are forming one of these special types of nonprofits, skip ahead to "Filling Out the Schedules" and look over the instructions for the schedule you need to complete. That way, you'll have a better understanding of what the IRS is looking for in your statement about your nonprofit activities.

Schedules For Special Groups

Type of Organization	See Schedule
Church	A
School, College, or University	B
Hospital and Medical Research Organization	C
Home for the Aged or Handicapped	F
Student Aid or Scholarship Benefit Organization	H

Your description should indicate your organization's anticipated sources of financial support —preferably in the order of magnitude (most money to least money). Here are a few tips to help you address this portion of your response:

- Your sources of support should be related to your exempt purposes—particularly if you plan to be classified as a public charity

under the support test described in "Exempt Activities Support Test," in Chapter 4, where the group's primary support is derived from the performance of tax-exempt activities.

- If you plan to qualify as a publicly supported public charity (described in "Public Support Test," in Chapter 4), your responses here should show significant support from various governmental grants, private agency funding, or individual contributions.

- If you expect your principal sources of support to fluctuate substantially, attach a statement describing and explaining anticipated changes—see the specific instructions to Part II, line 2, in the 1023 package.

Your description should show how you will fund your activities. For example, if you will give classes, state how you will recruit instructors and attract students. If you will rely on grants, state your likely sources of grant support—for example, the particular or general categories of grant agencies you plan to approach. If your nonprofit expects to obtain funds through grant solicitations or other fundraising efforts—that is, by soliciting contributions from donors either directly or through paid fundraising—make sure you provide a narrative description of these efforts here, and also refer to Part VIII, line 4, of your application, where you will provide additional information on your fundraising activities (see instructions to Part VIII, below).

Include as exhibits any literature you plan to distribute to solicit support and indicate that this material is attached to your application.

Fundraising activities include unrelated business activities that will bring cash into your nonprofit. If you have concrete plans to engage in unrelated activities (which, of course, you should be able to clearly describe as an insubstantial part of your overall activities), include the details if you have not done so already in your response.

If your organization has or plans to have a website, provide information on the existing site (including its URL) or the planned site. The existing or proposed website content and any revenue it generates should be related to and further the exempt purposes of the group. If your website is used to solicit contributions or generate other revenue, explain how this is or will be done.

Finally, if your group intends to operate under a fictitious business name (an "aka"—also known as—or "dba"—doing business as—name) that differs from your formal corporate name as stated in your articles (see "File Fictitious or Assumed Business Name Statement" in Chapter 9), make sure to mention the alternate name here, and state why you want to use an alternate name.

Part V: Compensation and Financial Arrangements With Your Officers, Directors, Trustees, Employees, and Independent Contractors

The IRS has expanded this part of the application to try and prevent people from creating and operating nonprofits simply to benefit one or more of the nonprofit's founders, insiders, or major contributors. We've already explained the basic 501(c)(3) prohibition against private inurement and the excess benefit rules that penalize nonprofits and their managers if they pay unreasonable compensation to insiders and outsiders (see "Limitation on Profits and Benefits" in Chapter 3). In this part of the application, the IRS tries to find out if your nonprofit runs the risk of violating any of these rules. So if you have compensation

or other financial arrangements with any of your founders, directors, officers, employees, contractors, contributors, and others, now is the time to disclose this information. It's better to find out ahead of time that the IRS objects to your proposed financial arrangements rather than pay hefty excess benefit taxes later and run the risk of losing your tax exemption.

Line 1(a): Provide the names, titles, mailing addresses, and proposed compensation of the initial directors named in your articles and your initial officers. You can ignore the instructions concerning trustees—your directors are the trustees of your nonprofit corporation. List your initial directors and your top-tier officer team, if you know who will fill these officer positions (such as President or Chief Executive Officer, Vice President, Secretary, and Treasurer or Chief Financial Officer, or any other title used in your organization). For director or officer mailing addresses, you can state the mailing address of the corporation.

At this stage in the organization of your nonprofit, you may not be absolutely certain what you will pay your initial directors and officers. However, if you have a good ballpark estimate or a maximum amount in mind, it's better to state it in your response instead of "unknown" or "not yet decided." In the sample bylaws included in this book, we say that directors will not be paid a salary but may be paid a per-meeting fee and reimbursed expenses (see Article 3, Section 6). Therefore, you may wish to respond along the following lines:

"Pursuant to Article 3, Section 6, of the corporation's bylaws, directors will not be paid a salary. They may be paid a reasonable fee for attending meetings of the board [you may mention a specific amount or a range if you have decided on a per diem fee] and may be allowed reasonable reimbursement or advancement for expenses incurred in the performance of their duties." This response will not fit in the "Compensation amount" column, so you'll need to prepare your response as an attachment if you use this wording.

If you have decided on officers' salaries or a range or maximum compensation level for officers, you can state it in your response. If you are not sure who your board will appoint as initial officers and do not know the compensation level for your officers, you may wish to respond as follows: "The persons who will serve as officers and the compensation they will receive, if any, have not yet been determined by the board of directors. Any such compensation will be reasonable and will be paid in return for the performance of services related to the tax-exempt purposes of the corporation." This response will not easily fit in the space provided for your 1(a) response, so you'll probably need to prepare your response as an attachment if you use this wording.

If you have decided who will be elected to serve as officers, provide the details of these officer arrangements, including the amount of any salaries to be paid.

Line 1(b): In this section, state the names, titles, mailing addresses, and compensation for your five top-paid employees who will earn more than $50,000 per year. You should include employer contributions made to employee benefit plans, 401(k)s, IRAs, expected bonus payments, and the like in computing the amount of compensation paid to your employees. You should list only employees who are not officers (all officer salaries should be reported in line 1(a) of this Part). It's best to anticipate who will be paid more than $50,000 by providing estimated compensation figures rather than leaving this information blank. However, if you really don't know yet which officers you will pay or how much you will pay them, you can respond as follows: "This

corporation is newly formed and has not yet hired employees nor determined the amount of compensation to pay employees it may hire. However, all compensation will be reasonable and will be paid to employees in return for furthering the exempt purposes of this nonprofit corporation."

There is nothing special or suspect about paying an employee more than $50,000. In fact, compensation paid to employees who make less than $80,000 (a figure that is adjusted for cost of living increases) normally is not subject to scrutiny under the excess benefit rules. (See "Limitation on Profits and Benefits," in Chapter 3, for more on the excess benefit rules. If you are interested in the $80,000 category and how it fits within the excess benefit rules, see IRS Regulation 53.4985-3(d)(3)(i) and IRC Section 414(q)(1)(B)(i).) For this line item, the IRS wants to see exactly how much your top five highest-paid employees are getting paid if they make more than $50,000. Ignoring all the fine print of the excess benefit rules and regulations, just remember that the salary and other benefits you pay each employee should be no more than what a comparably paid person in a similar position in a similar organization would receive. With nonprofit symphony orchestra leaders getting paid millions in annual salaries, it is questionable that using a comparability standard always produces the best or even reasonable results. And we're sure that readers of this book, who work long, hard hours getting paid less than they should in pursuit of their public purposes, should have little to worry about when it comes to the question of receiving unreasonably large salaries or other excess benefits from their nonprofit.

Line 1(c): Indicate the names of individuals (or names of businesses), titles (if individual), mailing addresses, and compensation for your five top paid independent contractors who will earn more than $50,000 per year. Independent contractors are people and companies who provide nonemployee services to the nonprofit, such as a paid lawyer, accountant, outside bookkeeper, financial consultant, fundraiser, and other outside individuals and companies hired by the nonprofit who are not on the nonprofit's employee payroll. Typically, your nonprofit will have a separate contract for services with its independent contractors— particularly if it will pay them more than $50,000 per year. If your newly formed nonprofit has plans to contract more than $50,000 with one or more outside individuals or companies, list them here and provide the expected amount of business you plan to do with each contractor annually. If, as is typical, your newly formed nonprofit does not have plans to contract for outside services, you can respond (in the blanks or on an attachment) as follows: "This newly formed nonprofit corporation has no current plans to contract for services with outside persons or companies. If and when it does, any such contracts will provide for payment in commercially reasonable amounts in return for services related to the exempt functions of this nonprofit."

Lines 2(a)–9(a): The remaining questions in this Part V seek to determine if your nonprofit may run afoul of the excess benefit restrictions that apply to 501(c)(3) public charities—the type of nonprofit you are trying to establish. The excess benefit rules apply to "disqualified persons," as defined under the Internal Revenue Code, Section 4958. For these purposes, a disqualified person means anyone who exercises substantial influence over the nonprofit, such as founders, directors, officers, and substantial contributors. People who fall within the definition of disqualified persons are not prohibited from being paid by your nonprofit. Instead, their salaries and benefits are subject to scrutiny

under the excess benefit rules. If the IRS finds that a disqualified person was overpaid—that is, the person received a salary, bonus, or benefits that exceeded the fair market value of the services provided or was excessive compared to amounts paid to similar people in other nonprofits—the disqualified person and the nonprofit and its managers can be subject to sanctions. The sanctions include being required to pay back previously paid salaries and stiff penalty taxes. (For more information on disqualified persons and the excess benefit rules, see "Limitation on Profits and Benefits" in Chapter 3).

The IRS will review your answers in this section to see if there is any indication that an intentional or incidental purpose of your nonprofit is to financially benefit the private interests of any board members, officers, employees, or contractors. If the IRS determines that you are using nonprofit funds to excessively compensate any of these people, it will deny your tax exemption.

If you answer "yes" to any of the remaining items in Part V, make sure to explain your response. Provide any additional information needed to show why you marked "yes" on an attachment page.

TIP

There are numerous definitions of "disqualified persons" in the Internal Revenue Code. Don't get confused or concerned if you run up against different definitions of "disqualified persons" that apply to nonprofits. For example, a different definition of disqualified person (under IRC § 4946) is used to determine permitted sources of public support for 501(c)(3) public charity support tests and when applying the excise tax restrictions that apply to private foundations (see Chapter 4 and "Who Are Disqualified Persons?" in Chapter 8).

Line 2(a): Check "yes" if any of your directors or officers are related to each other or have a business relationship with one another. A family relationship includes an individual's spouse, ancestors, children, brothers, and sisters (see the instructions to Form 1023 for a description of family and business relationships that must be disclosed). If you check "yes," provide a list of names and a description of the family or business relationship between the individuals on an attachment page.

Line 2(b): Check "yes" if your organization ("you" means your nonprofit) has an outside business relationship with its directors or officers (see the Form 1023 instructions for the types of business relationships that must be disclosed). Again, these relationships will not be an absolute bar to your obtaining a tax exemption, but the IRS will scrutinize payments made to these "related" parties to make sure they are being fairly, not excessively, compensated by your nonprofit (either through salaries and benefits or through separate business contracts with your nonprofit). Of course, it looks best if your board and officers do not have an outside business relationship with your nonprofit—and we expect, even just for appearances' sake, that most smaller nonprofits will not appoint board members or officers with whom the nonprofit plans to do outside business. If you check "yes," disclose the names of the individuals and their business relationships with your nonprofit on an attachment page.

Line 2(c): This item asks if any of your directors or officers are related to the people listed in 1(b) or 1(c)—that is, related to your highest-paid employees or independent contractors who make more than $50,000. If you answer "yes," specify the names of the directors and officers and their relationship to the highest-paid people. Again, it looks best if your board and officers are not related

to your more highly compensated employees or contractors. But in the real world of small nonprofits, it may be impossible to start your nonprofit without getting Uncle Bill or Aunt Sally to provide their expertise by volunteering as an unpaid board member. As long as you disclose these arrangements and make sure to fairly pay—and not overpay—anyone, the IRS should conclude that your nonprofit is on the up-and-up and is entitled to its exemption if it meets all the substantive requirements.

Line 3(a): This item requests very important information (on an attachment page), which the IRS uses to determine if your nonprofit will pay excessive benefits to any insider or outsider. Specifically, it asks you to list the qualifications, average hours worked (or to be worked), and duties of your directors and officers listed in 1(a) and highly compensated employees and contractors (listed in 1(b) and 1(c), respectively). Your responses here should justify any high salaries, benefits, or per diem amounts paid to your officers or directors. For example, if you plan to pay officers a significant salary that may raise IRS examiner eyebrows, make sure to list the extra qualifications and experience of the highly compensated officer. Don't hold back or be shy in touting the credentials (academic degrees, teaching positions, awards), experience (past associations as advisors or directors with other nonprofits), and other qualifications or community affiliations of your well-paid people. The IRS really wants to know why you pay people well (if, in fact, you are lucky enough to pay or plan to pay your officers and other employees a competitive wage, salary, or benefits). On the flip side, obviously, if you pay your part-time administrative aid, who just happens to be your cousin Joe, a lavish hourly wage plus full benefits, expect the IRS to balk. Unless Joe has special skills that are in high demand by other organizations and companies, the IRS will question this special arrangement.

Line 3(b): If any of the directors, officers, and highly paid people listed in 1(a) through 1(c) get paid by another organization or company that has "common control" with your nonprofit, you will need to mark "yes" on this item and provide an explanation on an attachment page. As the instructions to Form 1023 explain, organizations with common control include those that have their boards or officers appointed or elected by the same parent or overseeing organization. In addition, if a majority of your board and/or officers and a majority of the board and/or officers of another organization consist of the same individuals, then you share common control. If common control between your nonprofit and another organization exists, expect the IRS to attribute the total compensation paid by both commonly controlled organizations to your board and officers, and also expect the IRS to judge the purposes and activities of your nonprofit in light of the control exercised or shared by the other organization. For example, if a majority of your officers are officers of another nonprofit, the IRS will want to know whether your nonprofit exists to serve the purposes or foster the activities of the related nonprofit. This may be fine if the other nonprofit is, itself, a 501(c)(3) tax-exempt nonprofit. But if it isn't, the common control aspect probably will adversely affect your ability to obtain your tax exemption—your nonprofit can't be formed to promote nonexempt purposes.

Line 4(a)–4(g): This item asks whether your group has established the procedures and practices recommended under the safe harbor rules of the excess benefit provisions and regulations (see "Limitation on Profits and Benefits," in Chapter 3, for a brief summary of the safe harbor rules). These procedures are meant to minimize the risk that nonprofits will pay out excess benefits. You don't have to adopt and follow them, but you should if you want the IRS to look kindly on your tax exemption.

If you adopt the standard bylaws contained in this book, you can mark "yes" to each question and provide the responses to each item shown below on an attachment page. The IRS instructions to this line do not ask for more information if you answer "yes" to an item, but we think you should offer more, stating in your response where the IRS can look in your bylaws to verify that you have adopted each practice (as explained for each item, below).

Line 4(a): Check "yes" and state on an attachment page: "This organization has adopted a conflict of interest policy that controls the approval of salaries to directors, officers, and other 'disqualified persons' as defined in Section 4958 of the Internal Revenue Code. See Article 9, as well as Article 3, Section 6, and Article 4, Section 10, of the bylaws attached to this application. Also, Article 9, Section 5, of this organization's bylaws applies additional conflict of interest requirements on the board and compensation committee when approving compensation arrangements."

Line 4(b): Check "yes" and state on an attachment page: "Article 9, Section 3, of this organization's bylaws requires the approval of compensation of directors, officers, and any 'disqualified person' as defined in Section 4958 of the Internal Revenue Code in advance after full disclosure of the surrounding facts and approval by disinterested members of the governing board or committee and prior to entering into the compensation agreement or arrangement. Further, Article 9, Section 5(a), of this organization's bylaws requires specific approval of compensation arrangements prior to the first payment of compensation under such arrangements."

Line 4(c): Check "yes" and state on an attachment page: "Article 9, Section 4, of the organization's bylaws, which are attached to this application, require the taking of written minutes of meetings at which compensation paid to any director, officer, or other 'disqualified person' as defined in Section 4958 of the Internal Revenue Code, are approved. The minutes must include the date and the terms of the approved compensation arrangements. Further, and specifically with respect to the approval by the board or compensation committee of compensation arrangements, Article 9, Section 5(d), of the organization's bylaws requires the recordation of the date and terms of compensation arrangements as well as other specific information concerning the basis for the approval of compensation arrangements."

Line 4(d): Check "yes" and state on an attachment page: "Article 9, Section 4, of the organization's bylaws requires the written recordation of the approval of compensation and other financial arrangements between this organization and a director, officer, employee, contractor, and any other 'disqualified person' as defined in Section 4958 of the Internal Revenue Code, including the names of the persons who vote on the arrangement and their votes. Further, and specifically with respect to the approval by the board or compensation committee of compensation arrangements, Article 9, Section 5(d), of the organization's bylaws requires the recordation of the board or committee who were present during discussion of the approval of compensation arrangements, those who voted on it, and the votes cast by each board or committee member."

Line 4(e): Check "yes" and state on an attachment page: "Article 9, Section 5(c), of the organization's bylaws requires that the board or compensation committee considering the approval of a compensation arrangement obtain compensation levels paid by similarly situated organizations, both taxable and tax-exempt, for functionally comparable positions; the availability of similar services in the geographic area of this organization; current compensation surveys compiled by independent firms; and actual written offers from similar institutions competing for the services of the person who is the subject of the compensation arrangement. This article also provides that it is sufficient for these purposes to rely on compensation data obtained from three comparable organizations in the same or similar communities for similar services if this organization's three-years' average gross receipts are less than $1 million (as allowed by IRS Regulation 53.4958-6)."

Line 4(f): Check "yes" and state on an attachment page: "Article 9, Section 5(d), of the organization's bylaws requires that the written minutes of the board or compensation committee meeting at which a compensation arrangement was discussed and approved include the terms of compensation and the basis for its approval. This bylaw provision includes a list of specific information that must be included in the required written minutes."

If you haven't adopted the bylaws included with this book or have deleted or changed the provisions in Article 9 of the bylaws, you may need to mark "no" to one or more of the items in line 4. And whether you mark "yes" or "no," you will need to provide responses on an attachment page that explains your particular conflicts of interest and compensation approval standards and procedures. Your responses should be sufficient to convince the IRS that your directors, officers, employees, and contractors will be paid fairly for work done to further your organization's exempt purposes and that disinterested directors or compensation committee members—for example, nonpaid directors or committee members who are not related to anyone paid by your organization—set the salaries and other compensation of your officers, employees, and contractors.

Line 5(a)–5(c): Mark "yes" if you have adopted the bylaws included with this book. State on the attachment page for this item: "The board of directors of this organization has adopted bylaws that contain a conflicts of interest policy. The policy is set out in Article 9 of the attached bylaws. This policy is based on the sample conflict of interest policy contained in Appendix A of the official instructions to IRS Form 1023. The organization has added additional requirements in Article 9, Section 5, of its bylaws for the approval of compensation arrangements that are based on the additional requirements contained in IRS Regulation Section 53.4958-6 to help ensure that all compensation arrangements are made by disinterested members of the organization's board or a duly constituted compensation committee of the board and are fair, reasonable, and in furtherance of the tax-exempt purposes of this organization."

If you mark "yes" to 5(a), you can skip 5(b) and 5(c). If you marked "no" to 5(a) because you did not adopt the bylaws included with this book or changed them to adopt a different conflict of interest policy, include responses to questions 5(a) and 5(b) on an attachment page. Your responses should show that you will follow your own practices to make sure that your directors, officers, employees, and others who exert significant influence over your nonprofit cannot feather their own nests by setting their own salary levels and making their own self-serving business deals with your nonprofit.

Line 6(a)–6(b): The IRS instructions to Form 1023 explain what the terms "fixed payment" and "non-fixed payment" mean. Essentially, question 6(a) asks if your organization will pay its directors, officers, highly paid employees, or highly paid contractors (those listed in this part, lines 1(a) through 1(c)) any discretionary amounts (such as bonuses) or amounts based on your organization's revenues (such as a salary kicker or bonus computed as a percentage of annual contributions received by your nonprofit). Question 6(b) asks this same question with respect to all the other employees of your nonprofit who receive compensation of more than $50,000 per year. Obviously, it looks best if your nonprofit's principals and employees do not receive these types of revenue-driven incentives, which are more typical in a business, not a nonprofit, setting. We assume most small nonprofits will be able to answer "no" to this question. If, however, you have an overriding need to pay directors, officers, and employees discretionary bonuses or provide them with revenue- or performance-based compensation or commissions, you need to provide the information requested on an attachment page. Your response should show that these nonfixed payments will be fairly and reasonably paid as incentives to promote the nonprofit purposes of your organization (this may not be easy to show), and that it won't be used simply to pay out revenues to your principals. Remember—private inurement is a nonprofit no-no—so siphoning over revenue to nonprofit principals is not allowed, even in the guise of bonus or performance-based employee incentives.

Line 7(a)–7(b): Question 7(a) asks if your organization will purchase goods, services, or assets from its directors, officers, highly paid employees, or highly paid contractors (those listed in this Part V, lines 1(a)–1(c)). Question 7(b) asks if your organization will sell goods, services, or assets to these people.

Most nonprofits will be able to answer "no" to both these questions because they will want to stay clear of insider sales and purchase transactions, simply to avoid the appearance (if not the actuality) of self-dealing. That said, it's also a fact of life that some smaller nonprofits have to look to their directors, officers, and principal employees or contractors to buy or sell goods or services—these may be the only people willing to do business with the nonprofit at the start of its operations. Even more typically, a small nonprofit may want to buy goods at a special discount offered by a director or officer. If you answer "yes" to one of these questions, provide the requested information in your response on an attachment page. Your response should make clear that any such purchases or sales will be at arm's length—that is, your nonprofit will pay no more and sell at no less than the commercially competitive, fair market value price for the goods, services, or assets. If you plan to buy goods, services, or assets at a discount from a director, officer, employee, or contractor, make sure to say so, since this sort of bargain purchase is better than an arm's-length deal from the perspective of the nonprofit.

The official instructions to Form 1023, line 7(a) and 7(b), indicate that you can ignore purchases and sales of goods and services in the normal course of operations that are available to the general public under similar terms or conditions. In other words, if you buy normal inventory items from a contractor listed in Part V, line 1(c), at standard terms paid by the general public for these inventory items, you do not have to mark "yes" to 7(a). Frankly, if your organization plans to purchase any type of goods or services from a director, officer, or employee, we think it should be disclosed in your application, since deals of this sort may have the appearance of a self-dealing transaction. In such a case, you can check "yes" to line 7(a), then make it clear in your response that your organization will pay the same price

for the inventory or other standard items purchased from a director, officer, or employee as the price paid by the general public (the current commercially competitive fair market value price).

If you answer "yes" to either question and have adopted the bylaws included with this book, you can add in your response that "Article 9, Section 3, of the organization's bylaws requires the approval of conflict-of-interest transactions or arrangements, such as the purchase or sale of goods, services, or assets between the organization and one of its directors, officers, or any other 'disqualified person' as defined in Section 4958(f)(1) of the Internal Revenue Code and as amplified by Section 53.4958-3 of the IRS Regulations, by the vote of a majority of disinterested directors or members of a board committee, only after a finding that a more advantageous transaction or arrangement is not available to the organization and that the proposed transaction or arrangement is in the organization's best interest, is for its own benefit, and is fair and reasonable."

Line 8(a)–8(f): Question 8(a) asks if your organization will enter into leases, contracts, or other agreements with its directors, officers, highly paid employees, or highly paid contractors (those listed in this part, lines 1(a) through (c)). If you answer "yes," you must supply responses to items 8(b) through 8(f) on an attachment page.

To rephrase an observation made in the instructions to line 7, above, to avoid the appearance if not the actuality of self-dealing, it's best not to deal with nonprofit insiders when leasing property or contracting for goods, services, or making other business arrangements. Most nonprofits will shy away from doing this, and will answer "no" to 8(a).

However, newly formed nonprofits sometimes find it most practical (and economical) to lease or rent property owned by a founder, director, or officer, or may otherwise have to enter into a contract or arrangement with one of these people. There is nothing absolutely forbidden about doing so, but you will want to make sure that any lease, contract, or agreement between your nonprofit and one of these people reflects fair market value terms or better. For example, it looks best if a director leases property owned by the director to the nonprofit at a lower-than-market value rate (best of all, of course, is when the director lets the nonprofit use the lease premises rent free).

If you answer "yes" to 8(a), provide the information requested in 8(b) through 8(f) on an attachment page. If possible, attach a copy of any lease, rental, or other agreement as requested in 8(f). For a discussion of leases together with a sample assignment of lease, see "Prepare Assignments of Leases and Deeds" in Chapter 9. Also, if you have adopted the bylaws included with this book, you can add in your response to item 8(d) or 8(e) that "Article 9, Section 3, of the organization's bylaws requires the approval of conflict-of-interest transactions or arrangements, such as a lease, contract, or other agreement between this organization and any of its directors, officers, or any other 'disqualified person' as defined in Section 4958(f)(1) of the Internal Revenue Code and as amplified by Section 53.4958-3 of the IRS Regulations, by the vote of a majority of disinterested directors or members of a board committee, only after a finding that a more advantageous transaction or arrangement is not available to the organization and that the proposed transaction or arrangement is in the organization's best interest, is for its own benefit, and is fair and reasonable."

Line 9(a)–9(f): These questions are similar to those in 8(a) through 8(f) above, except they apply to leases, contracts, and agreements between your nonprofit and another business or organization associated with or controlled by your directors or officers. Specifically, these questions apply to business deals between your nonprofit and another company or organization in which one or more of your directors or officers also serves as a director or officer or one of your directors or officers owns a 35% or greater interest (for example, a 35% voting stock ownership interest in a profit-making corporation). You can ignore deals made between your corporation and another 501(c)(3) tax-exempt nonprofit organization, even if one or more of your directors or officers also serves on the board or as an officer of the other 501(c)(3) tax-exempt nonprofit organization.

EXAMPLE 1:

If one of your directors also serves as a board member on a nonprofit cooperative that is not tax exempt under 501(c)(3) and your nonprofit enters in leases, contracts, or other agreements with the other nonprofit, answer "yes" to 9(a) and provide the information requested in items 9(b) through 9(f).

EXAMPLE 2:

If one of your officers owns a 35% or greater stock interest in a business corporation, and your nonprofit buys goods and services from the business corporation (either through a formal contract or a verbal agreement), answer "yes" to 9(a) and provide the information requested in items 9(b) through 9(f).

The discussion in line 8, above, about leases and agreements between your nonprofit and individuals applies here to leases and agreements between your nonprofit and affiliated or controlled companies and organizations. If you answer "yes," provide the information requested in items 9(b) through 9(f). Also, if you have adopted the bylaws included with this book, you can add in your response to item 9(d) or 9(e) that "Article 9, Section 3, of the organization's bylaws requires the approval of conflict-of-interest transactions or arrangements, such as a lease, contract, or other agreement between this organization and any 'disqualified person' as defined in Section 4958(f)(1) of the Internal Revenue Code and as amplified by Section 53.4958-3 of the IRS Regulations, which includes 35% controlled entities, by the vote of a majority of disinterested directors or members of a board committee, only after a finding that a more advantageous transaction or arrangement is not available to the organization and that the proposed transaction or arrangement is in the organization's best interest, is for its own benefit, and is fair and reasonable."

Part VI: Your Members and Other Individuals and Organizations That Receive Benefits From You

Line 1(a): If you plan to implement programs that provide goods, services, or funds to individuals, check "yes" and describe these programs on an attachment page. Many smaller nonprofits will provide goods or services as part of their exempt-purpose activities, such as a nonprofit dance studio (dance lessons or admissions to dance performances), formal and informal nonprofit schools (tuition or fees for classes and instructional services), hospitals (health care costs), and other educational or charitable groups. Of course, charitable-purpose groups often provide goods or services free to the public or at lower than market-rate cost—such as free or low-cost meals, shelter, and clothing. But educational-purpose groups often charge standard or slightly reduced rates for admissions, tuition, and services. Doing the latter is permissible. What the IRS wants to see

is that your nonprofit is set up to provide goods and services as part of a valid nonprofit tax-exempt program, and that all members of the public—or at least a segment of the public that is not limited to particular individuals—will have access to your goods or services. What you can't do is set up a tax-exempt nonprofit that intends to benefit a private class or specific group of individuals, as individuals (such as your uncle Bob and Aunt Betty, or all your relatives and in-laws). The broader the class of people that your nonprofit benefits, the better. Making your nonprofit programs available to the public-at-large normally looks best to the IRS. And providing goods and services at rates below market rates also helps bolster your credibility as a nonprofit, as opposed to revenue-driven, organization.

At this point in the process, most groups have not fully determined what they will charge for goods and services. If this is the case, describe in your response the services and benefits that will be provided to the public (or a segment of the public) and explain generally how you will determine fees. For example, you may wish to indicate that "charges for the described benefits, products, and services are at present undetermined, but will be reasonable and related to the cost of the service to be provided." And again, if you plan to provide goods or services at a discount or free of charge, make sure you say so.

Line 1(b): If your nonprofit will provide goods or services to other organizations, check "yes" and describe your program plans on an attachment page. If you donate or sell goods and services to another 501(c)(3) tax-exempt nonprofit at fair or discounted rates for use in their tax-exempt programs, your program should pass muster with the IRS. But if you simply plan to obtain revenue by selling goods and services provided to profit-making businesses, expect to have to justify this sort of commercial-looking activity. For example, an educational group may provide seminars to the human resource managers of business corporations on how to comply with federal and state fair employment regulations. This sort of program that serves the needs of employees should be fine with the IRS. But simply trafficking in goods and services for a profit with other organizations and companies will look like (and probably is in fact) a commercially-driven, profit-making enterprise that won't qualify as a tax-exempt activity.

Indicate whether you are a membership organization. If you have included membership provisions in your bylaws or you have used the tear-out or CD-ROM membership provisions, as explained in Chapter 7, you should check "yes" and answer the questions in lines 11(a), (b), and (c). If you have not formed a formal membership organization, check "no" and go on to line 12.

Line 2: Most groups will answer "no" to this question because the IRS frowns on groups that limit benefits, services, or funds to a specific individual or group of individuals. However, if the group of people benefited by the nonprofit is broad (not limited to specific individuals) and related to the exempt purposes of the nonprofit group, the IRS should have no objection (see the discussion to line 1(a) of this part, above). If you answer "yes," provide an explanation on an attachment page. You may be able to refer to information already provided in your response to line 1(a) of this part.

EXAMPLE:

A nonprofit musical heritage organization plans to provide programs and benefits to needy musicians residing in the community. If the overall tax-exempt purpose of the organization is allowed, the IRS will permit

this limitation of benefits to a segment of the community.

Line 3: In this question, the IRS is looking for prohibited self-inurement—in this case, whether your nonprofit is set up primarily or directly to provide goods, services, or funds to individuals who have a family or business relationship with your directors, officers, or highest-paid employees or contractors listed in Part V, lines 1(a) through 1(c). Most groups will answer "no" here. However, if you think someone who fits in one of these categories may receive goods, products, or services incidentally from your nonprofit as a member of the public, check "yes" and explain how these related people will have access to your nonprofit's benefits. If your response makes it clear that these related people are not the focus of your nonprofit programs, but as members of the general public only coincidentally qualify, you should be okay.

Part VII: Your History

Line 1: Most groups will answer "no" to this question. However, if you are a successor to an incorporated or preexisting organization (such as an unincorporated association), mark "yes."

Successor has a special technical meaning, which is explained in the official IRS instructions to this item. Basically, you are most likely to be a successor organization if your nonprofit corporation has:

- taken over the activities of a prior organization—this is presumably the case if your nonprofit corporation has appointed initial directors or officers who are the same people who served as the directors or officers of the prior association, and your nonprofit has the same purposes as the prior association

- taken over 25% or more of the assets of a preexisting nonprofit, or

• been legally converted from the previous association to a nonprofit—typically by filing special articles of incorporation to state the name of the prior association and a declaration by the prior officers of the association that the conversion to a nonprofit corporation was properly approved by the association, or by filing articles of conversion to convert a profit-making entity to your new nonprofit corporation.

We assume most readers will be starting new nonprofits, not inheriting the assets, people, and activities of a preexisting formal nonprofit association. We also assume most readers have not adopted special articles to legally convert a prior association or profit-making entity to a nonprofit corporation. In the real world, this formal conversion of a prior association to a nonprofit corporation only occurs if the prior group was a highly organized and visible entity with a solid support base that it wants to leverage by formally converting the association to a nonprofit corporation. However, in most cases, a small nonprofit that existed previously as an informal nonprofit group with few assets, little support, and hardly any formal infrastructure normally starts out fresh with a newly formed corporation that is not a successor to the prior group. If you think your nonprofit corporation is a "successor" organization, we suggest you get help from a nonprofit expert to complete Schedule G and make sure all the paperwork for your new nonprofit as well as the prior group is in order.

If you are a successor to a prior organization, mark "yes," and complete Schedule G of the 1023 application. (See "Filling Out the Schedules," below, for instructions on filling out Schedule G.) The IRS will take the history, activities, and financial data of your prior organization as well as your responses to Schedule G into account when deciding whether your nonprofit corporation is entitled to its tax exemption. It may also ask you to file tax returns for the prior organization if it has not already done so for all preceding tax years during which the prior nonexempt organization was in operation.

Line 2: Most new groups will be able to answer "no" here because they will be submitting their exemption application within 27 months after the end of month when their nonprofit corporation was formed. The date of formation is the date the corporation's articles of incorporation were filed by the secretary of state and became effective. For example, if you filed your articles on January 12, 2010 you have until the end of April 2012 to submit (postmark) your exemption application.

If you are submitting your exemption application after this 27-month deadline, check "yes" and fill in and submit Schedule E with your 1023 exemption application. (See "Filling Out the Schedules," below, for instructions on completing Schedule E.)

Part VIII: Your Specific Activities

This part asks about certain types of activities, such as political activity and fundraising, that the IRS looks at more closely. These are activities that a 501(c)(3) is prohibited from engaging in or can do only within certain strict limitations—namely, without benefiting or catering to the special interests of particular individuals or organizations. Please read the official instructions to this Part in the 1023 instructions before reading our instructions below.

Line 1: A 501(c)(3) nonprofit organization may not participate in political campaigns (although some voter education drives and political debate activities are permitted—

see "Limitation on Political Activities" in Chapter 3). The IRS may deny or revoke your tax-exempt status if you participate in or donate to a campaign. Most groups should answer "no" here.

If you think you should answer "yes" to this question, check with a nonprofit lawyer or tax consultant—a "yes" response means you do not qualify for a 501(c)(3) tax exemption. However, you may qualify for a 501(c)(4) tax exemption.

Line 2(a): This question concerns your group's plans, if any, to affect legislation. Most groups will answer "no" to this question. If you answer "no," you can move on to line 3.

If you plan to engage in efforts to influence legislation, check "yes" and read the discussion in "Limitation on Political Activities," in Chapter 3. Then complete 2(b).

Line 2(b): Check "yes" if you plan to elect to fall under the alternate political expenditures test discussed in "Limitation on Political Activities," in Chapter 3, and attach a completed IRS Form 5768, *Election/Revocation of Election by an Eligible Section 501(c)(3) Organization To Make Expenditures To Influence Legislation.* We assume you have not already filed this form; if you have, attach a copy of the filed form. A copy of this simple, one-page consent form is included on the CD-ROM provided with this book. The political expenditures test is complicated, and you'll probably need the help of a seasoned nonprofit advisor to decide whether you will be able to meet the requirements and gain a benefit from electing this special test for political legislative activities. Before using the Form 5768 included on the CD-ROM, go to the IRS website, at www.irs.gov, and make sure it is the latest version of the form. If the IRS site has a more current version, use the website's form, not the form included on the CD-ROM.

If you checked "yes" to line 2(a) and do not plan to elect the political expenditures test,

check "no" to line 2(b). On an attachment, you must describe the extent and percentage of time and money you expect to devote to your legislative activities compared to your total activities. Be as specific as you can about the political activities you expect to promote and how you will promote them. If possible (and accurate), make it clear that your legislative activities will make up an "insubstantial" part of your overall nonprofit programs and activities. If the IRS feels that your political program will be substantial, it will deny your 501(c)(3) tax exemption.

Line 3(a)–3(c): Most 501(c)(3) nonprofits do not engage in bingo and gaming activities. If you plan to do so, read the IRS official instruction for this line as well as IRS Publication 3079, *Gaming Publication for Tax-Exempt Organizations,* before checking "yes" to any of the questions in line 3 and providing the requested information.

Line 4(a): Read the official instructions to this line to learn the definition of fundraising and some of the different ways it may be conducted. Note that fundraising includes raising funds for your own organization, raising funds for other organizations, as well as having some other individual or organization raise funds for your group. If your nonprofit is one that will be obtaining revenue and operating funds only from the performance of its exempt functions— that is by providing services or goods related to your exempt purpose—you can check "no" here. Make sure that none of the specific fundraising activity boxes listed in 4(a) apply to your group. However, if you expect your nonprofit to do any type of fundraising, such as soliciting government grants, attracting private and public donations or contributions, or going whole hog and hiring a professional fundraiser, check "yes" and then check each box that describes a fundraising activity that you plan to or may pursue in your quest for program funds and revenue. On an attachment page, describe each activity whose box you have checked. If your nonprofit plans to engage in a type of fundraising not listed under 4(a), check the "other" box and describe it in your attachment response. Be as specific and as thorough as you can in your response about the people you will use, any compensation you will pay, the amount and type of support you hope to raise, and the use to which you will put raised funds for each fundraising activity. If you check "no" to 4(a), you can skip ahead to line 5.

Line 4(b): Mark "yes" if you plan to hire paid fundraisers, and provide the financial and contract information requested on an attachment page. Any financial information should be actual or projected figures that cover the same periods as the financial information you will provide in Part IX (see the official 1023 Part IX instructions and our Part IX instructions, below, to determine the period for which you should provide financial information). Many beginning nonprofits will not plan to use paid fundraisers right away and can state: "This newly formed nonprofit has not entered into oral or written contracts with individuals or organizations for the raising of funds, and has no specific plans to do so in the foreseeable future."

Line 4(c): If your nonprofit will do fundraising for other organizations, state "yes" and provide the information requested on an attachment page. Most nonprofit organizers using this book will not raise funds for other organizations even if they plan to raise funds for themselves and will mark "no" here.

Line 4(d): If you checked "yes" to 4(a), provide the information requested for this item. You should provide this information for states or localities where you will raise funds for your organization or for other organizations, or

where an individual or another organization, including a paid fundraiser, will raise funds for your organization.

Line 4(e): See the official instructions for this item—it concerns the special practice of soliciting and using "donor-advised" or "donor-directed" funds. Most nonprofits will not have plans to use this practice, but if you do, provide the information requested on an attachment page. The IRS will want to make sure that your organization does not use funds to meet the private needs of donors, but instead will use donor-directed funds for purposes that are consistent with the tax-exempt purposes of the nonprofit.

Here is a statement from the 2005 IRS Exempt Organization (EO) Report that explains why the IRS is concerned about donor-advised funds, and indicates that it will be keeping an eye out for abuse in this area:

> Donor-advised funds allow private donors to provide input as to how their charitable contributions will be spent. A number of organizations have come to light through examinations, referrals from other parts of the IRS, and public scrutiny which appear to have abused the basic concepts underlying donor-advised funds. These organizations, while promoted as legitimate donor-advised funds, appear to be established for the purpose of generating questionable charitable deductions, providing impermissible economic benefits to the donors and their families (including tax-sheltered investment income for the donors), and providing management fees for the promoters. EO Examinations will identify organizations with a high potential for abuse in this area and commence examinations during FY 2005.

Line 5: This item is for special government-affiliated groups (see the instructions to the 1023 form). If you check "yes," your nonprofit needs special assistance responding to this item and being able to meet the requirements for a 501(c)(3) tax exemption. If you check "yes," consult a nonprofit legal adviser.

Line 6: See the 1023 instructions. If you are an economic development nonprofit and mark "yes," you'll need expert help filling out your tax exemption to make sure your activities meet the 501(c)(3) requirements.

Below is a statement from the 2005 IRS Exempt Organization (EO) Report that explains why the IRS is applying special scrutiny to economic development nonprofits:

> In response to referrals from HUD concerning abuse by individuals setting up exempt organizations for the purpose of participating in a number of HUD programs, EO initiated a compliance project in this area in FY 2004. Potential abuses include lack of charitable activity, personal use of program property, and most often, private benefit provided to for-profit construction contractors hired to complete the repairs to program properties. In these cases, contractors were usually related to the organizations' officers or board members, and were often the same individuals. Costs were overstated and work was substandard or completely lacking. The project is currently focusing on abuses by exempt organizations in HUD's housing rehabilitation/resale and down payment assistance programs, and will expand to other HUD programs as staffing permits.

Line 7(a): Line 7 applies to nonprofits that will own or develop real estate, such as land or a building, in pursuit of its nonprofit activities. See the 1023 instructions for line 7(a) through 7(c) for more information. If you plan to develop or improve real estate, including land or buildings, mark "yes" to 7(a) and provide the information requested on an attachment page. Mostly the IRS wants to make sure that your nonprofit is not planning to make any "sweetheart" real estate development deals that benefit people associated with your nonprofit and its directors and officers through family or business ties.

Line 7(b): If your nonprofit will maintain facilities, such as a building or office space or other physical address, and plans to use anyone other than employees or volunteers to manage the facilities—for example, if it plans to hire a management company to manage property—check "yes" and provide the information requested on an attachment page. Again, the IRS wants you to show that the managers are not getting special breaks or excess payments because they are family members or business associates of the nonprofit's directors or officers.

Line 7(c): This line wants you to provide information on all developers and managers of real estate or facilities owned or used by your nonprofit if any of these developers or managers have a business or family relationship with your nonprofit directors or officers. If this question applies to your nonprofit, provide the information requested on an attachment page. If you have already provided the information in response to 7(a) and/or 7(b), you can refer to your previous response. The IRS will scrutinize any contracts you provide and negotiation processes you describe to make sure your nonprofit is not paying more than fair market value for real property development and management services.

Line 8: First read the 1023 instructions for this line. If your nonprofit plans to enter into joint ventures (business deals) with individuals or other nonprofits or commercial business entities, see a legal adviser before providing the information requested and completing your 1023 tax exemption application. Nonprofit organization joint ventures raise complex issues that require expert help to make sure they are structured properly to meet the requirements of the 501(c)(3) tax exemption.

Line 9(a)–9(d): If you are forming a child care organization, you may qualify for your tax exemption either under 501(k) of the Internal Revenue Code or 501(c)(3) as a school. Read the instructions before answering these questions. If you check "yes" to 9(a), answer 9(b) through 9(d). If you answer "no," go on to line 10.

Line 10: This question asks if your nonprofit plans to publish, own, or have rights in intellectual property, such as art, books, patents, trademarks, and the like (see the 1023 instructions for definitions). If you answer "yes," provide the information requested on an attachment page about ownership of the intellectual property, if and how you will derive revenue from the property, and generally how the property will be used as part of your nonprofit activities. In essence, the IRS wants to know whether your nonprofit plans to acquire and exploit copyrights, patents, and other forms of intellectual property and, if so, how. Examples of groups that would answer "yes" include a visual arts exhibit studio, educational book publisher, scientific research center that engages in original (patentable) research, and any group that plans to market its trade name (a name used by the nonprofit and associated with its activities), trademark, or servicemark (logos, words, and images used by the nonprofit to market its goods and services).

501(c)(3) nonprofits that conduct scientific research in the public interest are expected to make their patents, copyrights, processes, or formulae available to the public, not simply develop and exploit results of their research for their own use (see "Scientific Purposes" in Chapter 3). There is nothing wrong or underhanded, however, about a nonprofit owning and exploiting intellectual property related to its exempt purpose—for example, a qualified literary or education nonprofit

owning and obtaining royalty revenue from the sale of its published educational works, or a nonprofit selling donated art to raise funds for its exempt purpose. Be careful though: If a nonprofit deals in intellectual property as a routine method of raising operating revenue—for example, if a nonprofit licenses its trade name to obtain revenue—the IRS is likely to consider this income unrelated business income. If this unrelated income is clearly more than a small portion of the group's overall revenue, the IRS will likely question or deny the group's 501(c)(3) tax exemption.

The issue of copyright ownership sometimes is key to this issue. Remember: If copyrights in published works are owned by a 501(c)(3) nonprofit, this means that the copyrights, like all other assets owned by the nonprofit, are irrevocably dedicated to tax-exempt purposes and must be distributed (transferred) to another tax-exempt nonprofit when the organization dissolves. Hence, the IRS is apt to look more favorably on an educational nonprofit that holds copyrights in its published works. Conversely, if a nonprofit education group does not own the copyright to its published works, but instead publishes the works owned by others under the terms of standard commercial royalty contracts, the IRS may feel that the group is simply a commercial publisher that is not entitled to a 501(c)(3) educational tax exemption. However, if the group publishes education material written by volunteers or its employees or under "work for hire" contracts with outside authors, copyrights in the works are owned by the nonprofit, not by the authors. Publication of this material is clearly in the public interest and contains content related to the educational purpose of the nonprofit. Thus, the IRS is more likely to agree that the group is entitled to a tax exemption.

The sale of art by nonprofits often piques the interest of IRS examiners. For example, if an educational nonprofit exhibits artwork owned by artists and collects a commission on each sale, the IRS may conclude that the organization runs a commercial art gallery that is not entitled to a tax exemption. There is no bright-line test for groups that deal in art or sell goods and services. The IRS looks at all the facts and circumstances related to a group's activities and operations to determine if the group's primary purpose is a charitable, educational, or another 501(c)(3) purpose or, instead, represents a commercial enterprise. For examples of when the IRS has reached different conclusions after examining the activities of groups that sell art as part of their activities, see the summaries of selected IRS revenue rulings below:

TIP

How to read IRS revenue rulings. Each IRS revenue ruling is referenced with a two- or four-digit year prefix followed by a number—for example, revenue ruling 2004-98 is a 2004 ruling and revenue ruling 80-106 is a 1980 ruling. The rulings are distinguished from other rulings during the year by the second number.

- Rev. Rul. 80-106. Thrift shop; consignment sales. An organization operated a thrift shop that sold items that were either donated or received on consignment. Substantially all of the work in operating the thrift shop was performed without compensation, all transactions were at arm's length, and all profits were distributed to Section 501(c)(3) organizations. The organization qualified for exemption as an organization operated for charitable purposes.
- Rev. Rul. 76-152. Art gallery. A nonprofit educational organization, formed by art

patrons to promote community understanding of modern art trends by selecting for exhibit, exhibiting, and selling artworks of local artists, and which retained a commission on sales that was less than customary commercial charges and was not sufficient to cover the cost of operating the gallery, did not qualify for exemption under Section 501(c)(3). The following statement in the ruling provides perhaps the best clue as to why the IRS rejected the group's application: "Since ninety percent of all sales proceeds are turned over to the individual artists, such direct benefits are substantial by any measure and the organization's provision of them cannot be dismissed as being merely incidental to its other purposes and activities."

- Rev. Rul. 71-395. Art selling. A cooperative art gallery, which was formed and operated by a group of artists for the purpose of exhibiting and selling their works, did not charge admission but received a commission from sales and rental of art sufficient to cover the cost of operating the gallery. It did not qualify for exemption under Section 501(c)(3) as an educational organization.
- Rev. Rul. 66-178. Art exhibits. A nonprofit organization was created to foster and develop the arts by sponsoring a public art exhibit at which the works of unknown but promising artists were selected by a panel of qualified judges for display. Artists eligible to have their works displayed were those who were not affiliated with art galleries and who had no medium for exhibiting their creations. The organization did not charge the artists any fees, nor did the organization sell or offer the displayed works for sale. For the exhibit, the organization prepared a catalog that listed each work displayed, the name of its creator, and the artist's

home or studio address. The catalog was sold for a small fee to the public. The organization also received income from nominal admission fees to the exhibit and from contributions. Funds were paid out for renting the exhibition hall, printing the catalogs, and administrative expenses. The organization qualified for a 501(c)(3) tax exemption.

If nothing else, the above rulings reinforce one fundamental fact about seeking and obtaining a tax exemption: The IRS looks at the full context of a nonprofit's operations—including its sources and uses of revenue—when deciding whether a group qualifies for 501(c)(3) tax exemption. Normally, no one fact is fatal or determinative. The more a group demonstrates that its operations are public rather than private or commercial, the better its chances of obtaining a tax exemption. And on a more subjective note, the above rulings also hint at the importance of couching your nonprofit activities in the most acceptable (least commercial) terms—for example, it may sound and look better to the IRS if your group collects admission or consignment fees rather than commissions, since the latter term typically connotes overt commercial activity.

Below are two revenue rulings related to educational nonprofits that involve the publication of books and music. The first repeats the theme that the more a group looks and acts like a regular commercial venture, the less its chances of qualifying for 501(c)(3) tax-exempt status. The second shows that nonprofits that cater to a small, traditionally noncommercial, segment of public education stand a better chance of obtaining a tax exemption, at least partially because the nonprofit activity is, in fact, less likely to reap significant profits.

- Rev. Rul. 66-104. Educational publishing. An education organization was created to meet the need for more satisfactory teaching materials and textbooks in economics and related fields. The organization contracted with commercial publishing firms for the publication of these materials, which were used primarily by colleges and universities. The organization did not hold the copyright in its published material. The contracts between the organization and the publishers provided that the publishers pay all publication costs and a royalty to the organization on sales of the publication. In return, the publisher received the copyright, publishing, and selling rights. The agreement between the organization and the editors and authors provided that the royalty income would first be applied to pay for the costs of preparing the materials for publication, including funds to authors and editors. The remaining royalty was divided into specific percentages between the organization and the editors and authors. The IRS concluded that: "Although educational interests are served by the publication of better teaching materials, the facts in this case show only an enterprise conducted in an essentially commercial manner, in which all the participants expect to receive a monetary return." The IRS denied the organization's 501(c)(3) tax exemption.

- Rev. Rul. 79-369. Musical recording. The organization was created to stimulate, promote, encourage, and sustain interest in and appreciation of contemporary symphonic and chamber music. The organization recorded the new works of unrecognized composers as well as the neglected works of more established composers. The music selected for recording had a limited commercial market and was not generally produced by the commercial music publishing and recording industry for sale to the public. The organization sold its recordings primarily to libraries and educational institutions. Some records were provided free to radio stations operated by educational institutions. The organization also made sales to individuals. The records were not made available for sale through commercial record dealers except in a few specialty shops, but were sold through mail orders. The organization did not engage in any advertising, but relied upon those who were interested in this type of music to communicate the availability of the records. All sales were facilitated by the use of a catalog published by the organization. The catalog contents included information about the compositions and the composers. This information was retained in the catalog so that the catalog served as an archive with respect to these compositions and recordings. Copies of all recordings were maintained for availability in the future. The liner notes on the album covers contained a biography of the composer and a description of the composition by its composer. Composers received royalties from the sale of recordings as required by federal law. Due to the limited commercial market for this type of music, the royalties received by the composers were not significant. The group qualified for a 501(c)(3) tax exemption.

Line 11: This question asks if your nonprofit will accept contributions of various types of property, including works of art and automobiles. If you answer "yes," provide the information requested. If you receive contributions of art, you may be able to refer to portions of your response to line 10, if you used

line 10 to provide information on how you sell contributed art works. The IRS mostly wants to make sure your nonprofit is not simply setting up a contribution-conduit organization formed and operated primarily to generate income tax contributions for wealthy individuals associated with your group. See IRS Publication 526, *Charitable Contributions,* for the latest rules on the deductibility of contributions to qualified 501(c)(3) charities, available on the IRS wesite at www.irs.gov.

Line 12(a)–12(d): If your nonprofit plans to operate in one or more foreign countries, answer "yes" to 12(a) and provide the information requested in 12(b) through 12(d) on an attachment page. Special tax-exemption and deductibility of contribution rules apply to nonprofits created or operated abroad. If you answer "yes," see a nonprofit adviser who has experience in advising nonprofits that operate in the foreign countries where you plan to operate for help in completing your 1023 application. Also see "Foreign Organizations in General," in the official 1023 instructions for basic information on nonprofits formed abroad. Finally, realize that a big part of the IRS's energy is now devoted to scrutinizing the operations of foreign-based nonprofits as part of the service's participation in antiterrorism. Here is an excerpt from the IRS 2005 EO (Exempt Organization) report:

> In FY 2005, EO will examine a sample of foreign grant making organizations; the primary focus of the examinations is to ensure that funds are used for their intended charitable purpose and not diverted for terrorist activity. The project will gather information about current practices, that is, the existence and effectiveness of controls put in place to monitor the distribution of overseas grants and other assistance. This committee will also address the need for possible guidance or other modifications to the laws in this area.

Line 13(a)–13(g): If your nonprofit will make grants or loans to other organizations or receive and disburse funds (for example, as a fiscal agent) for other organizations, answer "yes" to line 13(a), then answer 13(b) through 13(g). Most smaller nonprofits do not make grants or loans to other nonprofits, but may receive grant money as a fiscal agent for another nonprofit. If your group plans to do this, your responses should show that the groups you sponsor promote activities that are related to your tax-exempt purposes and that you exercise oversight in making sure the funds are accounted for and used properly by the groups you sponsor. If your responses demonstrate or imply that you disburse funds as a "feeder" group to promote regular commercial or nonexempt activities, the IRS will deny your exemption. The questions listed here should give you an indication of what the IRS is looking for—formal applications, grant proposals, fiscal reporting controls, and other procedures that you will use to select, monitor, and assess the groups that you sponsor.

Line 14(a)–14(f): This question is similar to line 13, except it applies only to foreign groups that you assist or sponsor. If you answer "yes" to 14(a), it asks additional questions (14(b) through 14(f)) to make sure you apply extra scrutiny to any foreign groups you sponsor (see the antiterrorism note in the line 12 instructions, above—it is one of the drivers for this extra IRS scrutiny of groups that sponsor or assist foreign organizations).

Line 15: First read the instructions to this line in the official 1023 instructions. They provide a definition of what "close connection" means, and the definitions cover a lot of helpful material. If you answer "yes," provide a thorough explanation on an attachment page of how your structure and/or operations are connected to those of another group. Obviously, if you do share space, people,

programs, or other attributes or activities with another group, the IRS will want to see that you are not diverting your tax-exempt purposes or revenue to nontax-exempt ends or purposes promoted by the group with which you are connected.

Line 16: See the instructions before answering this question. A cooperative hospital service organization is a very special type of organization that is tax exempt under Section 501(e) of the Internal Revenue Code, which like a 501(c)(3) group, uses the 1023 application to apply for its tax exemption. You will need expert help completing your tax exemption application if you answer "yes" here.

Line 17: See the instructions before answering this question. A cooperative service organization of operating educational organizations is another special type of organization that is tax exempt under Section 501(f) of the Internal Revenue Code. Like a 501(c)(3) group, it also uses the 1023 application to apply for its tax exemption. You will need expert help completing your tax exemption application if you answer "yes" here.

Line 18: We assume readers of this book are not setting up a charitable risk pool under Section 501(n) of the Internal Revenue Code (see the instructions to the 1023 form). If you are, get help from an expert in this special field of nonprofit activity before completing your tax exemption application.

Line 19: As explained in the 1023 instructions to this line, a school is defined as an educational organization that has the primary function of presenting formal instruction, normally maintains a regular faculty and curriculum, normally has a regularly enrolled body of students, and has a place where its educational activities are carried on (for example, private primary or secondary schools and colleges).

Check the "yes" box and fill in Schedule B if one of your purposes, whether primary or otherwise, is operating a nonprofit school. (See "Filling Out the Schedules," below, for instructions on completing Schedule B.)

Line 20: If your nonprofit is setting up a hospital or medical care facility, including a medical research facility (see the definitions in the 1023 instructions), answer "yes" and complete Schedule C. (See "Filling Out the Schedules," below, for instructions on completing Schedule C.)

Line 21: If you are forming a low-income housing facility or housing for the elderly or handicapped (see the 1023 instructions for definitions of these terms), check "yes" and complete Schedule F. (See "Filling Out the Schedules," below, for instructions on completing Schedule F.)

Line 22: Refer to the 1023 instructions for definitions of terms before answering this question. If your nonprofit, whether it is a school or otherwise, will provide scholarships or other education or educational-related financial aid or assistance to individuals, check "yes" and fill in Schedule H. (See "Filling Out the Schedules," below, for instructions on completing Schedule H.)

Part IX: Financial Data

All groups should complete the financial data tables in Section A (Statement of Revenues and Expenses) and Section B (Balance Sheet) of this Part IX. Start by reading the 1023 instructions for this part.

We have replaced the official instructions to the June 2006 form with updated instructions that reflect new rules adopted by the IRS (and summarized at the beginning of the 1023 form). Remember to check whether an updated Form 1023 is available (see "Check that your IRS 1023 form is current" in "Getting Started," above).

Under the latest regulations, there is no advance ruling period. If a new nonprofit shows in the financial information provided in its 1023 application that it can reasonably expect to receive qualifying public support during its first five years, it will be granted a definitive ruling as a public charity for the first five years. If it can't do this, it will be classified as a private foundation. The initial five year definitive public charity status, if granted, is uncontestable—the nonprofit will retain this status during those five years regardless of its actual sources of support during this period. In other words, even if it guessed wrong in its 1023 exemption application projections, it will keep its public charity status. After the five-year period, however, the IRS will look at current and past year annual Form 990 or 990-EZ returns to see if the group continues to qualify as a public charity. (See Chapter 10 for more on Form 990s.)

EXAMPLE:
The Free Food Program gets its 501(c)(3) tax exemption and public charity tax status starting in 2010. FFP will be treated as a public charity for the five-year period from 2010 to and through 2014. At the end of 2015, the IRS will look at the group's 2011 through 2015 Form 990 returns to see if it qualifies as a public charity for the year 2015.

For more information, go to the IRS website (www.irs.gov) and type "Elimination of the Advance Ruling Process" in the search box. This will display a link to an FAQ on the new rules.

Statement of Revenues and Expenses

The financial data listed here includes your group's past and current receipts and expenses (many groups will need to show proposed receipts and expenses, as explained below). The IRS will use this financial data to make sure that:

- your group's actual and/or proposed receipts and expenses correspond to the exempt-purpose activities and operational information you describe in your application

- you do not plan to engage substantially in unrelated business activities, and

- you do or most likely will meet the appropriate 501(c)(3) public charity support test (see our instructions to Part X, below).

The number of columns you use in Section A will depend on the number of full and partial tax years your group has been in existence. Most nonprofits will have a tax year that goes from January 1 to December 31, but some will have a tax year that ends on the last day of another month—see your response to Part 1, line 5, above.

New groups without prior tax years. If your nonprofit is newly formed, it probably has not been in existence for a full tax year. Put projected numbers for the current year in column (a), and projections for the next two years in columns (b) and (c) for a total of three years.

EXAMPLE:

You are a new nonprofit formed on February 15 of the current year, with a tax year that goes from January 1 to December 31, and you are applying for your tax exemption in June of the corporation's first tax year. The beginning "from" date of the period shown at the top of column (a) is the date

you filed your articles—February 15 of the current year. The "to" date for this period should be December 31, the end of the current tax year. Use columns (b) and (c) to show projected figures for your next two tax years, going from January 1 to December 31 of each of the next two years. Many new groups will repeat much of the information from their first tax year for the next two proposed tax years, unless they anticipate a major change in operations or sources of support. Use column (e) to show the total for columns (a) through (f).

Don't expect to fill in all the items. The IRS knows you've just commenced operations and that you are estimating possible sources of revenue and items of expense, and it expects to see a few blank lines. Also realize that some of your projected revenues and expenses may not neatly fit the categories shown in the printed revenue and expense table. You can use revenue item 7 (other income) and expense item 23 (other expenses) to list totals for these items, and attach a list that itemizes these additional items of revenue and expense on an attachment page. The IRS does not like to see large lump sum amounts, so break down these additional items of revenue and expense as much as possible.

Groups with prior tax years. If your nonprofit has been in existence for five or more prior tax years, show actual revenue and expense amounts for your last five completed tax years in columns (a) through (d). Note that you will have to add a column between (d) and (e) for your fifth year—column (e) is for totals for all five years. You can provide this extra column of information on an attachment page (or you can split column (e) in half and use the left side of (e) for your fifth-year data). Note that the current year, column (a), will be your last completed tax year, not the partially completed current tax year. You will be supplying figures for five completed tax years, and no projected information.

Alternatively, if your nonprofit has been in existence more than one full tax year, but less than five tax years, you must show projected financial information for your current tax year in column (a), then show figures for your prior completed tax year(s) in the other column or columns. You also may need to show projected revenue and expense information in one of the columns for a future tax year depending on how many years you have been in existence. Here is how it works:

If your group has been existence one full prior tax year, show projected figures for the full current tax year in column (a), and your prior completed tax year in column (b). Then show projected figures for the next two years' revenues and expenses (the two tax years after the current tax year) in columns (c) and (d). This information represents four full tax years' worth of information—one completed tax year and three projected tax years.

If your group has been existence two full prior tax years, show projected figures for the full current tax year in column (a), your most recent completed tax year in column (b), and your first completed tax year in column (c). Then show projected figures for the next year's (the year after the current year) revenues and expenses in column (d). This information represents four full tax years' worth of information—two completed tax years and two projected tax years. Use column (e) for totals of the other columns.

Line 12 of the revenue and expense statement asks you to list any "unusual grant" revenue. This term is explained in the instructions for this line in the 1023 instructions, and we explain it in more detail in "Public Support Test" and

"Exempt Activities Support Test," in Chapter 4, as it applies to the different public charity support tests. Also see the specific rules on unusual grants contained in IRS Publication 557 (included on the CD-ROM).

Basically, unusual grants are permitted grants which can throw a kink in your public charity support computations because they come from one source, as opposed to several smaller grants from different sources. Remember, 501(c)(3) public support revenue is supposed to be spread out and come from a number of public sources, not just one or two. It is unlikely that you expect to receive an unusual grant this early in your nonprofit life—unusual grants normally happen only as a result of a sustained and successful outreach program that attracts one or two large grants that surprise the modest expectations of a small nonprofit. In effect, an unusual grant represents both good and bad news. The good news is the unusually large amount of the grant; the bad news is its potential damage to the group's ability to meet the technical public support requirements that apply to 501(c)(3) public charities. If you have received or expect to receive one or more unusual grants, insert the total number here on line 12 in the appropriate column (past, present, or future tax year), and list on an attachment page a description of each grant (what the grant was for, whether it was restricted to a specific use, and other terms of the grant), together with the donor's name, date, and amount of each unusual grant. If a large grant qualifies as an unusual grant, it will be disregarded by the IRS when it computes whether your support qualifies under the technical public charity support test rules (see Part X, below).

Balance Sheet

Prepare the balance sheet to show assets and liabilities of your corporation as of your last completed tax year, if any, or the current tax year if you have not yet completed one full tax year.

EXAMPLE:

You have organized a new nonprofit corporation, formed on April 1. You are preparing your 1023 application in November of the same year. Your tax year goes from January 1 to December 31. The current tax year period covered by column (a) of your Statement of Revenue and Expenses is from April 1 to December 31. Your balance sheet ending date will be the same ending date, December 31, the eventual ending date of your first tax year. This date should appear as the "year-end" date in the blank at the top right of the balance sheet page. Even though this is a future end date, you should base your statement of assets and liabilities on current information—that is on your organization's current assets and liabilities at the time of the preparation of your exemption application.

It's not uncommon for a small starting nonprofit without liabilities and accounts receivable to simply show a little cash as its only reportable balance sheet item. Other common items reported are line 8 depreciable assets—equipment owned by the corporation and used to conduct its exempt activities.

Line 17 of the balance sheet asks for fund balance or net asset information. Typically, this is the amount by which your assets exceed your liabilities—in other words, the net value of your assets. If you have difficulty preparing the financial information under this part, get the help of a tax or legal adviser.

Line 19 asks if there have been substantial changes in your assets and liabilities since the year-end date for your balance sheet. This question should be answered "no" by most groups. However, if your nonprofit is submit-

ting a balance sheet for a prior completed period and your assets and liabilities have undergone significant change—as a result, perhaps of a sale or purchase of assets, a refinancing of debt, or other major structural change—answer "yes" and provide an explanation on an attachment page.

Part X: Public Charity Status

You should be familiar with the material in Chapter 4 to answer the questions in this part of the form. This is where terms such as "public charity" and "private foundation" become important. We will refer to earlier explanations as we go along, but you may want to look over Chapter 4 now before you proceed. The questions in this part relate to whether you are seeking to be classified as a 501(c)(3) public charity or as a 501(c)(3) private foundation. As you know by now, we assume you want your nonprofit to qualify as a 501(c)(3) public charity, not as a 501(c)(3) private foundation.

Line 1(a)–(b): In Chapter 4, we discussed the distinction between the public charity and private foundation classifications and the reasons that you should try to meet one of the three primary tests for being classified as a public charity. The 1023 instructions provide a list of groups that qualify for public charity status, which lumps all publicly supported groups together ("groups that have broad financial support"). We use a different classification scheme in Chapter 4, which puts public charities into one of three categories:

(1) Automatic Public Charity Status: groups that are set up for a specific purpose or special function, such as churches, schools, hospitals, and public safety organizations, qualify as public charities (we say they "automatically" qualify because these groups, unlike the other two types of

public charities listed below, do not have to meet public support tests).

(2) Public Support Test Groups: these are groups that are supported by contributions and grants and that meet the one-third or one-tenth public support tests described in "Public Support Test" in Chapter 4.

(3) Exempt Activities Support Test Groups: these are groups that obtain support through the performance of their exempt purposes, such as admissions, tuition, seminar fees, and receipts from goods and services related to the group's exempt purposes.

We assume your nonprofit will either be setting up one of the special public charities that automatically qualify under (1), above, or a nonprofit that has or can reasonably expect to receive the type of support listed in (2) or (3), above.

Line 1(a): Check "yes" or "no" on line 1(a) to indicate whether or not you are a private foundation. Again, we assume you expect to qualify as a public charity and will mark "no" to this question. If your response is "no," go on to line 5. If you are forming a 501(c)(3) private foundation, check "yes" and go on to line 1(b).

Line 1(b): This line only applies if you answered "yes" to line 1(a). Line 1(b) asks you to check the box as a reminder that your private foundation requires special provisions in your articles or reliance on special provisions of state law. This book and its forms do not address these extra requirements, and you will need the help of a nonprofit adviser to form your 501(c)(3) private foundation and prepare your articles properly.

Lines 2–4: As with line 1(b) above, these lines only apply if you answered "yes" to line 1(a) indicating that you are applying for a tax exemption for a 501(c)(3) private foundation. These questions ask even more specific questions

to help pigeonhole the private foundation into special subcategories—private operating and private nonoperating foundation categories. We assume you will get the help of an experienced legal or tax person who works with private foundations before answering these questions. After answering these questions, groups that are preparing their 1023 application for a private foundation should skip the remaining lines in this part of the form and go on to Part XI.

Line 5: Check the box (letters (a)–(i)) that corresponds to the basis of your claim to public charity status. First, absorb what you can of the technical material given in the 1023 line 5 instructions. Then reread "How to Qualify for Public Charity Status," in Chapter 4—this section provides the names of these public charity organizations, the requirements they must meet, and the Internal Revenue Code sections that apply to them. Note that letter (i) is a special case that allows certain groups to have the IRS determine which public charity support test best suits their activities and sources of revenue. We cover this special choice in more detail in line (i), below.

The following chart shows how the different types of groups listed in this part of the application fit within the three different categories of public charity status discussed in "How to Qualify for Public Charity Status," in Chapter 4. If you concentrate on our basic division of these different groups into the three public charity categories, rather than focusing on the individual Internal Revenue Code sections, this part will go more smoothly.

Let's look a little more closely at each of the lettered boxes in line 5:

Line 5(a): If you seek to qualify automatically for public charity status as a church, see the 1023 instructions to this item. You will need to complete Schedule A and include it with your 1023 application. (See "Filling Out the Schedules," below, for instructions on completing Schedule A.)

Line 5(b): Check this box if your primary purpose is to set up and operate a formal school. If you check this box, make sure you have completed Schedule B. See the separate 1023 instructions to Schedule B, in "Automatic Public Charity Status," in Chapter 4 (see the section "Schools"), and our instructions for filling out Schedule B in "Filling Out the Schedules," below.

If you will set up and operate a school, but operating the school is not your primary purpose, do not check this box—you will need to qualify as a public charity by checking one of the other line 5 boxes. However, you must complete Schedule B and attach it to your exemption application if you plan to operate a school, even if operating the school is not your primary purpose and the basis for your claim to public charity status—see the instruction to line 5(b) in the 1023 instructions.

Line 5(c)–5(f): Read the instructions for these lines in the 1023 instructions. Few groups will choose one of these boxes—each applies to a special type of organization such as a hospital, supporting organization, public safety organization, or government agency.

Line 5(c) hospitals and medical research groups will need to complete Schedule C—you should refer to the 1023 instructions for this schedule, the section "Hospitals and Medical Research Organizations" in "Automatic Public Charity Status," in Chapter 4, and our instructions for filling out Schedule C in "Filling Out the Schedules," below.

Line 5(d) supporting organizations are a special type of nonprofit set up to support other public charities. They are operated solely for the benefit of, or in connection with, any of the other public charity organizations (except one testing for public safety). A supporting organization must complete Schedule D. This information helps the IRS determine whether this type of organization supports other qualified public charities.

IRS Line 9 Public Charities Covered in Chapter 4		
Line 5(a)	church	Chapter 4, Automatic Public Charity Status
Line 5(b)	school	Chapter 4, Automatic Public Charity Status
Line 5(c)	hospital or medical research	Chapter 4, Automatic Public Charity Status
Line 5(d)	supporting organizations	Chapter 4, Automatic Public Charity Status
Line 5(e)	public safety organizations	Chapter 4, Automatic Public Charity Status
Line 5(f)	government organization supporting colleges	Chapter 4, Automatic Public Charity Status
Line 5(g)	public support test groups	Chapter 4, Public Support Test
Line 5(h)	exempt activities support test groups	Chapter 4, Exempt Activities Support Test
Line 5(i)	either public support or exempt activities support test group	Chapter 4, Public Support Test and Exempt Activities Support Test

TIP

Get help when applying for an exemption for a special type of nonprofit. If you check one of the 5(c) through 5(f) boxes, the lawyer, accountant, or other adviser who is helping you organize one of these special corporations should help you with your application and any additional schedules you have to prepare and include with your application.

Line 5(g): First read the 1023 instructions for this line. This box is for organizations that receive a substantial part of their support from government agencies or from the general public. These are the public support test groups discussed in Chapter 4. If you believe this is the public charity best suited to your organization's sources of support, check the box on this line. If you are unsure whether this is the best support test to use for your group (that is, if you think that the exempt activities support test in line 5(h) also may apply to your organization), you may wish to let the IRS make this decision for you as explained in the line 5(i) instructions, below.

As discussed in "Public Support Test," in Chapter 4, many groups will not want to fall under this public charity test because it does not allow your receipts from the performance of services related to the corporation's exempt purposes to be included as "qualified public support."

Groups checking line 5(g), go on to Part X, line 6.

Line 5(h): Start by reading the 1023 instructions for this line. This box is for organizations that normally receive one-third of their support from contributions, membership fees, and gross receipts from activities related to the exempt functions of the organization (subject to certain exceptions) but not more than one-third from unrelated trades and businesses or gross investment income. This exempt activities support test is discussed in Chapter 4. This is the most common and often the easiest way to qualify a new nonprofit organization as a public charity. So reread the requirements of this test and the definition of terms associated with it in Chapter 4. If you believe this public charity test best suits your expected sources of support, check this box. If you are unsure, see the instructions to line 5(i), just below.

Groups checking line 5(h), go on to Part X, line 6.

Line 5(i): If you feel that your group may qualify as a public charity either under line 5(g) or 5(h) but aren't sure which to choose, you can check this box. The IRS will decide which of these two public charity classifications best suits your organization based upon the financial data and other financial support information included in your 1023 application. For many new groups, line 5(i) is the best way to go. Rather than working through the math and the technical definitions necessary to approximate whether you will qualify as a public charity under line 5(g) or 5(h), by checking this box you let the IRS do the hard work for you.

Groups checking line 5(i), go on to Part X, line 6.

Here are some sample responses to line 5 by some typical, hypothetical nonprofit groups:

The First Fellowship Church, a religious organization that plans to maintain a space to provide weekly religious services to its congregation, checks line 5(a) to request automatic public charity status as a church.

The Workshop for Social Change, an educational group that plans to receive support from public and private grant funds and from individual and corporate contributions, checks line 5(g) to request public charity status as a publicly supported organization.

Everybody's Dance Studio and Dinner Theater, a group that expects to derive most of its operating revenue from student tuitions, special workshops, and ticket sales (as well as from other exempt-purpose activities), selects line 5(h) to be classified as a group that meets the exempt activities support test, discussed in Chapter 4.

The School for Alternative Social Studies, an accredited private postgraduate school with a formal curriculum, full-time faculty, and regularly enrolled student body, checks line 5(b) to request automatic public charity status as a formal private school.

The Elder Citizens' Collective and Information Exchange, which plans to derive support from contributions and grants as well as subscriptions to its weekly newsletter (and other exempt-purpose services and products made available to members and the public at large), checks line 5(i) to have the IRS decide whether line 5(g) or 5(h) is the appropriate public charity classification.

Line 6: Only groups that have checked line 5(g), 5(h), or 5(i)—groups that are seeking to be classified as a publicly-supported public charity—should look at line 6. To start with, all of these groups should ignore line 6(a) and the following blank lines that appear under the Consent portion of this part of the form. Line 6(a) and the Consent portion used to apply if a publicly-supported group wanted to or was required to seek an advance ruling as to its public charity status. Since the federal tax regulations have eliminated the advance ruling period for all groups, line 6(a) no longer applies. *Ignore it!*

If you checked line 5(g), 5(h), or 5(i), but your nonprofit has not been in existence for five or more completed tax years, you also should ignore lines 6(b) and 7, and you should go on to Part XI.

If you checked 5(g), 5(h), or 5(i) and your nonprofit has been in existence for five or more completed tax years, you should complete line 6(b) and line 7 of Part X. The IRS will use this additional information to determine if your nonprofit qualifies as a publicly-supported public charity.

Line 6(b): If you checked line 5(g), 5(h), or 5(i) and your nonprofit has completed five or more tax years (ignore the requirements for completing line 6(b) on the June 2006 form—these requirements are based on the old law). Check the line 6(b) box and answer the remaining line 6(b) questions, as explained in the next several paragraphs. First read the official 1023 instructions to these additional line 6(b) items before following our instructions below.

Line 6(b)(i)(a): Enter 2% (0.02) of the amount shown in Part IX-A (Revenues and Expenses), line 8, column (e)—this is 2% of your organization's total public support received over the tax years shown in Part IX-A. The IRS will use this number in computing whether your group meets the appropriate public charity support test.

Line 6(b)(i)(b): If any individual, organization, or company has contributed more than the 2% amount shown in 6(b)(i)(a) during the prior tax years covered in Part IX-A (Revenues and Expenses) of your application, supply the name(s) of the contributor(s) and the amount(s) contributed on an attachment page. Conversely, if no individual, organization, or company contributes more than this 2% amount, check the box at the right. Why does the IRS want this information? For line 5(g) public support test charities, the IRS generally does not count amounts that exceed 2% of the group's total support as qualified public support (for more on the 2% rule and its exceptions, see "Public Support Test" in Chapter 4 and IRS Publication 557, "Support From the General Public").

Line 6(b)(ii)(a)–6(b)(ii)(b): These questions require you to disclose sources of support that the IRS does not consider qualified public support for groups that are seeking public charity status under the exempt activities support test (the groups covered in "Exempt Activities Support Test," in Chapter 4, that rely on support received primarily from their exempt-purpose activities). We're talking here about contributions from disqualified persons or gross receipts from other individuals that exceed the larger of 1% of the organization's total support or $5,000 in any tax year.

Line 6(b)(ii)(a): For a definition of disqualified persons, including a "substantial contributor," see the official instructions to the form. We provide a somewhat friendlier set of definitions of these terms in "Who Are Disqualified Persons?" below. If a disqualified person provided gifts, grants, or contributions, membership fees, or payments for admissions, or other exempt-purpose services or products (these are the categories listed in lines 1, 2, and 9 of Part IX-A, Revenues and Expenses) during any tax year shown in Part IX-A, list the disqualified persons and amounts contributed or paid on an attachment page. If no disqualified person paid or contributed any of these amounts, check the box to the right.

Line 6(b)(ii)(b): If any person (other than a disqualified person) has paid more than the larger of either $5,000 or 1% of the amount shown in line 9 of Part IX, Revenues and Expenses (admissions or other exempt-purpose services or products), during any completed tax year shown in Part IX-A, provide the name of the person or organization who made the payment and the amount of each payment on an attachment page. The list should be broken down year by year. If no individual (other than a disqualified person) made such a payment for any of the completed tax years shown in Part IX-A, check the box to the right of this item.

Line 7: As with line 6(b), line 7 only applies to groups that checked line 5(g), 5(h), or 5(i), and have completed five or more tax years. To answer this question, first refer to our instructions to Part IX-A above (Statement of Revenue and Expenses). If you have listed any unusual grants on line 12 of the Statement of Revenue and Expenses in any of the columns, check "yes" and list them on an attachment page along with the donor's name, date, and amount and the nature of the grant (what the grant was for, whether it was restricted to a specific use, and other terms of the grant). If you provided this information in an attachment to Part IX-A, you can refer to your earlier response. For further explanation of what constitutes unusual grants, see "Unusual Grants," below. If you have not listed any unusual grants in the Part IX-A Revenue and Expense statement, check the "no" box.

Who Are Disqualified Persons?

People who are disqualified in the eyes of the IRS are not necessarily prohibited from participating in the operation of the 501(c)(3) nonprofit corporation. Instead, their contributions to the nonprofit may not count when figuring the public support received by public charities. (Note that the definitions of disqualified persons discussed here are different from the definitions of disqualified persons under IRC § 4958—see the instructions to Part V, above, for information on this separate set of definitions.) If the corporation is classified as a 501(c)(3) private foundation, the corporation and the disqualified individual can be held liable for certain private foundation excise taxes. Disqualified persons for purposes of meeting the public charity support tests include:

1. Substantial contributors. These are donors who give more than $5,000, if the amount they contributed is more than 2% of the total contributions and bequests received by the organization. For example, suppose Ms. X makes a gift of $20,000 to your nonprofit corporation. If this gift exceeds 2% of all contributions and bequests made to your organization from the time it was created until the end of the corporate tax year in which Ms. X made the contribution, Ms. X is a substantial contributor.

For purposes of determining whether a substantial donor is a disqualified person, gifts and bequests made by that individual include all contributions and bequests made by the individual's spouse. Once a person is classified as a substantial contributor, he generally remains classified as one (regardless of future contributions made, or not made, by the individual or future support received by the organization). However, if other conditions are met, a person will lose his status as a substantial contributor if he makes no contribution to the organization for ten years.

2. All foundation managers. Directors, trustees, and officers (or people with similar powers or responsibilities), or any employee with final authority to act on a matter, are disqualified as foundation managers—this means the bigwigs in a nonprofit who exercise executive control. Officers include persons specifically designated as "officers" in the articles, bylaws, or minutes, and persons who regularly make administrative and policy decisions. Officers do not include independent contractors, such as accountants, lawyers, financial and investment advisers, and managers. Generally, any person who simply makes recommendations for action but cannot implement these recommendations will not qualify as an officer.

3. Owners and substantial players in entities that contribute. An owner of more than 20% of the total combined voting power of a corporation, the profits of a partnership, or the beneficial interest of a trust or unincorporated enterprise are all disqualified, if any of these entities is a substantial contributor.

4. Family members. A member of the family —including ancestors, spouse, and lineal descendants, such as children and grandchildren, but not brothers and sisters—of any of the individuals described in 1, 2, or 3 above, is disqualified.

5. Other business entities. Corporations, partnerships, trusts, and so on in which the persons described in 1 through 4 above have at least a 35% ownership interest.

For more information on disqualified persons, see the "Private Foundations" link in the Public Charities & Non-Profits section of the IRS website at www.irs.gov.

Unusual Grants

Unusual grants are contributions, bequests, or grants that your organization receives because it is publicly supported but that are so large that they could jeopardize your ability to meet your public support test. The benefit of having a large grant qualify as an unusual grant is that it does not jeopardize the group's public charity status (as do other large sums received from a single source). It is unlikely that your beginning nonprofit has received sums that should be classified as unusual grants. For further information on this technical area, see the 1023 instructions to line 7 of Part X, the discussion and examples of unusual grants in "What Is Public Support?" in Chapter 4 (see "Money From Unusual Grants" and "Unusual Grants Drop Out of the Support Computation"), and the specific rules on unusual grants contained in IRS Publication 557.

Part XI: User Fee Information

You must pay a user fee when you submit your 1023 tax exemption application. The fee is determined according to the amount of gross receipts your group has or expects to receive annually (averaged over a four-year period). See the 1023 instructions to this part first before reading our instructions below.

CAUTION

Always check that the fee amount is current. Your user fee check should be made payable to the "United States Treasury," and show "User fee Form 1023 [name of your group]" on the check memo line. Before writing your check, go to the IRS website at www.irs.gov to make sure you have the current fee amounts. (Fees were increased in 2010.) Type "User Fee" in the keyword box to find fee amounts. Alternatively, call the IRS Exempt

Organization Customer Service telephone number at 877-829-5500 to ask for current 1023 user fee amounts.

Ignore the amounts listed in Part XI of the 2006 form. Here are the latest amounts (which are noted in the instructions at the top of the 2006 1023 form).

Line 1: Groups that qualify for a reduced user fee of $400 (the 2006 form has the old $300 fee) check "yes." Your organization qualifies for this reduced fee if it is submitting its initial exemption application and:

- it is a new organization (in operation for less than four years) that anticipates annual gross receipts averaging not more than $10,000 during its first four tax years, or

- it has been in operation for four tax years or more and has had annual gross receipts averaging not more than $10,000 during the preceding four years.

Line 2: If you check "yes" in line 1, also check the line 2 box, cross out $300, and insert "$400" (the current reduced fee). If you did not check "yes" to line 1, do not check box 2.

Line 3: If you did not check "yes" to line 1, check the line 3 box and include a user fee check for $850 (cross out the old fee amount of $750 and replace it with "$850"). If you checked the line 1 box, do not check this box.

Sometime after 2010, the IRS expects to release an online application process called "Cyber Assistant" that will have a reduced $200 user fee. Check the IRS website to see if it is available.

TIP

What happens if you guess incorrectly? You may be concerned about what will happen if you estimate that your gross receipts will average no more than $10,000 during your first four tax years, but your actual gross receipts exceed this amount in one or more years. We don't know for sure, but if you make more than this threshold amount, it seems reasonable to assume that the IRS would monitor your annual information returns and ask you to pay the remaining balance later. Of course, if the financial information you submit with your 1023 exemption application shows that your group has, or expects to have, average gross receipts exceeding $10,000 for its first four years and you check the wrong box here, expect the IRS to return your exemption application due to insufficient payment or to send out a request for an additional payment before it continues processing your application.

Signature, Name, Title, and Date Lines: Have one of your initial directors or officers sign, type his or her name and title (director, president, chief operations officer, or the like), and insert the date on the lines provided at the bottom of Part XI.

Write a check payable to the United States Treasury for the amount of the user fee. *Do not staple* or otherwise attach your check to your application. You will simply place your check at the top of your assembled exemption application package, as explained in the next section. The check does not have to be an organizational check. The person preparing the application or any other incorporator may write a personal check. The user fee is kept by the IRS in almost all circumstances, even if your application is denied. The only time it is refunded is if the IRS decides that it cannot issue a determination as to your exempt status one way or the other—because it has insufficient information or cannot resolve some of the issues associated with your tax exemption request. By the way, this rarely happens. For example, if you don't respond to any follow-up questions that the IRS may ask in response to your application, it normally denies your exemption (and keeps the check).

Whew! You're just about done. Follow the instructions below for assembling your entire federal exemption package.

Filling Out the Schedules

Certain groups must complete and submit schedules with their Form 1023 application. In the line-by-line instructions to the 1023 form, above, we let you know when you are required to complete a schedule. For example, in Part VII, line 1, of the application, we tell you that if you answered "yes" to that item, you must complete Schedule G. If you do not need to submit any schedules with your Form 1023, you can skip this section.

Schedule A. Churches

See the separate instructions to Schedule A, included in the last portion of the official 1023 instructions, for help in filling out this schedule. We've discussed the requirements for churches in "Automatic Public Charity Status," in Chapter 4. The questions here seek to determine whether your organization possesses conventional institutional church attributes—the more the better as far as the IRS is concerned. Some also relate to whether your organization unduly benefits, or was created to serve the personal needs of, your pastor or the pastor's family and relatives. Obviously, doing so is an IRS no-no.

Schedule B. Schools, Colleges, and Universities

See the official 1023 instructions to Schedule B for help in completing this schedule. Your responses to this schedule should show that your operations are nondiscriminatory and in accordance with a nondiscrimination statement included in your bylaws and published in the community in which you serve (you must attach this bylaw resolution to Schedule B). For information on drafting and publishing this statement of nondiscrimination, see "Educational Purposes" in Chapter 3. Also see IRS Publication 557, "Private Schools" (included on the CD-ROM).

Schedule C. Hospitals and Medical Research Organizations

Make sure to check the appropriate boxes at the top of the schedule and fill out the appropriate section of the form. Generally this schedule seeks to determine two things:

- whether the hospital is charitable in nature and qualifies for 501(c)(3) tax-exempt status, and

- whether the hospital or medical research organization qualifies for automatic public charity status (see the Schedule C instructions in the official 1023 instructions and IRS Publication 557, "Hospitals and Medical Research Organizations").

A 501(c)(3) charitable hospital normally has many of the following characteristics:

- staff doctors selected from the community at large

- a community-oriented board of directors (directors come from the community served by the hospital)

- emergency room facilities open to the public

- a policy of allowing at least some patients to be treated without charge (on a charity basis)

- a nondiscrimination policy with respect to patient admissions (it doesn't pick and choose its patient population) and particularly does not discriminate against Medicare or Medicaid patients, and

- a medical training and research program that benefits the community.

Hospitals need to be careful when it comes to renting space to physicians who are members of the board—and carrying out a private practice that's unrelated to the community service programs of the hospital. The IRS will be particularly suspicious if such physicians are prior tenants and their rent is below fair market value. Section 1, question 7, of Schedule C addresses this issue.

Hospitals should adopt a suitable conflict of interest policy in their bylaws (see Schedule C, Section 1, line 14). Article 9 of the bylaws included with this book contains most of the provisions in the sample conflict of interest policy provided in Appendix A of the official 1023 instructions. However, it does not include the special bracketed provisions that apply specifically to hospitals. There are two, which are clearly marked in Appendix A of the 1023 instructions with the words "*[Hospital Insert— for hospitals that complete Schedule C...].*" Make sure you insert these additional bracketed provisions to the provisions in Article 9 of the bylaws included with this book.

Schedule D. Section 509(a)(3) Supporting Organizations

Refer to the 1023 instructions for this schedule, Chapter 4, "Automatic Public Charity Status" (see "Supporting Organizations") and Publication 557, "Section 509(a)(3) Organizations." This is a complicated schedule—you must meet a number of technical tests. Your nonprofit legal or tax adviser can help you qualify for this special type of public charity classification.

Schedule E. Organizations Not Filing Form 1023 Within 27 Months of Formation

Before filling in Schedule E, read the official IRS 1023 instructions to Schedule E, which are contained in the instructions for separate schedules at the end of the 1023 instructions. This material will give you some basic definitions and information that will help you work your way through the schedule.

Lines 1–3: Three groups are not required to file Form 1023: churches; public charities that normally have gross receipts of not more than $5,000 in each year (see the extra instructions for line 2(b) below); and subordinate organizations exempt under a group exemption letter (see Section B, above). If you decide that you fall within one of these exceptions (after reading any additional instructions for the line below), check the "yes" box or boxes on the appropriate line (either line 1, 2, or 3) and go on to Part VIII of the 1023 form. You do not need to complete the rest of Schedule E. If the IRS agrees that you qualify as one of these three special groups, your federal exemption will be effective retroactively from the date of your incorporation, even though you filed your exemption application late (after more than 27 months from the end of the month when you filed your articles).

If you fall within one of the three groups, you are filing an exemption application even though you believe you are not required to do so and even though you are filing more than 27 months after your nonprofit corporation was formed. As we said in Section B, above, we agree that this is the best way to go because by submitting your exemption application you are making sure the IRS agrees that your group is entitled to a tax exemption in one of these three special 501(c)(3) categories.

Line 2(a)–2(b): The 2(a) exception is often applicable to new nonprofits. Your group qualifies if:

- it is a public charity rather than a private foundation (because one of the purposes of completing your 1023 application is to establish that you are eligible for public charity status, we assume that you meet this requirement), and
- it "normally" has gross receipts of not more than $5,000 in each tax year.

Groups that have been in existence for two tax years qualify if they had total gross receipts of $12,000 or less during the first two years. We assume your group has been in existence for at least two years because it is filing more than 27 months after it was formed. If you have been in existence for three or more tax years, your gross receipts over the three years must be $15,000 or less to qualify for the "normally $5,000" exception. Many new groups without outside sources of support can meet this gross receipts test during their beginning tax years. And, if you can't check "yes" to line 2(a), there's a technical loophole in line 2(b): It says that groups that are filing their 1023 application within 90 days after the end of the tax year when they qualified for the "normally $5,000 gross receipts" test also can file their application late.

EXAMPLE:

You form a new nonprofit corporation in January of 2007 and file your tax exemption application more than four years later—in February 2011. Your group had gross receipts of less than $5,000 for 2007 through 2009, but 2010 was a really good year so the total gross receipts for your organization over the three-tax-year period from January 2008 through December 2010 was $25,000. This is well over the three-year $15,000 cumulative total maximum amount. If you submit your 1023 application in February of 2011, which is within 90 days of the end of 2010, you can check box 2(b) and have the tax exemption extend all the way back to the date of incorporation because it meets this special line 2(b) exception. Obviously, this 2(b) exception is intended for groups that file quickly after determining that their past three-year cumulative gross receipts put them over the $15,000 mark. Once they go over this mark, they become a group that is required to file a 1023 application—the IRS will let them have their tax exemption for all prior years, even though the last three-year cumulative total exceeded the $15,000 threshold, as long as the group files the 1023 within 90 days of the end of the high-receipts tax year.

Line 4: Here is where you end up if your group is filing the 1023 application more than 27 months from the date of your incorporation and you don't meet one of the three exceptions listed in lines 1 through 3 of this part. Groups formed on or before October 9, 1969 get a special break. Of course, we assume you were formed recently, and will check "no" and move on to line 5.

Line 5: Since your group is not one of the special groups listed in the previous lines on Schedule E, your group can only qualify for an exemption that extends back to its date of formation if it asks the IRS to qualify for late filing. To do this, check "yes" and attach a statement giving the reasons why you failed to complete the 1023 application process within the 27-month period after your incorporation. Federal rules, contained in Treasury Regulations 301.9100-1 and 301.9100-3, also include a list of the acceptable reasons for late filing, as well as those that aren't. For example, acceptable reasons include the following: you relied on the advice of a lawyer, accountant, or an IRS employee, and received inaccurate information or were not informed of the deadline. These acceptable reasons are summarized in the 1023 instructions for this line. After attaching your statement, perhaps with the help of your tax adviser, go on to Part VIII of the 1023 application—you should not complete the rest of Schedule E.

If you don't think you can qualify for an extension (or if you decide not to bother—see "If You End Up on Schedule E, Line 5, Should You Ask for an Extension?" below), check "no" and go on to line 6.

If You End Up on Schedule E, Line 5, Should You Ask for an Extension?

Most groups will not end up on Schedule E, line 5—they will submit their 1023 application within 27 months from the date of their incorporation. If your group does end up here, you may decide not to bother seeking an extension and simply check "no" on line 5. This means that your 501(c)(3) exemption, if granted, will be effective only from the application's postmark date, not from the date of your incorporation. Is this so terrible? Often, it isn't. Here's why. Many nonprofits will not have any taxable income or contributions from donors during these early start-up months (the 27-plus months of operation prior to filing their 1023 application). Consequently, obtaining a tax exemption for these early months will not provide a tax benefit. However, if your group is facing tax liability for early operations, the need to provide donors with tax deductions for gifts contributed during the first 27-plus months, or the need to obtain 501(c)(3) tax-exempt status from the date of its creation for some other pressing reason, then it makes sense to prepare a special statement under line 5 as explained in the text. If you are unsure, check with your tax adviser.

Line 6 (a): If you checked "no" on line 5 (you don't want to qualify for an extension of time to file), you should check "yes" to 6(a). This means that you agree that your 501(c)(3) exemption can be recognized only from its postmark date, not retroactively to the date of your incorporation. By the way, if you check "no" to 6(a), you are saying that you are applying for a tax exemption as a 501(c)(3) private foundation, not a public charity—this is something you definitely will not want to do. We assume all readers will want to form a 501(c)(3) public charity, as mentioned earlier in this chapter and explained in more detail in Chapter 4. So check "yes" to 6(a) and move on to 6(b).

Even though the 1023 instructions say that checking "yes" to 6(a) means that you will have to request an advance ruling period for your public charity status (by completing Part X, 6(a)), this is no longer true. As mentioned earlier, advance rulings have been eliminated and you should ignore Part X, line 6(a)—see our instructions to Part X, earlier in this chapter.

Line 6(b): Most groups that are applying late for their tax exemption are not planning to substantially change how they get financial support, so they will check "no" to 6(b) and ignore the table in line 7—they will move on to line 8 of Schedule E. However, some groups that are applying late realize that their past operations and sources of financial support may or may not qualify them to meet one of the public charity support tests (as more fully explained in our instructions to Part X), and will want to change their plans for financial support now. If this is the case for your late-filing nonprofit, mark "yes" to 6(b), then fill in the projected revenue table in line 7 to show your expected sources of future financial support.

Line 7: If you marked "yes" to line 6(b), fill in projected sources of financial support for the next two full years following the current tax year. For example, if you are applying for your tax exemption late in July of 2011, and your nonprofit's tax year goes from January to December (the typical case), supply financial figures for the period from January 2012 to December 2014 in the table. You don't have to fill in items for all rows, but you should be able to supply figures that show that you expect your nonprofit to obtain support from sources that qualify it for public charity status under one of the two basic financial support categories discussed in Part X.

Line 8: If you are filing your 1023 application late and checked "yes" to line 6(a) on Schedule E, you should complete line 8 of the Schedule, regardless of how you responded to 6(b). If you end up here, your application for 501(c)(3) status will be considered only from the date of its postmark. If you check "yes" to line 8, you are asking the IRS to grant your group tax-exempt status as a 501(c)(4) organization—a social welfare group or a civic league—during your late filing period (the 27-month-plus period from the date your articles were filed up to the date your 1023 application postmark). What does this do for you? If your request for 501(c)(4) status is approved, your organization will be exempt from paying federal corporate income taxes as a 501(c)(4) organization from the date of its formation until the date of approval of your 501(c)(3) tax-exempt status (the 1023 postmark date). For most newly formed groups without taxable income during this initial period, obtaining this extra tax exemption will not be necessary and you can ignore this box.

However, if you or your tax adviser determines that your organization is subject to tax liability for this initial period, check this box and call 800-TAX-FORM to order IRS Publication 1024 (or go to www.irs.gov). Fill in page 1 of

Form 1024 and submit it with your exemption application. If you qualify as a 501(c)(4) social welfare group (as many 501(c)(3)s do—see "501(c)(4) Organizations," below)—your 501(c) (3) tax determination letter will indicate that you qualify as a 501(c)(4) organization during your initial late filing (your pre-501(c)(3)) period.

501(c)(4) Organizations

Internal Revenue Code Section 501(c)(4) provides a federal corporate income tax exemption for nonprofit social welfare groups and civic leagues (see *Special Nonprofit Tax-Exempt Organizations*, in Appendix C). Since the promotion of public welfare is defined as "promoting the common good and general welfare of the people of the community," many 501(c)(3) nonprofits also qualify as 501(c)(4) social welfare organizations. Although 501(c)(4) nonprofits are exempt from federal corporate income taxation, they are not eligible to receive tax-deductible contributions from donors. They also do not enjoy many of the other advantages associated with 501(c)(3) tax-exempt status, such as eligibility to receive public and private grant funds, participate in local, state, and federal nonprofit programs, obtain county real and personal property tax exemptions, and other benefits.

But 501(c)(4) organizations do enjoy one advantage not available to 501(c)(3) groups: They may engage in substantial legislative activities and may support or oppose candidates to public office. For further information on 501(c)(4) tax-exempt status, see IRS Publication 557.

Schedule F. Homes for the Elderly or Handicapped and Low-Income Housing

See the 1023 instructions for help in filling out this schedule. In part, this schedule attempts to determine whether elderly or handicapped housing facilities are made available to members of the public or the particular community at reasonable rates, whether provision is made for indigent residents, whether health care arrangements are adequate, and whether facilities are adequate to house a sufficient number of residents.

Schedule G. Successors to Other Organizations

Line 1(a): We assume your nonprofit is not a successor to a prior profit-making company, which is one such as a sole proprietorship, partnership, limited liability company, or a business corporation that allows its owners to have a proprietary (financial) interest in its assets. In the unlikely case that you check "yes" to line 1(a) because you are a successor to a profit organization, we think you will need help from a nonprofit expert when filing out Schedule G and the rest of your tax exemption application to explain to the IRS why you decided to convert a prior profit-making activity to nonprofit corporate status, and why the new nonprofit is entitled to its tax exemption.

Successor groups that check "no" to line 1(a) will have to check "yes" to line 2(a) to indicate that they are successors to a nonprofit groups (remember, a successor group is one that meets one of the successor tests listed above—if you are not a successor group, you shouldn't be filling in Schedule G). Even these groups may need help responding to Schedule G. For example, it asks for the prior tax status and

EIN of your predecessor group, and whether it has previously applied for a tax exemption. If the predecessor group was required to file tax returns and/or pay taxes but did not, expect the IRS to ask for these returns (and late filing and late payment penalties too). If the prior group was denied a tax exemption, you will need to clearly explain what has changed that makes you believe you qualify for an exemption now. The schedule also attempts to determine if the new nonprofit has been set up to benefit or serve the private interests of the people associated with the predecessor organization. If assets were transferred from the prior nonprofit association to the new nonprofit corporation, you are asked to provide a sales or transfer agreement (Schedule G, line 6(c)). If you have prepared this formal paperwork, attach a copy to your application. If you haven't (this is normally the case for small nonprofits that are formally converting a prior nonprofit association to a nonprofit corporation), you should prepare (perhaps with help from someone with financial savvy associated with your nonprofit) and put together a simple term sheet that lists the assets and liabilities transferred to the new nonprofit and the terms of the transfer. This simple agreement should be signed by officers of the prior association and directors or officers of your new nonprofit, and attached to Schedule G.

If your nonprofit corporation will lease property or equipment previously owned or used by the predecessor organization or will lease property from people associated with the prior group, include an explanation and copies of any leases as requested in line 8. The IRS will scrutinize a lease to make sure that it does not provide for excessive rent payments to the people associated with the former organization. If a nonprofit corporation is a successor to a prior nonprofit association, it's usually best, if possible, for the prior association simply to assign any leases to the nonprofit corporation without payment (or for a $1 consideration to keep things legal) or have the corporation renegotiate the leases with the landlord. That way, the successor nonprofit corporation can deal with the landlord directly rather than have people from the former organization retain the lease and require rent payments from the successor nonprofit corporation. (For an example of an assignment of lease form, see "Prepare Assignments of Leases and Deeds" in Chapter 9.) If your successor nonprofit will lease property back to the people associated with the prior group, line 9 also asks for a copy of the lease agreement. Obviously, a leaseback of property will be strictly scrutinized by the IRS to see if the payments are reasonable—the IRS also will wonder why the new nonprofit transferred the assets in the first place, since after the transfer it decided to lease them back to the people associated with the prior group. Leaseback deals like this look fine in the normal business world, but raise IRS examiner eyebrows when they are disclosed on tax-exemption applications.

Schedule H. Organizations Providing Scholarships, Educational Loans, or Other Educational Grants

Schedule H is used by the IRS to determine whether your nonprofit will provide financial aid on a nondiscriminatory basis. The IRS wants to know that financial aid funds will not be set aside specifically to help put family and friends of people associated with your nonprofit through school and that the providing of funds in general will promote your group's tax-exempt public purposes, which typically will be charitable and/or educational. For further information on IRS guidelines, see IRS Publication 557, "Charitable Organization

Supporting Education" and "Organization Providing Loans." Section II of this schedule can be used to get IRS approval of your organization's grant-making procedures if your organization is classified as a private foundation (in the event your request for public charity classification under Part X is denied). If you wish to plan for this contingency, consult your tax adviser to help you select the appropriate IRC section on line 1(b) of Section II.

Assemble and Mail Your Application to the IRS

You've accomplished the most difficult part of your paperwork. The only task left is to gather up your application forms and papers and send them off to the IRS. Follow these steps:

Complete the Checklist: The IRS wants you to complete and include the checklist with your mailed materials. The checklist is included as the last two pages of the 1023 application form. To complete the checklist, check each box to show you completed all the checklist tasks. If you followed the previous steps in this chapter, you should be able to check each box and complete each checklist task as follows:

- **Assemble your application materials in order.** Put your materials together in the order shown in the checklist. Note that Forms 2848 and 8821, as well as amendments to articles of incorporation, nondiscriminatory school statement, and Form 5768, will not apply to most groups.
- **User fee.** Place your user fee check at the top of your materials. Do not staple it to your application papers.
- **EIN.** Make sure you have obtained an Employer Identification Number (it should be stated in Part I, line 4, of your application).

- **Completed Parts I through XI of your application.** We assume you can check this checklist box to show you have completed all parts of the 1023 form.
- **Schedules.** Check "yes" or "no" to show which, if any, schedules you have completed and included with your application. Many groups will mark "no" to all schedules. Only submit schedules with your application that you have completed—do not include blank schedules.
- **Articles.** We assume you have included a file-stamped or certified copy of your articles in response to Part II, line 1, of the application. Fill in the two blanks here to show (1) your purpose clause (repeat the reference to your articles you inserted in response to Part III, line 1) and (2) your dissolution clause (repeat the reference to your articles you inserted in response to Part III, line 2(b)—we assume you did not refer to a state law provision in line 2(c)—see our instructions to Part II above).
- **Signature.** Make sure a director or officer has signed, filled in the name and title lines, and dated the form at the bottom of Part XI (and, if applicable, completed and signed the Consent lines in Part X, line 6(a)—see our instructions to this line, above).
- **Name of Organization.** The name you insert in Part I, line 1, of the 1023 application must be the same as the name of your corporation in your articles of incorporation.

Make Copies. After completing the checklist and including it as the first page of your exemption materials, make at least one photocopy of all pages and attachments to your application and file them in your corporate records book.

Mail Your Application. Mail your package to the IRS address listed in the checklist. You may want to send it certified mail, return receipt requested, to obtain proof of mailing and/or of receipt by the IRS. You can check for the current mailing address on the IRS website, at www.irs.gov. At this writing, the address is:

Internal Revenue Service
P.O. Box 12192
Covington, KY 41012-0192

As an alternative to regular mail, you may want to send your application papers to the IRS via an express mail service (see the approved list of private delivery services in the 1023 instructions, "Private Delivery Services"). The express mail address currently shown on the 1023 checklist is:

Internal Revenue Service
201 West Rivercenter Blvd.
Attn: Extracting Stop 312
Covington, KY 41011

Your next step is to wait. Although the IRS turnaround time to respond to your application is usually about three months, you may have to wait three to six months or more for a response to your exemption application. To see the timetables for the review process, go to the Charities & Non-Profits section of the IRS website at www.irs.gov and type in the search box "Where is My Exemption Application?".

You can request expedited filing of your 1023 application by submitting a written request along with your exemption application. The IRS may approve the request and speed up the processing of your application if your reason for the request is an impending grant deadline, if your nonprofit provides disaster relief, or if the IRS has already delayed a prior application or response to a previous application by the group. See "Expedite request," in the 1203 instructions, for more information.

CAUTION

You must file annual federal and state information returns for your organization while your federal tax exemption application is pending (see "Annual Filing Requirements" in the 1023 instructions and in Chapter 10). Indicate on your annual returns that your federal 1023 application is pending approval by the IRS.

What to Expect From the IRS

After reviewing your application, the IRS will do one of three things:

- grant your federal tax exemption
- request further information, or
- issue a proposed adverse determination (a denial of tax exemption that becomes effective 30 days from the date of issuance).

If the IRS asks for more information and you are not sure what they want from you—or you just feel that you are in over your head—consult a nonprofit attorney or tax adviser. If you receive a proposed denial and you wish to appeal, see a lawyer immediately. For further information on appeal procedures, see IRS Publication 557, *Tax-Exempt Status for Your Organization*, and type "Appeal Procedures" in the Search box on the IRS website at www.irs.gov for links to other appeals procedure information.

The Federal Determination Letter

The fortunate among you—and we trust it will be most of you—will get good news from the IRS. It will come in the form of a favorable determination letter, telling you that you are exempt from federal corporate income taxes under Section 501(c)(3) of the Internal

Revenue Code, as a public charity. Unless you filed your application late and were not entitled to an extension, your tax exemption and public charity status will be effective retroactively to the date when your articles were filed with the secretary of state.

CAUTION

If your determination letter tells you that you are exempt as a private foundation, see a tax or legal adviser immediately. Most nonprofits will not want to maintain a nonprofit private foundation, and often either contest the determination or decide to dissolve their nonprofit corporation immediately.

Resist the natural temptation to file the letter without reading past the first sentences. In fact, the letter contains important information regarding the basis for your exemption and the requirements for maintaining it. Here's what to look for:

- **Are you properly classified?** Check to make sure that the public charity section listed by the IRS corresponds to the kind of public charity status you asked for. (You will find the various public charity code sections listed in Part X, line 5, of your copy of the 1023 form.) Some groups will have checked Part X, line 5(i), to let the IRS determine the proper public charity support test category support test for the organization.

- **Must you file a federal tax return?** The determination letter will tell you whether you must file a federal annual information return, IRS Form 990 or Form 990-EZ. Most 501(c)(3) groups must file a 990 return (it's explained in Chapter 10).

- **Are you liable for excise taxes?** The determination letter also should state that you are not liable for excise taxes under Chapter 42 of the Internal Revenue Code. These are the taxes applicable to private foundations. The letter will also refer to other excise taxes for which you may be liable. These are the regular excise taxes applicable to all businesses that engage in certain activities, such as the sale of liquor, the manufacturing of certain products, and so on. For further information, see IRS Publication 510, *Excise Taxes.*

- **Information on deductions for donors.** Your letter will include information on the deductibility of charitable contributions made to your organization, and will refer to Internal Revenue Code sections that cover the deductibility of such donations.

- **Must you pay FUTA taxes?** Most groups will be told in their letter that they are exempt from federal unemployment (FUTA) taxes. You are, however, subject to filing nonprofit unrelated business income tax returns (Form 990-T). Nonprofits and their employees, however, are subject to Social Security (FICA) taxes—see "Federal and State Corporate Employment Taxes" in Chapter 10.

Congratulations! You've just finished the most complicated, and indeed most crucial, part of your nonprofit incorporation process. The remaining formal incorporation steps are explained in the next chapter. ●

Final Steps in Organizing Your Nonprofit Corporation

Most of the hard work is over, but there are still a few important details to attend to. Don't be overwhelmed by the number of steps that follow—many will not apply to your nonprofit corporation and others are very simple.

To chart your way through the tasks that follow, we recommend you use the Incorporation Checklist, included in Appendix C and on the CD-ROM.

Obtain State Corporate Income Tax Exemption

Most states impose an annual corporate income, franchise, or other tax based on the net earnings of the corporation. In these states, your corporation must obtain an exemption from payment of these corporate taxes. In many cases, obtaining this state tax exemption is a formality—you will generally receive it once you file nonprofit articles in your state and obtain a federal 501(c)(3) tax exemption.

We suggest you browse your state corporate tax agency website now and request all information and forms necessary for you to apply for your state exemption from corporate taxes (see Appendix B).

The state tax exemption application process will be simple and self-explanatory in most cases. In the few instances where you must answer detailed questions or submit separate financial data, the responses and attachments to your federal 1023 package should serve as sufficient responses on the state form.

Make sure to take care of your state tax exemption in a timely fashion (usually by the end of your first tax year). As with the federal form, if you reach the deadline date for your annual state tax return and your state tax exemption is pending, make sure to file your required annual state return, indicating that the state tax-exemption application is pending. Remember, like the IRS, state tax departments can impose severe fines and penalties for failing to file required tax returns, whether or not your corporation is subject to, or liable for, any corporate taxes.

Set Up a Corporate Records Book

Now take a few minutes to set up or order a corporate records book—this is an important part of your incorporation process.

Corporate Records Book

You will need a corporate records book to keep all your papers in an orderly fashion. These documents include articles of incorporation, bylaws, minutes of your first board meeting and ongoing director and shareholder meetings, tax exemption applications and determination letters, membership certificates (for those nonprofits with formal members), and any other related documents. You should keep your corporate records book at the principal office of your corporation at all times to make sure you always know where to find it.

To set up a corporate records book, you can simply place all your incorporation documents in a three-ring binder. If you prefer, however, you can order a custom-designed corporate records book.

Corporate Kits

You can order a nonprofit corporate kit through a legal stationery store. These nonprofit corporate kits typically include:

- a corporate records book with minute paper and index dividers for charter (articles of incorporation), bylaws, minutes, and membership certificates

- a metal corporate seal (a circular stamp with the name of your corporation, the state's name, and year of incorporation), which you can use on important corporate documents, and

- membership certificates, printed with the name of your corporation.

Corporate Seals

Placing a corporate seal on a document is a formal way of showing that the document is the authorized act of the corporation. Nonprofits don't normally use a seal on everyday business papers (such as invoices and purchase orders), but they do use them for more formal documents, such as leases, membership certificates, deeds of trust, and certifications of board resolutions. A corporation is not legally required to have or use a corporate seal, but many find it convenient to do so.

A customized metal seal is usually included as part of a corporate kit you can order from a legal stationery store.

Corporate Membership Certificates

If you have decided to adopt a formal membership structure with members entitled to vote for the board of directors, you may want to use membership certificates. Unlike stock certificates used in profit corporations, membership certificates in nonprofit 501(c)(3) corporations do not represent an ownership interest in the assets of the corporation. They serve only as a formal reminder of membership status.

The certificates that you issue should be numbered sequentially. Type the certificate number at the top of the form. Type the name of the corporation in the heading and the name of the member in the blank in the first paragraph. Have the certificate signed by your president and secretary, then place an impression of the seal of the corporation at the bottom. You should also record the name and address of the member and the number of the issued membership certificate in the membership list in your corporate records.

Prepare the Minutes of Your First Board of Directors Meeting

Your next step is to prepare minutes of your first board of directors meeting. The initial board of directors named in your articles of incorporation attends this meeting. If you did not name an initial board in your articles, see "If You Have Not Named Initial Directors in Your Articles," below, for instructions on having your incorporator(s) appoint the initial board. The purpose of this meeting is to transact the initial business of the corporation (elect officers, fix the legal address of the corporation, and so on) and to authorize the newly elected officers to take actions necessary to get your nonprofit corporation going (set up bank accounts, admit members if appropriate, and so on). Your directors should also discuss any other steps necessary at this point to get your nonprofit activities and operations started.

Prepare the minutes by filling in the blanks on the tear-out Minutes of First Meeting of Board of Directors, included in Appendix C, or on the Minutes form, on the CD-ROM, following the instructions below.

TIP

We have flagged optional resolutions in the special instructions below. If an optional resolution does not apply to you, do not include the optional resolution page in your final minutes.

Here are some instructions to help you prepare your minutes.

Waiver of Notice form. You can find this Waiver of Notice form preceding the tear-out minutes in Appendix C; a copy is also included on the CD-ROM. The purpose of this form is to obtain the prior written consent of each initial director to hold your first board meeting. Under the statutes of many states, if the directors consent in writing the corporation may dispense with special notice procedures that would otherwise apply to this first unscheduled meeting of the board. Even if this written consent procedure does not apply in your state, you can use this form to notify each of your directors of the upcoming first meeting of the board.

Fill in this form showing the name and address of your corporation and the date, time, and place of the meeting. Date the form and have each initial director sign.

Preamble to minutes. The first page of the minutes contains several standard paragraphs reciting facts necessary to hold a meeting of directors. Type the name of your corporation, the date and time of the meeting, and the address of the corporation, in the first few blanks. Next, list the names of the initial directors present at and, if applicable, absent from, the meeting. Remember, a quorum of the board, as specified in the bylaws, must be in attendance to carry out corporate business.

Name one of the directors as chairperson and another as secretary of the meeting. You will elect permanent officers later in the meeting.

Articles of incorporation. Indicate the name of the state corporate filings office (usually the secretary of state) where the articles were filed and the date of this filing.

Bylaws. This resolution shows that your directors accept the contents of the bylaws.

Corporate tax exemptions. This resolution shows that your organization has obtained a favorable IRS determination of its 501(c)(3) tax-exempt status and is exempt from any applicable state corporate income taxes as well. Put the date of your federal determination letter in the blank in the first paragraph.

Election of officers. Type the names of the persons that the directors elect as officers of your corporation. Most nonprofits will wish to fill each of the four officer positions listed in this resolution. In many cases, particularly in larger nonprofits, officers are selected from among the board of directors.

RELATED TOPIC

Most states require a nonprofit to have a president, treasurer, and secretary, and allow one person to fill more than one or all of the officer positions. See your state's nonprofit law and check our sidebar, "How Many People Are Needed to Form a Nonprofit Corporation?," in Chapter 2.

If You Have Not Named Initial Directors in Your Articles

In some states, initial directors need not be named in the articles. If this is the case, then the incorporators (the person or persons who signed the articles) must appoint the initial board of directors. To do this, type the following form, fill in the name of the persons appointed to the board, and have each incorporator sign the form. Then prepare the minutes of your first board meeting as explained in the text. Make sure to place a copy of this form in your corporate minutes.

Meeting of Incorporators

On _____, 20__,
at _____ o'clock, a meeting of the incorporator(s) of (name of corporation) was held to elect the initial members of the board of directors. After nomination and discussion, the following persons were unanimously voted to serve on the board of directors of this corporation until their successors shall be elected and qualified:

_____

_____

_____

_____

There being no further business, the meeting was adjourned.

Dated: _____

[signature(s) of incorporator(s)]

Principal office. Article 1, Section 1, of the bylaws indicates the county of the principal office of your corporation. Here you should provide the street address and city of this office. You should not list a post office box.

Bank account. You must keep corporate funds separate from any personal funds by depositing corporate funds into, and writing corporate checks out of, at least one corporate checking account. Indicate the bank and branch office where you will maintain corporate accounts in the first blank. In the second blank, indicate the number of persons (one or more) who must cosign corporate checks. In the remaining blanks, list the names of individuals allowed to cosign checks. Many corporations list the president and treasurer, among others.

Optional compensation of officers. Indicate any salaries to be paid to the officers in the blanks in this resolution. Type a zero to show unpaid officers' resolutions. Most nonprofits do not compensate officers, or do so only minimally. If you do provide for real officer salaries, make sure they are reasonable and are related to what other people in the nonprofit sector make for providing similar services.

Optional corporate seal. If you've ordered a corporate seal, impress the seal in the space to the right of this resolution.

Optional corporate certificates. This is an optional resolution. Include this page in your final minutes if you have ordered director, sponsor, membership, or other certificates for your corporation and attach a sample of each certificate to your completed minutes.

Secretary certification page. Your secretary should date and sign the blanks on the last page of the minutes.

Place Minutes and Attachments in Corporate Records Book

You are now through preparing your minutes. Place your minutes and all attachments in your corporate records book. Your attachments may include the following forms or documents:

- Waiver of Notice and Consent to Holding of First Meeting of Board of Directors
- copy of your articles, or certificate of incorporation, file-stamped or certified by the secretary of state
- copy of your bylaws
- federal 501(c)(3) tax exemption determination letter
- copy of state tax exemption application determination letter or other correspondence, and
- sample director, sponsor, or membership certificates.

Remember, you should continue to place an original or copy of all formal corporate documents in your corporate records book (including minutes of director, committee, and membership meetings) and keep this book at your principal office.

Issue Membership Certificates

If you have set up a membership corporation and have membership certificates, you will want to issue them to members after they have applied for membership in the corporation and paid any fees required by the membership provisions in your bylaws. The corporate president and secretary should sign each certificate before giving it to the member.

If you have ordered membership materials, record each member's name and address, together with the number of the certificate, in the membership register in your corporate records book. When you prepare your membership certificates, complete each certificate by typing the number of the certificate, the name of the corporation, and the name of the member on the certificate. Then execute the certificate by filling in the date and having the president and secretary sign at the bottom (if you have a seal, impress it at the bottom of each certificate). Give the certificate to the member, then record the member's name, address, certificate number, and date of issuance on a separate page in your corporate records book. The information on these pages, kept in the corporate records book, constitutes the membership book of the corporation.

File Fictitious or Assumed Business Name Statement

If your nonprofit corporation will engage in activities (raise funds, apply for grants, advertise, sell goods or services, and so on) under a name other than the exact corporate name given in your articles of incorporation, you will need to file an assumed or fictitious business name statement with your secretary of state and/or county clerk's office.

EXAMPLE:

If the name stated in your articles is "THE ART WORKS, INC.," and the corporation plans to continue using the name of the preexisting organization which was incorporated as "THE ART STUDIO" (or chooses another name different from the one set out in the articles), you should file an assumed corporate name statement.

Your secretary of state website should contain information on assumed corporate name statements. If not, call or email your secretary of state or other corporate filings office and ask if this filing is made at the state or county level (or both). Order the form from the appropriate office and prepare and file the statement. In most cases, a small fee is charged for this filing. Also, the statement may need to be published locally in a legal newspaper and a proof of publication filed with your county clerk. Check the instructions to the form for the requirements in your state.

Filing an assumed or fictitious business name statement does not authorize you to use a name that another business is already using as a trademark, trade name, or service mark. Before you settle on a fictitious name, make sure the name is not already in use (just as you did with your corporate name—see "Choose a Corporate Name," in Chapter 6, for details).

Apply for a Federal Nonprofit Mailing Permit

Most 501(c)(3) tax-exempt nonprofit corporations will qualify for and want to obtain a third-class nonprofit mailing permit from the U.S. Post Office. This permit entitles you to lower rates on mailings, an important advantage for many groups since the nonprofit rate is considerably lower than the regular third-class rate.

To obtain your permit, bring to your local or main post office branch:

- a file-stamped or certified copy of your articles
- a copy of your bylaws
- a copy of your federal and state tax-exemption determination letters, and

- copies of program literature, newsletters, bulletins, and any other promotional materials.

The post office clerk will ask you to fill out a short application and take your papers. If your local post office branch doesn't handle this, the clerk will send you to a classifications office at the main post office. You'll pay a one-time fee and an annual permit fee. The clerk will forward your papers to the classification office at the regional post office for a determination. In a week or so, you will receive notice of the post office's determination.

Once you have your permit, you can mail letters and parcels at the reduced rate by affixing stamps to your mail; taking the mail to your post office and filling out a special mailing form; or by using the simpler methods of either stamping your mail with an imprint stamp (made by a stampmaker) or leasing a mail stamping machine that shows your imprint information. Ask the classifications clerk for further information.

Apply for Property Tax Exemptions

We've already discussed state tax exemptions for real and personal property taxes, in Chapter 5. Now is the time to apply for any property tax exemptions available to your group. Remember:

- Apply for an exemption from local personal property taxes if real property is owned or leased by the corporation.
- If you establish an exemption on leased premises, your landlord should give you a corresponding reduction in rent payments.
- Even if your federal tax exemption is pending, you may want to submit your application for a property tax exemption as soon as possible. When you get your federal

tax exemption, forward a copy to the taxing agency. This way, you may be able to obtain at least a partial exemption for the current property tax year.

The procedure for applying for an exemption from local personal and real property taxes varies. Often you will need to submit a completed application form, copies of your articles and bylaws, and current and projected financial statements. You can copy the initial financial statements from, or base them on, the financial statement information you submitted with your federal 1023 form.

Call your county tax assessor or collector to find out what property tax exemptions are available for your tax-exempt 501(c)(3) nonprofit corporation and the procedures for applying. In some cases, you must apply to an office in the state capital; in others, the county office will process the papers locally. There may be multiple exemption categories to choose from. For example, a religious group may qualify for a church property tax exemption and for a separate property exemption available to 501(c)(3) nonprofit organizations. The county office should be able to advise you as to the most appropriate property exemption available to your group.

File an Initial Corporate Report Form

In most states you must file a periodic nonprofit corporate report form or statement with the secretary of state's office. Most states require you to file this form annually.

RESOURCE

Your state corporate filing office website should contain information on any periodic corporate report requirements and provide a downloadable form you can use. (See Appendix B.)

While the nature and extent of the information required in each state varies, most states require certain basic organizational information, such as the address of your principal office, the names and addresses of your directors and officers, your registered agent and office, and so on. In some cases, you must also submit financial information, such as directors' and officers' salaries, officer and supervisory staff compensation, fundraising receipts, and so on. Usually, the secretary of state makes this information available to the public.

Because failing to file a periodic report may lead to a fine or, for repeated failures, a suspension or forfeiture of corporate powers, make sure to file your corporate reports on time.

Register With the Attorney General

In some states, 501(c)(3) nonprofit corporations must register and report to the state attorney general's office. The attorney general scrutinizes nonprofit activities to make sure that the assets of the 501(c)(3) organization are being used for valid charitable or public purposes, not for private purposes.

The information sought on attorney general reporting forms varies. Most commonly, the financial reporting requirements seek to determine whether funds solicited from the public are being used for their stated purpose and whether any of the principals of the nonprofit (directors, officers, staff) are benefiting unduly from nonprofit funds or programs.

In some states, you must file an initial registration form, with a periodic report required each succeeding year or so. We suggest you check with the attorney general's office by calling the main office in your state capital (the website of your state filing office may provide a link to the state attorney general's office). Ask if your 501(c)(3) tax-exempt nonprofit corporation must register or report to this office. In many states, this reporting function is handled by the charitable trusts division or department. Ask if your state has a similar division or department in the attorney general's office.

Check Local Ordinances

If you plan to solicit contributions locally (for example, as part of a door-to-door fundraising drive), make sure to comply with all local solicitation ordinances and regulations. Some counties and cities enforce local registration and reporting requirements. Other localities require you to furnish specific statements and disclose information to persons solicited by the nonprofit corporation.

Comply With Political Reporting Requirements

If your nonprofit corporation plans to lobby for legislation, hire a lobbyist, or otherwise be politically active (for example, by supporting or opposing state, county, or city measures to be voted on by the public), we suggest you check to see if your state imposes political registration or reporting requirements. (See "Limitation on Political Activities," in Chapter 3, for more on political activities and 501(c)(3) nonprofits.) Often, a Fair Political Practices Commission or similar body in the state capital oversees and administers these requirements. Another politically active nonprofit organization in your community should have experience with these requirements and should be able to direct you to the proper state office.

If you are active in campaigns for candidates to federal political office, also check whether you are subject to the registration and reporting rules under the Federal Election Campaign Act. For information on FECA and the rules and regulations administered under this act by the Federal Election Commission, go to www.fec.gov.

SKIP AHEAD
The final three steps of this chapter apply only to groups that have incorporated a preexisting organization.

Prepare Assignments of Leases and Deeds

If you have transferred a prior business or organization to your corporation, the prior owners or nonprofit organization may want to prepare assignments of leases or deeds if they are transferring real property interests to the corporation. Under an assignment, you step into the shoes of the old tenant—the terms and conditions of the lease don't change.

Here is a basic Assignment of Lease form you can use, or modify for use.

Assignment of Lease

[Name of original lessee, for example, the
unincorporated nonprofit organization],
Lessee of those premises commonly
known as   *[address of leased property]*   ,
hereby assigns the attached Lease relating to
the above premises, executed *[date original*
lease was signed] , and all rights, liabilities,
and obligations thereunder, to a proposed
corporation, *[name of corporation]* .

Dated: _____

[name of Lessee] _____

By: *[signature of Lessee representative]* _____

      [typed name of representative] _____

The undersigned Lessor of the above premises
hereby assents to this Assignment of Lease.

Dated: _____

By: *[signature of Lessor]* _____

      [typed name of Lessor], Lessor

TIP

Renegotiate rental agreements or leases.
Of course, assignments can be dispensed with if
rental agreements or leases are simply renegotiated
between the landlord and the new corporation.
Even if you do prepare an assignment, the terms
of the lease itself will normally require you to get
the landlord's consent (the sample assignment of
lease form above includes a clause showing the
lessor's consent to the assignment). It is particularly
important to communicate with the landlord
if the nonprofit corporation expects to obtain
an exemption from local real property taxes on
the leased premises (see "Apply for Property Tax
Exemptions," above). Nonprofit groups in this
situation will want to insert a clause in their new
lease allowing them a credit against rent payments
for the amount of the decrease in the landlord's
property tax bill as a result of obtaining their real
property tax exemption.

A real estate broker or agent can help you
obtain and prepare new leases and deeds. If a
mortgage or deed of trust is involved, you may
need the permission of the lender.

File Final Papers for Prior Organization

If you have incorporated a preexisting group,
you may need to file final sales tax, employment
tax, and other returns for the prior organization.
You will also want to cancel any permits or
licenses issued to the prior organization or its
principals, obtaining new licenses in the name
of the nonprofit corporation.

Notify Others of Your Incorporation

If a preexisting group has been incorporated,
notify creditors and other interested parties,
in writing, of the termination and dissolution
of the prior organization and of its transfer to
the new corporation. This is advisable as a legal
precaution and as a courtesy to those who have
dealt with the prior organization.

To notify past creditors, suppliers, organizations, and businesses of your incorporation,
send a friendly letter that shows the date of your
incorporation, your corporate name, and its
principal office address. Retain a copy of each
letter for inclusion in your corporate records
book.

TIP

If the prior group was organized as a partnership (not a common situation), some states require the publication of a Notice of Dissolution of Partnership in the county or judicial district where the partnership office or property was located. To do this, call a local legal newspaper and ask if this notice form is published by the paper. If so, the newspaper will charge a small fee to publish the statement the required number of times and send you a proof of publication form for your files. If required, the newspaper should also file the proof of publication with the county clerk, the county recorder, or other appropriate county office.

After Your Corporation Is Organized

You have now incorporated your nonprofit and have handled many initial organizational details. But before you close this book, read just a little more. After incorporating, you need to become familiar with the formalities of corporate life, such as filing tax returns, paying employment taxes, and preparing minutes of formal corporate meetings. In this chapter, we look at some tax and other routine filings required by federal, state, and local governmental agencies. At the end, we give you an overview of what's involved in dissolving a nonprofit corporation.

The information presented here won't tell you everything you will need to know about these subjects, but will provide some of the basics and indicate some of the major areas that you (or your tax adviser) will need to go over in more detail.

Piercing the Corporate Veil—If You Want to Be Treated Like a Corporation, It's Best to Act Like One

After you've set up a corporation of any kind, your organization should act like one. Although filing your articles of incorporation with the secretary of state brings the corporation into existence as a legal entity, this is not enough to ensure that a court or the IRS will treat your organization as a corporation. What we are referring to here is not simply maintaining your various tax exemptions or even your nonprofit status with the state—we are talking about being treated as a valid corporate entity in court and for tax purposes. Remember, it is your legal corporate status that allows your organization to be treated as an entity apart from its directors, officers, and employees and allows it to be taxed (or not taxed), sue, or be sued, on its own. It is the corporate entity that insulates the people behind the corporation from taxes and lawsuits.

Courts and the IRS do, on occasion, scrutinize the organization and operation of a corporation, particularly if it is directed and operated by a small number of people who wear more than one hat (such as those who fill both director and officer positions). If you don't take care to treat your corporation as a separate legal entity, a court may decide to disregard the corporation and hold the principals (directors and officers) personally liable for corporate debts. This might happen if the corporation doesn't have adequate money to start with, making it likely that creditors or people who have claims against the corporation won't be able to be paid; if corporate and personal funds are commingled; if the corporation doesn't keep adequate corporate records (such as minutes of meetings); or generally doesn't pay much attention to the theory and practice of corporate life. Also, the IRS may assess taxes and penalties personally against those connected with managing the affairs of the corporation if it concludes that the corporation is not a valid legal or tax entity. In legal jargon, holding individuals responsible for corporate deeds or misdeeds is called piercing the corporate veil.

To avoid problems of this type, be careful to operate your corporation as a separate legal entity. Hold regular and special meetings of your board and membership as required by your bylaws and as necessary to take formal corporate action. It is critical that you document formal corporate meetings with neat and thorough minutes. Also, it is wise to have enough money in your corporate account to pay foreseeable debts and liabilities that may arise in the course of carrying out your activities—even nonprofits should start with a small cash reserve. Above all, keep corporate funds separate from the personal funds of the individuals who manage or work for the corporation.

Federal Corporate Tax Returns

In this section, we list and briefly discuss the main IRS tax paperwork you can expect to face as a 501(c)(3) nonprofit corporation.

Your 990 and 990-T (unrelated business income return) forms must be made available for public inspection (go to the IRS website, at www.irs.gov, for more information).

CAUTION

Make sure your tax forms are current. IRS forms, instructions, fees, and penalties are subject to constant change. Be sure to get the most current information (on return deadlines, tax rates, penalties, and so on) when you file. You can download the federal tax forms discussed in this section from the IRS website, at www.irs.gov.

Public Charities: Annual Exempt Organization Return

Nonprofit corporations exempt from federal corporate income tax under Section 501(c)(3) and treated or classified as public charities must file IRS Form 990, *Return of Organization Exempt From Income Tax* (together with Form 990, Schedule A). The filing deadline is on or before the 15th day of the fifth month (within four and a half months) following the close of their accounting period (tax year). You should file this even if your 1023 federal application for exemption is still pending.

Some groups may be eligible to file IRS Form 990-EZ instead of Form 990. This is a short form annual return that can be used by small tax-exempt public charities—those with gross receipts of less than specified amounts—see the instructions to the current Form 990 on the IRS website, at www.irs.gov, for more

information. Any 501(c)(3) public charities that file Form 990 or 990-EZ must also complete and submit Form 990, Schedule A (with additional schedules if required), with their return. This form is used to test whether the publicly-supported charity meets the applicable support test for the year (see Chapter 4).

CAUTION

Watch out for short deadlines. Your first 990 return deadline may come up sooner than you expect if your first tax year is a "short year"—a tax year of fewer than 12 months.

EXAMPLE: If your accounting period as specified in your bylaws runs from January 1 to December 31 and your articles were filed on December 1, your first tax year consists of one month, from December 1 to December 31. In this situation, your first Form 990 would have to be filed within four and a half months of December 31 (by May 15 of the following year), only five and a half months after your articles were filed. It is likely that your federal tax exemption application would still be pending at this time.

Groups Exempt From Filing Form 990

The Internal Revenue Code exempts certain public charities from filing Form 990, including certain churches, schools, mission societies, religious activity groups, state institutions, corporations organized under an Act of Congress, tax-exempt private foundations, certain trusts, religious and apostolic organizations, and public charities. In general, these groups cannot normally have more than $25,000 in gross receipts in each taxable year. See the official instructions to IRS Form 990 for the details of these exemptions.

Your federal exemption determination letter should state whether you must file Form 990. Most public charities will be publicly supported organizations or receive a majority of their support from exempt-purpose revenue (see "Public Support Test" and "Exempt Activities Support Test" in Chapter 4). Because these groups are not institutional public charities falling under one of the automatic exemptions to filing listed above, they will have to file Form 990 unless they meet the normally not more than $25,000 gross receipts exemption. To rely on this exemption, fill in the top portion of the 990 form and check the box indicating that you are eligible for this exemption.

If your nonprofit corporation makes the political expenditures election by filing Federal Election Form 5768 (discussed in "Limitation on Political Activities" in Chapter 3), indicate on Form 990, Schedule A, that you made this election and fill in the appropriate part of the schedule showing your actual lobbying expenditures during the year.

> **CAUTION**
>
> **IRS e-Postcard, Form 990-N, annual filing requirement for small nonprofits.** Small tax-exempt organizations that are not required to file 990 returns with the IRS are required to file an annual electronic notice with the IRS—Form 990-N, *Electronic Notice (e-Postcard) for Tax-Exempt Organizations not Required To File Form 990 or 990-EZ*. Organizations that do not file the e-Postcard or an information return Form 990 or 990-EZ for three consecutive years will have their tax-exempt status revoked.
>
> For more information and to file a 990-N online, visit the IRS website, at www.irs.gov (the direct link to fill in and file 990-N is http://epostcard.form990.org).

Private Foundations: Annual Exempt Organization Return

Very few 501(c)(3) nonprofits will be classified as private foundations. If you are one, however, you must file a federal annual *Return of Private Foundation or Section 4947(a)(1) Nonexempt Charitable Trust Treated as a Private Foundation*, Form 990-PF, within four and one-half months of the close of your tax year. You file this Form 990-PF instead of Form 990 discussed above. You'll provide information on receipts and expenditures, assets and liabilities, and other information that will help the IRS determine whether you are liable for private foundation excise taxes. You should receive the form and separate instructions for completing it close to the end of your accounting period. Again, watch out for a short first year and an early deadline for filing your Form 990-PF.

The foundation manager(s) must publish a notice telling the public that they may see the annual report. Do so in a local county newspaper before the filing deadline for the 990-PF. The notice must state that the annual report is available for public inspection, at the principal office of the corporation, within 180 days after the publication of the inspection notice. A copy of the published notice must be attached to the 990-PF.

Unrelated Business Income: Annual Exempt Organization Tax Return

With a few minor exceptions, Section 501(c)(3) federal tax-exempt corporations that have gross incomes of $1,000 or more during the year from an unrelated trade or business must file an *Exempt Organization Business Income Tax Return* (Form 990-T). The form is due within two and a half months after the close of their tax year. For a definition and discussion of unrelated trades and businesses, see "Federal Unrelated Business Income Tax," in Chapter 5, and obtain Federal Publication 598, *Tax on Unrelated Business Income of Exempt Organizations*. Use booklet 598 and the separate instructions to Form 990-T to prepare this form.

The taxes imposed on unrelated business income are the same rates applied to normal federal corporate income. Remember that too much unrelated business income may indicate to the IRS that you are engaging in nonexempt activities to a "substantial" degree and may jeopardize your tax exemption.

More Information on Taxes

We suggest all nonprofits obtain IRS Publication 509, *Tax Calendars*, prior to the beginning of each year. This pamphlet contains tax calendars showing the dates for corporate and employer filings during the year.

Information on withholding, depositing, reporting, and paying federal employment taxes can be found in IRS Publication 15 (Circular E) *Employer's Tax Guide*, and the Publication 15-A and 15-B Supplements.

Other helpful IRS publications are Publication 542, *Corporations*, and Publication 334, *Tax Guide for Small Business*.

Helpful information on accounting methods and bookkeeping procedures is contained in IRS Publication 538, *Accounting Periods and Methods*, and Publication 583, *Starting a Business and Keeping Records*.

You can get IRS publications online, at www.irs.gov. You can also pick them up at your local IRS office (or order them by phone—call your local IRS office or try the toll-free IRS forms and publications request telephone number, 800-TAX-FORM).

File Your Returns on Time

The IRS and states are notoriously efficient in assessing and collecting late filing and other penalties. So, while it may be true that your nonprofit corporation does not have to worry about paying income taxes (because of its federal and state income exemptions), you should worry a bit about filing your annual information returns on time (including your employment tax returns and payments). Too many nonprofit corporations have had to liquidate when forced to pay late filing penalties (which add up quickly) for a few years' worth of simple informational returns that they inadvertently forgot to file.

Another important aspect of late filing penalties and delinquent employment taxes is that the IRS (and state) can, and often do, try to collect these often substantial amounts from individuals associated with the corporation if the corporation doesn't have sufficient cash to pay them. Remember, one of the exceptions to the concept of limited liability is liability for unpaid taxes and tax penalties. The IRS and state can go after the person (or persons) associated with the corporation who are determined to be responsible for reporting and/or paying taxes.

RESOURCE

For guidance on avoiding IRS problems and retaining your tax-exempt status, see *Every Nonprofit's Tax Guide*, by Stephen Fishman (Nolo).

State Corporate Tax Returns and Reports

Make sure to file your state corporate tax returns on time. In many states, the state forms are based on or follow the federal nonprofit corporate tax returns discussed above and are due on the same date. You can obtain state tax corporate forms online at your state tax office website (see Appendix B). Or you can make a call to your state department of taxation and revenue (or similar state tax agency or department) to order annual nonprofit corporation tax forms, schedules, and instructions.

Federal and State Corporate Employment Taxes

You must withhold and pay federal and state employment (payroll) taxes on behalf of the people who work for your nonprofit corporation. Directors, with certain exceptions, are not considered employees if they are paid only for attending board meetings. However, if they are paid for other services or as salaried employees of the corporation, the IRS will consider them employees whose wages are subject to employment taxes. Check with the IRS and your local state employment tax office for further information.

501(c)(3)s are exempt from paying federal unemployment insurance (FUTA) taxes but must collect, withhold, report, and pay federal Social Security (FICA) and individual income taxes on employees' salaries. Your tax-exempt nonprofit may be exempt from having to pay some state employment taxes as well.

For information and help in computing your federal withholding and employer contribution payments, obtain the IRS publications listed in "More Information on Taxes," above. To register as an employer in your state and for information on meeting state payroll tax requirements, call the state employment tax office in your vicinity (or go to the employer registration office online—your state tax office website may provide a link).

Generally, independent contractors, such as consultants, who are not subject to the control of the corporation—both as to what shall be done and how the work is to be performed—are not considered employees. Wages paid to these people are not subject to payroll tax withholding or payment by the nonprofit corporation.

> **CAUTION**
>
> **Be careful when classifying people as independent contractors.** The law in this area is fuzzy, and the IRS (as well as the state employment tax office) is obstinate about trying to prove that outsiders really work for the corporation (and must be covered by payroll taxes). For more information, see IRS Publication 1779. An excellent legal guide to the ins and outs of independent contractor status is *Working for Yourself: Law & Taxes for Independent Contractors, Freelancers & Consultants*, by Stephen Fishman (Nolo).

Employee Income Tax Returns

Corporate staff and other compensated corporate personnel must report and pay taxes on employment compensation on their individual annual federal income tax returns (IRS Form 1040). If your state imposes a personal income tax, state income taxes are computed and paid with the employee's state personal income tax return.

Sales Tax Forms and Exemption From Sales Tax

Your corporation may be required to charge and collect state, county, and city sales, use, transit, excise, and other state taxes from customers or clients. In some cases, nonprofit exemptions from one or more of these state taxes may be available to your 501(c)(3) nonprofit corporation. Contact your state department of revenue, taxation, or similar state agency to register your corporation for sales tax and obtain any exemptions to which you may be entitled.

Licenses and Permits

Many businesses, whether operating as profit or nonprofit corporations, partnerships, or sole proprietorships, are required to obtain state licenses and permits before commencing business. So, while you may not be subject to the usual kind of red tape applicable to strictly profit-making enterprises (such as contractors, real estate brokers, or engineers), you should check with your state department of consumer affairs (or similar state licensing agency or department) for information concerning any state licensing requirements for your activities or type of organization. Many nonprofit institutions, such as schools or hospitals, will need to comply with a number of registration and reporting requirements administered by the state and, possibly, county government. A local business license or permit may also be required for your activities—check with your city business license department.

Workers' Compensation

Workers' compensation insurance coverage compensates workers for losses caused by work-related injuries and protects the corporation from lawsuits brought to recover these amounts. In some states, this coverage is mandatory; in others it is optional. Specific exemptions from coverage may be available to directors and officers in some instances. Make sure to check with your insurance agent or broker, or call your state compensation insurance commission, for names of carriers, rates, and extent of required coverage.

Private Insurance Coverage

Nonprofit corporations, like other organizations, should carry the usual types of commercial insurance to prevent undue loss in the event of an accident, fire, theft, and so on. Although the corporate form may insulate directors, officers, and members from personal loss, it won't prevent corporate assets from being jeopardized by such eventualities. Examine coverage for general liability, product liability, and fire and theft. You should also consider liability insurance for directors and officers, particularly if your nonprofit corporation wants to reassure any passive directors on the board that they will be protected from personal liability in the event of a lawsuit.

Dissolving a Nonprofit Corporation

A corporation may be dissolved either voluntarily or involuntarily. Voluntary dissolution occurs when a corporation decides to wind up its affairs by a vote of the board of directors, or a vote of the board in conjunction with the formal membership. The corporation might decide to dissolve because it runs out of program or administrative funds, because of an internal dispute within the nonprofit, or simply because the nonprofit program has accomplished its purposes or done as much as is reasonably possible in its area of endeavor.

A corporation dissolves voluntarily by filing articles of dissolution (or a similar document) with the secretary of state and, in some cases, obtaining a tax clearance from the state department of taxation or revenue. (Your secretary of state's website should contain forms and instructions to dissolve a nonprofit corporation in your state.)

Involuntary dissolution may occur if the corporation has failed to file its required annual financial report or pay state taxes for which it is liable for a given number of years. In such instances, the secretary of state or the attorney general will initiate the dissolution, depending on which department has jurisdiction over the misfeasance. The nonprofit corporation itself may petition the court to involuntarily dissolve it if its board is deadlocked, if it has been inactive for a number of years, or for other reasons specified under state statutes.

After a board decision to dissolve, the corporation must cease transacting business except to the extent necessary to wind up its affairs. All corporate debts and liabilities, to the extent of the corporation's remaining assets, must be paid or provided for. If any corporate assets are left after paying corporate debts, a 501(c)(3) tax-exempt nonprofit corporation must distribute them to another 501(c)(3) group. ●

Lawyers and Accountants

While we believe you can take care of the bulk of the work required to organize and operate your nonprofit corporation, you may need to consult a lawyer or accountant on complicated or special issues. It also makes sense to have a lawyer or accountant experienced in forming nonprofits and preparing tax exemption applications look over your papers. Reviewing your incorporation papers with an attorney or accountant is a sensible way to ensure that all of your papers are up to date and meet your needs. Besides, making contact with a legal and tax person early in your corporate life is often a sensible step. As your group grows and its programs expand, you'll be able to consult these professionals for help with ongoing legal and tax questions.

The professionals you contact should have experience in nonprofit incorporations and tax exemption applications. They should also be prepared to help you help yourself—to answer your questions and review, not rewrite, the forms you have prepared.

The next sections provide a few general suggestions on how to find the right lawyer or tax adviser and, if you wish to do your own legal research, how to find the law.

Lawyers

Finding the right lawyer is not always easy. Obviously, the best lawyer to choose is someone you personally know and trust, who has lots of experience advising smaller nonprofits. Of course, this may be a tall order. The next best is a nonprofit adviser whom a friend, another nonprofit incorporator, or someone in your nonprofit network recommends. A local nonprofit resource center, for example, may be able to steer you to one or more lawyers who maintain active nonprofit practices. With patience and persistence (and enough phone calls), this second word-of-mouth approach almost always brings positive results.

Another approach is to locate a local non-profit legal referral panel. Local bar associations or another nonprofit organization typically run panels of this sort. A referral panel in your area may be able to give you the names of lawyers who are experienced in nonprofit law and practice and who offer a discount or free consultation as part of the referral panel program. Ask about (and try to avoid) referral services that are operated on a strict rotating basis. With this system, you'll get the name of the next lawyer on the list, not necessarily one with nonprofit experience. You can also check the lawyer directory at www.nolo.com.

When you call a prospective lawyer, speak with the lawyer personally, not just the reception desk. You can probably get a good idea of how the person operates by paying close attention to the way your call is handled. Is the lawyer available, or is your call returned promptly? Is the lawyer willing to spend at least a few minutes talking to you to determine if he or she is really the best person for the job? Does the lawyer seem sympathetic to, and compatible with, the nonprofit goals of your group? Do you get a good personal feeling from your conversation? Oh, and one more thing: Be sure to get the hourly rate the lawyer will charge set in advance. If you are using this book, you will probably want to eliminate lawyers who charge top dollar to support an office on top of the tallest building in town.

What About Low-Cost Law Clinics?

Law clinics advertise their services regularly on TV and radio. Can they help you form a nonprofit organization? Perhaps, but usually at a rate well above their initial low consultation rate. Because the lawyer turnover rate at these clinics is high and the degree of familiarity with nonprofit legal and tax issues is usually low, we recommend you spend your money more wisely by finding a reasonably priced nonprofit lawyer elsewhere.

Legal Research

Many incorporators may want to research legal information on their own. You can browse most state nonprofit laws online (see Appendix B). And in most states, county law libraries are open to the public (you need not be a lawyer to use them) and are not difficult to use once you understand how the information is categorized and stored. They are an invaluable source of corporate and general business forms, federal and state corporate tax procedures, and other information. Research librarians will usually go out of their way to help you find the right statute, form, or background reading on any corporate or tax issue.

Whether you are leafing through your own copy of your state's nonprofit corporation law or browsing corporate statutes online or at your local county law library, finding a particular corporate provision is usually a straightforward process. First define and, if necessary, narrow down the subject matter of your search to essential key words associated with your area of interest. For example, if one of the directors on your board resigns and you want to determine whether your state has any statutory rules for filling vacancies on the board, you will define and restrict your search to the key areas of "directors" and "vacancies." Look for these headings in your state's nonprofit corporation law.

At the beginning of your corporation law, a main table of contents will show headings for the major topics covered in the corporation law. One of these major topics will probably be labeled "Directors," followed by a range of code sections devoted to this subject area. Just before the first of these code sections in the corporation code, a subsidiary table of contents should be included showing individual headings for each code section in this range. In this mini table of contents for the "Directors" code sections, one heading may be listed for a code section devoted to "Vacancies."

Another search strategy is to simply start at the beginning of the corporation law and leaf through all the major and minor headings. Eventually—usually after just a few minutes or so—you will hit upon your area of interest or will satisfy yourself that the area in question is not covered by your corporate statutes. By the way, after going through your nonprofit law this way once or twice, you should become acquainted with most of its major headings. This will help you locate specific nonprofit subject areas and statutes quickly when searching this material in the future.

Legal Shorthand and Definitions

A number of the rules contained in the corporate statutes are often given in legal shorthand—in short legal catchwords and phrases that are defined elsewhere in the code. For example, a common requirement contained in corporate statutes is that a matter or transaction be "approved by the board" or "approved by a majority of the board." Each of these phrases is defined in separate sections of the corporations code. (By the way, the first phrase usually means approval by a majority of directors present at a meeting at which a quorum of directors is present; the second usually means approval by a majority of the full board.) Special definitions of this sort are usually listed at the beginning of the state's nonprofit corporation law—read this starting definition section first to understand any special rules and legal shorthand used throughout your nonprofit corporation statutes.

When you look up a nonprofit statute, whether online or in a book, you might want to use an "annotated" version of the codes. Annotated codes include not only the text of the statutes themselves, but also brief summaries of court cases that mention and interpret each statute. After you find a relevant statute, you may want to scan these case summaries—and perhaps even read some of the cases—to get an idea of how courts have interpreted the language of the statute.

RESOURCE

If you are interested in doing your own legal research, an excellent source of information is *Legal Research: How to Find & Understand the Law*, by Stephen Elias (Nolo).

Accountants and Tax Advice

As you already know, organizing and operating a nonprofit corporation involves a significant amount of financial and tax work. While much of it is easy, some of it requires a nitpicking attention to definitions, cross-references, formulas, and other elusive or downright boring details, particularly when preparing your federal 1023 tax exemption application. As we often suggest in the book, you may find it sensible to seek advice or help from an accountant or other tax adviser when organizing your nonprofit corporation.

For example, you may need help preparing the income statements, balance sheets, and other financial and tax information submitted with your IRS tax exemption application. Also, if your organization will handle any significant amount of money, you will need an accountant or bookkeeper to set up your double-entry accounting books (cash receipts and disbursement journals, general ledger, and so on). Double-entry accounting techniques are particularly important to nonprofits that receive federal or private grant or program funds— accounting for these "restricted funds" usually requires setting up a separate set of books for each fund (and the assistance of a professional).

Nonprofit corporation account books should be designed to allow for easy transfer of financial data to state and federal nonprofit corporate tax returns and disclosure statements. It should be easy to use the books to determine, at any time, whether receipts and expenditures fall into the categories proper for maintaining your 501(c)(3) tax exemption, public charity status, and grant or program eligibility. You will also want to know whether your operations are likely to subject you to an unrelated business income tax under federal and state rules.

Once your corporation is organized and your books are set up, corporate personnel with experience in bookkeeping and nonprofit tax matters can do the ongoing work of keeping the books and filing tax forms. Whatever your arrangement, make sure to at least obtain the tax publications listed in "More Information on Taxes," in Chapter 10. These pamphlets contain essential information on preparing and filing IRS corporation and employment tax returns.

When you select an accountant or book-keeper, the same considerations apply as when selecting a lawyer. Choose someone you know or whom a friend or nonprofit contact recommends. Be as specific as you can regarding the services you want performed. Make sure the adviser has had experience with nonprofit taxation and tax exemption applications, as well as regular payroll, tax, and accounting procedures. Many nonprofit bookkeepers work part-time for several nonprofit organizations. Again, calling people in your nonprofit network is often the best way to find this type of person. ●

How to Use the CD-ROM

The CD-ROM included with this book can be used with Windows computers. It installs files that use software programs that need to be on your computer already. It is not a stand-alone software program.

In accordance with U.S. copyright laws, the CD-ROM and its files are for your personal use only.

Two types of files are included:

- Word processing (RTF) files that you can open, complete, print, and save with your word processing program (see "Using the Word Processing Files to Create Documents," below), and

- Portable Document Format (PDF) files that can be viewed only with Adobe Reader (see "Using the Print Only Files," below). These files are designed to be printed out and filled in by hand or with a typewriter.

See the end of this appendix for a list of files, their file names, and their file formats.

Please read this appendix and the "ReadMe. htm" file included on the CD-ROM for instructions on using the CD-ROM.

Note to Macintosh users: This CD-ROM and its files should also work on Macintosh computers. Please note, however, that Nolo cannot provide technical support for non-Windows users.

Note to eBook users: You can access the CD files mentioned here from the bookmarked section of the eBook, located on the left-hand side.

How to View the README File

To view the "Readme.htm" file, insert the CD-ROM into your computer's CD-ROM drive and follow these instructions:

Windows *XP, Vista*, and 7

1. On your PC's desktop, double-click the **My Computer** icon.

2. Double-click the icon for the CD-ROM drive into which the CD-ROM was inserted.

3. Double-click the file "Readme.htm."

Macintosh

1. On your Mac desktop, double-click the icon for the CD-ROM that you inserted.

2. Double-click the file "Readme.htm."

Installing the Files Onto Your Computer

To work with the files on the CD-ROM, you first need to install them onto your hard disk. Here's how:

Windows *XP, Vista*, and 7

Follow the CD-ROM's instructions that appear on the screen.

If nothing happens when you insert the CD-ROM, then:

1. Double-click the **My Computer** icon.

2. Double-click the icon for the CD-ROM drive into which the CD-ROM was inserted.

3. Double-click the file "Setup.exe."

Macintosh

If the **Nonprofit Forms CD** window is not open, double-click the **Nonprofit Forms CD** icon. Then:

1. Select the **Nonprofit Forms** folder icon.
2. Drag and drop the folder icon onto your computer.

Where Are the Files Installed?

Windows

By default, all the files are installed to the **Nonprofit Forms** folder in the **Program Files** folder of your computer. A folder called **Nonprofit Forms** is added to the **Programs** folder of the **Start** menu.

Macintosh

All the files are located in the **Nonprofit Forms** folder.

Using the Word Processing Files to Create Documents

The CD-ROM includes word processing files that you can open, complete, print, and save with your word processing program. All word processing files come in rich text format and have the extension ".rtf." For example, the file for the Articles of Incorporation discussed in Chapter 6 is on the file "Articles.rtf." RTF files can be read by most recent word processing programs including MS *Word*, Windows *WordPad*, and recent versions of *WordPerfect*.

The following are general instructions. Because each word processor uses different commands to open, format, save, and print documents, refer to your word processor's help file for specific instructions.

Do not call Nolo's technical support if you have questions on how to use your word processor or your computer.

Opening a File

You can open word processing files any of the three following ways:

1. Windows users can open a file by selecting its "shortcut."

- Click the Windows **Start** button.
- Open the **Programs** folder.
- Open the **Nonprofit Forms** folder.
- Open the **RTF** subfolder.
- Click the shortcut to the file you want to work with.

2. Both Windows and Macintosh users can open a file by double-clicking it.

- Use **My Computer** or **Windows Explorer** (Windows *XP*, *Vista*, or *7*) or the **Finder** (Macintosh) to go to the **Nonprofit Forms** folder.
- Double-click the file you want to open.

3. Windows and Macintosh users can open a file from within their word processor.

- Open your word processor.
- Go to the File menu and choose the **Open** command. This opens a dialog box.
- Select the location and name of the file. (You will navigate to the version of the **Nonprofit Forms** folder that you've installed on your computer.)

Editing Your Document

Here are tips for working on your document.

Refer to the book's instructions and sample agreements for help.

Underlines indicate where to enter information, frequently including bracketed instructions. Delete the underlines and instructions before finishing your document.

Signature lines should appear on a page with at least some text from the document itself.

Editing Forms That Have Optional or Alternative Text

Some files have optional or alternative text:

- With optional text, you choose whether to include or exclude the given text.
- With alternative text, you select one alternative to include and exclude the other alternatives.

When editing these files, we suggest you do the following:

Optional text

Delete optional text you do not want to include and keep that which you do. In either case, delete the italicized instructions. If you choose to delete an optional numbered clause, renumber the subsequent clauses after deleting it.

Alternative text

Delete all the alternatives that you do not want to include first. Then delete the italicized instructions.

Printing Out the Document

Use your word processor's or text editor's **Print** command to print out your document.

Saving Your Document

Use the **Save As** command to save and rename your document. You will be unable to use the **Save** command because the files are "read-only." If you save the file without renaming it, the underlines that indicate where you need to enter your information will be lost, and you will be unable to create a new document with this file without recopying the original file from the CD-ROM.

Using Print-Only Files

The CD-ROM includes useful files in Adobe Acrobat PDF format. To use them, you need Adobe Reader installed on your computer. If you don't already have this software, you can download it for free at www.adobe.com.

Opening PDF Files

PDF files, like the word processing files, can be opened one of three ways:

1. Windows users can open a file by selecting its "shortcut."

- Click the Windows **Start** button.
- Open the **Programs** folder.
- Open the **Nonprofit Forms** subfolder.
- Open the **PDF** subfolder
- Click the shortcut to the form you want to work with.

2. Both Windows and Macintosh users can open a file directly by double-clicking it.

- Use **My Computer** or **Windows Explorer** (Windows *XP*, *Vista*, or *7*) or the **Finder** (Macintosh) to go to the **Nonprofit Forms** folder.
- Double-click the specific file you want to open.

3. Both Windows and Macintosh users can open a PDF file from within Adobe *Reader*.

- Open Adobe *Reader*.
- Go to the **File** menu and choose the **Open** command. This opens a dialog box.
- Select the location and name of the file. (You will navigate to the version of the **Nonprofit Forms folder** that you've installed on your computer).

Filling in PDF Files

The PDF files cannot be filled out using your computer. To create your document using one of these files, print it out and then complete it by hand or typewriter.

Files on the CD-ROM

The following files are in rich text format (RTF):

Form/Document Title	File Name
Incorporation Checklist	CHECKLIST.RTF
Application for Reservation of Corporate Name	RESERVE.RTF
Articles of Incorporation	ARTICLES.RTF
Articles Filing Letter	FILING.RTF
Bylaws (including Adoption of Bylaws and Membership	BYLAWS.RTF
Waiver of Notice and Consent to Holding of First Meeting of Board of Directors	MINUTES.RTF
Minutes of First Board Meeting	MINUTES.RTF
IRS Revenue Procedure 75-50	IRS7550.RTF
IRC Section 4958, Taxes on Excess Benefit Transactions	IRS4598.RTF
IRS Regulations Section 53.4598-0, Table of Contents	IRS4958R.RTF

The following files are in Adobe Acrobat PDF Format:

Form/Document Title	File Name
Form 1023: *Application for Recognition of Exemption*	f1023.pdf
Instructions for Form 1023 (with Notice 1382)	i1023.pdf
Form SS-4: *Application for Employer Identification Number*	fss4.pdf
Instructions for Form SS-4	iss4.pdf
Form 5768 *Election/Revocation To Make Expenditures To Influence Legislation*	f5768.pdf
Publication 557 *Tax-Exempt Status for Your Organization*	f557.pdf
Publication 4220: *Applying for 501(c)(3) Tax-Exempt Status*	p4220.pdf
Publication 4221-PC: *Compliance Guide for 501(c)(3) Public Charities*	p4221pc.pdf

Form/Document Title	File Name
Publication 4221-PF: *Compliance Guide for 501(c)(3) Private Foundations*	p4221pf.pdf
Publication 1828: *Tax Guide for Churches and Religious Organizations*	p1828.pdf
Public Charity or Private Foundation Status Issues under IRC §§ 509(a)(1)–(4), 4942(j)(3), and 507	eotopicb03.pdf
Disclosure, FOIA and the Privacy Act	eotopicc03.pdf
Update: The Final Regulations on the Disclosure Requirements for Annual Information Returns and Applications for Exemption	topico00.pdf
Education, Propaganda, and the Methodology Test	eotopich97.pdf
Election Year Issues	eotopici02.pdf
Lobbying Issues	topic-p.pdf
Private School Update	topicn00.pdf
UBIT: Current Developments	topic-o.pdf
Intermediate Sanctions (IRC 4958) Update	eotopice03.pdf
IRS Revenue Ruling 2007-41 *Political Campaign Prohibition Guidance*	rr-07-41.pdf
Internal Revenue Bulletin (IRB 2008-18) with T.D. 9390 Final Regulation changes to Section 4958 regulations	irb08-18.pdf

How to Locate Incorporation Resources Online

This appendix explains how you can locate your state's websites that have the legal and tax rules for forming and operating your nonprofit corporation. We show you methods for locating corporate offices and information online using other websites that automate the process of locating links for these websites, instead of asking you to manually type in often complicated webpage addresses in your browser's address bar. Another advantage of using these online links is that they are maintained and updated on a regular basis and are less likely to go out of date than links that are listed in an appendix and manually updated only with each edition of this book.

How to Find Your State's Corporate Filing Office Website

The corporate filing office is where you file articles (or a similar document) to form a corporation. You can go to this site (or call the office at the telephone number listed on the site) to check the availability of your proposed corporate name and to reserve your name if you wish to do so. State filing office websites typically provide downloadable articles, name reservation request forms, and the latest corporate filing fee information. Many websites allow you to reserve your name and form your corporation online from the website,

without having to prepare, print, and mail paper forms for filing to the state corporate filing office.

To find your state's corporate filing office website, go to www.statelocalgov.net. In the left pane, go to the "Select Topic" box and choose "SOS" (for secretary of state) on the pull-down menu. Choose your state's secretary of state office, then search the tabs and menus to find the filing or form information you need.

If you don't mind having to provide some information, you can find a direct link to your state's filing office at the website of the National Association of Secretaries of State (NASS) at www.nass.org. Register on the site (for free), then select "Issues," "Business Services," then "Corporate Registration" in the left pane, and choose your state to go to the main page for your state's business entity filing office.

How to Find Your State's Tax Office Website

The state tax office website provides state nonprofit tax exemption forms and information, as well as other corporate and individual tax forms and information. To find your state's tax office website, go to the Federation of Tax Administrators website at www.taxadmin.org/fta/link/forms.html, then click your state on the map.

How to Find Your State's Corporation Law Lookup Website

To find your state's Nonprofit Corporation Act or similarly titled law, visit the state law legal research area of Nolo's website at www.nolo.com/legal-rsearch/state-law.html. Click your state's name. This will bring you to your state's statutory lookup webpage. You will see either a list of state law headings with title and chapter numbers and the name of each state law, or a search box that asks for a statute number. Just look for a Nonprofit Corporations heading. If you don't see one, look for a Business Entities or Corporations heading, then drill down to find the Nonprofit Corporation law heading.

If you are browsing through your state's nonprofit law for a general subject, select the heading from the heading list in your law that seems most appropriate for the subject. For example, open the "Directors" heading to look for statutes about directors or directors' meeting requirements, then select the particular statute of interest listed under the heading. Nonprofit corporation laws normally are not extremely long, so it should not be difficult to search through heading or statute lists to find the subject areas you're seeking. With practice, you'll soon get to know how your nonprofit corporation law is organized, and future generalized searches should take less and less time.

Wyoming's 50-State Online Information Locator

The Wyoming Secretary of State publishes and maintains an online listing of links to online resources of state agencies at http://soswy.state.wy.us/Business/Business50.aspx. If the links provided above do not lead you to the online resource you are seeking, try using the Wyoming 50-state locator service.

Information and Tear-Out Forms

Incorporation Checklist

Special Nonprofit Tax-Exempt Organizations

Application for Reservation of Corporate Name

Articles of Incorporation

Articles Filing Letter

Bylaws (including Membership Provisions and Adoption of Bylaws clause)

Waiver of Notice and Consent to Holding of First Meeting of Board of Directors

Minutes of First Meeting of Board of Directors

IRS Form 1023: *Application for Recognition of Exemption* (June 2006) (with Notice 1382)

IRS Form SS-4: *Application for Employer Identification Number* (January 2010)

IRS Form 5768: *Election/Revocation of Election By an Eligible Section 501(c)(3) Organization To Make Expenditures To Influence Legislation* (September 2009)

Incorporation Checklist

Step	Location of Instructions
☐ Go Online to Your Secretary of State's Website	Chapter 6
☐ Choose a Corporate Name	Chapter 6
☐ Reserve Your Corporate Name	Chapter 6
☐ Perform a Name Search	Chapter 6
☐ Protect Your Name	Chapter 6
☐ Prepare Articles of Incorporation	Chapter 6
☐ File Articles of Incorporation	Chapter 6
☐ Prepare Bylaws	Chapter 7
☐ Prepare Membership Provisions	Chapter 7
☐ Prepare and File Your Federal Tax Exemption Application	Chapter 8
☐ Obtain State Corporate Income Tax Exemption	Chapter 9
☐ Set Up a Corporate Records Book	Chapter 9
☐ Prepare Minutes of First Board of Directors Meeting	Chapter 9
☐ Place Minutes and Attachments in Corporate Records Book	Chapter 9
☐ Prepare Assignments of Leases and Deeds	Chapter 9
☐ File Final Papers for Prior Organization (existing groups only)	Chapter 9
☐ Notify Others of Your Incorporation (existing groups only)	Chapter 9
☐ File Assumed Business Name Statement	Chapter 9
☐ Apply for Federal Nonprofit Mailing Permit	Chapter 9
☐ Apply for Property Tax Exemptions	Chapter 9
☐ File Corporate Report Form	Chapter 9
☐ Register With Attorney General	Chapter 9
☐ Comply With Political Reporting Requirements	Chapter 9

Special Nonprofit Tax-Exempt Organizations

IRC §	Organization and Description	Application Form	Annual Return	Deductibility of Contributions[1]
501(c)(1)	**Federal Corporations:** Corporations organized under an Act of Congress as federal corporations specifically declared to be exempt from payment of federal income taxes.	No Form	None	Yes, if made for public purposes
501(c)(2)	**Corporations Holding Title to Property for Exempt Organizations:** Corporations organized for the exclusive purpose of holding title to property, collecting income from property, and turning over this income, less expenses, to an organization which, itself, is exempt from payment of federal income taxes.	1024	990	No
501(c)(4)	**Civic Leagues, Social Welfare Organizations, or Local Employee Associations:** Civic leagues or organizations operated exclusively for the promotion of social welfare, or local associations of employees, the membership of which is limited to the employees of a particular employer within a particular municipality, and whose net earnings are devoted exclusively to charitable, educational, or recreational purposes. Typical examples of groups which fall under this category are volunteer fire companies, home owners or real estate development associations, or employee associations formed to further charitable community service.	1024	990	Generally, No[2]
501(c)(5)	**Labor, Agricultural, or Horticultural Organizations:** Organizations of workers organized to protect their interests in connection with their employment (e.g., labor unions) or groups organized to promote more efficient techniques in production or the betterment of conditions for workers engaged in agricultural or horticultural employment.	1024	990	No
501(c)(6)	**Business Leagues, Chambers of Commerce, Etc.:** Business leagues, chambers of commerce, real estate boards, or boards-of-trade organized for the purpose of improving business conditions in one or more lines of business.	1024	990	No
501(c)(7)	**Social and Recreational Clubs:** Clubs organized for pleasure, recreation, and other nonprofit purposes, no part of the net earnings of which inure to the benefit of any member. Examples of such organizations are hobby clubs and other special-interest social or recreational membership groups.	1024	990	No
501(c)(8)	**Fraternal Beneficiary Societies:** Certain groups which operate under the lodge system for the exclusive benefit of their members, which provide benefits such as the payment of life, sick, or accident insurance to members.	1024	990	Yes, if for 501(c)(3) purposes
501(c)(9)	**Volunteer Employee Beneficiary Associations:** Associations of employees which provide benefits to their members, enrollment in which is strictly voluntary and none of the earnings of which inure to the benefit of any individual members except in accordance with the association's group benefit plan.	1024	990	No
501(c)(10)	**Domestic Fraternal Societies:** Certain domestic fraternal organizations operating under the lodge system which devote their net earnings to religious, charitable, scientific, literary, educational, or fraternal purposes and which do not provide for the payment of insurance or other benefits to members.	1024	990	Yes, if for 501(c)(3) purposes

Special Nonprofit Tax-Exempt Organizations (continued)

IRC §	Organization and Description	Application Form	Annual Return	Deductibility of Contributions[1]
501(c)(11)	**Local Teacher Retirement Fund Associations:** Associations organized to receive amounts received from public taxation, from assessments on the teaching salaries of members, or from income from investments, to devote solely to providing retirement benefits to its members.	No Form[3]	990	No
501(c)(12)	**Benevolent Life Insurance Associations, Mutual Water and Telephone Companies, Etc.:** Organizations organized on a mutual or cooperative basis to provide the above and similar services to members, 85% of whose income is collected from members, and whose income is used solely to cover the expenses and losses of the organization.	1024	990	No
501(c)(13)	**Cemetery Companies:** Companies owned and operated exclusively for the benefit of members solely to provide cemetery services to their members.	1024	990	Generally, Yes
501(c)(14)	**Credit Unions:** Credit unions and other mutual financial organizations organized without capital stock for nonprofit purposes.	1024	990	No
501(c)(15)	**Mutual Insurance Companies:** Certain mutual insurance companies whose gross receipts are from specific sources and are within certain statutory limits.	1024	990	No
501(c)(16)	**Farmers' Cooperatives:** Associations organized and operated on a cooperative basis for the purpose of marketing the products of members or other products.	1024	990	No
501(c)(19)	**War Veteran Organizations:** Posts or organizations whose members are war veterans and which are formed to provide benefits to their members.	1024	990	Generally, No
501(c)(20)	**Group Legal Service Organizations:** Organizations created for the exclusive function of forming a qualified group legal service plan.	1024	990	No
501(d)	**Religious and Apostolic Organizations:** Religious associations or corporations with a common treasury which engage in business for the common benefit of members. Each member's share of the net income of the corporation is reported on his individual tax return. This is a rarely used section of the Code used by religious groups which are ineligible for 501(c)(3) status because they engage in a communal trade or business.	No Form	1065	No
521(a)	**Farmers' Cooperative Associations:** Farmers, fruit growers, and like associations organized and operated on a cooperative basis for the purpose of marketing the products of members or other producers, or for the purchase of supplies and equipment for members at cost.	1028	990-C	No

For specific information on the requirements of several of these special-purpose tax exemption categories, see IRS publication 557, *Tax-Exempt Status for Your Organization.*

[1] An organization exempt under a subsection of IRC Section 501 other than (c)(3)—the types listed in this table—may establish a fund exclusively for 501(c)(3) purposes, contributions to which are deductible. Section 501(c)(3) tax-exempt status should be obtained for this separate fund of a non-501(c)(3) group. See IRS publication 557 for further details.

[2] Contributions to volunteer fire companies and similar organizations are deductible, but only if made for exclusively public purposes.

[3] Application is made by letter to the key District Director.

Date: _____

_____

_____

_____

_____

Re: Corporate Name Reservation

Please reserve the following corporate name for my use for the allowable period specified under the state's corporation statutes.

_____

I enclose the required payment of $_____. My name, address, and phone number are included below if you wish to contact me regarding this request.

Name: _____

Address: _____

Phone: _____

Thank you for your assistance.

_____

Articles of Incorporation

of

_____

A Nonprofit Corporation

Pursuant to the provision of the Nonprofit Corporation Act of this state, the undersigned incorporators hereby adopt the following Articles of Incorporation:

Article 1

The name of this corporation is: _____

_____

Article 2

The name and address of the registered agent and registered office of this corporation is: _____

_____

_____

Article 3

The purposes for which this corporation is organized are: _____

_____

_____

_____

_____

_____

_____

_____

_____

_____

_____

_____

_____

Article 4

The number of initial directors of this corporation shall be _____ and the names and addresses of the initial directors are as follows: _____

_____

_____

_____

_____

Article 5

The name(s) and address(es) of the incorporator(s) of this corporation is/are: _____

_____

_____

Article 6

The period of the duration of this corporation is: _____ .

Article 7

The classes, rights, privileges, qualifications, and obligations of members of this corporation are as follows:

_____

_____

_____

_____

Article 8

Additional provisions (attach separate pages if necessary): _____

_____

_____

_____

_____

_____

_____

_____

_____

_____

_____

_____

_____

_____

_____

_____

_____

_____

_____

_____

_____

_____

_____

_____

_____

_____

_____

_____

_____

_____

_____

The undersigned incorporators hereby declare under penalty of perjury that the statements made in the foregoing Articles of Incorporation are true.

Dated: _____

_____

_____

_____

_____

Name and Address of Incorporator: _____

_____

_____

Name and Address of Incorporator: _____

_____

_____

Name and Address of Incorporator: _____

_____

_____

Name and Address of Incorporator: _____

_____

_____

_____

_____

_____

_____

Date: _____

_____

_____

_____

_____

Re: Articles of Incorporation Filing

I enclose an original and _____ copies of the proposed Articles of Incorporation of

_____.

Please file the Articles of Incorporation and return a Certificate of Incorporation (or file-stamped copy of the original Articles) to me at the above address.

A check/money order in the amount of $_____, made payable to your office, for total filing and processing fees is enclosed.

The above corporate name was reserved for my use pursuant to reservation # _____ issued on

_____.

Sincerely,

_____

_____, Incorporator

Bylaws

of

_____

Article 1
Offices

Section 1. Principal Office

The principal office of the corporation is located in _____ County, State of _____ .

Section 2. Change of Address

The designation of the county or state of the corporation's principal office may be changed by amendment of these bylaws. The board of directors may change the principal office from one location to another within the named county by noting the changed address and effective date below, and such changes of address shall not be deemed, nor require, an amendment of these bylaws:

New Address: _____

Dated: _____ , 20_____

New Address: _____

Dated: _____ , 20_____

New Address: _____

Dated: _____ , 20_____

Section 3. Other Offices

The corporation may also have offices at such other places, within or without its state of incorporation, where it is qualified to do business, as its business and activities may require, and as the board of directors may, from time to time, designate.

Article 2
Nonprofit Purposes

Section 1. IRC Section 501(c)(3) Purposes

This corporation is organized exclusively for one or more of the purposes as specified in Section 501(c)(3) of the Internal Revenue Code, including, for such purposes, the making of distributions to organizations that qualify as exempt organizations under Section 501(c)(3) of the Internal Revenue Code.

Section 2. Specific Objectives and Purposes

The specific objectives and purposes of this corporation shall be: _____

_____

_____

_____

_____

_____

_____

_____

_____

_____

_____

_____

_____

_____

_____

_____

_____

_____

_____

_____

_____

_____

_____

_____

_____

_____

_____

_____

_____

_____

_____

_____

Article 3
Directors

Section 1. Number

The corporation shall have _____ directors and collectively they shall be known as the board of directors.

Section 2. Qualifications

Directors shall be of the age of majority in this state. Other qualifications for directors of this corporation shall be as follows: _____

_____

_____

_____

_____

_____

Section 3. Powers

Subject to the provisions of the laws of this state and any limitations in the articles of incorporation and these bylaws relating to action required or permitted to be taken or approved by the members, if any, of this corporation, the activities and affairs of this corporation shall be conducted and all corporate powers shall be exercised by or under the direction of the board of directors.

Section 4. Duties

It shall be the duty of the directors to:

    a. Perform any and all duties imposed on them collectively or individually by law, by the articles of incorporation, or by these bylaws;

    b. Appoint and remove, employ and discharge, and, except as otherwise provided in these bylaws, prescribe the duties and fix the compensation, if any, of all officers, agents, and employees of the corporation;

    c. Supervise all officers, agents, and employees of the corporation to assure that their duties are performed properly;

    d. Meet at such times and places as required by these bylaws;

    e. Register their addresses with the secretary of the corporation, and notices of meetings mailed or telegraphed to them at such addresses shall be valid notices thereof.

Section 5. Term of Office

Each director shall hold office for a period of _____ and until his or her successor is elected and qualifies.

Section 6. Compensation

Directors shall serve without compensation except that a reasonable fee may be paid to directors for attending regular and special meetings of the board. In addition, they shall be allowed reasonable advancement or reimbursement of expenses incurred in the performance of their duties. Any payments to directors shall be approved in advance in accordance with this corporation's conflict of interest policy, as set forth in Article 9 of these bylaws.

Section 7. Place of Meetings

Meetings shall be held at the principal office of the corporation unless otherwise provided by the board or at such other place as may be designated from time to time by resolution of the board of directors.

Section 8. Regular Meetings

Regular meetings of directors shall be held on _____ at _____ _____.m., unless such day falls on a legal holiday, in which event the regular meeting shall be held at the same hour and place on the next business day.

If this corporation makes no provision for members, then, at the regular meeting of directors held on _____, directors shall be elected by the board of directors. Voting for the election of directors shall be by written ballot. Each director shall cast one vote per candidate, and may vote for as many candidates as the number of candidates to be elected to the board. The candidates receiving the highest number of votes up to the number of directors to be elected shall be elected to serve on the board.

Section 9. Special Meetings

Special meetings of the board of directors may be called by the chairperson of the board, the president, the vice president, the secretary, by any two directors, or, if different, by the persons specifically authorized under the laws of this state to call special meetings of the board. Such meetings shall be held at the principal office of the corporation or, if different, at the place designated by the person or persons calling the special meeting.

Section 10. Notice of Meetings

Unless otherwise provided by the articles of incorporation, these bylaws, or provisions of law, the following provisions shall govern the giving of notice for meetings of the board of directors:

   a. **Regular Meetings.** No notice need be given of any regular meeting of the board of directors.

   b. **Special Meetings.** At least one week prior notice shall be given by the secretary of the corporation to each director of each special meeting of the board. Such notice may be oral or written, may be given personally, by first class mail, by telephone or by facsimile machine, and shall state the place, date, and time of the meeting and the matters proposed to be acted upon at the meeting. In the case of facsimile notification, the director to be contacted shall acknowledge personal receipt of the facsimile notice by a return message or telephone call within twenty-four hours of the first facsimile transmission.

c. **Waiver of Notice.** Whenever any notice of a meeting is required to be given to any director of this corporation under provisions of the articles of incorporation, these bylaws, or the law of this state, a waiver of notice in writing signed by the director, whether before or after the time of the meeting, shall be equivalent to the giving of such notice.

Section 11. Quorum for Meetings

A quorum shall consist of _____ of the members of the board of directors.

Except as otherwise provided under the articles of incorporation, these bylaws, or provisions of law, no business shall be considered by the board at any meeting at which the required quorum is not present, and the only motion which the chair shall entertain at such meeting is a motion to adjourn.

Section 12. Majority Action as Board Action

Every act or decision done or made by a majority of the directors present at a meeting duly held at which a quorum is present is the act of the board of directors, unless the articles of incorporation, these bylaws, or provisions of law require a greater percentage or different voting rules for approval of a matter by the board.

Section 13. Conduct of Meetings

Meetings of the board of directors shall be presided over by the chairperson of the board, or, if no such person has been so designated, or in his or her absence, the president of the corporation, or in his or her absence, by the vice president of the corporation, or in the absence of each of these persons, by a chairperson chosen by a majority of the directors present at the meeting. The secretary of the corporation shall act as secretary of all meetings of the board, provided that, in his or her absence, the presiding officer shall appoint another person to act as secretary of the meeting.

Meetings shall be governed by _____,
insofar as such rules are not inconsistent with or in conflict with the articles of incorporation, these bylaws, or with provisions of law.

Section 14. Vacancies

Vacancies on the board of directors shall exist (1) on the death, resignation, or removal of any director, and (2) whenever the number of authorized directors is increased.

Any director may resign effective upon giving written notice to the chairperson of the board, the president, the secretary, or the board of directors, unless the notice specifies a later time for the effectiveness of such resignation. No director may resign if the corporation would then be left without a duly elected director or directors in charge of its affairs, except upon notice to the Office of the Attorney General or other appropriate agency of this state.

Directors may be removed from office, with or without cause, as permitted by and in accordance with the laws of this state.

Unless otherwise prohibited by the articles of incorporation, these bylaws, or provisions of law, vacancies on the board may be filled by approval of the board of directors. If the number of directors then in office is less than a quorum, a vacancy on the board may be filled by approval of a majority of the directors then in office or by a sole remaining director. A person elected to fill a vacancy on the board shall hold office until the next election of the board of directors or until his or her death, resignation, or removal from office.

Section 15. Nonliability of Directors

The directors shall not be personally liable for the debts, liabilities, or other obligations of the corporation.

Section 16. Indemnification by Corporation of Directors and Officers

The directors and officers of the corporation shall be indemnified by the corporation to the fullest extent permissible under the laws of this state.

Section 17. Insurance for Corporate Agents

Except as may be otherwise provided under provisions of law, the board of directors may adopt a resolution authorizing the purchase and maintenance of insurance on behalf of any agent of the corporation (including a director, officer, employee, or other agent of the corporation) against liabilities asserted against or incurred by the agent in such capacity or arising out of the agent's status as such, whether or not the corporation would have the power to indemnify the agent against such liability under the articles of incorporation, these bylaws, or provisions of law.

Article 4
Officers

Section 1. Designation of Officers

The officers of the corporation shall be a president, a vice president, a secretary, and a treasurer. The corporation may also have a chairperson of the board, one or more vice presidents, assistant secretaries, assistant treasurers, and other such officers with such titles as may be determined from time to time by the board of directors.

Section 2. Qualifications

Any person may serve as officer of this corporation.

Section 3. Election and Term of Office

Officers shall be elected by the board of directors, at any time, and each officer shall hold office until he or she resigns or is removed or is otherwise disqualified to serve, or until his or her successor shall be elected and qualified, whichever occurs first.

Section 4. Removal and Resignation

Any officer may be removed, either with or without cause, by the board of directors, at any time. Any officer may resign at any time by giving written notice to the board of directors or to the president or secretary of the corporation. Any such resignation shall take effect at the date of receipt of such notice or at any later date specified therein, and, unless otherwise specified therein, the acceptance of such resignation shall not be necessary to make it effective. The above provisions of this section shall be superseded by any conflicting terms of a contract which has been approved or ratified by the board of directors relating to the employment of any officer of the corporation.

Section 5. Vacancies

Any vacancy caused by the death, resignation, removal, disqualification, or otherwise, of any officer shall be filled by the board of directors. In the event of a vacancy in any office other than that of president, such vacancy may be filled temporarily by appointment by the president until such time as the board shall fill the vacancy. Vacancies occurring in offices of officers appointed at the discretion of the board may or may not be filled as the board shall determine.

Section 6. Duties of President

The president shall be the chief executive officer of the corporation and shall, subject to the control of the board of directors, supervise and control the affairs of the corporation and the activities of the officers. He or she shall perform all duties incident to his or her office and such other duties as may be required by law, by the articles of incorporation, or by these bylaws, or which may be prescribed from time to time by the board of directors. Unless another person is specifically appointed as chairperson of the board of directors, the president shall preside at all meetings of the board of directors and, if this corporation has members, at all meetings of the members. Except as otherwise expressly provided by law, by the articles of incorporation, or by these bylaws, he or she shall, in the name of the corporation, execute such deeds, mortgages, bonds, contracts, checks, or other instruments which may from time to time be authorized by the board of directors.

Section 7. Duties of Vice President

In the absence of the president, or in the event of his or her inability or refusal to act, the vice president shall perform all the duties of the president, and when so acting shall have all the powers of, and be subject to all the restrictions on, the president. The vice president shall have other powers and perform such other duties as may be prescribed by law, by the articles of incorporation, or by these bylaws, or as may be prescribed by the board of directors.

Section 8. Duties of Secretary

The secretary shall:

Certify and keep at the principal office of the corporation the original, or a copy, of these bylaws as amended or otherwise altered to date.

Keep at the principal office of the corporation or at such other place as the board may determine, a book of minutes of all meetings of the directors, and, if applicable, meetings of committees of directors and of members, recording therein the time and place of holding, whether regular or special, how called, how notice thereof was given, the names of those present or represented at the meeting, and the proceedings thereof.

Ensure that the minutes of meetings of the corporation, any written consents approving action taken without a meeting, and any supporting documents pertaining to meetings, minutes, and consents shall be contemporaneously recorded in the corporate records of this corporation. "Contemporaneously" in this context means that the minutes, consents, and supporting documents shall be recorded in the records of this corporation by the later of 1) the next meeting of the board, committee, membership, or other body for which the minutes, consents, or supporting documents are being recorded, or 2) sixty (60) days after the date of the meeting or written consent.

See that all notices are duly given in accordance with the provisions of these bylaws or as required by law.

Be custodian of the records and of the seal of the corporation and affix the seal, as authorized by law or the provisions of these bylaws, to duly executed documents of the corporation.

Keep at the principal office of the corporation a membership book containing the name and address of each and any members, and, in the case where any membership has been terminated, he or she shall record such fact in the membership book together with the date on which such membership ceased.

Exhibit at all reasonable times to any director of the corporation, or to his or her agent or attorney, on request therefor, the bylaws, the membership book, and the minutes of the proceedings of the directors of the corporation.

In general, perform all duties incident to the office of secretary and such other duties as may be required by law, by the articles of incorporation, or by these bylaws, or which may be assigned to him or her from time to time by the board of directors.

Section 9. Duties of Treasurer

The treasurer shall:

Have charge and custody of, and be responsible for, all funds and securities of the corporation, and deposit all such funds in the name of the corporation in such banks, trust companies, or other depositories as shall be selected by the board of directors.

Receive, and give receipt for, monies due and payable to the corporation from any source whatsoever.

Disburse, or cause to be disbursed, the funds of the corporation as may be directed by the board of directors, taking proper vouchers for such disbursements.

Keep and maintain adequate and correct accounts of the corporation's properties and business transactions, including accounts of its assets, liabilities, receipts, disbursements, gains, and losses.

Exhibit at all reasonable times the books of account and financial records to any director of the corporation, or to his or her agent or attorney, on request therefor.

Render to the president and directors, whenever requested, an account of any or all of his or her transactions as treasurer and of the financial condition of the corporation.

Prepare, or cause to be prepared, and certify, or cause to be certified, the financial statements to be included in any required reports.

In general, perform all duties incident to the office of treasurer and such other duties as may be required by law, by the articles of incorporation of the corporation, or by these bylaws, or which may be assigned to him or her from time to time by the board of directors.

Section 10. Compensation

The salaries of the officers, if any, shall be fixed from time to time by resolution of the board of directors. In all cases, any salaries received by officers of this corporation shall be reasonable and given in return for services actually rendered to or for the corporation. All officer salaries shall be approved in advance in accordance with this corporation's conflict of interest policy, as set forth in Article 9 of these bylaws.

Article 5
Committees

Section 1. Executive Committee

The board of directors may, by a majority vote of its members, designate an Executive Committee consisting of _____ board members and may delegate to such committee the powers and authority of the board in the management of the business and affairs of the corporation, to the extent permitted, and, except as may otherwise be provided, by provisions of law.

By a majority vote of its members, the board may at any time revoke or modify any or all of the executive committee authority so delegated, increase or decrease but not below two (2) the number of the members of the executive committee, and fill vacancies on the executive committee from the members of the board. The executive committee shall keep regular minutes of its proceedings, cause them to be filed with the corporate records, and report the same to the board from time to time as the board may require.

Section 2. Other Committees

The corporation shall have such other committees as may from time to time be designated by resolution of the board of directors. These committees may consist of persons who are not also members of the board and shall act in an advisory capacity to the board.

Section 3. Meetings and Action of Committees

Meetings and action of committees shall be governed by, noticed, held, and taken in accordance with the provisions of these bylaws concerning meetings of the board of directors, with such changes in the context of such bylaw provisions as are necessary to substitute the committee and its members for the board of directors and its members, except that the time for regular and special meetings of committees may be fixed by resolution of the board of directors or by the committee. The board of directors may also adopt rules and regulations pertaining to the conduct of meetings of committees to the extent that such rules and regulations are not inconsistent with the provisions of these bylaws.

Article 6
Execution of Instruments, Deposits, and Funds

Section 1. Execution of Instruments

The board of directors, except as otherwise provided in these bylaws, may by resolution authorize any officer or agent of the corporation to enter into any contract or execute and deliver any instrument in the name of and on behalf of the corporation, and such authority may be general or confined to specific instances. Unless so authorized, no officer, agent, or employee shall have any power or authority to bind the corporation by any contract or engagement or to pledge its credit or to render it liable monetarily for any purpose or in any amount.

Section 2. Checks and Notes

Except as otherwise specifically determined by resolution of the board of directors, or as otherwise required by law, checks, drafts, promissory notes, orders for the payment of money, and other evidence of indebtedness of the corporation shall be signed by the treasurer and countersigned by the president of the corporation.

Section 3. Deposits

All funds of the corporation shall be deposited from time to time to the credit of the corporation in such banks, trust companies, or other depositories as the board of directors may select.

Section 4. Gifts

The board of directors may accept on behalf of the corporation any contribution, gift, bequest, or devise for the nonprofit purposes of this corporation.

Article 7
Corporate Records, Reports, and Seal

Section 1. Maintenance of Corporate Records

The corporation shall keep at its principal office:

a. Minutes of all meetings of directors, committees of the board, and, if this corporation has members, of all meetings of members, indicating the time and place of holding such meetings, whether regular or special, how called, the notice given, and the names of those present and the proceedings thereof;

b. Adequate and correct books and records of account, including accounts of its properties and business transactions and accounts of its assets, liabilities, receipts, disbursements, gains, and losses;

c. A record of its members, if any, indicating their names and addresses and, if applicable, the class of membership held by each member and the termination date of any membership;

d. A copy of the corporation's articles of incorporation and bylaws as amended to date, which shall be open to inspection by the members, if any, of the corporation at all reasonable times during office hours.

Section 2. Corporate Seal

The board of directors may adopt, use, and at will alter, a corporate seal. Such seal shall be kept at the principal office of the corporation. Failure to affix the seal to corporate instruments, however, shall not affect the validity of any such instrument.

Section 3. Directors' Inspection Rights

Every director shall have the absolute right at any reasonable time to inspect and copy all books, records, and documents of every kind and to inspect the physical properties of the corporation, and shall have such other rights to inspect the books, records, and properties of this corporation as may be required under the articles of incorporation, other provisions of these bylaws, and provisions of law.

Section 4. Members' Inspection Rights

If this corporation has any members, then each and every member shall have the following inspection rights, for a purpose reasonably related to such person's interest as a member:

a. To inspect and copy the record of all members' names, addresses, and voting rights, at reasonable times, upon written demand on the secretary of the corporation, which demand shall state the purpose for which the inspection rights are requested.

b. To obtain from the secretary of the corporation, upon written demand on, and payment of a reasonable charge to, the secretary of the corporation, a list of the names, addresses, and voting rights of those members entitled to vote for the election of directors as of the most recent record date for which the list has been compiled or as of the date specified by the member subsequent to the date of demand. The demand shall state the purpose for which the list is requested. The membership list shall be made available within a reasonable time after the demand is received by the secretary of the corporation or after the date specified therein as of which the list is to be compiled.

c. To inspect at any reasonable time the books, records, or minutes of proceedings of the members or of the board or committees of the board, upon written demand on the secretary of the corporation by the member, for a purpose reasonably related to such person's interests as a member.

Members shall have such other rights to inspect the books, records, and properties of this corporation as may be required under the articles of incorporation, other provisions of these bylaws, and provisions of law.

Section 5. Right to Copy and Make Extracts

Any inspection under the provisions of this article may be made in person or by agent or attorney and the right to inspection shall include the right to copy and make extracts.

Section 6. Periodic Report

The board shall cause any annual or periodic report required under law to be prepared and delivered to an office of this state or to the members, if any, of this corporation, to be so prepared and delivered within the time limits set by law.

Article 8
IRC 501(c)(3) Tax Exemption Provisions

Section 1. Limitations on Activities

No substantial part of the activities of this corporation shall be the carrying on of propaganda, or otherwise attempting to influence legislation (except as otherwise provided by Section 501(h) of the Internal Revenue Code), and this corporation shall not participate in, or intervene in (including the publishing or distribution of statements), any political campaign on behalf of, or in opposition to, any candidate for public office.

Notwithstanding any other provisions of these bylaws, this corporation shall not carry on any activities not permitted to be carried on (a) by a corporation exempt from federal income tax under Section 501(c)(3) of the Internal Revenue Code, or (b) by a corporation, contributions to which are deductible under Section 170(c)(2) of the Internal Revenue Code.

Section 2. Prohibition Against Private Inurement

No part of the net earnings of this corporation shall inure to the benefit of, or be distributable to, its members, directors or trustees, officers, or other private persons, except that the corporation shall be authorized and empowered to pay reasonable compensation for services rendered and to make payments and distributions in furtherance of the purposes of this corporation.

Section 3. Distribution of Assets

Upon the dissolution of this corporation, its assets remaining after payment, or provision for payment, of all debts and liabilities of this corporation, shall be distributed for one or more exempt purposes within the meaning of Section 501(c)(3) of the Internal Revenue Code or shall be distributed to the federal government, or to a state or local government, for a public purpose. Such distribution shall be made in accordance with all applicable provisions of the laws of this state.

Section 4. Private Foundation Requirements and Restrictions

In any taxable year in which this corporation is a private foundation as described in Section 509(a) of the Internal Revenue Code, the corporation (1) shall distribute its income for said period at such time and manner as not to subject it to tax under Section 4942 of the Internal Revenue Code; (2) shall not engage in any act of self-dealing as defined in Section 4941(d) of the Internal Revenue Code; (3) shall not retain any excess business holdings as defined in Section 4943(c) of the Internal Revenue Code; (4) shall not make any investments in such manner as to subject the corporation to tax under Section 4944 of the Internal Revenue Code; and (5) shall not make any taxable expenditures as defined in Section 4945(d) of the Internal Revenue Code.

Article 9
Conflict of Interest and
Compensation Approval Policies

Section 1. Purpose of Conflict of Interest Policy

The purpose of this conflict of interest policy is to protect this tax-exempt corporation's interest when it is contemplating entering into a transaction or arrangement that might benefit the private interest of an officer or director of the corporation or any "disqualified person" as defined in Section 4958(f)(1) of the Internal Revenue Code and as amplified by Section 53.4958-3 of the IRS Regulations and which might result in a possible "excess benefit transaction" as defined in Section 4958(c)(1)(A) of the Internal Revenue Code and as amplified by Section 53.4958 of the IRS Regulations. This policy is intended to supplement but not replace any applicable state and federal laws governing conflict of interest applicable to nonprofit and charitable organizations.

Section 2. Definitions

a. Interested Person. Any director, principal officer, member of a committee with governing board delegated powers, or any other person who is a "disqualified person" as defined in Section 4958(f)(1) of the Internal Revenue Code and as amplified by Section 53.4958-3 of the IRS Regulations, who has a direct or indirect financial interest, as defined below, is an interested person.

b. Financial Interest. A person has a financial interest if the person has, directly or indirectly, through business, investment, or family:

1. An ownership or investment interest in any entity with which the corporation has a transaction or arrangement,

2. A compensation arrangement with the corporation or with any entity or individual with which the corporation has a transaction or arrangement, or

3. A potential ownership or investment interest in, or compensation arrangement with, any entity or individual with which the corporation is negotiating a transaction or arrangement.

Compensation includes direct and indirect remuneration as well as gifts or favors that are not insubstantial.

A financial interest is not necessarily a conflict of interest. Under Section 3, paragraph B, a person who has a financial interest may have a conflict of interest only if the appropriate governing board or committee decides that a conflict of interest exists.

Section 3. Conflict of Interest Avoidance Procedures

a. Duty to Disclose. In connection with any actual or possible conflict of interest, an interested person must disclose the existence of the financial interest and be given the opportunity to disclose all material facts to the directors and members of committees with governing board delegated powers considering the proposed transaction or arrangement.

b. Determining Whether a Conflict of Interest Exists. After disclosure of the financial interest and all material facts, and after any discussion with the interested person, he/she shall leave the governing board or committee meeting while the determination of a conflict of interest is discussed and voted upon. The remaining board or committee members shall decide if a conflict of interest exists.

c. Procedures for Addressing the Conflict of Interest. An interested person may make a presentation at the governing board or committee meeting, but after the presentation, he/she shall leave the meeting during the discussion of, and the vote on, the transaction or arrangement involving the possible conflict of interest.

The chairperson of the governing board or committee shall, if appropriate, appoint a disinterested person or committee to investigate alternatives to the proposed transaction or arrangement.

After exercising due diligence, the governing board or committee shall determine whether the corporation can obtain with reasonable efforts a more advantageous transaction or arrangement from a person or entity that would not give rise to a conflict of interest.

If a more advantageous transaction or arrangement is not reasonably possible under circumstances not producing a conflict of interest, the governing board or committee shall determine by a majority vote of the disinterested directors whether the transaction or arrangement is in the corporation's best interest, for its own benefit, and whether it is fair and reasonable. In conformity with the above determination, it shall make its decision as to whether to enter into the transaction or arrangement.

d. Violations of the Conflicts of Interest Policy. If the governing board or committee has reasonable cause to believe a member has failed to disclose actual or possible conflicts of interest, it shall inform the member of the basis for such belief and afford the member an opportunity to explain the alleged failure to disclose.

If, after hearing the member's response and after making further investigation as warranted by the circumstances, the governing board or committee determines the member has failed to disclose an actual or possible conflict of interest, it shall take appropriate disciplinary and corrective action.

Section 4. Records of Board and Board Committee Proceedings

The minutes of meetings of the governing board and all committees with board delegated powers shall contain:

a. The names of the persons who disclosed or otherwise were found to have a financial interest in connection with an actual or possible conflict of interest, the nature of the financial interest, any action taken to determine whether a conflict of interest was present, and the governing board's or committee's decision as to whether a conflict of interest in fact existed.

b. The names of the persons who were present for discussions and votes relating to the transaction or arrangement, the content of the discussion, including any alternatives to the proposed transaction or arrangement, and a record of any votes taken in connection with the proceedings.

Section 5. Compensation Approval Policies

A voting member of the governing board who receives compensation, directly or indirectly, from the corporation for services is precluded from voting on matters pertaining to that member's compensation.

A voting member of any committee whose jurisdiction includes compensation matters and who receives compensation, directly or indirectly, from the corporation for services is precluded from voting on matters pertaining to that member's compensation.

No voting member of the governing board or any committee whose jurisdiction includes compensation matters and who receives compensation, directly or indirectly, from the corporation, either individually or collectively, is prohibited from providing information to any committee regarding compensation.

When approving compensation for directors, officers and employees, contractors, and any other compensation contract or arrangement, in addition to complying with the conflict of interest requirements and policies contained in the preceding and following sections of this article as well as the preceding paragraphs of this section of this article, the board or a duly constituted compensation committee of the board shall also comply with the following additional requirements and procedures:

a. the terms of compensation shall be approved by the board or compensation committee prior to the first payment of compensation;

b. all members of the board or compensation committee who approve compensation arrangements must not have a conflict of interest with respect to the compensation arrangement as specified in IRS Regulation Section 53.4958-6(c)(iii), which generally requires that each board member or committee member approving a compensation arrangement between this organization and a "disqualified person" (as defined in Section 4958(f)(1) of the Internal Revenue Code and as amplified by Section 53.4958-3 of the IRS Regulations):

   1. is not the person who is the subject of the compensation arrangement, or a family member of such person;

   2. is not in an employment relationship subject to the direction or control of the person who is the subject of the compensation arrangement;

   3. does not receive compensation or other payments subject to approval by the person who is the subject of the compensation arrangement;

   4. has no material financial interest affected by the compensation arrangement; and

   5. does not approve a transaction providing economic benefits to the person who is the subject of the compensation arrangement, who in turn has approved or will approve a transaction providing benefits to the board or committee member.

c. the board or compensation committee shall obtain and rely upon appropriate data as to comparability prior to approving the terms of compensation. Appropriate data may include the following:

   1. compensation levels paid by similarly situated organizations, both taxable and tax-exempt, for functionally comparable positions. "Similarly situated" organizations are those of a similar size, purpose, and with similar resources;

   2. the availability of similar services in the geographic area of this organization;

   3. current compensation surveys compiled by independent firms;

4. actual written offers from similar institutions competing for the services of the person who is the subject of the compensation arrangement.

As allowed by IRS Regulation 4958-6, if this organization has average annual gross receipts (including contributions) for its three prior tax years of less than $1 million, the board or compensation committee will have obtained and relied upon appropriate data as to comparability if it obtains and relies upon data on compensation paid by three comparable organizations in the same or similar communities for similar services.

d. the terms of compensation and the basis for approving them shall be recorded in written minutes of the meeting of the board or compensation committee that approved the compensation. Such documentation shall include:

1. the terms of the compensation arrangement and the date it was approved;

2. the members of the board or compensation committee who were present during debate on the transaction, those who voted on it, and the votes cast by each board or committee member;

3. the comparability data obtained and relied upon and how the data was obtained;

4. If the board or compensation committee determines that reasonable compensation for a specific position in this organization or for providing services under any other compensation arrangement with this organization is higher or lower than the range of comparability data obtained, the board or committee shall record in the minutes of the meeting the basis for its determination;

5. If the board or committee makes adjustments to comparability data due to geographic area or other specific conditions, these adjustments and the reasons for them shall be recorded in the minutes of the board or committee meeting;

6. any actions taken with respect to determining if a board or committee member had a conflict of interest with respect to the compensation arrangement, and if so, actions taken to make sure the member with the conflict of interest did not affect or participate in the approval of the transaction (for example, a notation in the records that after a finding of conflict of interest by a member, the member with the conflict of interest was asked to, and did, leave the meeting prior to a discussion of the compensation arrangement and a taking of the votes to approve the arrangement);

7. the minutes of board or committee meetings at which compensation arrangements are approved must be prepared before the later of the date of the next board or committee meeting or 60 days after the final actions of the board or committee are taken with respect to the approval of the compensation arrangements. The minutes must be reviewed and approved by the board and committee as reasonable, accurate, and complete within a reasonable period thereafter, normally prior to or at the next board or committee meeting following final action on the arrangement by the board or committee.

Section 6. Annual Statements

Each director, principal officer, and member of a committee with governing board delegated powers shall annually sign a statement which affirms such person:

a. has received a copy of the conflicts of interest policy;

b. has read and understands the policy;

c. has agreed to comply with the policy; and

d. understands the corporation is charitable and in order to maintain its federal tax exemption it must engage primarily in activities which accomplish one or more of its tax-exempt purposes.

Section 7. Periodic Reviews

To ensure the corporation operates in a manner consistent with charitable purposes and does not engage in activities that could jeopardize its tax-exempt status, periodic reviews shall be conducted. The periodic reviews shall, at a minimum, include the following subjects:

a. Whether compensation arrangements and benefits are reasonable, based on competent survey information, and the result of arm's-length bargaining.

b. Whether partnerships, joint ventures, and arrangements with management organizations conform to the corporation's written policies, are properly recorded, reflect reasonable investment or payments for goods and services, further charitable purposes, and do not result in inurement, impermissible private benefit, or in an excess benefit transaction.

Section 8. Use of Outside Experts

When conducting the periodic reviews as provided for in Section 7, the corporation may, but need not, use outside advisors. If outside experts are used, their use shall not relieve the governing board of its responsibility for ensuring periodic reviews are conducted.

Article 10
Amendment of Bylaws

Section 1. Amendment

Subject to the power of the members, if any, of this corporation to adopt, amend, or repeal the bylaws of this corporation and except as may otherwise be specified under provisions of law, these bylaws, or any of them, may be altered, amended, or repealed, and new bylaws adopted by approval of the board of directors.

Construction and Terms

If there is any conflict between the provisions of these bylaws and the articles of incorporation of this corporation, the provisions of the articles of incorporation shall govern.

Should any of the provisions or portions of these bylaws be held unenforceable or invalid for any reason, the remaining provisions and portions of these bylaws shall be unaffected by such holding.

All references in these bylaws to the articles of incorporation shall be to the articles of incorporation, articles of organization, certificate of incorporation, organizational charter, corporate charter, or other founding document of this corporation filed with an office of this state and used to establish the legal existence of this corporation.

All references in these bylaws to a section or sections of the Internal Revenue Code shall be to such sections of the Internal Revenue Code of 1986 as amended from time to time, or to corresponding provisions of any future federal tax code.

[The following provisions are for use in your bylaws ONLY if you have chosen to adopt a membership structure for your corporation. If you have decided to form a nonmembership corporation (as most nonprofits do), you should not include the "Membership Provisions" clauses in your bylaws. Instead, delete them from this document.

NOTE: Take care not to delete the "Adoption of Bylaws" clause at the end of this document. This clause will be the last page of your bylaws, whether you include the "Membership Provisions" or not.]

[Optional]:
Membership Provisions of the Bylaws

of

_____

Article 12
Members

Section 1. Determination and Rights of Members

The corporation shall have only one class of members. No member shall hold more than one membership in the corporation. Except as expressly provided in or authorized by the articles of incorporation, the bylaws of this corporation, or provisions of law, all memberships shall have the same rights, privileges, restrictions, and conditions.

Section 2. Qualifications of Members

The qualifications for membership in this corporation are as follows: _____

_____

_____

_____

_____ .

Section 3. Admission of Members

Applicants shall be admitted to membership_____

_____

_____

_____ .

Section 4. Fees and Dues

a. The following fee shall be charged for making application for membership in the corporation:

    _____ .

b. The annual dues payable to the corporation by members shall be _____ .

Section 5. Number of Members

There is no limit on the number of members the corporation may admit.

Section 6. Membership Book

The corporation shall keep a membership book containing the name and address of each member. Termination of the membership of any member shall be recorded in the book, together with the date of termination of such membership. Such book shall be kept at the corporation's principal office.

Section 7. Nonliability of Members

A member of this corporation is not, as such, personally liable for the debts, liabilities, or obligations of the corporation.

Section 8. Nontransferability of Memberships

No member may transfer a membership or any right arising therefrom. All rights of membership cease upon the member's death.

Section 9. Termination of Membership

The membership of a member shall terminate upon the occurrence of any of the following events:

1. Upon his or her notice of such termination delivered to the president or secretary of the corporation personally or by mail, such membership to terminate upon the date of delivery of the notice or date of deposit in the mail.

2. If this corporation has provided for the payment of dues by members, upon a failure to renew his or her membership by paying dues on or before their due date, such termination to be effective thirty (30) days after a written notification of delinquency is given personally or mailed to such member by the secretary of the corporation. A member may avoid such termination by paying the amount of delinquent dues within a thirty (30) day period following the member's receipt of the written notification of delinquency.

3. After providing the member with reasonable written notice and an opportunity to be heard either orally or in writing, upon a determination by the board of directors that the member has engaged in conduct materially and seriously prejudicial to the interests or purposes of the corporation. Any person expelled from the corporation shall receive a refund of dues already paid for the current dues period.

All rights of a member in the corporation shall cease on termination of membership as herein provided.

Article 13
Meetings of Members

Section 1. Place of Meetings

Meetings of members shall be held at the principal office of the corporation or at such other place or places as may be designated from time to time by resolution of the board of directors.

Section 2. Regular Meetings

A regular meeting of members shall be held on _____, at _____ ____.m., for the purpose of electing directors and transacting other business as may come before the meeting. The candidates receiving the highest number of votes up to the number of directors to be elected shall be elected. Each voting member shall cast one vote, with voting being by ballot only. The annual meeting of members for the purpose of electing directors shall be deemed a regular meeting.

Other regular meetings of the members shall be held on _____, at _____ ____.m.,

If the day fixed for a regular meeting falls on a legal holiday, such meeting shall be held at the same hour and place on the next business day.

Section 3. Special Meetings of Members

Special meetings of the members shall be called by the board of directors, the chairperson of the board, or the president of the corporation, or, if different, by the persons specifically authorized under the laws of this state to call special meetings of the members.

Section 4. Notice of Meetings

Unless otherwise provided by the articles of incorporation, these bylaws, or provisions of law, notice stating the place, day, and hour of the meeting and, in the case of a special meeting, the purpose or purposes for which the meeting is called, shall be delivered not less than ten (10) nor more than fifty (50) days before the date of the meeting, either personally or by mail, by or at the direction of the president, or the secretary, or the persons calling the meeting, to each member entitled to vote at such meeting. If mailed, such notice shall be deemed to be delivered when deposited in the United States mail addressed to the member at his or her address as it appears on the records of the corporation, with postage prepaid. Personal notification includes notification by telephone or by facsimile machine, provided however, in the case of facsimile notification, the member to be contacted shall acknowledge personal receipt of the facsimile notice by a return message or telephone call within twenty-four hours of the first facsimile transmission.

The notice of any meeting of members at which directors are to be elected shall also state the names of all those who are nominees or candidates for election to the board at the time notice is given.

Whenever any notice of a meeting is required to be given to any member of this corporation under provisions of the articles of incorporation, these bylaws, or the law of this state, a waiver of notice in writing signed by the member, whether before or after the time of the meeting, shall be equivalent to the giving of such notice.

Section 5. Quorum for Meetings

A quorum shall consist of _____ of the voting members of the corporation.

Except as otherwise provided under the articles of incorporation, these bylaws, or provisions of law, no business shall be considered by the members at any meeting at which the required quorum is not present, and the only motion which the chair shall entertain at such meeting is a motion to adjourn.

Section 6. Majority Action as Membership Action

Every act or decision done or made by a majority of voting members present in person or by proxy at a duly held meeting at which a quorum is present is the act of the members, unless the articles of incorporation, these bylaws, or provisions of law require a greater number.

Section 7. Voting Rights

Each member is entitled to one vote on each matter submitted to a vote by the members. Voting at duly held meetings shall be by voice vote. Election of directors, however, shall be by written ballot.

Section 8. Action by Written Ballot

Except as otherwise provided under the articles of incorporation, these bylaws, or provisions of law, any action which may be taken at any regular or special meeting of members may be taken without a meeting if the corporation distributes a written ballot to each member entitled to vote on the matter. The ballot shall:

1. set forth the proposed action;

2. provide an opportunity to specify approval or disapproval of each proposal;

3. indicate the number of responses needed to meet the quorum requirement and, except for ballots soliciting votes for the election of directors, state the percentage of approvals necessary to pass the measure submitted; and

4. shall specify the date by which the ballot must be received by the corporation in order to be counted. The date set shall afford members a reasonable time within which to return the ballots to the corporation.

Ballots shall be mailed or delivered in the manner required for giving notice of membership meetings as specified in these bylaws.

Approval of action by written ballot shall be valid only when the number of votes cast by ballot within the time period specified equals or exceeds the quorum required to be present at a meeting authorizing the action, and the number of approvals equals or exceeds the number of votes that would be required to approve the action at a meeting at which the total number of votes cast was the same as the number of votes cast by ballot.

Directors may be elected by written ballot. Such ballots for the election of directors shall list the persons nominated at the time the ballots are mailed or delivered.

Section 9. Conduct of Meetings

Meetings of members shall be presided over by the chairperson of the board, or, if there is no chairperson, or in his or her absence, by the president of the corporation or, in his or her absence, by the vice president of the corporation or, in the absence of all of these persons, by a chairperson chosen by a majority of the voting members present at the meeting. The secretary of the corporation shall act as secretary of all meetings of members, provided that, in his or her absence, the presiding officer shall appoint another person to act as secretary of the meeting.

Meetings shall be governed by _____, as such rules may be revised from time to time, insofar as such rules are not inconsistent with or in conflict with the articles of incorporation, these bylaws, or with provisions of law.

[End option]

ADOPTION OF BYLAWS

We, the undersigned, are all of the initial directors or incorporators of this corporation, and we consent to, and hereby do, adopt the foregoing bylaws, consisting of _____ preceding pages, as the bylaws of this corporation.

Dated: _____

_____

_____

_____

_____

Waiver of Notice and Consent to Holding
of First Meeting of Board of Directors

of

_____

We, the undersigned, being all the directors of _____

_____, hereby waive notice of the first

meeting of the board of directors of the corporation and consent to the holding of said meeting at

_____, on

_____, 20_____, at _____ _____.m., and consent to the

transaction of any and all business by the directors at the meeting, including, without limitation, the

adoption of bylaws, the election of officers, and the selection of the place where the corporation's bank

accounts will be maintained.

Date: _____

_____

_____, Director

_____

_____, Director

_____

_____, Director

_____

_____, Director

_____

_____, Director

_____

_____, Director

_____

_____, Director

Minutes of First Meeting of Board of Directors

of _____

The board of directors of _____

held its first meeting on _____, 20_____, at _____.m.

The following directors, constituting a quorum of the full board, were present at the meeting:

_____

_____

_____

_____

The following directors were absent:

_____

_____

_____

_____

   On motion and by unanimous vote, _____
was elected temporary chairperson and then presided over the meeting. _____
_____ was elected temporary secretary of the meeting.

   The chairperson announced that the meeting was held pursuant to written waiver of notice signed by each of the directors. Upon a motion duly made, seconded, and unanimously carried, the waiver was made a part of the records of the meeting. It now precedes the minutes of this meeting in the corporate records book.

Articles of Incorporation

The chairperson announced that the articles of incorporation or similar organizing instrument of this corporation was filed with the office of _____
_____ on _____.

   RESOLVED, that the secretary of this corporation is directed to see that a copy of the articles of incorporation or similar organizing instrument of this corporation, file-stamped or certified by the secretary of state or other appropriate state office or official, is kept at the corporation's principal office.

Bylaws

There was then presented to the meeting for adoption a proposed set of bylaws of the corporation. The bylaws were considered and discussed and, on motion duly made and seconded, it was unanimously

RESOLVED, that the bylaws presented to this meeting be and hereby are adopted as the bylaws of the corporation;

RESOLVED FURTHER, that the secretary of this corporation is directed to see that a copy of the bylaws is kept at the corporation's principal office.

Corporate Tax Exemptions

The chairperson announced that, upon application previously submitted to the Internal Revenue Service, the corporation was determined to be exempt from payment of federal corporate income taxes under Section 501(c)(3) of the Internal Revenue Code per Internal Revenue Service determination letter dated _____, 20_____. The chairperson then presented the federal tax exemption determination letter and the secretary was instructed to insert this letter in the corporate records book.

The chairperson announced that the corporation was exempt from applicable state corporate income, franchise, or similar taxes. The chairperson instructed the secretary to place a copy of any correspondence related to the corporation's state corporate tax exemption in the corporate records book.

Election of Officers

The chairperson then announced that the next item of business was the election of officers. Upon motion, the following persons were unanimously elected to the offices shown after their names:

_____ President

_____ Vice President

_____ Secretary

_____ Treasurer

Each officer who was present accepted his or her office. Thereafter, the president presided at the meeting as chairperson of the meeting, and the secretary of the corporation acted as secretary of the meeting.

Principal Office

After discussion as to the exact location of the corporation's principal office for the transaction of business in the county named in the bylaws, upon motion duly made and seconded, it was

RESOLVED, that the principal office of this corporation shall be located at _____

_____.

Bank Account

Upon motion duly made and seconded, it was

RESOLVED, that the funds of this corporation shall be deposited with _____

_____.

RESOLVED FURTHER, that the treasurer of this corporation be and hereby is authorized and directed to establish an account with said bank and to deposit the funds of this corporation therein.

RESOLVED FURTHER, that any officer, employee, or agent of this corporation be and is authorized to endorse checks, drafts, or other evidences of indebtedness made payable to this corporation, but only for the purpose of deposit.

RESOLVED FURTHER, that all checks, drafts, and other instruments obligating this corporation to pay money shall be signed on behalf of this corporation by any of the following persons:

_____

_____

_____

_____

RESOLVED FURTHER, that said bank be and hereby is authorized to honor and pay all checks and drafts of this corporation signed as provided herein.

RESOLVED FURTHER, that the authority hereby conferred shall remain in force until revoked by the board of directors of this corporation and until written notice of such revocation shall have been received by said bank.

RESOLVED FURTHER, that the secretary of this corporation be and hereby is authorized to certify as to the continuing authority of these resolutions, the persons authorized to sign on behalf of this corporation, and the adoption of said bank's standard form of resolution, provided that said form does not vary materially from the terms of the foregoing resolutions.

Compensation of Officers

There followed a discussion concerning the compensation to be paid by the corporation to its officers. Upon motion duly made and seconded, it was unanimously

RESOLVED, that the following annual salaries be paid to the officers of this corporation:

President	$_____
Vice President	$_____
Secretary	$_____
Treasurer	$_____

Corporate Seal

The secretary presented to the meeting for adoption a proposed form of seal of the corporation. Upon motion duly made and seconded, it was:

RESOLVED, that the form of corporate seal presented to this meeting be and hereby is adopted as the seal of this corporation, and the secretary of the corporation is directed to place an impression thereof in the space next to this resolution.

[Impress seal here]

Corporate Certificates

The secretary then presented to the meeting proposed director, sponsor, membership, or other forms of corporate certificates for approval by the board. Upon motion duly made and seconded, it was

RESOLVED, that the form of certificates presented to this meeting are hereby adopted for use by this corporation and the secretary is directed to attach a copy of each form of certificate to the minutes of this meeting.

Since there was no further business to come before the meeting, on motion duly made and seconded, the meeting was adjourned.

Dated: _____

_____

_____, Secretary

Department of the Treasury
Internal Revenue Service

Notice 1382

(Rev. September 2009)

Changes for Form 1023:

- Mailing address
- Parts IX, X and XI

Changes for Form 1023, Application for Recognition of Exemption Under Section 501(c)(3) of the Internal Revenue Code

Change of Mailing Address

The mailing address shown on Form 1023 Checklist, page 28, the first address under the last checkbox; and in the Instructions for Form 1023, page 4 under *Where to File,* has been changed to:

Internal Revenue Service
P.O. Box 12192
Covington, KY 41012-0192

Changes for Parts IX and X

Changes to Parts IX and X are necessary to comply with new regulations that eliminated the advance ruling process. Until Form 1023 is revised to reflect this change, please follow the directions on this notice when completing Part IX and Part X of Form 1023. For more information about the elimination of the advance ruling process, visit us at *www.irs.gov* and click on *Charities & Non-Profits.*

Part IX. Financial Data

The instructions at the top of Part IX on page 9 of Form 1023 are now as follows. For purposes of this schedule, years in existence refer to completed tax years.

1. If in existence less than 5 years, complete the statement for each year in existence and provide projections of your likely revenues and expenses based on a reasonable and good faith estimate of your future finances for a total of:

    a. Three years of financial information if you have not completed one tax year, or

    b. Four years of financial information if you have completed one tax year.

2. If in existence 5 or more years, complete the schedule for the most recent 5 tax years. You will need to provide a separate statement that includes information about the most recent 5 tax years because the data table in Part IX, has not been updated to provide for a 5th year.

Part X. Public Charity Status

Do not complete line 6a on page 11 of Form 1023, and **do not sign** the form under the heading "Consent Fixing Period of Limitations Upon Assessment of Tax Under Section 4940 of the Internal Revenue Code."

Only complete line 6b and line 7 on page 11 of Form 1023, if in existence 5 or more tax years.

Notice **1382** (Rev. 9-2009)
Cat. No. 52336F

Part XI. Increase in User Fees.

User fee increases are effective for all applications postmarked after January 3, 2010.

1. $400 for organizations whose gross receipts do not exceed $10,000 or less annually over a 4-year period.

2. $850 for organizations whose gross receipts exceed $10,000 annually over a 4-year period.

See *www.irs.gov* web page link on Form 1023, page 12, Part XI, User Fee Information, for the current user fees.

Cyber Assistant, a web-based software program designed to help organizations prepare a complete and accurate Form 1023 application, will become available during 2010. Once the IRS announces the availability of Cyber Assistant, the user fees will change again.

1. $200 for organizations using Cyber Assistant (regardless of size) to prepare their Form 1023, or

2. $850 for all other organizations not using Cyber Assistant (regardless of size) to prepare their Form 1023.

IRS will announce when Cyber Assistant is available and the effective date of the user fee change. Sign up for the *Exempt Organization (EO) Update,* EO's subscription newsletter, at *www.irs.gov/charities,* to automatically receive an alert that Cyber Assistant is available.

Form 1023
(Rev. June 2006)
Department of the Treasury
Internal Revenue Service

Application for Recognition of Exemption
Under Section 501(c)(3) of the Internal Revenue Code

OMB No. 1545-0056

Note: *If exempt status is approved, this application will be open for public inspection.*

*Use the instructions to complete this application and for a definition of all **bold** items.* For additional help, call IRS Exempt Organizations Customer Account Services toll-free at 1-877-829-5500. Visit our website at **www.irs.gov** for forms and publications. If the required information and documents are not submitted with payment of the appropriate user fee, the application may be returned to you.

Attach additional sheets to this application if you need more space to answer fully. Put your name and EIN on each sheet and identify each answer by Part and line number. Complete Parts I - XI of Form 1023 and submit only those Schedules (A through H) that apply to you.

Part I Identification of Applicant

1 Full name of organization (exactly as it appears in your **organizing document**)	2 c/o Name (if applicable)

3 **Mailing address** (Number and street) (see instructions)	Room/Suite	4 Employer Identification Number (EIN)
City or town, state or country, and ZIP + 4		5 Month the annual accounting period ends (01 – 12)

6 Primary contact (officer, director, trustee, or **authorized representative**)
  a Name:

b Phone:

c Fax: (optional)

7 Are you represented by an authorized representative, such as an attorney or accountant? If "Yes," provide the authorized representative's name, and the name and address of the authorized representative's firm. Include a completed Form 2848, *Power of Attorney and Declaration of Representative,* with your application if you would like us to communicate with your representative. ☐ **Yes** ☐ **No**

8 Was a person who is not one of your officers, directors, trustees, employees, or an authorized representative listed in line 7, paid, or promised payment, to help plan, manage, or advise you about the structure or activities of your organization, or about your financial or tax matters? If "Yes," provide the person's name, the name and address of the person's firm, the amounts paid or promised to be paid, and describe that person's role. ☐ **Yes** ☐ **No**

9a Organization's website:

  b Organization's email: (optional)

10 Certain organizations are not required to file an information return (Form 990 or Form 990-EZ). If you are granted tax-exemption, are you claiming to be excused from filing Form 990 or Form 990-EZ? If "Yes," explain. See the instructions for a description of organizations not required to file Form 990 or Form 990-EZ. ☐ **Yes** ☐ **No**

11 Date incorporated if a corporation, or formed, if other than a corporation. (MM/DD/YYYY)   /   /

12 Were you formed under the laws of a **foreign country**? If "Yes," state the country. ☐ **Yes** ☐ **No**

For Paperwork Reduction Act Notice, see page 24 of the instructions.   Cat. No. 17133K   Form **1023** (Rev. 6-2006)

Part II Organizational Structure

You must be a corporation (including a limited liability company), an unincorporated association, or a trust to be tax exempt. (See instructions.) **DO NOT file this form unless you can check "Yes" on lines 1, 2, 3, or 4.**

1 Are you a **corporation**? If "Yes," attach a copy of your articles of incorporation showing **certification of filing** with the appropriate state agency. Include copies of any amendments to your articles and be sure they also show state filing certification. ☐ Yes ☐ No

2 Are you a **limited liability company (LLC)**? If "Yes," attach a copy of your articles of organization showing certification of filing with the appropriate state agency. Also, if you adopted an operating agreement, attach a copy. Include copies of any amendments to your articles and be sure they show state filing certification. Refer to the instructions for circumstances when an LLC should not file its own exemption application. ☐ Yes ☐ No

3 Are you an **unincorporated association**? If "Yes," attach a copy of your articles of association, constitution, or other similar organizing document that is dated and includes at least two signatures. Include signed and dated copies of any amendments. ☐ Yes ☐ No

4a Are you a **trust**? If "Yes," attach a signed and dated copy of your trust agreement. Include signed and dated copies of any amendments. ☐ Yes ☐ No

b Have you been funded? If "No," explain how you are formed without anything of value placed in trust. ☐ Yes ☐ No

5 Have you adopted **bylaws**? If "Yes," attach a current copy showing date of adoption. If "No," explain how your officers, directors, or trustees are selected. ☐ Yes ☐ No

Part III Required Provisions in Your Organizing Document

The following questions are designed to ensure that when you file this application, your organizing document contains the required provisions to meet the organizational test under section 501(c)(3). Unless you can check the boxes in both lines 1 and 2, your organizing document does not meet the organizational test. **DO NOT file this application until you have amended your organizing document.** Submit your original and amended organizing documents (showing state filing certification if you are a corporation or an LLC) with your application.

1 Section 501(c)(3) requires that your organizing document state your exempt purpose(s), such as charitable, religious, educational, and/or scientific purposes. Check the box to confirm that your organizing document meets this requirement. Describe specifically where your organizing document meets this requirement, such as a reference to a particular article or section in your organizing document. Refer to the instructions for exempt purpose language. Location of Purpose Clause (Page, Article, and Paragraph): _____ ☐

2a Section 501(c)(3) requires that upon dissolution of your organization, your remaining assets must be used exclusively for exempt purposes, such as charitable, religious, educational, and/or scientific purposes. Check the box on line 2a to confirm that your organizing document meets this requirement by express provision for the distribution of assets upon dissolution. If you rely on state law for your dissolution provision, do not check the box on line 2a and go to line 2c. ☐

2b If you checked the box on line 2a, specify the location of your dissolution clause (Page, Article, and Paragraph). Do not complete line 2c if you checked box 2a. _____

2c See the instructions for information about the operation of state law in your particular state. Check this box if you rely on operation of state law for your dissolution provision and indicate the state: _____ ☐

Part IV Narrative Description of Your Activities

Using an attachment, describe your *past, present,* and *planned* activities in a narrative. If you believe that you have already provided some of this information in response to other parts of this application, you may summarize that information here and refer to the specific parts of the application for supporting details. You may also attach representative copies of newsletters, brochures, or similar documents for supporting details to this narrative. Remember that if this application is approved, it will be open for public inspection. Therefore, your narrative description of activities should be thorough and accurate. Refer to the instructions for information that must be included in your description.

Part V Compensation and Other Financial Arrangements With Your Officers, Directors, Trustees, Employees, and Independent Contractors

1a List the names, titles, and mailing addresses of all of your officers, directors, and trustees. For each person listed, state their total annual **compensation**, or proposed compensation, for all services to the organization, whether as an officer, employee, or other position. Use actual figures, if available. Enter "none" if no compensation is or will be paid. If additional space is needed, attach a separate sheet. Refer to the instructions for information on what to include as compensation.

Name	Title	Mailing address	Compensation amount (annual actual or estimated)

Part V	Compensation and Other Financial Arrangements With Your Officers, Directors, Trustees, Employees, and Independent Contractors *(Continued)*

b List the names, titles, and mailing addresses of each of your five highest compensated employees who receive or will receive compensation of more than $50,000 per year. Use the actual figure, if available. Refer to the instructions for information on what to include as compensation. Do not include officers, directors, or trustees listed in line 1a.

Name	Title	Mailing address	Compensation amount (annual actual or estimated)

c List the names, names of businesses, and mailing addresses of your five highest compensated **independent contractors** that receive or will receive compensation of more than $50,000 per year. Use the actual figure, if available. Refer to the instructions for information on what to include as compensation.

Name	Title	Mailing address	Compensation amount (annual actual or estimated)

The following "Yes" or "No" questions relate to *past, present, or planned* relationships, transactions, or agreements with your officers, directors, trustees, highest compensated employees, and highest compensated independent contractors listed in lines 1a, 1b, and 1c.

2a Are any of your officers, directors, or trustees **related** to each other through **family** or **business relationships**? If "Yes," identify the individuals and explain the relationship. ☐ **Yes** ☐ **No**

b Do you have a business relationship with any of your officers, directors, or trustees other than through their position as an officer, director, or trustee? If "Yes," identify the individuals and describe the business relationship with each of your officers, directors, or trustees. ☐ **Yes** ☐ **No**

c Are any of your officers, directors, or trustees related to your highest compensated employees or highest compensated independent contractors listed on lines 1b or 1c through family or business relationships? If "Yes," identify the individuals and explain the relationship. ☐ **Yes** ☐ **No**

3a For each of your officers, directors, trustees, highest compensated employees, and highest compensated independent contractors listed on lines 1a, 1b, or 1c, attach a list showing their name, qualifications, average hours worked, and duties.

b Do any of your officers, directors, trustees, highest compensated employees, and highest compensated independent contractors listed on lines 1a, 1b, or 1c receive compensation from any other organizations, whether tax exempt or taxable, that are related to you through **common control**? If "Yes," identify the individuals, explain the relationship between you and the other organization, and describe the compensation arrangement. ☐ **Yes** ☐ **No**

4 In establishing the compensation for your officers, directors, trustees, highest compensated employees, and highest compensated independent contractors listed on lines 1a, 1b, and 1c, the following practices are recommended, although they are not required to obtain exemption. Answer "Yes" to all the practices you use.

a Do you or will the individuals that approve compensation arrangements follow a conflict of interest policy? ☐ **Yes** ☐ **No**
b Do you or will you approve compensation arrangements in advance of paying compensation? ☐ **Yes** ☐ **No**
c Do you or will you document in writing the date and terms of approved compensation arrangements? ☐ **Yes** ☐ **No**

| Part V | Compensation and Other Financial Arrangements With Your Officers, Directors, Trustees, Employees, and Independent Contractors *(Continued)* |

d Do you or will you record in writing the decision made by each individual who decided or voted on compensation arrangements?   ☐ **Yes**   ☐ **No**

e Do you or will you approve compensation arrangements based on information about compensation paid by **similarly situated** taxable or tax-exempt organizations for similar services, current compensation surveys compiled by independent firms, or actual written offers from similarly situated organizations? Refer to the instructions for Part V, lines 1a, 1b, and 1c, for information on what to include as compensation.   ☐ **Yes**   ☐ **No**

f Do you or will you record in writing both the information on which you relied to base your decision and its source?   ☐ **Yes**   ☐ **No**

g If you answered "No" to any item on lines 4a through 4f, describe how you set compensation that is **reasonable** for your officers, directors, trustees, highest compensated employees, and highest compensated independent contractors listed in Part V, lines 1a, 1b, and 1c.

5a Have you adopted a **conflict of interest policy** consistent with the sample conflict of interest policy in Appendix A to the instructions? If "Yes," provide a copy of the policy and explain how the policy has been adopted, such as by resolution of your governing board. If "No," answer lines 5b and 5c.   ☐ **Yes**   ☐ **No**

b What procedures will you follow to assure that persons who have a conflict of interest will not have influence over you for setting their own compensation?

c What procedures will you follow to assure that persons who have a conflict of interest will not have influence over you regarding business deals with themselves?

Note: A conflict of interest policy is recommended though it is not required to obtain exemption. Hospitals, see Schedule C, Section I, line 14.

6a Do you or will you compensate any of your officers, directors, trustees, highest compensated employees, and highest compensated independent contractors listed in lines 1a, 1b, or 1c through **non-fixed payments**, such as discretionary bonuses or revenue-based payments? If "Yes," describe all non-fixed compensation arrangements, including how the amounts are determined, who is eligible for such arrangements, whether you place a limitation on total compensation, and how you determine or will determine that you pay no more than reasonable compensation for services. Refer to the instructions for Part V, lines 1a, 1b, and 1c, for information on what to include as compensation.   ☐ **Yes**   ☐ **No**

b Do you or will you compensate any of your employees, other than your officers, directors, trustees, or your five highest compensated employees who receive or will receive compensation of more than $50,000 per year, through non-fixed payments, such as discretionary bonuses or revenue-based payments? If "Yes," describe all non-fixed compensation arrangements, including how the amounts are or will be determined, who is or will be eligible for such arrangements, whether you place or will place a limitation on total compensation, and how you determine or will determine that you pay no more than reasonable compensation for services. Refer to the instructions for Part V, lines 1a, 1b, and 1c, for information on what to include as compensation.   ☐ **Yes**   ☐ **No**

7a Do you or will you purchase any goods, services, or assets from any of your officers, directors, trustees, highest compensated employees, or highest compensated independent contractors listed in lines 1a, 1b, or 1c? If "Yes," describe any such purchase that you made or intend to make, from whom you make or will make such purchases, how the terms are or will be negotiated at **arm's length**, and explain how you determine or will determine that you pay no more than **fair market value**. Attach copies of any written contracts or other agreements relating to such purchases.   ☐ **Yes**   ☐ **No**

b Do you or will you sell any goods, services, or assets to any of your officers, directors, trustees, highest compensated employees, or highest compensated independent contractors listed in lines 1a, 1b, or 1c? If "Yes," describe any such sales that you made or intend to make, to whom you make or will make such sales, how the terms are or will be negotiated at arm's length, and explain how you determine or will determine you are or will be paid at least fair market value. Attach copies of any written contracts or other agreements relating to such sales.   ☐ **Yes**   ☐ **No**

8a Do you or will you have any leases, contracts, loans, or other agreements with your officers, directors, trustees, highest compensated employees, or highest compensated independent contractors listed in lines 1a, 1b, or 1c? If "Yes," provide the information requested in lines 8b through 8f.   ☐ **Yes**   ☐ **No**

b Describe any written or oral arrangements that you made or intend to make.

c Identify with whom you have or will have such arrangements.

d Explain how the terms are or will be negotiated at arm's length.

e Explain how you determine you pay no more than fair market value or you are paid at least fair market value.

f Attach copies of any signed leases, contracts, loans, or other agreements relating to such arrangements.

9a Do you or will you have any leases, contracts, loans, or other agreements with any organization in which any of your officers, directors, or trustees are also officers, directors, or trustees, or in which any individual officer, director, or trustee owns more than a 35% interest? If "Yes," provide the information requested in lines 9b through 9f.   ☐ **Yes**   ☐ **No**

Part V **Compensation and Other Financial Arrangements With Your Officers, Directors, Trustees, Employees, and Independent Contractors** *(Continued)*

  b Describe any written or oral arrangements you made or intend to make.

  c Identify with whom you have or will have such arrangements.

  d Explain how the terms are or will be negotiated at arm's length.

  e Explain how you determine or will determine you pay no more than fair market value or that you are paid at least fair market value.

  f Attach a copy of any signed leases, contracts, loans, or other agreements relating to such arrangements.

Part VI **Your Members and Other Individuals and Organizations That Receive Benefits From You**

The following "Yes" or "No" questions relate to goods, services, and funds you provide to individuals and organizations as part of your activities. Your answers should pertain to *past, present,* and *planned* activities. (See instructions.)

1a In carrying out your exempt purposes, do you provide goods, services, or funds to individuals? If "Yes," describe each program that provides goods, services, or funds to individuals.	☐ **Yes** ☐ **No**
b In carrying out your exempt purposes, do you provide goods, services, or funds to organizations? If "Yes," describe each program that provides goods, services, or funds to organizations.	☐ **Yes** ☐ **No**
2 Do any of your programs limit the provision of goods, services, or funds to a specific individual or group of specific individuals? For example, answer "Yes," if goods, services, or funds are provided only for a particular individual, your members, individuals who work for a particular employer, or graduates of a particular school. If "Yes," explain the limitation and how recipients are selected for each program.	☐ **Yes** ☐ **No**
3 Do any individuals who receive goods, services, or funds through your programs have a family or business relationship with any officer, director, trustee, or with any of your highest compensated employees or highest compensated independent contractors listed in Part V, lines 1a, 1b, and 1c? If "Yes," explain how these related individuals are eligible for goods, services, or funds.	☐ **Yes** ☐ **No**

Part VII **Your History**

The following "Yes" or "No" questions relate to your history. (See instructions.)

1 Are you a **successor** to another organization? Answer "Yes," if you have taken or will take over the activities of another organization; you took over 25% or more of the fair market value of the net assets of another organization; or you were established upon the conversion of an organization from for-profit to non-profit status. If "Yes," complete Schedule G.	☐ **Yes** ☐ **No**
2 Are you submitting this application more than 27 months after the end of the month in which you were legally formed? If "Yes," complete Schedule E.	☐ **Yes** ☐ **No**

Part VIII **Your Specific Activities**

The following "Yes" or "No" questions relate to specific activities that you may conduct. Check the appropriate box. Your answers should pertain to *past, present,* and *planned* activities. (See instructions.)

1 Do you support or oppose candidates in **political campaigns** in any way? If "Yes," explain.	☐ **Yes** ☐ **No**
2a Do you attempt to **influence legislation**? If "Yes," explain how you attempt to influence legislation and complete line 2b. If "No," go to line 3a.	☐ **Yes** ☐ **No**
b Have you made or are you making an **election** to have your legislative activities measured by expenditures by filing Form 5768? If "Yes," attach a copy of the Form 5768 that was already filed or attach a completed Form 5768 that you are filing with this application. If "No," describe whether your attempts to influence legislation are a substantial part of your activities. Include the time and money spent on your attempts to influence legislation as compared to your total activities.	☐ **Yes** ☐ **No**
3a Do you or will you operate bingo or **gaming** activities? If "Yes," describe who conducts them, and list all revenue received or expected to be received and expenses paid or expected to be paid in operating these activities. **Revenue and expenses** should be provided for the time periods specified in Part IX, Financial Data.	☐ **Yes** ☐ **No**
b Do you or will you enter into contracts or other agreements with individuals or organizations to conduct bingo or gaming for you? If "Yes," describe any written or oral arrangements that you made or intend to make, identify with whom you have or will have such arrangements, explain how the terms are or will be negotiated at arm's length, and explain how you determine or will determine you pay no more than fair market value or you will be paid at least fair market value. Attach copies or any written contracts or other agreements relating to such arrangements.	☐ **Yes** ☐ **No**
c List the states and local jurisdictions, including Indian Reservations, in which you conduct or will conduct gaming or bingo.	

Part VIII   Your Specific Activities *(Continued)*

4a Do you or will you undertake **fundraising**? If "Yes," check all the fundraising programs you do or will conduct. (See instructions.)   ☐ **Yes**   ☐ **No**

☐ mail solicitations   ☐ phone solicitations
☐ email solicitations   ☐ accept donations on your website
☐ personal solicitations   ☐ receive donations from another organization's website
☐ vehicle, boat, plane, or similar donations   ☐ government grant solicitations
☐ foundation grant solicitations   ☐ Other

Attach a description of each fundraising program.

b Do you or will you have written or oral contracts with any individuals or organizations to raise funds for you? If "Yes," describe these activities. Include all revenue and expenses from these activities and state who conducts them. Revenue and expenses should be provided for the time periods specified in Part IX, Financial Data. Also, attach a copy of any contracts or agreements.   ☐ **Yes**   ☐ **No**

c Do you or will you engage in fundraising activities for other organizations? If "Yes," describe these arrangements. Include a description of the organizations for which you raise funds and attach copies of all contracts or agreements.   ☐ **Yes**   ☐ **No**

d List all states and local jurisdictions in which you conduct fundraising. For each state or local jurisdiction listed, specify whether you fundraise for your own organization, you fundraise for another organization, or another organization fundraises for you.

e Do you or will you maintain separate accounts for any contributor under which the contributor has the right to advise on the use or distribution of funds? Answer "Yes" if the donor may provide advice on the types of investments, distributions from the types of investments, or the distribution from the donor's contribution account. If "Yes," describe this program, including the type of advice that may be provided and submit copies of any written materials provided to donors.   ☐ **Yes**   ☐ **No**

5 Are you **affiliated** with a governmental unit? If "Yes," explain.   ☐ **Yes**   ☐ **No**

6a Do you or will you engage in **economic development**? If "Yes," describe your program.   ☐ **Yes**   ☐ **No**
  b Describe in full who benefits from your economic development activities and how the activities promote exempt purposes.

7a Do or will persons other than your employees or volunteers **develop** your facilities? If "Yes," describe each facility, the role of the developer, and any business or family relationship(s) between the developer and your officers, directors, or trustees.   ☐ **Yes**   ☐ **No**

b Do or will persons other than your employees or volunteers **manage** your activities or facilities? If "Yes," describe each activity and facility, the role of the manager, and any business or family relationship(s) between the manager and your officers, directors, or trustees.   ☐ **Yes**   ☐ **No**

c If there is a business or family relationship between any manager or developer and your officers, directors, or trustees, identify the individuals, explain the relationship, describe how contracts are negotiated at arm's length so that you pay no more than fair market value, and submit a copy of any contracts or other agreements.

8 Do you or will you enter into **joint ventures**, including partnerships or **limited liability companies** treated as partnerships, in which you share profits and losses with partners other than section 501(c)(3) organizations? If "Yes," describe the activities of these joint ventures in which you participate.   ☐ **Yes**   ☐ **No**

9a Are you applying for exemption as a childcare organization under section 501(k)? If "Yes," answer lines 9b through 9d. If "No," go to line 10.   ☐ **Yes**   ☐ **No**

b Do you provide child care so that parents or caretakers of children you care for can be **gainfully employed** (see instructions)? If "No," explain how you qualify as a childcare organization described in section 501(k).   ☐ **Yes**   ☐ **No**

c Of the children for whom you provide child care, are 85% or more of them cared for by you to enable their parents or caretakers to be gainfully employed (see instructions)? If "No," explain how you qualify as a childcare organization described in section 501(k).   ☐ **Yes**   ☐ **No**

d Are your services available to the general public? If "No," describe the specific group of people for whom your activities are available. Also, see the instructions and explain how you qualify as a childcare organization described in section 501(k).   ☐ **Yes**   ☐ **No**

10 Do you or will you publish, own, or have rights in music, literature, tapes, artworks, choreography, scientific discoveries, or other **intellectual property**? If "Yes," explain. Describe who owns or will own any copyrights, patents, or trademarks, whether fees are or will be charged, how the fees are determined, and how any items are or will be produced, distributed, and marketed.   ☐ **Yes**   ☐ **No**

Part VIII Your Specific Activities *(Continued)*

11 Do you or will you accept contributions of: real property; conservation easements; closely held securities; intellectual property such as patents, trademarks, and copyrights; works of music or art; licenses; royalties; automobiles, boats, planes, or other vehicles; or collectibles of any type? If "Yes," describe each type of contribution, any conditions imposed by the donor on the contribution, and any agreements with the donor regarding the contribution. ☐ **Yes** ☐ **No**

12a Do you or will you operate in a **foreign country** or **countries?** If "Yes," answer lines 12b through 12d. If "No," go to line 13a. ☐ **Yes** ☐ **No**

  b Name the foreign countries and regions within the countries in which you operate.

  c Describe your operations in each country and region in which you operate.

  d Describe how your operations in each country and region further your exempt purposes.

13a Do you or will you make grants, loans, or other distributions to organization(s)? If "Yes," answer lines 13b through 13g. If "No," go to line 14a. ☐ **Yes** ☐ **No**

  b Describe how your grants, loans, or other distributions to organizations further your exempt purposes.

  c Do you have written contracts with each of these organizations? If "Yes," attach a copy of each contract. ☐ **Yes** ☐ **No**

  d Identify each recipient organization and any **relationship** between you and the recipient organization.

  e Describe the records you keep with respect to the grants, loans, or other distributions you make.

  f Describe your selection process, including whether you do any of the following:

    (i) Do you require an application form? If "Yes," attach a copy of the form. ☐ **Yes** ☐ **No**

    (ii) Do you require a grant proposal? If "Yes," describe whether the grant proposal specifies your responsibilities and those of the grantee, obligates the grantee to use the grant funds only for the purposes for which the grant was made, provides for periodic written reports concerning the use of grant funds, requires a final written report and an accounting of how grant funds were used, and acknowledges your authority to withhold and/or recover grant funds in case such funds are, or appear to be, misused. ☐ **Yes** ☐ **No**

  g Describe your procedures for oversight of distributions that assure you the resources are used to further your exempt purposes, including whether you require periodic and final reports on the use of resources.

14a Do you or will you make grants, loans, or other distributions to foreign organizations? If "Yes," answer lines 14b through 14f. If "No," go to line 15. ☐ **Yes** ☐ **No**

  b Provide the name of each foreign organization, the country and regions within a country in which each foreign organization operates, and describe any relationship you have with each foreign organization.

  c Does any foreign organization listed in line 14b accept contributions earmarked for a specific country or specific organization? If "Yes," list all earmarked organizations or countries. ☐ **Yes** ☐ **No**

  d Do your contributors know that you have ultimate authority to use contributions made to you at your discretion for purposes consistent with your exempt purposes? If "Yes," describe how you relay this information to contributors. ☐ **Yes** ☐ **No**

  e Do you or will you make pre-grant inquiries about the recipient organization? If "Yes," describe these inquiries, including whether you inquire about the recipient's financial status, its tax-exempt status under the Internal Revenue Code, its ability to accomplish the purpose for which the resources are provided, and other relevant information. ☐ **Yes** ☐ **No**

  f Do you or will you use any additional procedures to ensure that your distributions to foreign organizations are used in furtherance of your exempt purposes? If "Yes," describe these procedures, including site visits by your employees or compliance checks by impartial experts, to verify that grant funds are being used appropriately. ☐ **Yes** ☐ **No**

Part VIII   Your Specific Activities *(Continued)*

15	Do you have a **close connection** with any organizations? If "Yes," explain.	☐ Yes ☐ No
16	Are you applying for exemption as a **cooperative hospital service organization** under section 501(e)? If "Yes," explain.	☐ Yes ☐ No
17	Are you applying for exemption as a **cooperative service organization of operating educational organizations** under section 501(f)? If "Yes," explain.	☐ Yes ☐ No
18	Are you applying for exemption as a **charitable risk pool** under section 501(n)? If "Yes," explain.	☐ Yes ☐ No
19	Do you or will you operate a **school**? If "Yes," complete Schedule B. Answer "Yes," whether you operate a school as your main function or as a secondary activity.	☐ Yes ☐ No
20	Is your main function to provide **hospital** or **medical care**? If "Yes," complete Schedule C.	☐ Yes ☐ No
21	Do you or will you provide **low-income housing** or housing for the **elderly** or **handicapped**? If "Yes," complete Schedule F.	☐ Yes ☐ No
22	Do you or will you provide scholarships, fellowships, educational loans, or other educational grants to individuals, including grants for travel, study, or other similar purposes? If "Yes," complete Schedule H.	☐ Yes ☐ No

Note: Private foundations may use Schedule H to request advance approval of individual grant procedures.

Part IX	Financial Data

For purposes of this schedule, years in existence refer to completed tax years. If in existence 4 or more years, complete the schedule for the most recent 4 tax years. If in existence more than 1 year but less than 4 years, complete the statements for each year in existence and provide projections of your likely revenues and expenses based on a reasonable and good faith estimate of your future finances for a total of 3 years of financial information. If in existence less than 1 year, provide projections of your likely revenues and expenses for the current year and the 2 following years, based on a reasonable and good faith estimate of your future finances for a total of 3 years of financial information. (See instructions.)

A. Statement of Revenues and Expenses

	Type of revenue or expense	Current tax year (a) From ___ To ___	3 prior tax years or 2 succeeding tax years (b) From ___ To ___	(c) From ___ To ___	(d) From ___ To ___	(e) Provide Total for (a) through (d)
Revenues	**1** Gifts, grants, and contributions received (do not include unusual grants)					
	2 Membership fees received					
	3 Gross investment income					
	4 Net unrelated business income					
	5 Taxes levied for your benefit					
	6 Value of services or facilities furnished by a governmental unit without charge (not including the value of services generally furnished to the public without charge)					
	7 Any revenue not otherwise listed above or in lines 9–12 below (attach an itemized list)					
	8 Total of lines 1 through 7					
	9 Gross receipts from admissions, merchandise sold or services performed, or furnishing of facilities in any activity that is related to your exempt purposes (attach itemized list)					
	10 Total of lines 8 and 9					
	11 Net gain or loss on sale of capital assets (attach schedule and see instructions)					
	12 Unusual grants					
	13 Total Revenue Add lines 10 through 12					
Expenses	**14** Fundraising expenses					
	15 Contributions, gifts, grants, and similar amounts paid out (attach an itemized list)					
	16 Disbursements to or for the benefit of members (attach an itemized list)					
	17 Compensation of officers, directors, and trustees					
	18 Other salaries and wages					
	19 Interest expense					
	20 Occupancy (rent, utilities, etc.)					
	21 Depreciation and depletion					
	22 Professional fees					
	23 Any expense not otherwise classified, such as program services (attach itemized list)					
	24 Total Expenses Add lines 14 through 23					

Part IX   Financial Data *(Continued)*

B. Balance Sheet (for your most recently completed tax year)

Year End:

Assets

(Whole dollars)

1	Cash	1	
2	Accounts receivable, net	2	
3	Inventories	3	
4	Bonds and notes receivable (attach an itemized list)	4	
5	Corporate stocks (attach an itemized list)	5	
6	Loans receivable (attach an itemized list)	6	
7	Other investments (attach an itemized list)	7	
8	Depreciable and depletable assets (attach an itemized list)	8	
9	Land	9	
10	Other assets (attach an itemized list)	10	
11	Total Assets (add lines 1 through 10)	11	

Liabilities

12	Accounts payable	12	
13	Contributions, gifts, grants, etc. payable	13	
14	Mortgages and notes payable (attach an itemized list)	14	
15	Other liabilities (attach an itemized list)	15	
16	Total Liabilities (add lines 12 through 15)	16	

Fund Balances or Net Assets

17	Total fund balances or net assets	17	
18	Total Liabilities and Fund Balances or Net Assets (add lines 16 and 17)	18	

19   Have there been any substantial changes in your assets or liabilities since the end of the period shown above? If "Yes," explain.   ☐ Yes   ☐ No

Part X   Public Charity Status

Part X is designed to classify you as an organization that is either a **private foundation** or a **public charity**. Public charity status is a more favorable tax status than private foundation status. If you are a private foundation, Part X is designed to further determine whether you are a **private operating foundation**. (See instructions.)

1a   Are you a private foundation? If "Yes," go to line 1b. If "No," go to line 5 and proceed as instructed. If you are unsure, see the instructions.   ☐ Yes   ☐ No

b   As a private foundation, section 508(e) requires special provisions in your organizing document in addition to those that apply to all organizations described in section 501(c)(3). Check the box to confirm that your organizing document meets this requirement, whether by express provision or by reliance on operation of state law. Attach a statement that describes specifically where your organizing document meets this requirement, such as a reference to a particular article or section in your organizing document or by operation of state law. See the instructions, including Appendix B, for information about the special provisions that need to be contained in your organizing document. Go to line 2.   ☐

2   Are you a private operating foundation? To be a private operating foundation you must engage directly in the active conduct of charitable, religious, educational, and similar activities, as opposed to indirectly carrying out these activities by providing grants to individuals or other organizations. If "Yes," go to line 3. If "No," go to the signature section of Part XI.   ☐ Yes   ☐ No

3   Have you existed for one or more years? If "Yes," attach financial information showing that you are a private operating foundation; go to the signature section of Part XI. If "No," continue to line 4.   ☐ Yes   ☐ No

4   Have you attached either (1) an affidavit or opinion of counsel, (including a written affidavit or opinion from a certified public accountant or accounting firm with expertise regarding this tax law matter), that sets forth facts concerning your operations and support to demonstrate that you are likely to satisfy the requirements to be classified as a private operating foundation; or (2) a statement describing your proposed operations as a private operating foundation?   ☐ Yes   ☐ No

5   If you answered "No" to line 1a, indicate the type of public charity status you are requesting by checking one of the choices below. You may check only one box.

The organization is not a private foundation because it is:

a   509(a)(1) and 170(b)(1)(A)(i)—a church or a convention or association of churches. Complete and attach Schedule A.   ☐

b   509(a)(1) and 170(b)(1)(A)(ii)—a **school**. Complete and attach Schedule B.   ☐

c   509(a)(1) and 170(b)(1)(A)(iii)—a **hospital**, a cooperative hospital service organization, or a medical research organization operated in conjunction with a hospital. Complete and attach Schedule C.   ☐

d   509(a)(3)—an organization supporting either one or more organizations described in line 5a through c, f, g, or h or a publicly supported section 501(c)(4), (5), or (6) organization. Complete and attach Schedule D.   ☐

Part X	**Public Charity Status** *(Continued)*

e 509(a)(4)—an organization organized and operated exclusively for testing for public safety. ☐

f 509(a)(1) and 170(b)(1)(A)(iv)—an organization operated for the benefit of a college or university that is owned or operated by a governmental unit. ☐

g 509(a)(1) and 170(b)(1)(A)(vi)—an organization that receives a substantial part of its financial support in the form of contributions from publicly supported organizations, from a governmental unit, or from the general public. ☐

h 509(a)(2)—an organization that normally receives not more than one-third of its financial support from gross **investment income** and receives more than one-third of its financial support from contributions, membership fees, and gross receipts from activities related to its exempt functions (subject to certain exceptions). ☐

i A publicly supported organization, but unsure if it is described in 5g or 5h. The organization would like the IRS to decide the correct status. ☐

6 If you checked box g, h, or i in question 5 above, you must request either an **advance** or a **definitive ruling** by selecting one of the boxes below. Refer to the instructions to determine which type of ruling you are eligible to receive.

a Request for Advance Ruling: By checking this box and signing the consent, pursuant to section 6501(c)(4) of the Code you request an advance ruling and agree to extend the statute of limitations on the assessment of excise tax under section 4940 of the Code. The tax will apply only if you do not establish public support status at the end of the 5-year advance ruling period. The assessment period will be extended for the 5 advance ruling years to 8 years, 4 months, and 15 days beyond the end of the first year. You have the right to refuse or limit the extension to a mutually agreed-upon period of time or issue(s). Publication 1035, *Extending the Tax Assessment Period,* provides a more detailed explanation of your rights and the consequences of the choices you make. You may obtain Publication 1035 free of charge from the IRS web site at *www.irs.gov* or by calling toll-free 1-800-829-3676. Signing this consent will not deprive you of any appeal rights to which you would otherwise be entitled. If you decide not to extend the statute of limitations, you are not eligible for an advance ruling. ☐

Consent Fixing Period of Limitations Upon Assessment of Tax Under Section 4940 of the Internal Revenue Code

For Organization

_____   _____   _____
(Signature of Officer, Director, Trustee, or other authorized official)   (Type or print name of signer)   (Date)

_____
(Type or print title or authority of signer)

For IRS Use Only

_____   _____
IRS Director, Exempt Organizations   (Date)

b Request for Definitive Ruling: Check this box if you have completed one tax year of at least 8 full months and you are requesting a definitive ruling. To confirm your public support status, answer line 6b(i) if you checked box g in line 5 above. Answer line 6b(ii) if you checked box h in line 5 above. If you checked box i in line 5 above, answer both lines 6b(i) and (ii). ☐

(i) (a) Enter 2% of line 8, column (e) on Part IX-A. Statement of Revenues and Expenses. _____

(b) Attach a list showing the name and amount contributed by each person, company, or organization whose gifts totaled more than the 2% amount. If the answer is "None," check this box. ☐

(ii) (a) For each year amounts are included on lines 1, 2, and 9 of Part IX-A. Statement of Revenues and Expenses, attach a list showing the name of and amount received from each **disqualified person.** If the answer is "None," check this box. ☐

(b) For each year amounts are included on line 9 of Part IX-A. Statement of Revenues and Expenses, attach a list showing the name of and amount received from each payer, other than a disqualified person, whose payments were more than the larger of (1) 1% of line 10, Part IX-A. Statement of Revenues and Expenses, or (2) $5,000. If the answer is "None," check this box. ☐

7 Did you receive any unusual grants during any of the years shown on Part IX-A. Statement of Revenues and Expenses? If "Yes," attach a list including the name of the contributor, the date and amount of the grant, a brief description of the grant, and explain why it is unusual. ☐ **Yes** ☐ **No**

Part XI   User Fee Information

You must include a user fee payment with this application. It will not be processed without your paid user fee. If your average annual gross receipts have exceeded or will exceed $10,000 annually over a 4-year period, you must submit payment of $750. If your gross receipts have not exceeded or will not exceed $10,000 annually over a 4-year period, the required user fee payment is $300. See instructions for Part XI, for a definition of **gross receipts** over a 4-year period. Your check or money order must be made payable to the United States Treasury. *User fees are subject to change. Check our website at www.irs.gov and type "User Fee" in the keyword box, or call Customer Account Services at 1-877-829-5500 for current information.*

1	Have your annual gross receipts averaged or are they expected to average not more than $10,000?	☐ **Yes**	☐ **No**
	If "Yes," check the box on line 2 and enclose a user fee payment of $300 (Subject to change—see above).		
	If "No," check the box on line 3 and enclose a user fee payment of $750 (Subject to change—see above).		
2	Check the box if you have enclosed the reduced user fee payment of $300 (Subject to change).		☐
3	Check the box if you have enclosed the user fee payment of $750 (Subject to change).		☐

I declare under the penalties of perjury that I am authorized to sign this application on behalf of the above organization and that I have examined this application, including the accompanying schedules and attachments, and to the best of my knowledge it is true, correct, and complete.

**Please
Sign
Here**   ▶

---   ---   ----------------------
(Signature of Officer, Director, Trustee, or other   (Type or print name of signer)   (Date)
authorized official)

(Type or print title or authority of signer)

Reminder: Send the completed Form 1023 Checklist with your filled-in-application.   Form **1023** (Rev. 6-2006)

Schedule A. Churches

1a Do you have a written creed, statement of faith, or summary of beliefs? If "Yes," attach copies of relevant documents.   ☐ **Yes**   ☐ **No**

b Do you have a form of worship? If "Yes," describe your form of worship.   ☐ **Yes**   ☐ **No**

2a Do you have a formal code of doctrine and discipline? If "Yes," describe your code of doctrine and discipline.   ☐ **Yes**   ☐ **No**

b Do you have a distinct religious history? If "Yes," describe your religious history.   ☐ **Yes**   ☐ **No**

c Do you have a literature of your own? If "Yes," describe your literature.   ☐ **Yes**   ☐ **No**

3 Describe the organization's religious hierarchy or ecclesiastical government.

4a Do you have regularly scheduled religious services? If "Yes," describe the nature of the services and provide representative copies of relevant literature such as church bulletins.   ☐ **Yes**   ☐ **No**

b What is the average attendance at your regularly scheduled religious services?   _____

5a Do you have an established place of worship? If "Yes," refer to the instructions for the information required.   ☐ **Yes**   ☐ **No**

b Do you own the property where you have an established place of worship?   ☐ **Yes**   ☐ **No**

6 Do you have an established congregation or other regular membership group? If "No," refer to the instructions.   ☐ **Yes**   ☐ **No**

7 How many members do you have?   _____

8a Do you have a process by which an individual becomes a member? If "Yes," describe the process and complete lines 8b–8d, below.   ☐ **Yes**   ☐ **No**

b If you have members, do your members have voting rights, rights to participate in religious functions, or other rights? If "Yes," describe the rights your members have.   ☐ **Yes**   ☐ **No**

c May your members be associated with another denomination or church?   ☐ **Yes**   ☐ **No**

d Are all of your members part of the same **family**?   ☐ **Yes**   ☐ **No**

9 Do you conduct baptisms, weddings, funerals, etc.?   ☐ **Yes**   ☐ **No**

10 Do you have a school for the religious instruction of the young?   ☐ **Yes**   ☐ **No**

11a Do you have a minister or religious leader? If "Yes," describe this person's role and explain whether the minister or religious leader was ordained, commissioned, or licensed after a prescribed course of study.   ☐ **Yes**   ☐ **No**

b Do you have schools for the preparation of your ordained ministers or religious leaders?   ☐ **Yes**   ☐ **No**

12 Is your minister or religious leader also one of your officers, directors, or trustees?   ☐ **Yes**   ☐ **No**

13 Do you ordain, commission, or license ministers or religious leaders? If "Yes," describe the requirements for ordination, commission, or licensure.   ☐ **Yes**   ☐ **No**

14 Are you part of a group of churches with similar beliefs and structures? If "Yes," explain. Include the name of the group of churches.   ☐ **Yes**   ☐ **No**

15 Do you issue church charters? If "Yes," describe the requirements for issuing a charter.   ☐ **Yes**   ☐ **No**

16 Did you pay a fee for a church charter? If "Yes," attach a copy of the charter.   ☐ **Yes**   ☐ **No**

17 Do you have other information you believe should be considered regarding your status as a church? If "Yes," explain.   ☐ **Yes**   ☐ **No**

Schedule B. Schools, Colleges, and Universities

If you operate a school as an activity, complete Schedule B

Section I	Operational Information		

1a Do you normally have a regularly scheduled curriculum, a regular faculty of qualified teachers, a regularly enrolled student body, and facilities where your educational activities are regularly carried on? If "No," do not complete the remainder of Schedule B. ☐ Yes ☐ No

b Is the primary function of your school the presentation of formal instruction? If "Yes," describe your school in terms of whether it is an elementary, secondary, college, technical, or other type of school. If "No," do not complete the remainder of Schedule B. ☐ Yes ☐ No

2a Are you a public school because you are operated by a state or subdivision of a state? If "Yes," explain how you are operated by a state or subdivision of a state. Do not complete the remainder of Schedule B. ☐ Yes ☐ No

b Are you a public school because you are operated wholly or predominantly from government funds or property? If "Yes," explain how you are operated wholly or predominantly from government funds or property. Submit a copy of your funding agreement regarding government funding. Do not complete the remainder of Schedule B. ☐ Yes ☐ No

3 In what public school district, county, and state are you located?

4 Were you formed or substantially expanded at the time of public school desegregation in the above school district or county? ☐ Yes ☐ No

5 Has a state or federal administrative agency or judicial body ever determined that you are racially discriminatory? If "Yes," explain. ☐ Yes ☐ No

6 Has your right to receive financial aid or assistance from a governmental agency ever been revoked or suspended? If "Yes," explain. ☐ Yes ☐ No

7 Do you or will you contract with another organization to develop, build, market, or finance your facilities? If "Yes," explain how that entity is selected, explain how the terms of any contracts or other agreements are negotiated at arm's length, and explain how you determine that you will pay no more than fair market value for services. ☐ Yes ☐ No

Note. Make sure your answer is consistent with the information provided in Part VIII, line 7a.

8 Do you or will you manage your activities or facilities through your own employees or volunteers? If "No," attach a statement describing the activities that will be managed by others, the names of the persons or organizations that manage or will manage your activities or facilities, and how these managers were or will be selected. Also, submit copies of any contracts, proposed contracts, or other agreements regarding the provision of management services for your activities or facilities. Explain how the terms of any contracts or other agreements were or will be negotiated, and explain how you determine you will pay no more than fair market value for services. ☐ Yes ☐ No

Note. Answer "Yes" if you manage or intend to manage your programs through your own employees or by using volunteers. Answer "No" if you engage or intend to engage a separate organization or independent contractor. Make sure your answer is consistent with the information provided in Part VIII, line 7b.

Section II	Establishment of Racially Nondiscriminatory Policy		

Information required by **Revenue Procedure 75-50.**

1 Have you adopted a racially nondiscriminatory policy as to students in your organizing document, bylaws, or by resolution of your governing body? If "Yes," state where the policy can be found or supply a copy of the policy. If "No," you must adopt a nondiscriminatory policy as to students before submitting this application. See Publication 557. ☐ Yes ☐ No

2 Do your brochures, application forms, advertisements, and catalogues dealing with student admissions, programs, and scholarships contain a statement of your racially nondiscriminatory policy? ☐ Yes ☐ No

a If "Yes," attach a representative sample of each document.

b If "No," by checking the box to the right you agree that all future printed materials, including website content, will contain the required nondiscriminatory policy statement. ▶ ☐

3 Have you published a notice of your nondiscriminatory policy in a newspaper of general circulation that serves all racial segments of the community? (See the instructions for specific requirements.) If "No," explain. ☐ Yes ☐ No

4 Does or will the organization (or any department or division within it) discriminate in any way on the basis of race with respect to admissions; use of facilities or exercise of student privileges; faculty or administrative staff; or scholarship or loan programs? If "Yes," for any of the above, explain fully. ☐ Yes ☐ No

Schedule B. Schools, Colleges, and Universities *(Continued)*

5 Complete the table below to show the racial composition for the current academic year and projected for the next academic year, of: (a) the student body, (b) the faculty, and (c) the administrative staff. Provide actual numbers rather than percentages for each racial category.

If you are not operational, submit an estimate based on the best information available (such as the racial composition of the community served).

Racial Category	(a) Student Body		(b) Faculty		(c) Administrative Staff	
	Current Year	Next Year	Current Year	Next Year	Current Year	Next Year
Total						

6 In the table below, provide the number and amount of loans and scholarships awarded to students enrolled by racial categories.

Racial Category	Number of Loans		Amount of Loans		Number of Scholarships		Amount of Scholarships	
	Current Year	Next Year	Current Year	Next Year	Current Year	Next Year	Current Year	Next Year
Total								

7a Attach a list of your incorporators, founders, board members, and donors of land or buildings, whether individuals or organizations.

b Do any of these individuals or organizations have an objective to maintain segregated public or private school education? If "Yes," explain. ☐ **Yes** ☐ **No**

8 Will you maintain records according to the non-discrimination provisions contained in Revenue Procedure 75-50? If "No," explain. (See instructions.) ☐ **Yes** ☐ **No**

Schedule C. Hospitals and Medical Research Organizations

Check the box if you are a **hospital**. See the instructions for a definition of the term "hospital," which includes an organization whose principal purpose or function is providing **hospital** or **medical care**. Complete Section I below.   ☐

Check the box if you are a **medical research organization** operated in conjunction with a hospital. See the instructions for a definition of the term "medical research organization," which refers to an organization whose principal purpose or function is medical research and which is directly engaged in the continuous active conduct of medical research in conjunction with a hospital. Complete Section II.   ☐

Section I	Hospitals		
1a	Are all the doctors in the community eligible for staff privileges? If "No," give the reasons why and explain how the medical staff is selected.	☐ Yes	☐ No
2a	Do you or will you provide medical services to all individuals in your community who can pay for themselves or have private health insurance? If "No," explain.	☐ Yes	☐ No
b	Do you or will you provide medical services to all individuals in your community who participate in Medicare? If "No," explain.	☐ Yes	☐ No
c	Do you or will you provide medical services to all individuals in your community who participate in Medicaid? If "No," explain.	☐ Yes	☐ No
3a	Do you or will you require persons covered by Medicare or Medicaid to pay a deposit before receiving services? If "Yes," explain.	☐ Yes	☐ No
b	Does the same deposit requirement, if any, apply to all other patients? If "No," explain.	☐ Yes	☐ No
4a	Do you or will you maintain a full-time emergency room? If "No," explain why you do not maintain a full-time emergency room. Also, describe any emergency services that you provide.	☐ Yes	☐ No
b	Do you have a policy on providing emergency services to persons without apparent means to pay? If "Yes," provide a copy of the policy.	☐ Yes	☐ No
c	Do you have any arrangements with police, fire, and voluntary ambulance services for the delivery or admission of emergency cases? If "Yes," describe the arrangements, including whether they are written or oral agreements. If written, submit copies of all such agreements.	☐ Yes	☐ No
5a	Do you provide for a portion of your services and facilities to be used for charity patients? If "Yes," answer 5b through 5e.	☐ Yes	☐ No
b	Explain your policy regarding charity cases, including how you distinguish between charity care and bad debts. Submit a copy of your written policy.		
c	Provide data on your past experience in admitting charity patients, including amounts you expend for treating charity care patients and types of services you provide to charity care patients.		
d	Describe any arrangements you have with federal, state, or local governments or government agencies for paying for the cost of treating charity care patients. Submit copies of any written agreements.		
e	Do you provide services on a sliding fee schedule depending on financial ability to pay? If "Yes," submit your sliding fee schedule.	☐ Yes	☐ No
6a	Do you or will you carry on a formal program of medical training or medical research? If "Yes," describe such programs, including the type of programs offered, the scope of such programs, and affiliations with other hospitals or medical care providers with which you carry on the medical training or research programs.	☐ Yes	☐ No
b	Do you or will you carry on a formal program of community education? If "Yes," describe such programs, including the type of programs offered, the scope of such programs, and affiliation with other hospitals or medical care providers with which you offer community education programs.	☐ Yes	☐ No
7	Do you or will you provide office space to physicians carrying on their own medical practices? If "Yes," describe the criteria for who may use the space, explain the means used to determine that you are paid at least fair market value, and submit representative lease agreements.	☐ Yes	☐ No
8	Is your board of directors comprised of a majority of individuals who are representative of the community you serve? Include a list of each board member's name and business, financial, or professional relationship with the hospital. Also, identify each board member who is representative of the community and describe how that individual is a community representative.	☐ Yes	☐ No
9	Do you participate in any joint ventures? If "Yes," state your ownership percentage in each joint venture, list your investment in each joint venture, describe the tax status of other participants in each joint venture (including whether they are section 501(c)(3) organizations), describe the activities of each joint venture, describe how you exercise control over the activities of each joint venture, and describe how each joint venture furthers your exempt purposes. Also, submit copies of all agreements. **Note.** Make sure your answer is consistent with the information provided in Part VIII, line 8.	☐ Yes	☐ No

Schedule C. Hospitals and Medical Research Organizations *(Continued)*

Section I　　Hospitals *(Continued)*

10 Do you or will you manage your activities or facilities through your own employees or volunteers? If "No," attach a statement describing the activities that will be managed by others, the names of the persons or organizations that manage or will manage your activities or facilities, and how these managers were or will be selected. Also, submit copies of any contracts, proposed contracts, or other agreements regarding the provision of management services for your activities or facilities. Explain how the terms of any contracts or other agreements were or will be negotiated, and explain how you determine you will pay no more than fair market value for services.　☐ **Yes**　☐ **No**

　　Note. Answer "Yes" if you do manage or intend to manage your programs through your own employees or by using volunteers. Answer "No" if you engage or intend to engage a separate organization or independent contractor. Make sure your answer is consistent with the information provided in Part VIII, line 7b.

11 Do you or will you offer recruitment incentives to physicians? If "Yes," describe your recruitment incentives and attach copies of all written recruitment incentive policies.　☐ **Yes**　☐ **No**

12 Do you or will you lease equipment, assets, or office space from physicians who have a financial or professional relationship with you? If "Yes," explain how you establish a fair market value for the lease.　☐ **Yes**　☐ **No**

13 Have you purchased medical practices, ambulatory surgery centers, or other business assets from physicians or other persons with whom you have a business relationship, aside from the purchase? If "Yes," submit a copy of each purchase and sales contract and describe how you arrived at fair market value, including copies of appraisals.　☐ **Yes**　☐ **No**

14 Have you adopted a **conflict of interest policy** consistent with the sample health care organization conflict of interest policy in Appendix A of the instructions? If "Yes," submit a copy of the policy and explain how the policy has been adopted, such as by resolution of your governing board. If "No," explain how you will avoid any conflicts of interest in your business dealings.　☐ **Yes**　☐ **No**

Section II　　Medical Research Organizations

1 Name the hospitals with which you have a relationship and describe the relationship. Attach copies of written agreements with each hospital that demonstrate continuing relationships between you and the hospital(s).

2 Attach a schedule describing your present and proposed activities for the direct conduct of medical research; describe the nature of the activities, and the amount of money that has been or will be spent in carrying them out.

3 Attach a schedule of assets showing their fair market value and the portion of your assets directly devoted to medical research.

Form **1023** (Rev. 6-2006)

Schedule D. Section 509(a)(3) Supporting Organizations

Section I   Identifying Information About the Supported Organization(s)

1   State the names, addresses, and EINs of the supported organizations. If additional space is needed, attach a separate sheet.

Name	Address	EIN
		−
		−

2   Are all supported organizations listed in line 1 public charities under section 509(a)(1) or (2)? If "Yes," go to Section II. If "No," go to line 3.   ☐ **Yes**   ☐ **No**

3   Do the supported organizations have tax-exempt status under section 501(c)(4), 501(c)(5), or 501(c)(6)?   ☐ **Yes**   ☐ **No**

   If "Yes," for each 501(c)(4), (5), or (6) organization supported, provide the following financial information:

   ● Part IX-A. Statement of Revenues and Expenses, lines 1–13 and
   ● Part X, lines 6b(ii)(a), 6b(ii)(b), and 7.

   If "No," attach a statement describing how each organization you support is a public charity under section 509(a)(1) or (2).

Section II   Relationship with Supported Organization(s)—Three Tests

To be classified as a supporting organization, an organization must meet one of three relationship tests:
   Test 1: "Operated, supervised, or controlled by" one or more publicly supported organizations, or
   Test 2: "Supervised or controlled in connection with" one or more publicly supported organizations, or
   Test 3: "Operated in connection with" one or more publicly supported organizations.

1   Information to establish the "operated, supervised, or controlled by" relationship (Test 1)
   Is a majority of your governing board or officers elected or appointed by the supported organization(s)? If "Yes," describe the process by which your governing board is appointed and elected; go to Section III. If "No," continue to line 2.   ☐ **Yes**   ☐ **No**

2   Information to establish the "supervised or controlled in connection with" relationship (Test 2)
   Does a majority of your governing board consist of individuals who also serve on the governing board of the supported organization(s)? If "Yes," describe the process by which your governing board is appointed and elected; go to Section III. If "No," go to line 3.   ☐ **Yes**   ☐ **No**

3   Information to establish the "operated in connection with" responsiveness test (Test 3)
   Are you a trust from which the named supported organization(s) can enforce and compel an accounting under state law? If "Yes," explain whether you advised the supported organization(s) in writing of these rights and provide a copy of the written communication documenting this; go to Section II, line 5. If "No," go to line 4a.   ☐ **Yes**   ☐ **No**

4   Information to establish the alternative "operated in connection with" responsiveness test (Test 3)
   a   Do the officers, directors, trustees, or members of the supported organization(s) elect or appoint one or more of your officers, directors, or trustees? If "Yes," explain and provide documentation; go to line 4d, below. If "No," go to line 4b.   ☐ **Yes**   ☐ **No**

   b   Do one or more members of the governing body of the supported organization(s) also serve as your officers, directors, or trustees or hold other important offices with respect to you? If "Yes," explain and provide documentation; go to line 4d, below. If "No," go to line 4c.   ☐ **Yes**   ☐ **No**

   c   Do your officers, directors, or trustees maintain a close and continuous working relationship with the officers, directors, or trustees of the supported organization(s)? If "Yes," explain and provide documentation.   ☐ **Yes**   ☐ **No**

   d   Do the supported organization(s) have a significant voice in your investment policies, in the making and timing of grants, and in otherwise directing the use of your income or assets? If "Yes," explain and provide documentation.   ☐ **Yes**   ☐ **No**

   e   Describe and provide copies of written communications documenting how you made the supported organization(s) aware of your supporting activities.

Schedule D. Section 509(a)(3) Supporting Organizations *(Continued)*

Section II	Relationship with Supported Organization(s)—Three Tests *(Continued)*

5 Information to establish the "operated in connection with" integral part test (Test 3)

Do you conduct activities that would otherwise be carried out by the supported organization(s)? If "Yes," explain and go to Section III. If "No," continue to line 6a. ☐ **Yes** ☐ **No**

6 Information to establish the alternative "operated in connection with" integral part test (Test 3)

a Do you distribute at least 85% of your annual **net income** to the supported organization(s)? If "Yes," go to line 6b. (See instructions.) ☐ **Yes** ☐ **No**

If "No," state the percentage of your income that you distribute to each supported organization. Also explain how you ensure that the supported organization(s) are attentive to your operations.

b How much do you contribute annually to each supported organization? Attach a schedule.

c What is the total annual revenue of each supported organization? If you need additional space, attach a list.

d Do you or the supported organization(s) **earmark** your funds for support of a particular program or activity? If "Yes," explain. ☐ **Yes** ☐ **No**

7a Does your organizing document specify the supported organization(s) by name? If "Yes," state the article and paragraph number and go to Section III. If "No," answer line 7b. ☐ **Yes** ☐ **No**

b Attach a statement describing whether there has been an historic and continuing relationship between you and the supported organization(s).

Section III	Organizational Test

1a If you met relationship Test 1 or Test 2 in Section II, your organizing document must specify the supported organization(s) by name, or by naming a similar purpose or charitable class of beneficiaries. If your organizing document complies with this requirement, answer "Yes." If your organizing document does not comply with this requirement, answer "No," and see the instructions. ☐ **Yes** ☐ **No**

b If you met relationship Test 3 in Section II, your organizing document must generally specify the supported organization(s) by name. If your organizing document complies with this requirement, answer "Yes," and go to Section IV. If your organizing document does not comply with this requirement, answer "No," and see the instructions. ☐ **Yes** ☐ **No**

Section IV	Disqualified Person Test

You do not qualify as a supporting organization if you are **controlled** directly or indirectly by one or more **disqualified persons** (as defined in section 4946) other than **foundation managers** or one or more organizations that you support. Foundation managers who are also disqualified persons for another reason are disqualified persons with respect to you.

1a Do any persons who are disqualified persons with respect to you, (except individuals who are disqualified persons only because they are foundation managers), appoint any of your foundation managers? If "Yes," (1) describe the process by which disqualified persons appoint any of your foundation managers, (2) provide the names of these disqualified persons and the foundation managers they appoint, and (3) explain how control is vested over your operations (including assets and activities) by persons other than disqualified persons. ☐ **Yes** ☐ **No**

b Do any persons who have a family or business relationship with any disqualified persons with respect to you, (except individuals who are disqualified persons only because they are foundation managers), appoint any of your foundation managers? If "Yes," (1) describe the process by which individuals with a family or business relationship with disqualified persons appoint any of your foundation managers, (2) provide the names of these disqualified persons, the individuals with a family or business relationship with disqualified persons, and the foundation managers appointed, and (3) explain how control is vested over your operations (including assets and activities) in individuals other than disqualified persons. ☐ **Yes** ☐ **No**

c Do any persons who are disqualified persons, (except individuals who are disqualified persons only because they are foundation managers), have any influence regarding your operations, including your assets or activities? If "Yes," (1) provide the names of these disqualified persons, (2) explain how influence is exerted over your operations (including assets and activities), and (3) explain how control is vested over your operations (including assets and activities) by individuals other than disqualified persons. ☐ **Yes** ☐ **No**

Schedule E. Organizations Not Filing Form 1023 Within 27 Months of Formation

Schedule E is intended to determine whether you are eligible for tax exemption under section 501(c)(3) from the postmark date of your application or from your date of incorporation or formation, whichever is earlier. If you are not eligible for tax exemption under section 501(c)(3) from your date of incorporation or formation, Schedule E is also intended to determine whether you are eligible for tax exemption under section 501(c)(4) for the period between your date of incorporation or formation and the postmark date of your application.

1	Are you a church, association of churches, or integrated auxiliary of a church? If "Yes," complete Schedule A and stop here. Do not complete the remainder of Schedule E.	☐ **Yes**	☐ **No**
2a	Are you a public charity with annual **gross receipts** that are normally $5,000 or less? If "Yes," stop here. Answer "No" if you are a private foundation, regardless of your gross receipts.	☐ **Yes**	☐ **No**
b	If your gross receipts were normally more than $5,000, are you filing this application within 90 days from the end of the tax year in which your gross receipts were normally more than $5,000? If "Yes," stop here.	☐ **Yes**	☐ **No**
3a	Were you included as a subordinate in a group exemption application or letter? If "No," go to line 4.	☐ **Yes**	☐ **No**
b	If you were included as a subordinate in a group exemption letter, are you filing this application within 27 months from the date you were notified by the organization holding the group exemption letter or the Internal Revenue Service that you cease to be covered by the group exemption letter? If "Yes," stop here.	☐ **Yes**	☐ **No**
c	If you were included as a subordinate in a timely filed group exemption request that was denied, are you filing this application within 27 months from the postmark date of the Internal Revenue Service final adverse ruling letter? If "Yes," stop here.	☐ **Yes**	☐ **No**
4	Were you created on or before October 9, 1969? If "Yes," stop here. Do not complete the remainder of this schedule.	☐ **Yes**	☐ **No**
5	If you answered "No" to lines 1 through 4, we cannot recognize you as tax exempt from your date of formation unless you qualify for an extension of time to apply for exemption. Do you wish to request an extension of time to apply to be recognized as exempt from the date you were formed? If "Yes," attach a statement explaining why you did not file this application within the 27-month period. Do not answer lines 6, 7, or 8. If "No," go to line 6a.	☐ **Yes**	☐ **No**
6a	If you answered "No" to line 5, you can only be exempt under section 501(c)(3) from the postmark date of this application. Therefore, do you want us to treat this application as a request for tax exemption from the postmark date? If "Yes," you are eligible for an advance ruling. Complete Part X, line 6a. If "No," you will be treated as a private foundation.	☐ **Yes**	☐ **No**
	Note. Be sure your ruling eligibility agrees with your answer to Part X, line 6.		
b	Do you anticipate significant changes in your sources of support in the future? If "Yes," complete line 7 below.	☐ **Yes**	☐ **No**

Schedule E. Organizations Not Filing Form 1023 Within 27 Months of Formation *(Continued)*

7 Complete this item only if you answered "Yes" to line 6b. Include projected revenue for the first two full years following the current tax year.

Type of Revenue	Projected revenue for 2 years following current tax year		
	(a) From ⸱⸱⸱⸱⸱⸱⸱⸱⸱⸱⸱⸱⸱⸱ 　　To	**(b)** From ⸱⸱⸱⸱⸱⸱⸱⸱⸱⸱⸱⸱⸱ 　　To	**(c)** Total
1 Gifts, grants, and contributions received (do not include unusual grants)			
2 Membership fees received			
3 Gross investment income			
4 Net unrelated business income			
5 Taxes levied for your benefit			
6 Value of services or facilities furnished by a governmental unit without charge (not including the value of services generally furnished to the public without charge)			
7 Any revenue not otherwise listed above or in lines 9–12 below (attach an itemized list)			
8 Total of lines 1 through 7			
9 Gross receipts from admissions, merchandise sold, or services performed, or furnishing of facilities in any activity that is related to your exempt purposes (attach itemized list)			
10 Total of lines 8 and 9			
11 Net gain or loss on sale of capital assets (attach an itemized list)			
12 Unusual grants			
13 Total revenue. Add lines 10 through 12			

8 According to your answers, you are only eligible for tax exemption under section 501(c)(3) from the postmark date of your application. However, you may be eligible for tax exemption under section 501(c)(4) from your date of formation to the postmark date of the Form 1023. Tax exemption under section 501(c)(4) allows exemption from federal income tax, but generally not deductibility of contributions under Code section 170. Check the box at right if you want us to treat this as a request for exemption under 501(c)(4) from your date of formation to the postmark date.　　▶ ☐

Attach a completed Page 1 of Form 1024, Application for Recognition of Exemption Under Section 501(a), to this application.

Schedule F. Homes for the Elderly or Handicapped and Low-Income Housing

Section I   **General Information About Your Housing**

1 Describe the type of housing you provide.

2 Provide copies of any application forms you use for admission.

3 Explain how the public is made aware of your facility.

4a Provide a description of each facility.
  b What is the total number of residents each facility can accommodate?
  c What is your current number of residents in each facility?
  d Describe each facility in terms of whether residents rent or purchase housing from you.

5 Attach a sample copy of your residency or homeownership contract or agreement.

6 Do you participate in any joint ventures? If "Yes," state your ownership percentage in each joint venture, list your investment in each joint venture, describe the tax status of other participants in each joint venture (including whether they are section 501(c)(3) organizations), describe the activities of each joint venture, describe how you exercise control over the activities of each joint venture, and describe how each joint venture furthers your exempt purposes. Also, submit copies of all joint venture agreements. ☐ Yes ☐ No

  Note. Make sure your answer is consistent with the information provided in Part VIII, line 8.

7 Do you or will you contract with another organization to develop, build, market, or finance your housing? If "Yes," explain how that entity is selected, explain how the terms of any contract(s) are negotiated at arm's length, and explain how you determine you will pay no more than fair market value for services. ☐ Yes ☐ No

  Note. Make sure your answer is consistent with the information provided in Part VIII, line 7a.

8 Do you or will you manage your activities or facilities through your own employees or volunteers? If "No," attach a statement describing the activities that will be managed by others, the names of the persons or organizations that manage or will manage your activities or facilities, and how these managers were or will be selected. Also, submit copies of any contracts, proposed contracts, or other agreements regarding the provision of management services for your activities or facilities. Explain how the terms of any contracts or other agreements were or will be negotiated, and explain how you determine you will pay no more than fair market value for services. ☐ Yes ☐ No

  Note. Answer "Yes" if you do manage or intend to manage your programs through your own employees or by using volunteers. Answer "No" if you engage or intend to engage a separate organization or independent contractor. Make sure your answer is consistent with the information provided in Part VIII, line 7b.

9 Do you participate in any government housing programs? If "Yes," describe these programs. ☐ Yes ☐ No

10a Do you own the facility? If "No," describe any enforceable rights you possess to purchase the facility in the future; go to line 10c. If "Yes," answer line 10b. ☐ Yes ☐ No

  b How did you acquire the facility? For example, did you develop it yourself, purchase a project, etc. Attach all contracts, transfer agreements, or other documents connected with the acquisition of the facility.

  c Do you lease the facility or the land on which it is located? If "Yes," describe the parties to the lease(s) and provide copies of all leases. ☐ Yes ☐ No

Schedule F. Homes for the Elderly or Handicapped and Low-Income Housing *(Continued)*

Section II   Homes for the Elderly or Handicapped

1a Do you provide housing for the elderly? If "Yes," describe who qualifies for your housing in terms of age, infirmity, or other criteria and explain how you select persons for your housing.   ☐ **Yes**   ☐ **No**

b Do you provide housing for the handicapped? If "Yes," describe who qualifies for your housing in terms of disability, income levels, or other criteria and explain how you select persons for your housing.   ☐ **Yes**   ☐ **No**

2a Do you charge an entrance or founder's fee? If "Yes," describe what this charge covers, whether it is a one-time fee, how the fee is determined, whether it is payable in a lump sum or on an installment basis, whether it is refundable, and the circumstances, if any, under which it may be waived.   ☐ **Yes**   ☐ **No**

b Do you charge periodic fees or maintenance charges? If "Yes," describe what these charges cover and how they are determined.   ☐ **Yes**   ☐ **No**

c Is your housing affordable to a significant segment of the elderly or handicapped persons in the community? Identify your **community**. Also, if "Yes," explain how you determine your housing is affordable.   ☐ **Yes**   ☐ **No**

3a Do you have an established policy concerning residents who become unable to pay their regular charges? If "Yes," describe your established policy.   ☐ **Yes**   ☐ **No**

b Do you have any arrangements with government welfare agencies or others to absorb all or part of the cost of maintaining residents who become unable to pay their regular charges? If "Yes," describe these arrangements.   ☐ **Yes**   ☐ **No**

4 Do you have arrangements for the healthcare needs of your residents? If "Yes," describe these arrangements.   ☐ **Yes**   ☐ **No**

5 Are your facilities designed to meet the physical, emotional, recreational, social, religious, and/or other similar needs of the elderly or handicapped? If "Yes," describe these design features.   ☐ **Yes**   ☐ **No**

Section III   Low-Income Housing

1 Do you provide low-income housing? If "Yes," describe who qualifies for your housing in terms of income levels or other criteria, and describe how you select persons for your housing.   ☐ **Yes**   ☐ **No**

2 In addition to rent or mortgage payments, do residents pay periodic fees or maintenance charges? If "Yes," describe what these charges cover and how they are determined.   ☐ **Yes**   ☐ **No**

3a Is your housing affordable to low income residents? If "Yes," describe how your housing is made affordable to low-income residents.   ☐ **Yes**   ☐ **No**

Note. Revenue Procedure 96-32, 1996-1 C.B. 717, provides guidelines for providing low-income housing that will be treated as charitable. (At least 75% of the units are occupied by low-income tenants or 40% are occupied by tenants earning not more than 120% of the very low-income levels for the area.)

b Do you impose any restrictions to make sure that your housing remains affordable to low-income residents? If "Yes," describe these restrictions.   ☐ **Yes**   ☐ **No**

4 Do you provide social services to residents? If "Yes," describe these services.   ☐ **Yes**   ☐ **No**

Schedule G. Successors to Other Organizations

1a Are you a **successor** to a **for-profit organization**? If "Yes," explain the relationship with the **predecessor** organization that resulted in your creation and complete line 1b.   ☐ **Yes** ☐ **No**

  b Explain why you took over the activities or assets of a for-profit organization or converted from for-profit to nonprofit status.

2a Are you a successor to an organization other than a for-profit organization? Answer "Yes" if you have taken or will take over the activities of another organization; or you have taken or will take over 25% or more of the fair market value of the net assets of another organization. If "Yes," explain the relationship with the other organzation that resulted in your creation.   ☐ **Yes** ☐ **No**

  b Provide the tax status of the predecessor organization.

  c Did you or did an organization to which you are a successor previously apply for tax exemption under section 501(c)(3) or any other section of the Code? If "Yes," explain how the application was resolved.   ☐ **Yes** ☐ **No**

  d Was your prior tax exemption or the tax exemption of an organization to which you are a successor revoked or suspended? If "Yes," explain. Include a description of the corrections you made to re-establish tax exemption.   ☐ **Yes** ☐ **No**

  e Explain why you took over the activities or assets of another organization.

3 Provide the name, last address, and EIN of the predecessor organization and describe its activities.
Name: _____   **EIN:** ___ - _____
Address: _____

4 List the owners, partners, principal stockholders, officers, and governing board members of the predecessor organization. Attach a separate sheet if additional space is needed.

Name	Address	Share/Interest (If a for-profit)

5 Do or will any of the persons listed in line 4, maintain a working relationship with you? If "Yes," describe the relationship in detail and include copies of any agreements with any of these persons or with any for-profit organizations in which these persons own more than a 35% interest.   ☐ **Yes** ☐ **No**

6a Were any assets transferred, whether by gift or sale, from the predecessor organization to you?   ☐ **Yes** ☐ **No**
If "Yes," provide a list of assets, indicate the value of each asset, explain how the value was determined, and attach an appraisal, if available. For each asset listed, also explain if the transfer was by gift, sale, or combination thereof.

  b Were any restrictions placed on the use or sale of the assets? If "Yes," explain the restrictions.   ☐ **Yes** ☐ **No**

  c Provide a copy of the agreement(s) of sale or transfer.

7 Were any debts or liabilities transferred from the predecessor for-profit organization to you?   ☐ **Yes** ☐ **No**
If "Yes," provide a list of the debts or liabilities that were transferred to you, indicating the amount of each, how the amount was determined, and the name of the person to whom the debt or liability is owed.

8 Will you lease or rent any property or equipment previously owned or used by the predecessor for-profit organization, or from persons listed in line 4, or from for-profit organizations in which these persons own more than a 35% interest? If "Yes," submit a copy of the lease or rental agreement(s). Indicate how the lease or rental value of the property or equipment was determined.   ☐ **Yes** ☐ **No**

9 Will you lease or rent property or equipment to persons listed in line 4, or to for-profit organizations in which these persons own more than a 35% interest? If "Yes," attach a list of the property or equipment, provide a copy of the lease or rental agreement(s), and indicate how the lease or rental value of the property or equipment was determined.   ☐ **Yes** ☐ **No**

Schedule H. Organizations Providing Scholarships, Fellowships, Educational Loans, or Other Educational Grants to Individuals and Private Foundations Requesting Advance Approval of Individual Grant Procedures

Section I	Names of individual recipients are not required to be listed in Schedule H. Public charities and private foundations complete lines 1a through 7 of this section. See the instructions to Part X if you are not sure whether you are a public charity or a private foundation.

1a Describe the types of educational grants you provide to individuals, such as scholarships, fellowships, loans, etc.

b Describe the purpose and amount of your scholarships, fellowships, and other educational grants and loans that you award.

c If you award educational loans, explain the terms of the loans (interest rate, length, forgiveness, etc.).

d Specify how your program is publicized.

e Provide copies of any solicitation or announcement materials.

f Provide a sample copy of the application used.

2 Do you maintain case histories showing recipients of your scholarships, fellowships, educational loans, or other educational grants, including names, addresses, purposes of awards, amount of each grant, manner of selection, and relationship (if any) to officers, trustees, or donors of funds to you? If "No," refer to the instructions. ☐ **Yes** ☐ **No**

3 Describe the specific criteria you use to determine who is eligible for your program. (For example, eligibility selection criteria could consist of graduating high school students from a particular high school who will attend college, writers of scholarly works about American history, etc.)

4a Describe the specific criteria you use to select recipients. (For example, specific selection criteria could consist of prior academic performance, financial need, etc.)

b Describe how you determine the number of grants that will be made annually.

c Describe how you determine the amount of each of your grants.

d Describe any requirement or condition that you impose on recipients to obtain, maintain, or qualify for renewal of a grant. (For example, specific requirements or conditions could consist of attendance at a four-year college, maintaining a certain grade point average, teaching in public school after graduation from college, etc.)

5 Describe your procedures for supervising the scholarships, fellowships, educational loans, or other educational grants. Describe whether you obtain reports and grade transcripts from recipients, or you pay grants directly to a school under an arrangement whereby the school will apply the grant funds only for enrolled students who are in good standing. Also, describe your procedures for taking action if the terms of the award are violated.

6 Who is on the selection committee for the awards made under your program, including names of current committee members, criteria for committee membership, and the method of replacing committee members?

7 Are relatives of members of the selection committee, or of your officers, directors, or **substantial contributors** eligible for awards made under your program? If "Yes," what measures are taken to ensure unbiased selections? ☐ **Yes** ☐ **No**

Note. If you are a private foundation, you are not permitted to provide educational grants to **disqualified persons**. Disqualified persons include your substantial contributors and foundation managers and certain family members of disqualified persons.

Section II	Private foundations complete lines 1a through 4f of this section. Public charities do not complete this section.

1a If we determine that you are a private foundation, do you want this application to be considered as a request for advance approval of grant making procedures? ☐ **Yes** ☐ **No** ☐ **N/A**

b For which section(s) do you wish to be considered?
- 4945(g)(1)—Scholarship or fellowship grant to an individual for study at an educational institution ☐
- 4945(g)(3)—Other grants, including loans, to an individual for travel, study, or other similar purposes, to enhance a particular skill of the grantee or to produce a specific product ☐

2 Do you represent that you will (1) arrange to receive and review grantee reports annually and upon completion of the purpose for which the grant was awarded, (2) investigate diversions of funds from their intended purposes, and (3) take all reasonable and appropriate steps to recover diverted funds, ensure other grant funds held by a grantee are used for their intended purposes, and withhold further payments to grantees until you obtain grantees' assurances that future diversions will not occur and that grantees will take extraordinary precautions to prevent future diversions from occurring? ☐ **Yes** ☐ **No**

3 Do you represent that you will maintain all records relating to individual grants, including information obtained to evaluate grantees, identify whether a grantee is a disqualified person, establish the amount and purpose of each grant, and establish that you undertook the supervision and investigation of grants described in line 2? ☐ **Yes** ☐ **No**

Schedule H. Organizations Providing Scholarships, Fellowships, Educational Loans, or Other Educational Grants to Individuals and Private Foundations Requesting Advance Approval of Individual Grant Procedures *(Continued)*

Section II	Private foundations complete lines 1a through 4f of this section. Public charities do not complete this section. *(Continued)*

4a Do you or will you award scholarships, fellowships, and educational loans to attend an educational institution based on the status of an individual being an *employee of a particular employer?* If "Yes," complete lines 4b through 4f. ☐ **Yes** ☐ **No**

b Will you comply with the seven conditions and either the percentage tests or facts and circumstances test for scholarships, fellowships, and educational loans to attend an educational institution as set forth in Revenue Procedures 76-47, 1976-2 C.B. 670, and 80-39, 1980-2 C.B. 772, which apply to inducement, selection committee, eligibility requirements, objective basis of selection, employment, course of study, and other objectives? (See lines 4c, 4d, and 4e, regarding the percentage tests.) ☐ **Yes** ☐ **No**

c Do you or will you provide scholarships, fellowships, or educational loans to attend an educational institution to employees of a particular employer? ☐ **Yes** ☐ **No** ☐ **N/A**

If "Yes," will you award grants to 10% or fewer of the eligible applicants who were actually considered by the selection committee in selecting recipients of grants in that year as provided by Revenue Procedures 76-47 and 80-39? ☐ **Yes** ☐ **No**

d Do you provide scholarships, fellowships, or educational loans to attend an educational institution to children of employees of a particular employer? ☐ **Yes** ☐ **No** ☐ **N/A**

If "Yes," will you award grants to 25% or fewer of the eligible applicants who were actually considered by the selection committee in selecting recipients of grants in that year as provided by Revenue Procedures 76-47 and 80-39? If "No," go to line 4e. ☐ **Yes** ☐ **No**

e If you provide scholarships, fellowships, or educational loans to attend an educational institution to children of employees of a particular employer, will you award grants to 10% or fewer of the number of employees' children who can be shown to be eligible for grants (whether or not they submitted an application) in that year, as provided by Revenue Procedures 76-47 and 80-39? ☐ **Yes** ☐ **No** ☐ **N/A**

If "Yes," describe how you will determine who can be shown to be eligible for grants without submitting an application, such as by obtaining written statements or other information about the expectations of employees' children to attend an educational institution. If "No," go to line 4f.

Note. Statistical or sampling techniques are not acceptable. See Revenue Procedure 85-51, 1985-2 C.B. 717, for additional information.

f If you provide scholarships, fellowships, or educational loans to attend an educational institution to *children of employees of a particular employer* without regard to either the 25% limitation described in line 4d, or the 10% limitation described in line 4e, will you award grants based on facts and circumstances that demonstrate that the grants will not be considered compensation for past, present, or future services or otherwise provide a significant benefit to the particular employer? If "Yes," describe the facts and circumstances that you believe will demonstrate that the grants are neither compensatory nor a significant benefit to the particular employer. In your explanation, describe why you cannot satisfy either the 25% test described in line 4d or the 10% test described in line 4e. ☐ **Yes** ☐ **No**

Form 1023 Checklist

(Revised June 2006)

Application for Recognition of Exemption under Section 501(c)(3) of the Internal Revenue Code

Note. *Retain a copy of the completed Form 1023 in your permanent records. Refer to the* General Instructions *regarding Public Inspection of approved applications.*

Check each box to finish your application (Form 1023). Send this completed Checklist with your filled-in application. If you have not answered all the items below, your application may be returned to you as incomplete.

☐ Assemble the application and materials in this order:
- Form 1023 Checklist
- Form 2848, *Power of Attorney and Declaration of Representative* (if filing)
- Form 8821, *Tax Information Authorization* (if filing)
- Expedite request (if requesting)
- Application (Form 1023 and Schedules A through H, as required)
- Articles of organization
- Amendments to articles of organization in chronological order
- Bylaws or other rules of operation and amendments
- Documentation of nondiscriminatory policy for schools, as required by Schedule B
- Form 5768, Election/Revocation of Election by an Eligible Section 501(c)(3) Organization To Make Expenditures To Influence Legislation (if filing)
- All other attachments, including explanations, financial data, and printed materials or publications. Label each page with name and EIN.

☐ User fee payment placed in envelope on top of checklist. DO NOT STAPLE or otherwise attach your check or money order to your application. Instead, just place it in the envelope.

☐ Employer Identification Number (EIN)

☐ Completed Parts I through XI of the application, including any requested information and any required Schedules A through H.
- You must provide specific details about your past, present, and planned activities.
- Generalizations or failure to answer questions in the Form 1023 application will prevent us from recognizing you as tax exempt.
- Describe your purposes and proposed activities in specific easily understood terms.
- Financial information should correspond with proposed activities.

☐ Schedules. Submit only those schedules that apply to you and check either "Yes" or "No" below.

Schedule A Yes ____ No ____		Schedule E Yes ____ No ____
Schedule B Yes ____ No ____		Schedule F Yes ____ No ____
Schedule C Yes ____ No ____		Schedule G Yes ____ No ____
Schedule D Yes ____ No ____		Schedule H Yes ____ No ____

☐ An exact copy of your complete articles of organization (creating document). Absence of the proper purpose and dissolution clauses is the number one reason for delays in the issuance of determination letters.

- Location of Purpose Clause from Part III, line 1 (Page, Article and Paragraph Number)_____
- Location of Dissolution Clause from Part III, line 2b or 2c (Page, Article and Paragraph Number) or by operation of state law _____

☐ Signature of an officer, director, trustee, or other official who is authorized to sign the application.
- Signature at Part XI of Form 1023.

☐ Your name on the application must be the same as your legal name as it appears in your articles of organization.

Send completed Form 1023, user fee payment, and all other required information, to:

Internal Revenue Service
P.O. Box 192
Covington, KY 41012-0192

If you are using express mail or a delivery service, send Form 1023, user fee payment, and attachments to:

Internal Revenue Service
201 West Rivercenter Blvd.
Attn: Extracting Stop 312
Covington, KY 41011

Form **SS-4**
(Rev. January 2010)

Department of the Treasury
Internal Revenue Service

Application for Employer Identification Number

(For use by employers, corporations, partnerships, trusts, estates, churches, government agencies, Indian tribal entities, certain individuals, and others.)

▶ See separate instructions for each line. ▶ Keep a copy for your records.

OMB No. 1545-0003

EIN

Type or print clearly.

1	Legal name of entity (or individual) for whom the EIN is being requested

2	Trade name of business (if different from name on line 1)	3	Executor, administrator, trustee, "care of" name

4a	Mailing address (room, apt., suite no. and street, or P.O. box)	5a	Street address (if different) (Do not enter a P.O. box.)
4b	City, state, and ZIP code (if foreign, see instructions)	5b	City, state, and ZIP code (if foreign, see instructions)

6	County and state where principal business is located

7a	Name of responsible party	7b	SSN, ITIN, or EIN

8a	Is this application for a limited liability company (LLC) (or a foreign equivalent)? . . . . ☐ Yes ☐ No	8b	If 8a is "Yes," enter the number of LLC members . . . . ▶

8c If 8a is "Yes," was the LLC organized in the United States? . . . . ☐ Yes ☐ No

9a **Type of entity** (check only one box). **Caution.** If 8a is "Yes," see the instructions for the correct box to check.

☐ Sole proprietor (SSN) _____
☐ Partnership
☐ Corporation (enter form number to be filed) ▶_____
☐ Personal service corporation
☐ Church or church-controlled organization
☐ Other nonprofit organization (specify) ▶_____
☐ Other (specify) ▶

☐ Estate (SSN of decedent) _____
☐ Plan administrator (TIN) _____
☐ Trust (TIN of grantor) _____
☐ National Guard   ☐ State/local government
☐ Farmers' cooperative   ☐ Federal government/military
☐ REMIC   ☐ Indian tribal governments/enterprises
Group Exemption Number (GEN) if any ▶

9b	If a corporation, name the state or foreign country (if applicable) where incorporated	State	Foreign country

10 **Reason for applying** (check only one box)

☐ Started new business (specify type) ▶ _____
_____
☐ Hired employees (Check the box and see line 13.)
☐ Compliance with IRS withholding regulations
☐ Other (specify) ▶

☐ Banking purpose (specify purpose) ▶_____
☐ Changed type of organization (specify new type) ▶_____
☐ Purchased going business
☐ Created a trust (specify type) ▶_____
☐ Created a pension plan (specify type) ▶_____

11	Date business started or acquired (month, day, year). See instructions.	12	Closing month of accounting year

13 Highest number of employees expected in the next 12 months (enter -0- if none).

If no employees expected, skip line 14.

Agricultural	Household	Other

14 If you expect your employment tax liability to be $1,000 or less in a full calendar year **and** want to file Form 944 annually instead of Forms 941 quarterly, check here. (Your employment tax liability generally will be $1,000 or less if you expect to pay $4,000 or less in total wages.) If you do not check this box, you must file Form 941 for every quarter. ☐

15 First date wages or annuities were paid (month, day, year). **Note.** If applicant is a withholding agent, enter date income will first be paid to nonresident alien (month, day, year) . . . . ▶

16 Check **one** box that best describes the principal activity of your business.

☐ Construction ☐ Rental & leasing ☐ Transportation & warehousing
☐ Real estate ☐ Manufacturing ☐ Finance & insurance

☐ Health care & social assistance ☐ Wholesale-agent/broker
☐ Accommodation & food service ☐ Wholesale-other ☐ Retail
☐ Other (specify)

17 Indicate principal line of merchandise sold, specific construction work done, products produced, or services provided.

18 Has the applicant entity shown on line 1 ever applied for and received an EIN? ☐ Yes ☐ No
If "Yes," write previous EIN here ▶

Third Party Designee	Complete this section **only** if you want to authorize the named individual to receive the entity's EIN and answer questions about the completion of this form.	
	Designee's name	Designee's telephone number (include area code) ( )
	Address and ZIP code	Designee's fax number (include area code) ( )

Under penalties of perjury, I declare that I have examined this application, and to the best of my knowledge and belief, it is true, correct, and complete.

Name and title (type or print clearly) ▶

Applicant's telephone number (include area code) ( )

Applicant's fax number (include area code) ( )

Signature ▶   Date ▶

For Privacy Act and Paperwork Reduction Act Notice, see separate instructions.   Cat. No. 16055N   Form **SS-4** (Rev. 1-2010)

Do I Need an EIN?

File Form SS-4 if the applicant entity does not already have an EIN but is required to show an EIN on any return, statement, or other document.[1] See also the separate instructions for each line on Form SS-4.

IF the applicant...	AND...	THEN...
Started a new business	Does not currently have (nor expect to have) employees	Complete lines 1, 2, 4a–8a, 8b–c (if applicable), 9a, 9b (if applicable), and 10–14 and 16–18.
Hired (or will hire) employees, including household employees	Does not already have an EIN	Complete lines 1, 2, 4a–6, 7a–b (if applicable), 8a, 8b–c (if applicable), 9a, 9b (if applicable), 10–18.
Opened a bank account	Needs an EIN for banking purposes only	Complete lines 1–5b, 7a–b (if applicable), 8a, 8b–c (if applicable), 9a, 9b (if applicable), 10, and 18.
Changed type of organization	Either the legal character of the organization or its ownership changed (for example, you incorporate a sole proprietorship or form a partnership)[2]	Complete lines 1–18 (as applicable).
Purchased a going business[3]	Does not already have an EIN	Complete lines 1–18 (as applicable).
Created a trust	The trust is other than a grantor trust or an IRA trust[4]	Complete lines 1–18 (as applicable).
Created a pension plan as a plan administrator[5]	Needs an EIN for reporting purposes	Complete lines 1, 3, 4a–5b, 9a, 10, and 18.
Is a foreign person needing an EIN to comply with IRS withholding regulations	Needs an EIN to complete a Form W-8 (other than Form W-8ECI), avoid withholding on portfolio assets, or claim tax treaty benefits[6]	Complete lines 1–5b, 7a–b (SSN or ITIN optional), 8a, 8b–c (if applicable), 9a, 9b (if applicable), 10, and 18.
Is administering an estate	Needs an EIN to report estate income on Form 1041	Complete lines 1–6, 9a, 10–12, 13–17 (if applicable), and 18.
Is a withholding agent for taxes on non-wage income paid to an alien (i.e., individual, corporation, or partnership, etc.)	Is an agent, broker, fiduciary, manager, tenant, or spouse who is required to file Form 1042, Annual Withholding Tax Return for U.S. Source Income of Foreign Persons	Complete lines 1, 2, 3 (if applicable), 4a–5b, 7a–b (if applicable), 8a, 8b–c (if applicable), 9a, 9b (if applicable), 10, and 18.
Is a state or local agency	Serves as a tax reporting agent for public assistance recipients under Rev. Proc. 80-4, 1980-1 C.B. 581[7]	Complete lines 1, 2, 4a–5b, 9a, 10, and 18.
Is a single-member LLC	Needs an EIN to file Form 8832, Classification Election, for filing employment tax returns and excise tax returns, or for state reporting purposes[8]	Complete lines 1–18 (as applicable).
Is an S corporation	Needs an EIN to file Form 2553, Election by a Small Business Corporation[9]	Complete lines 1–18 (as applicable).

[1] For example, a sole proprietorship or self-employed farmer who establishes a qualified retirement plan, or is required to file excise, employment, alcohol, tobacco, or firearms returns, must have an EIN. A partnership, corporation, REMIC (real estate mortgage investment conduit), nonprofit organization (church, club, etc.), or farmers' cooperative must use an EIN for any tax-related purpose even if the entity does not have employees.

[2] However, do not apply for a new EIN if the existing entity only (a) changed its business name, (b) elected on Form 8832 to change the way it is taxed (or is covered by the default rules), or (c) terminated its partnership status because at least 50% of the total interests in partnership capital and profits were sold or exchanged within a 12-month period. The EIN of the terminated partnership should continue to be used. See Regulations section 301.6109-1(d)(2)(iii).

[3] Do not use the EIN of the prior business unless you became the "owner" of a corporation by acquiring its stock.

[4] However, grantor trusts that do not file using Optional Method 1 and IRA trusts that are required to file Form 990-T, Exempt Organization Business Income Tax Return, must have an EIN. For more information on grantor trusts, see the Instructions for Form 1041.

[5] A plan administrator is the person or group of persons specified as the administrator by the instrument under which the plan is operated.

[6] Entities applying to be a Qualified Intermediary (QI) need a QI-EIN even if they already have an EIN. See Rev. Proc. 2000-12.

[7] See also *Household employer* on page 4 of the instructions. **Note.** State or local agencies may need an EIN for other reasons, for example, hired employees.

[8] See *Disregarded entities* on page 4 of the instructions for details on completing Form SS-4 for an LLC.

[9] An existing corporation that is electing or revoking S corporation status should use its previously-assigned EIN.

Form **5768**

(Rev. September 2009)

Department of the Treasury
Internal Revenue Service

Election/Revocation of Election by an Eligible Section 501(c)(3) Organization To Make Expenditures To Influence Legislation

(Under Section 501(h) of the Internal Revenue Code)

For IRS
Use Only ▶

Name of organization	Employer identification number

Number and street (or P.O. box no., if mail is not delivered to street address)	Room/suite

City, town or post office, and state	ZIP + 4

1 Election—As an eligible organization, we hereby elect to have the provisions of section 501(h) of the Code, relating to expenditures to influence legislation, apply to our tax year ending _____and all subsequent tax years until revoked.

(Month, day, and year)

Note: *This election must be signed and postmarked within the first taxable year to which it applies.*

2 Revocation—As an eligible organization, we hereby revoke our election to have the provisions of section 501(h) of the Code, relating to expenditures to influence legislation, apply to our tax year ending _____

(Month, day, and year)

Note: *This revocation must be signed and postmarked before the first day of the tax year to which it applies.*

Under penalties of perjury, I declare that I am authorized to make this (check applicable box) ▶ ☐ election   ☐ revocation
on behalf of the above named organization.

(Signature of officer or trustee)	(Type or print name and title)	(Date)

General Instructions

Section references are to the Internal Revenue Code.

Section 501(c)(3) states that an organization exempt under that section will lose its tax-exempt status and its qualification to receive deductible charitable contributions if a substantial part of its activities are carried on to influence legislation. Section 501(h), however, permits certain eligible section 501(c)(3) organizations to elect to make limited expenditures to influence legislation. An organization making the election will, however, be subject to an excise tax under section 4911 if it spends more than the amounts permitted by that section. Also, the organization may lose its exempt status if its lobbying expenditures exceed the permitted amounts by more than 50% over a 4-year period. For any tax year in which an election under section 501(h) is in effect, an electing organization must report the actual and permitted amounts of its lobbying expenditures and grass roots expenditures (as defined in section 4911(c)) on its annual return required under section 6033. See Part II-A of Schedule C (Form 990 or Form 990-EZ). Each electing member of an affiliated group must report these amounts for both itself and the affiliated group as a whole.

To make or revoke the election, enter the ending date of the tax year to which the election or revocation applies in item **1** or **2**, as applicable, and sign and date the form in the spaces provided.

Eligible organizations. A section 501(c)(3) organization is permitted to make the election if it is not a disqualified organization (see below) and is described in:

1. Section 170(b)(1)(A)(ii) (relating to educational institutions),

2. Section 170(b)(1)(A)(iii) (relating to hospitals and medical research organizations),

3. Section 170(b)(1)(A)(iv) (relating to organizations supporting government schools),

4. Section 170(b)(1)(A)(vi) (relating to organizations publicly supported by charitable contributions),

5. Section 509(a)(2) (relating to organizations publicly supported by admissions, sales, etc.), or

6. Section 509(a)(3) (relating to organizations supporting certain types of public charities other than those section 509(a)(3) organizations that support section 501(c)(4), (5), or (6) organizations).

Disqualified organizations. The following types of organizations are not permitted to make the election:

a. Section 170(b)(1)(A)(i) organizations (relating to churches),

b. An integrated auxiliary of a church or of a convention or association of churches, or

c. A member of an affiliated group of organizations if one or more members of such group is described in **a** or **b** of this paragraph.

Affiliated organizations. Organizations are members of an affiliated group of organizations only if (1) the governing instrument of one such organization requires it to be bound by the decisions of the other organization on legislative issues, or (2) the governing board of one such organization includes persons (i) who are specifically designated representatives of another such organization or are members of the governing board, officers, or paid executive staff members of such other organization, and (ii) who, by aggregating their votes, have sufficient voting power to cause or prevent action on legislative issues by the first such organization.

For more details, see section 4911 and section 501(h).

Note. A private foundation (including a private operating foundation) is not an eligible organization.

Where to file. Mail Form 5768 to the Department of the Treasury, Internal Revenue Service Center, Ogden, UT 84201-0027.

Cat. No. 12125M

Form **5768** (Rev. 9-2009)

Index

H

Health care nonprofits
  IRS Form 1023, Schedule C, 184, 191
  medical clinic statement of purpose, 111
  overview, 45
  public charity status, 63–64
  See also Hospitals
History of the nonprofit on IRS Form 1023,
  169–170
Hospitals
  cooperative hospital service organizations,
    178
  and IRS Form 1023, 178, 179
  IRS Form 1023, Schedule C, 184, 191
  public charity status, 63–64
Housing provider nonprofits
  EO statement on fraud, 173
  improvement statement of purpose, 110–111
  and IRS Form 1023, 179
  IRS Form 1023, Schedule F, 195
Human societies, 43

I

Income
  donations, 77, 80–81, 172
  estimating, 180, 181
  from goods and services, 86, 166, 168–169,
    175, 183
  gross receipts, 74–75
  membership dues, 10, 69, 73, 139
  passive income, 17, 72
  See also Fundraising; Grants; Taxes; *entries
    beginning with* "Activities"
Income taxes. *See* Tax exemptions
Incorporation
  costs and fees, 13–14
  decision-making process, 9, 12, 18–19
  notifying others of, 210–211
  online resources, 233–234
  overview, 7, 17–18, 90
  restrictions on usage of funds, 14–15

  time and energy requirements, 14
Incorporators
  appointing initial board of directors, 205
  legal research, 223–224
  names and addresses in articles of
    incorporation, 111–112
  overview, 23, 25–28
Indemnification for legal expenses, 26, 35, 153,
  219
Independent contractors
  classifying, 218
  fundraisers, 85, 171–172
  on IRS Form 1023, 160–161, 162
  See also Lawyers, consulting with; Tax
    advisers, consulting with
Indirect contributions, 66
Initial quorum rule, 31
Insider sales and purchase transactions,
  165–166
In-state (domestic) corporations, 8, 18–19
Insurance
  commercial, 219
  D&O errors and omissions insurance, 26,
    35, 153, 219
  for likely risks, 35
Internal Revenue Manual, 57
Internet
  databases of names, 101
  incorporation resources, 233–234
  IRS website, 56–57, 61, 90, 146
  nonprofit's own website, 153, 159
  secretaries of state websites, 103, 233
  state law websites, 234
  state taxes websites, 233
Investment of corporate assets, 34, 69–70, 72,
  75–76, 83–84, 173
Involuntary dissolution, 219–220
Iowa articles of incorporation, 105
IRS (Internal Revenue Service)
  appealing status decision, 198
  "Cyber Assistant," 13–14, 146–147, 189
  Employer Identification Number, 145, 147,
    151

 Go to Nolo.com/newsletters to sign up for free newsletters and discounts on Nolo products.

- **Nolo Briefs.** Our monthly email newsletter with great deals and free information.

- **Nolo's Special Offer.** A monthly newsletter with the biggest Nolo discounts around.

- **BizBriefs.** Tips and discounts on Nolo products for business owners and managers.

- **Landlord's Quarterly.** Deals and free tips just for landlords and property managers, too.

 Don't forget to check for updates. Find this book at **Nolo.com** and click "Legal Updates."

Let Us Hear From You

 Register your Nolo product and give us your feedback at Nolo.com/book-registration.

- Once you've registered, you qualify for technical support if you have any trouble with a download or CD (though most folks don't).

- We'll also drop you an email when a new edition of your book is released—and we'll send you a coupon for 15% off your next Nolo.com order!

NNP10

NOLO Bestsellers

**The Small Business
Start-Up Kit**

$29.99

**How to Write a
Business Plan**

$34.99

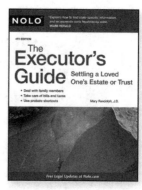

The Executor's Guide

$39.99

**The Criminal Law
Handbook**

$39.99

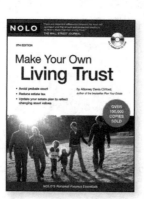

**Make Your Own
Living Trust**

$39.99

Patent It Yourself

$49.99

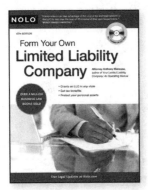

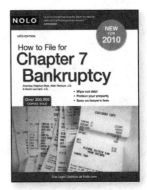
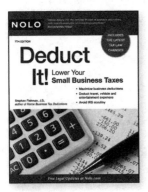

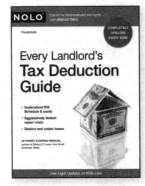